Date Due

MAY 3 1985			
MAR 2 0 1986			
MAY 1 4 1986			
MAR 2 2 1993			
MAR 1 2 2001			

FOR BETTER, FOR WORSE

FOR BETTER, FOR WORSE

A Feminist Handbook on Marriage and Other Options

Jennifer Baker Fleming and Carolyn Kott Washburne

Charles Scribner's Sons   New York

Copyright © 1977 Jennifer Baker Fleming and Carolyn Kott Washburne

Library of Congress Cataloging in Publication Data

Fleming, Jennifer Baker.
    For better, for worse.

    Bibliography: p. 363
    Includes index.
    1. Married women.   2. Marriage.   3. Women—Psychology.
4. Women—Sexual behavior.   I. Washburne, Carolyn Kott, joint author.
II. Title.   HQ1221.F53   301.42′72′042   77-8017
ISBN 0-684-14919-2
ISBN 0-684-14920-6 pbk.

The material on page 138 is excerpted from "The Manufacture of House-work" by Barbara Ehrenreich and Deirdre English as it appeared in *Social-ist Revolution* Magazine, #26, October-December 1975. Copyright © 1975 *Socialist Revolution* Magazine.

The material on page 144 is excerpted from "Welfare Is a Women's Issue" by Johnnie Tillmon as it appeared in *Ms.* Magazine, Spring 1972. Copy-right © *Ms.* Magazine Corporation 1972.

The material on page 254 is reprinted courtesy the *Chicago Tribune*. Copy-right © 1976 *Chicago Tribune*.

The material on page 263 is excerpted from *The Future of Marriage* by Jessie Bernard, published originally by the World Publishing Company. Copyright © 1972 Jessie Bernard. Reprinted by permission of Thomas Y. Crowell Company, Inc.

The poem on page 287 by Jennie Orvino first appeared in *Amazon Quar-terly*, February 1973. Copyright © 1973 Jennie Orvino.

The material on pages 387 to 390 first appeared in *Ms.* Magazine, March 1976. Copyright © *Ms.* Magazine Corporation 1976.

The material on pages 392 to 396 first appeared in *Ms.* Magazine, August 1976. Copyright © *Ms.* Magazine Corporation 1976.

1 3 5 7 9 11 13 15 17 19 M/C 20 18 16 14 12 10 8 6 4 2

1 3 5 7 9 11 13 15 17 19 M/P 20 18 16 14 12 10 8 6 4 2

Printed in the United States of America

Acknowledgments

General editing: Miriam Galper

Legal research: Linda Backiel

Typing: Linda Waltman
Joseph Waltman

Contributors: Alice W. Ballard,
Samuel, Ballard, and Hyman

Barbara Bloom, Coordinator
Regional Continuing Education
for Women Program

Dianne L. Chambless

Marion D. Cohen

Jeffry Galper

Ian M. Harris

Schree Hicks

Maureen Kelly

Lynn C. Malmgren

Options for Women, Inc.

Kathleen Riordan, Women's Bureau,
Department of Labor
Region III, Philadelphia

Lianne C. Scherr

Jean MacBryde Swenson, Director
Continuing Education for Women
Temple University

Betsy Warrior

Jacket photographs: Emiko Tonooka

Our special thanks go to our good friend Miriam Galper,
for her excellent editing, her sense of humor, and for
keeping down the melodrama and the rhetoric; to Linda
Backiel for her expertise and clearheadedness; to Schree
Hicks for her insight and contributions on minority women;
to our agent, Virginia Barber, for her encouragement and
"smarts"; and to our friends at Scribners, Kathie Ness,
Susan O'Connell, and Susan Richman.

Jennifer thanks her children, Robbie and Kathy Fleming,
for giving her enough space and time to write this book;
Carolyn thanks her parents, Shirley and Roland Kott, for
their support even though they do not always agree with
her ideas.

Jennifer Baker Fleming and Carolyn Kott Washburne were
among the founders of Women in Transition, Inc., a women's
counseling program in Philadelphia, Pennsylvania, and
two of the authors of *Women in Transition: A Feminist
Handbook on Separation and Divorce* (Scribners, 1975).
Jennifer is currently Director of the Women's Resource
Network in Philadelphia, a multifaceted resource system
for women. The first priority of the Network is the
Domestic Violence Project. Carolyn is now Assistant to the
Director of the Center for Advanced Studies in Human
Services, School of Social Welfare, University of
Wisconsin-Milwaukee.

Contents

Introduction: Why This Book?   1

1/Removing the Stardust   8
  Preconceived Notions   8
  Divorce and Remarriage in America   12
  Is This Book for You?   13

2/What about Love?   23
  Why Women Get Married   23
  What Our Mothers Didn't Tell Us   28
    Giving   29
    Dependency   33
    Power   34
    Sex   37
  The "His" and "Hers" Marriage   38
  Becoming a Separate Person within an Intimate
     Relationship   41
    Economic Independence   44
    Learn to Cope--and Share the Coping   46
    Emotional Independence   47
  Making It Work   51
  Women As Friends and Supports   58
  Professional Support   61

3/Marriage As a Legal Institution   71
  Does Marriage Benefit Women?   71

viii   Contents

The History of Our Marriage Laws   72
The Law Today   75
The Law in the Future   81
What You Can Do Yourself   83
Make a Contract   83
Know the Law   89
Conclusion   118

4/Who Controls the Pursestrings?   124
The First Step: How Do You Feel about Money?   128
Supporting Yourself   133
Support from a Spouse   137
The State   143
Women's Work   147
A Few Words about Discrimination   156
Insurance and Income Protection Plans   161
Education and Reeducation   163
Starting from the Bottom   163
Job Training Resources   165
Going (Back) to College   173
Credit   182

5/Motherhood   192
Redefining Motherhood   193
Thinking about Motherhood?   194
Once You've Decided   203
The Mother Role   207
Pressures   208
Identity Problems   212
Changing the Goals   214
The Mother Who Works outside the Home   223
The Single Mother   230
Stepfamilies   233
Economics   236
Child Abuse   238
Women As Support   239
In the End   240

6/Is That All There Is? Some Alternatives to Marriage 247
What Is an Alternative Life-style?   247
Being Single   253
"Open Marriage"   260
Equality   263
Togetherness   264
Sexuality and Jealousy   265
Common-Law Marriage and Living-Together Arrangements 272
Group Living   277

Contents   ix

7/Women Loving Women   286
    What Is Lesbianism?   286
    Who Are Lesbian Women? What Are Their Lives Like?   289
    Enter Feminism   291
    Lesbian Relationships   294
    If You Are Bisexual   297
    If You Are a Gay Woman   298
        Monogamy   300
        Sex   302
        The Outside World   302
        The Lesbian Community   303
        When There Are Children   304

8/Violence within Marriage   314
    The Police and the Courts   316
    So Why Doesn't She Leave Him? Women's Economic
        Dependence within Marriage   318
    How Does She Get in the Situation in the First
        Place? The Psychology of Powerlessness   319
    What Kind of Man Abuses His Wife?   322
    Wife Abuse and Child Abuse   322
    Class and Race Differences   323
    What Are the Solutions?   324
    How Does Wife Abuse Affect You?   325

9/Not for Men Only   340
    Taking the Risk   340
    What Does It Mean to Be a Man?   342
    Whey Men Get Married   347
    Making Changes in Your Life   349
        What the Women Do   350
        How the Men Respond   351
        What's in It for You?   352
        What You Have to Give Up   356
        Where to from Here?   357

Bibliography and Resources   363

Appendix/Common-Law Marriage   398

Index   402

Introduction:
Why This Book?

When a group of us were working as volunteer staff at the
Women's Liberation Center in Philadelphia, we dealt with
a great many calls from women who were in some kind of
marital transition--separated, divorced, raising children
alone--or who were being beaten by their husbands. Some
women wanted specific help, such as referrals to lawyers,
job information, or housing information; others needed
someone to talk to and assistance in coping with their
emotional needs.

Our group, Women in Transition, Inc., was organized to
provide help to all of these women in a systematic and
comprehensive manner. During the four years the program
operated in its original form* we provided two major
types of services: emotional support and legal support.
Emotional support took the form of small discussion groups
where women could come together to share experiences and

*Due to funding difficulties and our wish to broaden our
impact on the professional mental health community,
Women in Transition, Inc., is now focusing primarily on
consultation to other agencies rather than providing
direct individual service. The program is also
developing a component to deal with the problem of
wife abuse.

feelings about separation, marriage, children, anger, sexuality, needs, and goals. We also provided referrals to feminist therapists in private practice and in social agencies. The legal support services included individual legal counseling by our paralegal workers and referrals to lawyers or legal agencies. We conducted a *pro se* (for herself) divorce clinic to teach women how to obtain divorces without lawyers. We provided community outreach workshops where we shared information about issues of particular concern to low-income and minority women, such as common-law marriage, family court, "illegitimacy," and welfare. We also provided emotional and legal help to women who were victims of wife abuse.

The staff came from a variety of backgrounds and experiences--separated, divorced, single, married, with children, without children, lesbian, heterosexual, black, white, middle-class, lower-income, with professional credentials and without. The staff worked collectively, which meant we all had an equal share in policy-making and an equal share in the unglamorous aspects of running the program, such as taking out the trash, answering the telephone, or mimeographing.

We shared the basic conviction that with the right kinds of support, separation, divorce, and single parenthood didn't have to be the debilitating traumas they often are and might even become creative learning and growing processes. Most of us were separated or divorced ourselves and felt that the support of other women had been crucial to us, both during the transitional period and afterward as we settled into our new lives. It was our goal to help women realize their potential as strong, independent people regardless of whether they chose to remain in a marriage, follow through on divorce, or remarry.

Our book, the *Women's Survival Manual*, was published in 1972 in order to answer the questions most often asked and was directed to women in the Philadelphia area. It was followed in 1975 by a national version, *Women in Transition: A Feminist Handbook on Separation and Divorce*, which contains chapters on emotional supports, children in transition, what the law says, financial resources, housing, physical and mental health, and how to start a program similar to ours.

In the course of our travels promoting *Women in Transition* we were often asked by interviewers, "How can these

problems of adjustment to separation and divorce be
avoided in the first place? What advice would you give to
a person considering marriage? Are there special problems
for women in marriage? Isn't there a way of preventing
upheaval and unhappiness or at least dealing with potential
problems before they become *real* ones? What makes for a
good relationship?"

In this book we want to answer those questions and explore
many other issues which we have found to be of concern to
women. We are indebted to the thousands of women who
came to our program and whom we met across the country.
Their willingness to share their lives has made it possible for us to learn and grow, and we want to pass that
knowledge on to you.

EMIKO TONOOKA

EMIKO TONOOKA

EVA SHADEROWFSKY

1

ELSA

I was a very independent person. I lived my own life,
alone, with no supervision from the time that I was
eighteen. When I was about twenty I moved to Greenwich
Village and moved into the sophisticated areas of life.
My life had been very innocent before this. I developed
an interest in the arts, which followed naturally from my
interest in music. I did think about getting married,
though. I wanted to do what everybody else was doing, and
I felt deprived because I wasn't getting married when all
of my friends were, but I guess I made the best of it. I
didn't have much family to pressure me, but when I saw
aunts and they said, "Why aren't you getting married?" I
resented it very much. At the same time I felt that I
should be getting married. It was hard for me to say,
"Well, I would if I could, but I can't."

I met Manny under rather peculiar circumstances. I went
to work during the war in a factory that was producing
optical lenses for submarine sights, and he hired me. He
was the personnel manager. In a very short time I became
active in the union. I was thrilled about that, because
I had always been interested in the union movement. So
to me this was very productive because I felt I was really
growing and having experience with people. I worked

on a night shift because I had some kind of illusion that I could play the piano during the day, that I just didn't need to sleep. I worked the night shift, in the morning I would go to a union meeting, and then maybe to negotiations. For a short time I was on the negotiations committee, and he and I sat on opposite sides of the table in the negotiations. There seemed to be something within each of us that attracted the other, until we began to date. He was married. I enjoyed him and he enjoyed me.

He eventually left his wife and we moved in together. My expectation was to love somebody and to be loved. I didn't see myself as a typical housewife because--well, I had the piano, and I always wanted to be an independently educated and aware person who could participate in everything and not be a housewife. And I fought for that. I really fought for the opportunity to maintain my own growth as a person and not get stuck in the kitchen and the laundry room. I always worked. I didn't work full-time, but I always worked. And I considered my work at the piano as work, too.

We made a conscious decision not to have children. It was a necessary one. He had children, and the economic responsibilities would have been enormous. Manny had to send whatever unemployment insurance he got to his family-- he did have that responsibility. Although I accepted it intellectually, there must have been some part of me that resented it. His wife would never give him a divorce. It was the "over my dead body" kind of thing. We would have gotten married if she had, and that was a source of pain to me, mostly repressed, over the years. Every so often I would say to Manny, "Are you going to make an honest woman of me?" jokingly, and he would say, "You're more married than most of the people you know. Our relationship is a much more stable one. Part of it is knowing that you are always free to go. We each know that, and still we choose to stay."

I ran into extreme difficulty after he died because we weren't married. All his back pay and vacation pay went to his wife because that was the legal reality. I just had to take those losses.

He wasn't liberated. Theoretically Manny was very much opposed to male chauvinism, but I think there are a lot of radical men who are very good at exploiting women in spite of the fact that theoretically they don't believe

6

in it. When it comes to their own convenience, it's easier. As I remember, in the early days when we set up house together it was assumed that I would do all the things that every other woman does, and that for a while in the first glow, the whole thing was just so beautiful, to be living with a man, the companionship of somebody to go to bed with . . . It was assumed that this relationship for Manny was going to be the same as he had had with his mother and with his wife, with the added dimension that he had a talented woman. I played the piano, I was a nice girl—this was one of his favorite funny expressions, "She's a nice girl, she plays the piano." But do the dishes, do the laundry, do the marketing, you know, serve me, serve my needs. And I fought like hell about that. I'd say, "I want to read the paper, too. Why is it my role to go in the kitchen and do the dishes? I can't buy that. I did that all my life, so now that I have someone to share my life with, I want to share it."

I'm convinced that because I was an independent person in my marriage, it made it easier to adjust to his death. I didn't feel the loneliness that most women have when they're bereaved, when they feel that their life is over. Because he had certain strong interests, and because I was very strong in my conviction that I wanted to be a separate person, I felt I was able to make an adjustment to being alone again after twenty-five years of being with somebody else.

My friends came through for me after Manny died. And when I felt I had to ask for help, I asked, because I felt that much confidence. They had already shown that I could very freely ask for companionship, comfort, any kind of help, and I had extraordinary help from some of my friends. Now eight years or so have passed, and I have to say that in spite of the fact that I still do miss Manny very often, I'm not obsessed with it, and I have not felt the need to replace him. My life is very, very full with many things that I'm involved in, and I feel my needs are met.

1 / Removing the Stardust

Preconceived Notions

We want women to remove the stardust about marriage from
their eyes. Marriage is an institution which affects all
of our lives in one way or another, but which is obscured
by many myths and misconceptions. Most people, men and
women, romanticize marriage and develop unrealistic expectations for it rather than preparing themselves beforehand for the emotional, legal, and economic realities of
married life. We know that marriage is an institution
that is meaningful to many women. We know women who are
entering into marriage who want to avoid the problems
they have seen among their friends, in their families,
or perhaps in earlier marriages of their own. We have
met women who believe strongly in marriage and who want
to make the best of their own marriages without having
to deny their own needs. Other women have told us they
wish someone had told them before marrying what they were
getting into. They say that if they had known what to
expect, they would have made different choices about
such things as giving up their jobs, failing to develop
credit in their own names, allowing premarriage friendships to lapse, and in some cases even about having
children. We also know women who have made choices they

are not happy with and are exploring the alternatives
to marriage.

We believe there are special problems for women within
marriage, but there are ways to make the institution work
for you rather than against you. This, however, usually
involves going directly counter to all the advice women
have heard for years about how to "catch a man."

After working with thousands of women at Women in Transition, we now believe that it is not people who are failures
at marriage; it is the institution itself that contributes
to its own destruction. For women especially, marriage is
not, as most of us were led to believe, designed to
benefit and protect us. It has become clear to us that
marriage is a binding contract which the contracting
parties know very little about. Furthermore, it is a
contract in which the state plays an important role, a
fact which is *not* widely understood by the general public.
We discovered that women's obligations under the terms of
this contract, when combined with the economic power that
most husbands have over their wives, place wives in a
very handicapped position indeed. This becomes most obvious during the time of separation and divorce, when many
women first realize the extent of their vulnerability.
But the problems are not limited to separating and
divorcing women. Married and about-to-be-married women
who try to retain some independence within their marriages
meet with many frustrations and anxieties. This is true
economically, such as when women try to get credit in
their names, and emotionally, such as when women try to
develop friends and interests separate from their
husbands'.

MARSHA

*When I went to my Women in Transition group, I
couldn't believe my ears at first. I thought I had
problems in my marriage, but the stories I heard from
the other gals made my hair stand on end! There were
a couple of gals who couldn't collect child support
from their ex-husbands because the support court just
didn't have enough people to track the men down.
This really surprised me, because I always thought
the law said men were supposed to support their*

*children, especially when the wives couldn't
work. There was this other woman, a college teacher,
who got a good job in another city and her husband
didn't want to go. He said if she went he would
charge her with desertion, and he would probably get
the kids. Her lawyer told her the husband was in the
right, and furthermore if the husband wanted to move
and she didn't, she would still be charged with desertion. And this other one--the way her husband
used to beat her up, and she couldn't get the cops
or the judge to do anything about it. I don't even
want to talk about that one. Sometimes I felt like
my problems, which had to do with my husband's having
another girl friend, were nothing compared to theirs.
At least I was eating every day and didn't have any
bruises. But it was a real eye-opener, I'll tell you.*

At our counseling program we learned that the value system
that goes along with traditional marriage cripples both
spouses almost from the beginning. Ideally, marriage
should be the commitment of two people to love and support
each other throughout their lives, as equals. What
actually exists is an institution that too often succeeds
because of the woman's inferior status within it. That the
wives do most of the giving and make most of the sacrifices, that husbands fulfill themselves at the expense
of their wives, that the needs of husbands and children
come first--all of these assumptions can corrupt what might
have started out as a good relationship. The relationship
can be further distorted by the patterns of dominance and
submission which exist in most marriages and the prevalent
notion that wives are the property of their husbands. We
have seen some good relationships ruined by marriage. Even
those couples who think they can have a "liberated"
marriage often find themselves adopting the very values
they rejected before marriage. Very few people are immune
to the pressures from friends, family, media, and mental
health professionals about how married people are supposed
to think, act, and feel.

The Wooden Bowl

*Yetta, my mother
oiled the old wooden bowl
each season
"to keep it from looking
like a weathered board"*

She always sat
with the bowl on her lap
and propped it steady
between her knees
while she chopped

There's a difference
between a serving bowl
and a working bowl,
she'd say, scraping
the sides clean with a knife

The day I became
Joseph's wife my mother
gave me the bowl
wordlessly, her only
wedding gift

I rubbed the rough
surface with bacon grease
until it gleamed
and placed it alone
on the shelf

When Joseph used
the bowl for grating hard
parmesan cheese, his hand slipped
and he scarred the wood
with his blade

But the scar didn't
fade and finally he
left me
and the bowl behind
both empty

My wooden bowl,
scratched and worn thin at one end,
reminds me of my mother as a bride
carefully chopping eggs or liver or onions
inside its once-perfect hollow hemisphere

> *Maralyn Lois Polak*
> *August 13-14, 1973*
> *Contoocook, New Hampshire*

Divorce and Remarriage in America

Soap operas, statisticians, and friends all tell us that divorce and family disorganization are facts of American life. Some observers say that marriage is simply in a state of transition; the institution that served us well in years past is now being transformed into a viable one for the future. Others say that marriage is in deep trouble, a life-style that is doomed. Regardless of how you interpret them, government statistics indicate that two marriages in four end in divorce, separation, or desertion. Marriage counselors estimate that only 25 percent of American marriages can be considered happy and that the number of couples who have unhappy marriages far exceeds the number who actually seek counseling. Yet remarriage is also on the rise. What is happening?

When we ask the women in our program why their marriages are ending, many of them reply that they are tired of having to do most of the giving, make the compromises, be the martyrs. They feel that in their marriage they were the ones responsible for the family's emotional well-being as well as for day-to-day physical maintenance and in many cases also for contributing to the finances. Some are extremely disappointed in what marriage has turned out to be and wonder whether their expectations for marriage weren't so exaggerated that they couldn't possibly have found satisfaction. Even women who have been left by their husbands, while initially shattered, often say that they can now see ways in which the marriage limited their growth and happiness.

MIMI

There are times in life when it's a resting time. I don't want a serious relationship with anyone now. I'm resting up from a painful separation. I'm gathering my strength and I want to keep it all to myself for a while. I know I'm afraid that some of it will dissipate if I care about someone again. Will I become dependent again? Will I be able to maintain my sense of separateness, and not feel like I am merging into someone else? It's too shaky right now for me to even test it out. I want to go very slowly, and take time, and rest.

I want to see myself as a strong, independent woman. Does that mean if I ask for help that I will become weak and dependent? I find it so hard to announce that I am needy and can't do something alone. The thing is, I can do anything alone, but it can be so painful sometimes. And a person does need support.

Despite the fact that most of these women have been through at least one traumatic separation and divorce, many of them say they see remarriage in their future. Their reasons are usually similar to their reasons for getting married in the first place. It is difficult to be not married in a society that emphasizes being part of a couple. Marriage appears to be the best way to build some security into their lives, to find companionship and love, to "do the right thing" in the eyes of their family, friends, co-workers. Remarriage is just as enticing for them as marriage and probably more so, since most divorced women feel they made mistakes in their first marriages which they won't make the second time around. When we ask other women in our program why they are deciding to *stay* in their marriages, their reasons are similar to those of the women who are remarrying. Security, love, and respectability are high on the list. Often there are children involved, children who love both their parents and want the family to stay together. Many women feel they have put years of their lives into building their marriages and are reluctant to end them even though they are quite unhappy. They feel that what they are learning about themselves as women and about the institution of marriage will help them struggle with their husbands to make their marriages more satisfying.

Is This Book for You?

If this all sounds very negative to you, read on. We aren't suggesting that you never get married or that you divorce immediately if you are married. We think that the reasons women marry, remarry, and stay married are valid, given our upbringing, the messages about womanhood we get, and the lack of widely accepted alternatives.

We do believe there are ways to make marriage a supportive institution rather than the destructive one it has been for many women. This book is meant to give you new ways to look at your situation. We don't want to minimize the difficulties involved in making changes in a relationship that has been fixed for many years or of creating a new relationship along egalitarian lines. But we know it can be done, and we salute the courage of all the women we have met through the years who are struggling to make their relationships more fulfilling. In this book we want to share concrete information as well as personal stories and suggestions for new ways of interacting. We put a great deal of emphasis on the ways in which the economic and emotional aspects of a relationship interrelate and influence each other. It may not be terribly pleasant to speak of love and money in one breath, but it is very necessary.

MARYANNE

I definitely think marriage and motherhood get romanticized. Because it's not all it's cracked up to be and they want to make it sound a little bit better. I think society does it. Because a lot of people, once they get into it, realize that it's not candlelight and roses. The first year of our marriage and even now, Dennis and I learn things about each other--feelings that I never thought he had or that he thought I had. There are a lot of frightening things and terrible experiences that go along with getting used to someone else, and I think they romanticize it, they play it up to be only the good things.

This book is for you if you are a prospective bride. After you read it we hope you will have a better idea of what you are getting into. We hope your choice will be made not from what society expects but from your own understanding of what is best for you. If you want, you can take steps to ensure that your identity, your sense of self, is not submerged the minute you say, "I do." We hope this book will prepare you for the hard times as well as the good times. We want you to know ahead of time that the honeymoon will not last forever, but that there *are* ways to preserve and develop the love and caring which you and your partner now feel for each other.

This book is for you if you decide that marriage is not in your best interests. It will help you explore other options, deal with whatever feelings of doubt and guilt may exist, and reinforce your right to make a different choice.

This book is for you if you are already married and are not happy with your situation. We will probably contradict your friends, your family, and your therapist by saying that your problems may lie as much with the institution of marriage as they do with you or your husband, and maybe more so. Our suggestions for improving your situation may also contradict the advice of those around you, but they have been developed from the experiences of many women who were able to improve their lives.

This book is for you if you are considering remarriage. Having lived through one unhappy marriage (or a happy one), you have probably learned some of the things that make marriages work and some of the pitfalls. You may be feeling that you enjoy your single state and are reluctant to give up your independence. Or you may worry that there will be strains between your children and your pro- spective husband. Yet you look forward to the security and good times of a supportive relationship. Whatever your inclination at this point, you should explore all the possibilities for creating a new and satisfying life for yourself and your partner.

If you consider yourself happily married, we say congrat- ulations on accomplishing something that takes a great deal of perseverance and strength. We still think this book is for you. All of us need to find ways to grow, to change, and to improve the quality of our relationships. Most of us have a need for intimacy in our lives, and all of us have a need for self-understanding and a sense of self-worth. Developing these strengths is a lifelong process, of course, but the more we understand about the legal and economic influences on our emotional selves, and vice versa, the closer we will come to avoiding dependent, inhibiting relationships and to developing mature, fulfilling ones.

This book is also for you if you are a man. While we think that women are at the greatest disadvantage in marriage, most men also operate under destructive illusions about it.

JUDY

It's not that I couldn't live without him. We've both proven that we can. That's not the issue. But who the hell wants to? I'm so happy to have encountered somebody that living with him is better than living by myself. We all have to make adjustments, but there seems to be a maximum amount of grace going on in that. This is a list that I made up in September called "My Expectations for Marriage," which I submitted to Christian before we ever got very serious. These expectations are very personal, the product of my experiences in my first marriage and my relationship with Christian. They are, not in order of importance:

1. *Social acceptance.*

2. *Acceptance and respect of mate. That means that my efforts and ideas are to be taken seriously, acknowledged, not mocked, patronized, diminished, or belittled. Not necessarily agreed with or applauded, either--just accepted and acknowledged.*

3. *The marriage, the relationship, will not be static, will not be taken for granted, will not be used exclusively as a recharger of energy spent in other ways: work, play, change, etcetera. Energy will be spent on the relationship, in the certain knowledge that that is the most important way it can be spent. It is not secondary to other things. It will be spontaneous, creative. It will be taken very seriously by both.*

4. *Required reading: a women's lib book, The Joy of Sex, a Ginott book, The Death of Ivan Ilych, something about Pisces, and A Doll's House. Christian told me he won't read any of these.*

5. *An enclave of calm, comfort, quiet, and security.*

6. *Mutual support, protection, and help.*

7. *Greater financial security.*

8. *Openness and honesty in all dealings with each other. I need this very badly, cannot be secure without it. Trust.*

9. My needs are equal, not secondary.

10. My need to be alone, for privacy, must be respected. My needing to be alone at any given time is not a rejection of the other person or of his company.

11. I don't need much freedom of choice, sex, etcetera, if I have acceptance. One could quarrel with that, but that's the way I feel.

12. I will not be bound by custom, habit, expectation, passivity, and overprotection. I realize it is my responsibility to work on this one.

13. Help in raising my children.

14. More time and energy to devote to domestic concerns and inner space.

15. The best I have to offer is my best self. It is not helping the relationship or the other, much less myself, for me always to suppress, stifle, or subordinate my needs.

16. A stable relationship, constancy if not fidelity.

17. Sex must be taken seriously, too.

18. The man does the car things.

19. Lisa [her daughter] is a no-no.

MIRIAM GALPER

EVA SHADEROWFSKY

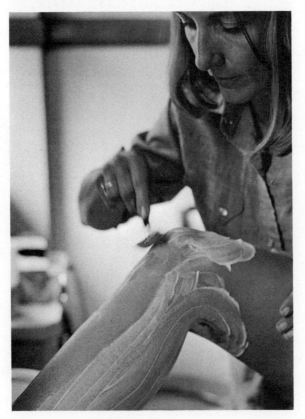

MIRIAM GALPER

BEA WEIDNER

EVA SHADEROWFSKY

EMIKO TONOOKA

JOANNE KANDER

FEMINIST RESOURCES

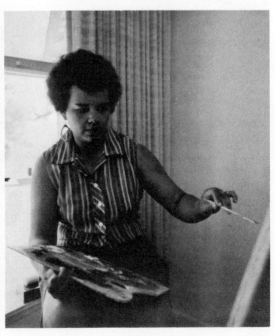

2

JORDAN

I'm going to be married next month. I'm twenty-two and I'm a student in dentistry. I grew up in a small town in western Pennsylvania. I have been very opposed to getting married for a long time. I never thought I would get married, and until Ron asked me to get married, I was saying to that minute, "I'll just live with someone." Then when he asked me, I was sort of . . . flattered is a good word for it. I appreciated the way that he thought. I felt honored in a way. Not the old-fashioned kind of honor, but he knew that he could have just lived with me. I had no intentions of leaving him; he didn't marry me to keep me. We would have lived together anyway. I think marriage means more to him than it does to me, maybe because his parents had a bad marriage. We've had something really good and he wants a good marriage.

I had a really good home life. My parents have a great marriage, and I was always brought up thinking you should be a virgin and get married. Then I sort of lost all my religion when I was a senior in high school. I started thinking that marriage was a stupid thing, too. I thought it was stupid because a little piece of paper doesn't mean anything. I said things to myself like, nobody can tell you what you feel, nobody can tell you that you're married, a lot of people who have their marriage certificate don't act like they're married, etcetera. I don't like the diamond rings and all that. I still didn't get a diamond ring. The idea of having a big wedding and a white gown and all these people coming and paying out vast amounts of money for a wedding--it just seems absurd to me. The whole idea of it--owning each other, saying that I'm yours and he's mine and I stick with him forever no matter what, promising that you're going to be there--it doesn't seem right to me. It seems like too many restrictions are put on people when they get married. I don't like that idea. Such as, when you do things, you do them together pretty much. I guess you don't have to have it that way. I know I won't be able to. I can't have a marriage like that.

I think that couples who live together and aren't married avoid those restrictions a lot more than people who are married. Because other people don't look at you and categorize you so much as being one entity then. You still have different names. You tend not to be able to think of that other person as always there because it is a lot easier to get up and walk out. There is a commitment, but not the commitment of the paper, and the families all saying that they're married. There's just a difference there, a difference in the way I think about it.

Ron and I are both agreed that after we are married our relationship will stay the same as it is now. We've been going together a little over a year. I still do entirely what I want to do. I still go partying with my other friends. I go to school with all guys; that's all my friends are, guys. And he's very good about it. I go swimming with some guys, I play paddle ball with other guys, I have a lot of friends that I do a lot of things with. If I want to go out to a party until four o'clock in the morning, there's a lot of trust there. He doesn't even wonder, "Well, what's she doing? Why isn't she home with me?" There seem to be no feelings like that at all. If that were to change, I couldn't handle it. He has the same freedom, but he doesn't seem to use it as much, maybe because he's in a different position. Most of his friends are males. Most of his friends from college are still around, and he goes and does things with them. I'm sure when they're drinking at the bar he probably dances with other girls, but I'd never want him to quit. That's part of the joy of living, being able to appreciate another person. I would feel dismayed if I thought that he was really untrue to me and sleeping with other girls. I would be really upset about that. I would feel very bad. We've talked about that, although we've never really said a lot. But enough has been said that we both know that we care. As far as something like that goes, that's too far for both of us to handle it.

I don't plan on having children. I'm really too selfish. I feel like I'm a big baby myself. I need to be pampered and cared for. I feel that you have to give so much time to children, and I don't think I'll have a lot of time because I'll be busy working. I don't intend to give up working, I like that. And in the time that I'm not working, I have so many other things that I enjoy doing, I just don't find time for children. Right now Ron doesn't see children as being a part of his future, but I think someday he might. I don't know how we're going to handle that, but he knows my feelings on that before he marries me. If I still feel the same, he can't ever put me down for it. Children bother me, too. I think they're really cute, I like children, but having one there constantly, having to be a companion to a kid all the time, would just drive me crazy. It would get boring to me after a while.

I'll be very disappointed if things change after the marriage. If I start feeling cramped or restricted, the very reasons that I didn't want to get married, I'll be really sorry. That's all I can say. I'll really be sorry. I just can't let it get that way. I think I can keep that from happening just by continuing to do the things I want to do.

A little bit more than me, he's going to want a traditional relationship. So I try to make him feel secure in all the ways that I can without losing myself. It's not like I don't want him to be happy or make him feel like he's the most important person, because he is. And I definitely want him to know that. But I still want him to let me continue doing the things I've always done. I think it will work out all right.

I'm not going to change my name. The school seems to get so hung up--"How can this be your wife if she has one name and you have another?" We checked into this, and you can call yourself anything you want to as long as you sign legal documents, such as taxes or if we ever bought something--I wouldn't care if it was in his name then. But as far as school goes and my friends, I'll keep my own name.

I think sleeping together before getting married is definitely a help, because we find out about each other. You wouldn't buy a horse without checking everything on it. So would you do that with a wife, somebody that you have to live with forever? And not even know what you're getting? Or a husband?

I have been able to picture myself going through life and not being part of a couple. I'm very independent. I don't need somebody else. I don't really feel like I need Ron. I love Ron, and I want to be with him, but if he died tomorrow or he left me tomorrow, I would be really sad, but I would get over it. I would always be able to get by. If my parents died tomorrow, I would be really sad, but I'd get through it. I really feel like I can make it through an awful lot on my own. I'd rather have someone to go through life with and make it with them. It makes it a lot easier to come home and cry your blues to someone else or laugh with someone else. I'd much prefer it that way, but I could do it otherwise. I think that's the only way two people should ever get married. You should never feel that you can't live without someone, or you're going to be a leech. Either they're going to get tired of your being a leech, or they're going to get burdened by you, one or the other. Unless you're independent enough to know that you can go through life alone, you shouldn't really try to hang someone else with yourself.

22

2 / What about Love?

Why Women Get Married

"I hated living with my parents and wanted to have a home of my own."

"I was pregnant. Nowadays it's easy to get an abortion, but then it wasn't. I figured I was better off married than dead on some butcher's table."

"All my girl friends were getting married. It seemed the thing to do."

"He was very sexy and I didn't want to sleep with him without being married first."

"My husband was the most dynamic person I had ever met. I could tell he was really going places, and I wanted to be right beside him. I couldn't imagine what he saw in me, but when he said he loved me I just had to love him back."

These are some of the answers we hear when we ask, "Why did
you get married?" The responses vary, but most women
agree that the romantic excitement of being a bride and
making a home for their husbands disguised their real
reasons for marrying--reasons they see clearly now. Low-
income and minority women are more likely to have married
for economic security, either to attach themselves to a
potentially steady moneyearner or to escape a difficult
family situation. Middle-class women, some of whom may
have had job or career plans, are more likely to have
married for romance or sex or companionship.

ANNA

*I was very conflicted in that whole period prior to
my wedding. I was depressed an awful lot. Years
later I found out that Don wasn't that interested in
getting married either, although it appeared to me
the whole time that he was really ready for it. And
he was in some ways. He had a whole different set
of neuroses that set him up for getting married. But
he was as conflicted as I was--he did and did not
want to. But once he had made the decision, which
is like everything else he does, when he actually
commits himself to something, he gets terribly
enthusiastic.*

*He and my mother got into this real trip together.
Planning the invitations and the seating and where it
was going to be. There's a lot of stuff that goes
into planning a wedding, I guess. I bowed out on the
excuse that it didn't really interest me, and I
think that was true to some extent, but what I think
it really was, was that if I had gotten as involved
as Don it would have meant more of a commitment to
the whole thing than I was prepared to make. This was
my way of rebelling, which is totally ineffectual.
It didn't stop the train from moving on.*

Fairy tales, romantic novels, soap operas, Hollywood movies,
parents, teachers, and neighbors have conditioned most of
us to think that men, marriage, and motherhood are our
whole reason for being. Girls were put on earth to become
wives and mothers, and any significant departure from that
is considered unnatural or pathetic or both. In recent
years there have been some changes in popular attitudes
about women's roles. These days it is more acceptable

for middle-class women to work outside the home as well as
in it. This is due in part to the now-popular idea that
home-bound women need stimulating contact with the outside
world, and in part to the worsening economic situation in
this country. Of course, low-income and minority women
for years have been forced to work outside the home for
their financial survival, and many say they would love
to experience the luxury of not having to hold down a job.
The prevalent notion, however, is that the roles of wife
and mother are the really important ones for women. It
is thought that a man should be able to support his family
on his income alone, and his job or career is considered
as important as his husband/father role, if not more so.

The reality is that most women don't have much choice
anyway. Higher education is just not a possibility for
many girls growing up in blue-collar and poor neighborhoods.
It may be difficult to study when there are family problems
or when a part-time job is necessary. Looking forward to
a lifetime of low wages and long hours of factory work,
waitressing, or typing seems hardly more appealing than
becoming a housewife, where there may at least be the
possibility of some creativity and control over the
surroundings. Women with college or graduate educations
may have more opportunities but are still subject to the
same pressures to marry, preferably an up-and-coming
professional man. That is how they must "complete"
themselves.

HARRIET

*I got married in 1941, two months before the outbreak
of Pearl Harbor. I actually thought marriage would
be kind of fun--being my own boss, along with my
husband. He lived with his mother and supported her
and I lived with my family and contributed heavily
to their support, but there was no great freedom
and our parents both kept very close track of us.
Not living at home if you weren't married was not
done in those days. Financially I probably couldn't
have done it anyway, but even if I had managed that,
having an apartment was frowned upon. There was
only one reason that you were going to take an
apartment with other girls, and that was to do bad
things. Now this is accepted.*

When you live with your parents your hours are very important--all-important, like Cinderella. You have to check in at a certain time and Lord help you if you don't. One time I stayed out all night, and all hell broke loose. So getting married was a form of independence. I thought it was going to be just wonderful to be on my own, and I really kind of liked housekeeping and cooking and that sort of thing, but done in my own way.

There is still relatively little encouragement for the woman who may feel that marriage and motherhood are not for her. Often she encounters resistance from friends and family and gets labeled a "women's libber." For the woman who feels restless, bored, or dissatisfied with her married life there are such labels as "neurotic," "selfish," "hostile." Women who are separated or divorced are often viewed with suspicion in their communities. Women and men alike are threatened by someone who is not part of a couple.

Popular culture in this country stresses "coupleness"; it also stresses women's subordination to men in general and to one man in particular. From childhood on we realize that our future status and security depend not on what we ourselves accomplish but rather on what man we "catch," and the competition for male approval begins. The message comes across loud and clear: the important people in the world are men. If you are white and middle-class, being female usually means acting weak, dumb, and passive whether you feel that way or not. If you come from a low-income or minority background, you are expected to be strong and independent in order to survive but often get mixed messages that assertive behavior is not appropriate for a "real woman." Even allowing for some cultural differences, strength, independence, assertiveness, self-confidence, bravery, courage, and self-reliance are all considered basically male qualities. Although almost no one would deny that these qualities are necessary for someone to be a complete human being, women are usually taught that acquiring them goes against our nature. Rather than enter into a fruitless and psychologically damaging struggle to develop these qualities ourselves, we are encouraged to find a man who has them. Through that union we will become complete.

Most of us are taught that our survival depends on
getting married, and how well we marry determines how
well we will survive. The old joke from mother to
daughter--"It's just as easy to fall in love with a rich
man as a poor one"--is no joke at all, but a lesson in
survival in a world where men have most of the power and
most of the options. How could we *not* want to marry
after all that pressure? Most of us can't wait to tie
the knot. Getting married gets us the approval of
friends and family, makes us the envy of other women, puts
us in the spotlight.

SARAH

*I wasn't trained for anything, so I started as a
ticket sorter at the bus company, which paid me
about twenty dollars a month, maybe. But I began
to meet people there. At that point I tried to do
what it looked like all the women were doing. I
even went to charm school to get trained to somehow
be a proper female. And I left my hundred-dollar
charm school course thinking, "I don't know how I
can do this. I'm not about to give up swearing."
There was a lot about me which seemed unacceptable
but was so much me that I didn't really want to
give it up and take on these refinements. So I
tried, but I never really made it as a proper,
man-hunting female in San Francisco.*

MIRNA

*Puerto Rican parents are really strict and they
didn't believe in dates. They believe if you like
a guy you wait a while to bring him home, and
when you bring him home it feels like you are
supposed to marry him. Fil went in the service--
he was in the Air Force and he was there for four
years. After three and a half years in the service
he came home and asked to marry me. At first I
didn't know what to say and I said yes. Then when
he left I was undecided. I didn't know if I
wanted to get married--I just didn't know. I wanted
to turn around and say no because I didn't know if
I was in love or not because he was my first boy
friend. It was really hard. I just felt like*

crying 'cause I wasn't sure if I was ready for it and I wanted to wait anyway and I am glad I did.

When I was at home my parents wouldn't let me go out. I was always home, and if I went out it was with my mother. I feel I am more free now that I am married.

JANICE

A couple of weeks before I got married I said to my mother, "I'm going to be married in a couple of weeks' time. Aren't there any things you want to tell me about sex?" She said, "Ask your girl friend. She just got married." That's the extent of the sexual information that my mother ever imparted to me. I thought you had to have an orgasm in order to get pregnant. So, not having orgasm, I knew I wasn't pregnant, and three months into the pregnancy I was still sure of that. Then my period stopped and that clicked. I knew that when your period stopped something else was wrong.

What Our Mothers Didn't Tell Us

Most marriages have bad times as well as good times, but many of us didn't have any idea how bad the bad times could be or what to do about them. We have learned from talking with other women that most of our mothers did not share the problems in their marriages with their daughters. They were perhaps afraid of being seen as failures in their daughters' eyes or felt that they had no right to complain and should keep a stiff upper lip. How many of us knew about our mothers' tears, or if we did, knew what was causing them? Those women who did share their disappointments usually insisted that the problems were their own fault for making a bad choice of husband or for not being better wives. As children we were usually aware when all was not well at home, but most of our mothers did not share their feelings with us because they were ashamed or frightened or could not even acknowledge those feelings in themselves.

Those of us who grew up in homes where our parents were separated or divorced got a slightly different picture. Some mothers were so disillusioned that they warned us to

stay away from men altogether and never get married; yet
we were bombarded daily with the confusing message that
marriage is women's most important goal. Other divorced
mothers felt that the failure of the marriage was totally
their fault. Since they hadn't been able to hold a man,
they would make sure that their daughters could, and they
pushed us into early or unsuitable marriages. In either
case, we were usually not told what had caused the divorce,
often because our mothers themselves were not clear about
it. Their own sense of failure and isolation often prevented them from looking at their lives objectively or
from seeing anything positive about the divorce.

Of course, there are women in happy marriages who would
choose to marry the same man again if they had it to do
over. But there are few, even among those, who don't
add that if they could live their lives again, they would
make some changes. They would have gotten more education
or kept their jobs or not had children or developed more
interests outside the home. Some older women say they can
only see this now because their husbands have died or
left them or their children are grown. They find that the
things that were supposed to fill their lives are gone and
there is little left to replace them.

When we married, we looked forward to a closeness with our
men which would give us stability and some good times. We
wanted to share life's joys and sorrows with them. Many
of us, in fact, do continue to share important events,
experiences, and feelings with our husbands and lovers,
but we have learned that the good things about intimate
relationships don't happen automatically. They have to be
created. We have also learned that the things we are
expected to do as wives are sometimes simply impossible,
and where we can live up to those expectations, it is
often at the expense of our time, energy, and happiness.
Lacking honest information from our mothers about marriage,
we have had to learn about the pitfalls and frustrations
by ourselves, the hard way. Such as . . .

GIVING

We have learned that giving is something that women are
expected to do a lot of, get rewarded for, and generally
feel good about. The standard arrangement in most marriages is that the husband brings in the major income;
the wife, who may or may not work outside the home, does

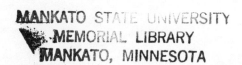

most or all of the housekeeping and childrearing. This
constitutes the partnership. Supposedly each spouse
contributes to the marriage the things she or he is best
at, and everybody benefits.

There are several problems with this notion of partnership.
First, since most wives aren't paid for housework and
child care, the husband is in fact getting these services
for free while he is able to build up skills and seniority
on his job. Should the marriage end, the wife will have
to start from scratch in the labor market and will be
dependent on his goodwill for support until she is earning
an adequate income. (If that sounds exaggerated to you,
see Chapter 3, "Marriage As a Legal Institution," for
some frightening facts on how little economic protection
wives and ex-wives have under the law.) If the wife
is working outside the home *and* doing most of the housework, she in effect has two jobs but is being paid for
only one.

Dinner Theater

*Let's reconstruct
the death
of this body
this love
the laughs
that came too easy
to be real
Neil Simon has
written our script
He gives you
a nervous stomach
and makes you forget
your Tums again
on the train
For the second week
in a row we will hear
your gut gurgle and churn
Remember this is
Sunday night
in Philadelphia All
the drugstores are closed
Meanwhile in my kitchen I
have cubed a whole lamb shoulder
half fat*

to make shishkabob
because you insist
beef is too American
and the only cheese
to use in omelets
is Vermont cheddar
But I am ready for your
ego   You say hello
with a hard-on
you bring behind your briefcase
all the way from Washington
It pops up like a bad joke
though you are
scarcely through the door
Times like this I
feel like a service station
and know you don't
give a damn about my
energy crisis   You have me
before dinner   I thought
this was a comedy   We eat
sitting on the floor
while the stereo blares
We share the last
skewer of meat
At 11 pm you feel
weak with fatigue
We do not speak
You undress in the dark
while I replace
our wineglasses
in the freezer
They'll chill in five minutes   No one
says goodnight
Something between us
is new   I know you
have changed but that is
an old feeling I always had
after five years as a wife
Why such silence
just when I need
applause

> *Maralyn Lois Polak*
> *June 26-28, 1973*
> *For JCG*

The other major problem with most marriage partnerships is
how unequal the emotional giving often is. Under the
guise of equality and compromise and sharing, it is
usually the woman who is giving in, sacrificing. This
happens in big and small ways and every couple has a different version of it. Bob and Sue, for example, have been
married for fifteen years. Bob has had several love
affairs during that time, which Sue tolerates, although
she is afraid his playing around will break up their
marriage. Bob, however, is enraged when Sue so much as
dances with another man at a party. Or, Mary is expected
to take care of Tom's children from his first marriage
when they visit weekends and one month in the summer.
Or, Will expects Betty to listen and be supportive about
his problems at work, but he refuses to take seriously
her problems with trying to care for the children and
taking refresher courses at the community college.

JUNE

> *I think the feeling of being needed by someone and
> having the satisfaction of knowing you're doing the
> best you can and that they appreciate that fact is
> important. I think there are times when you feel
> that little things mean a lot whereas you don't get
> them from men sometimes. Just a little compliment
> here and there could be encouraging you so much.*

> *I don't really get that. But many women I've talked
> to say the same thing. If men only realized that
> little things do mean an awful lot, that women
> could just go on and clean the whole house if their
> husband said, Gee, you really look sharp today,
> or Your hair looks nice. A little recognition
> could go a long way.*

> *As far as benefits of marriage, you enjoy watching
> your children together, sharing their growing up.
> And then you have to think what's going to happen
> when the children have grown up and gone off on
> their own. You'd feel very much alone if you didn't
> have some companionship.*

In most marriages the wife is the peacemaker, the mediator,
the family member who isn't supposed to get angry or
demand things for herself. Most men have been raised with
the expectation that there will be a woman in their lives--

mother, wife, secretary--who will take care of them, and
many of us fall into that role because it feels familiar
and comfortable. Sometimes this role makes us feel good--
we see ourselves as caring, loving people in a hostile
world. But more often than not the role of "the giver"
burdens our already stressful lives and turns us into
martyrs. It occurs to us that martyrs may be venerated
when they're dead, but they aren't particularly good
company when they're alive.

DOTTY

*I think most men are like that, and he just tries
to be like most men. Deep down inside I really
believe he wants to be kindhearted and a very cool
person, but he has to run around here and show
that he's a man, play Mr. Tough Guy. He has to be
able to say, "My old lady's at home," while he's
running around having a good time. I'm a good old
lady, he comes home and pats me on the back.
Because he's got to keep his image up.*

*What's the way out for him? Number one, just
consideration. Just being considerate. I really
think it would be easy for him and me to live
together if he would just do simple things around
the house, such as picking up after himself, cooking
dinner. Why do I have to ask? If something has to
be done, it should just be done. Then, taking part
in caring for the children. Why should it all be
on me? Because Tim wouldn't be here if it wasn't
for him, too. It's his child, too, and he has to
take part in raising him, caring for him, bathing,
everything. He's always saying he wants me to
inspire him, help him to do shit. So why doesn't
he inspire me? I write, and he never says anything
about my writing. I think he's threatened by it.*

DEPENDENCY

When we were younger, many of us dreamed of having someone
take care of us. Even if, as is the case with many low-
income women, we were warned that we had to depend on
ourselves because in the long run no man could be counted
on, we still had our hopes. If we married an up-and-coming,
dependable young man, we were relieved; our lives were

set; we no longer had to worry about what would become of us. Bit by bit we learned that being taken care of robbed us of ourselves. We became unsure of our abilities, our judgment; we became crippled. This handicap takes different forms depending on our backgrounds and life situations. For some women it is economic. If their husbands walked out tomorrow and refused to pay a cent or died without adequate insurance, they would be destitute. They have no skills (or the skills they once had are rusty) and no self-confidence. They are terrified to provoke a fight, to tell him what is really on their minds, for fear he will leave. And the thought of leaving him and making their own way is overwhelming.

The Garden of Eden

She reaches out to him.
He turns away
From wanting to respond.
He is afraid.
She looks in the mirror
Wondering what's the matter
With her.

Judith Bondy Brigham
October 29, 1975

For others the dependency is emotional. Each of them is the Woman Behind the Man. They need his ideas, his opinions, his interests, his friends, to make them feel like whole people. They are insecure about their own ideas, their friends. They have defined themselves through another person, and the thought of losing him panics them. If he becomes interested in another woman or simply less attentive to them, they feel worthless. They can't imagine coping with life on their own.

Some women are *both* economically and emotionally dependent on their husbands. Being so totally wrapped up in another person makes them feel warm and secure sometimes, but frightened and anxious other times.

POWER

We learned about power. Before marriage most of us wanted husbands we could look up to--husbands who were older, smarter, more educated, stronger. They would feel like real men and we would feel like real women. We expected to defer to our husbands when important decisions needed to be made. What actually happens is that often neither we nor our husbands fit the image. Our husbands don't like having to be towers of strength and we don't like having to take orders. Or they take the role of boss so seriously that any real cooperation is impossible. Those situations are hard on both partners because neither is living up to what was expected.

In most relationships there is a power struggle going on. *Power* is a word that is unpleasant to most women. We aren't supposed to think about it or try to acquire it, in either political terms or physical terms. As girls we weren't taught much about power--not how to run for public office or how to defend ourselves on the streets or how to demand what we want from an intimate relationship. It isn't ladylike. Few of us want to admit that in our marriages we are confronted with a daily struggle for power. Perhaps *negotiation, compromise,* and *communication* are nicer words. But much of what is usually called a personality clash in intimate relationships is in fact a struggle for power. Whose wishes will come first in a situation where the partners can't agree? Who is in control? Even in the best marriages there is a tremendous amount of back-and-forth that goes on in order for the family to live together. Since we can't all have everything we want all the time, we have to negotiate. Sometimes his needs take precedence, sometimes ours, sometimes the children's. That is bound to go on unless the family members are entirely isolated from each other. In good marriages this struggle is recognized for what it is and the family tries to develop ground rules for it. Family members try to figure out what they want and ask for it rather than manipulating others or denying themselves totally. Ideally no one should profit at the expense of others and everyone should have a chance to grow, develop, find out what makes her or him happy. In unhealthy marriages there are patterns of dominance and submission which are played out over and over again. The husband usually wields power over his wife except for what she has carved out by manipulation or deception. His word is law and everyone in the family has to abide by it or sneak around. The wife, in turn, often plays the same role with the children. She may have control over nothing else in her life, and in desperation she lives her life by running theirs.

We have found that women's experiences with power
relationships in marriage differ somewhat depending on
whether they are black or white; low-income, working-
class, or middle-income. In many marriages of low-income
couples it may appear that the women are under their
husbands' thumbs. Low-income men usually feel they have
little control over their own lives; they may feel trapped
in their jobs and trapped by having to support their
families. Consequently they take out those feelings of
frustration on those closest to them, their wives and
children, by being domineering and unreasonable at home.
Such a man can punish his family in many ways, sometimes
physical but usually verbal ("Aw, you're a slob just like
your mother!") and psychological ("I'm going to the bar
and I'll be back when I'm good and ready"). In some
lower-income families, on the other hand, it may appear
that the wife is the domineering one. She pays the bills,
keeps the kids in line, orders her "henpecked" husband
around. Yet women who have found themselves in this role
have told us that while they have the appearance of more
independence, they still feel trapped in a situation they
can't control. They feel that they have been maneuvered
into being the "grouch" so that their husbands can get
the sympathy of friends and family. They may have control
over what to have for dinner, but they are still tied to
the husband and children and the roles they have created
for each other.

In many middle-class families there appears to be more
equality. In some cases it reflects a real sharing, and
in other cases it just means that the husbands have stopped
openly criticizing their wives and ordering them around
Middle-class men often have more job options and get more
enjoyment from their jobs. Their manhood is not so much
in question, so they can be more flexible about their
roles, such as doing housework from time to time or taking
care of the children. When such flexibility reflects a
man's openness to change and sharing, it is exciting.
Sometimes, however, it can be a cover-up for a more subtle
form of psychological domination. The wives in such
situations, while appearing to have more options, are very
much dependent on their husbands' goodwill to make the
arrangement work. Such domination may be harder to
recognize and deal with because it is more subtle.

SEX

And we learned about sex. First we learned that we didn't
know very much and basically our husbands didn't either.
We didn't know how our bodies functioned. We didn't know
what kinds of pleasure we had a right to expect. We
didn't know how to ask for what we wanted. We expected
our husbands to know everything and to take the initiative
and if they seemed awkward or unsure of themselves (or
brutal and insensitive), we were confused and disappointed.
We were afraid even to talk about our feelings for fear
of insulting or angering them. As we have learned more
about our bodies and our feelings, some of us have tried
to share this knowledge with our husbands. Others of
us found it too threatening to them or to ourselves and
go unsatisfied, get our needs met elsewhere, or develop
a rich fantasy life. It is commonly thought that sex is
the biggest problem in unhappy marriages. Our experience
has been that problems in a couple's sexual life usually
reflect problems in the rest of their relationship. A
man who is tight with money probably isn't warm and giving
in bed either. A woman who keeps her marriage together
by always putting herself last is probably not getting her
sexual needs met, just as she is not getting her other
needs met.

ROBERTA

My husband didn't really like sex. I think he was
afraid of it. Anything except for straight screwing,
that is. He was afraid to deal with me as a sexual
person and as such, and in subtle ways, denied me
my sexuality. He didn't want to touch my clitoris.
I think now that he didn't want me to know pleasure.
But it all came down as me being the one who had
sexual problems and he as this loose, free sexual
spirit who was being held back by me, old tightass
herself. Before marriage I'd had a lot of sexual
experiences, which he could barely hear about, so
much so that I felt I had to lie to him about how
many men I'd slept with. When I did tell him about
some, he heaved a plate against the wall in rage and
frustration. And jealousy and anger. And maybe his
powerlessness to have control over my past. And he
made me deny that past by discouraging me from being
more free with him sexually. He didn't like it when
I talked or made noises during sex. So I stopped.

He didn't like me to touch myself, so I stopped.
I stopped being aggressive and active in sex. So,
of course, I also stopped being a sexual person.
It took me years and years to see all that, how
he couldn't deal with his own feelings of jealousy,
so he made me into a thing to not be jealous of.
If you're not married to a sexy woman, then you have
nothing to fear, right? At least, that's probably
how he figured it. It hurts me so much to think
about this, because I wanted him to love me so
much that I let it all happen. I didn't say,
"Wait a minute, I like to touch myself." I just
withdrew. And then he attacked me for withdrawing.
It was your basic lose-lose situation. The women's
movement gave me strength to say, "Wait a minute."
And I know I won't deny that part of me because of
any man any more.

The "His" and "Hers" Marriage

Sociologists and psychologists bear out what we learned
from the women who came to Women in Transition.* Their
writings indicate that there are actually "his" and "hers"
marriages. Husbands and wives have different perceptions
of almost everything--how long they courted before marriage,
how often they have sexual relations, the nature of
companionship and communication within the marriage, who
does household chores, and how decisions get made. There
is considerable evidence that marriage is actually good
for men, despite the bad reputation it has. Married men
live longer, are healthier, are more successful, and are
generally happier than unmarried men. Despite a lot
of male grumbling about marriage, statistics show that
once men have been married, they can't wait to get married
again. Divorced and widowed men marry in greater numbers
than single men, and many do so within just a few years
after being divorced or widowed.

Marriage for women, however, is another story. Once
married and raising a family, women often feel disillusioned, isolated, bored, sometimes crazy, wondering

*The *Future of Marriage* by Jessie Bernard is a fascinating
summary of this research. See Bibliography.

why they feel that way and feeling guilty that they do.
Married women show more symptoms of psychological stress--
that is, depression, fear, anxiety--than married men or
unmarried women. It appears that women are literally
being driven mad by marriage. Single women, despite
the extraordinarily bad reputation "spinsterhood" has,
consistently rate higher than the three other groups in
studies of mental stability, emotional maturity, and
happiness.

However, sociologists and psychologists also say that
even many of the wives who report that they are happy show
the anxieties and fears associated with acute stress or
mental illness. The researchers' analysis of this paradox
is that since most of these women were conditioned to think
that marriage would bring happiness, they define themselves as happy simply because they are married. Many of
them have adjusted to such a low level of expectation that
they are by clinical and common-sense standards actually
miserable. Jessie Bernard calls this phenomenon the
"housewife syndrome" and says it may very well be our
number-one public health problem.

AGORAPHOBIA--A LESSON FOR ALL WOMEN

I am a psychologist and have spent the last several years
working with women who have a problem labeled agoraphobia,
and I have learned something important about all women.
Agoraphobia literally translated means "fear of the
marketplace." Agoraphobics are often afraid of super-
markets but can also be afraid of any kind of closed space,
of traveling, of trains, buses, driving, bridges, eleva-
tors. The common denominator of all these fears is the
feeling of not being able to get to a place of safety or
to a safe person, usually a husband or parent. People
with this problem fear they will have a panic attack and
die, go crazy, have a heart attack, or start screaming and
embarrass themselves in public. A person will have this
kind of panic attack--and I imagine we've almost all had
them--and then is scared to go back to the place where it
happened. Eventually she or he worries about it so much
that the worrying brings on an attack. The remarkable
thing is that 85 percent of these victims are women,
primarily because parents and husbands often encourage a
woman's dependency and because such behavior in men is
tolerated less. When a man acts like this, everybody

asks if he's weird, but often a woman's parents or husband
have gone along with the problem and allowed her to be
dependent and not pushed her to go out on her own.
Agoraphobia is an extreme case which points up what we all
face: being expected to find a man to take care of us,
not developing our own coping skills. Discouraging
women from becoming self-sufficient can be a breeding
ground for pathology.

                                        Dianne

What are we to make of all this? You may not recognize
yourself in any of the situations we have described. But
if you do and want to make changes in your marriage or
primary relationship because you feel your needs are not
being met, read on. Most of us still have a need for love,
security, companionship, respect, and a long-term
commitment. For many women there is something necessary
and appealing about making that a legal commitment. If it
appears that our only options are a draining, confining
marriage or a lonely spinsterhood (or its modern equivalent, the swinging, lonely, sexually liberated life), many
of us would probably still choose marriage. Fortunately,
these are not the only options. Chapter 6, "Is That All
There Is?" discusses many options, including some of the
most common choices: living together without marriage,
communal living, and staying single combined with building
a network of close relationships. The next section of
this chapter discusses options within a more traditional
marriage relationship. The chapters on the law, finances,
and children are important to any discussion of the
emotional aspects of relationships, whether traditional or
nontraditional, because they are strong influences on the
quality of the love that's shared between partners. We
think it is possible to develop a relationship characterized by mutual respect and genuine sharing. But love can
become a healthy reality only when it is created by two
self-sufficient individuals who are working to eliminate
the crippling roles of "husband" and "wife."

Becoming a Separate Person within an
Intimate Relationship

Let us start by saying frankly that this is difficult to
accomplish, and we don't want to be glib about it or
underestimate the strength it takes. To become a separate
person within an intimate relationship requires going
against what we have been conditioned to believe and
against the advice of friends and family. It also requires
constant attention and a willingness to undergo tremendous
upheaval in your life, especially if you have been relating
in a rather traditional way for a number of years.

What do we mean by being a separate person within an intimate relationship? Many women started thinking about
themselves as separate people from their husbands as a
result of contacts with other women. That usually happened in women's consciousness-raising groups, which we
will talk about later, but it also happened at work, at
parties, or over the back fence--wherever women met and
felt they could be honest with one another. Why wouldn't
our husbands do the dishes? Why didn't we feel satisfied
sexually? Why was he threatened by our going out at
night with "the girls"? Many of us valued our relationships and weren't ready to separate or divorce. But
we wanted changes. We didn't like the idea that he was
supposed to be boss and we were supposed to serve him.
We wanted to be capable, interesting people ourselves and
to get credit for our accomplishments. We wanted to have
something real to offer another person, not just exist in
a close relationship because we were afraid (or could not
afford) to live alone or thought no one else could possibly want us. But at the same time as we wanted strength
and individuality, we also wanted to love and be loved.
We wanted to be open to another person and to the experiences we could share. We wanted a partnership in which
each person learned from the other, supported her or him,
and contributed to make the whole greater than the sum of
the parts. How to do this without one partner giving far
more than she (and sometimes he) got back? How to be
interdependent without being completely dependent?

We have talked a lot about dependency in our program and
among our friends. Some women use the phrase *healthy
dependency* to describe a situation where the partners
are truly partners--they can count on each other when they

are in trouble or depressed but don't feel swallowed up
or controlled by that other person. Other women feel
that the term *healthy dependency* is a contradiction, that
dependency in any form will always be destructive. Whatever words are used, what is important is to know we can
count on the other person but also to know we can step
back and live our own lives. The goal is to feel that
our partners know enough and care enough about us to be
sensitive to our needs and feelings (which, ideally, we
reciprocate) but not clutch at us or need our constant
attention or praise or support to keep themselves going.

There aren't Ten Easy Steps to Intimacy with Independence.
How you grow toward separateness, should you choose to do
so, will depend on your situation and your character. You
will need to come to terms with the issues of giving,
dependence, power, and sex in your own way and at your
own pace. We can only make a few suggestions, and we refer
you to the Bibliography for further readings. The problem
with books and articles on this subject, however, is that
they are usually written by white, middle-class, literary
or academic men. They do not take fully into account the
dependence which most women have developed and how that
dependence affects an intimate relationship. They also do
not take into account how the daily struggle for survival
can make discussions of personal growth irrelevant. These
writers usually talk about discovering and getting in
touch with your inner feelings, learning to communicate
them to your partner, developing commitment and trust,
learning to risk, and so on. All of these are important
qualities in a good relationship, but we as women must
develop our own understanding and interpretation of these
concepts. Otherwise, we run the risk of developing relationships that appear to be hip and liberated but are
still based on the old sex roles.

Let us say you are married or in a long-term relationship,
you are satisfied enough to want to work at it, but you are
unhappy about some aspects of the relationship. Or you
are planning to get married but have some reservations
about what life with him will be like. You want to do
everything possible to make the marriage work. You think
that the idea of being a separate person sounds good. The
suggestions we make here are simply guidelines, not rules
to be followed. Every woman must decide what will work
in her situation and at what pace she wants to change.

We stress that these suggestions are not about learning
to cope with men. Women have been sharing those tips for
centuries and have had to learn how to get what we want,
usually through manipulation or deception. We are talking
about learning to figure out what you want for yourself,
sharing those desires openly with your partner, finding
out what he wants, and together working out ways for
each of you to have what you want when that is possible.
When that is not possible, and it often isn't, the two of
you will have to learn how to negotiate fairly and honestly.

Your goal is emotional independence, a positive self-image,
and an understanding of who you are as a person. Without
those ingredients, a loving, mutually satisfying relationship will be difficult, if not impossible. Since we
have been conditioned to equate love with dependence
and need, we must begin to develop new definitions of what
is called "love." We believe that true love is based not
on how well someone can meet our needs, but on how well
we can express admiration, respect, and trust for other
human beings and experience those in return. Love must
grow from strength and self-confidence, not dependency
and desperation. How capable are we of loving? As women
we have been left with missing pieces, we have been
crippled by internalizing society's definition of womanhood. The extent to which we have accepted the myth of
our own inferiority determines the extent to which we
are incapable of loving. Without complete personhood,
without true belief in ourselves, without a healthy
amount of *self*-love, we can have little love for others.

It is not easy to develop self-love. Learning to love
yourself involves risk, involves recognizing needs that
have been artificially created in you and letting go of
them. Sometimes you will have to push yourself when you
are feeling weak or fearful or guilty. Other times you
will feel that your goal is impossible and you will want
to retreat to the comfort of life as it used to be. But
the rewards of self-respect and growth are great. Over
time you can develop the knowledge of what is best and
right for you. You can acquire the sense of yourself
which is necessary to enable you to share that self with
another. While no one can tell you exactly how to
develop yourself, here are some suggestions.

ECONOMIC INDEPENDENCE

Our first and most important suggestion to you is to take
a look at your economic situation and make plans for
developing your economic independence if at this time you
are not capable of supporting yourself. We cannot stress
this enough. From our experiences at Women in Transition
it is clear to us that even though relationships fall apart
for many reasons other than financial problems, the fact
that most women are economically dependent on their
husbands usually distorts their emotional honesty and
openness. No matter how good you may feel about each other
now, you must face the fact that almost every relationship
runs into hard times. If you have to stay with him because
you need his money, you will both know it and it will
affect the quality of caring between you.

How quickly and in what ways you move toward economic
independence will vary depending on your situation. Chapter
4, "Who Controls the Pursestrings?" outlines what you need
to know about financial independence, and Chapter 3,
"Marriage As a Legal Institution," will surprise you about
how little economic protection you and your children actually have under the law. We do not mean that you should
rush out tomorrow and get a paying job if you do not have
one. That may be unrealistic for women with no job skills
or small children to care for. What we are suggesting is
that you plan for your future. Think about further schooling, job training, advancement at your current job. Think
about getting credit in your own name. You may not be
able to act on those plans for some time, but it is important to formulate them. If you do not have children,
consider what impact they would have on your finances as
well as on your emotional and social life. (See Chapter 5,
"Motherhood.") We hope your relationship will not de-
teriorate to the point that you have to support yourself if
you do not want to. If that does happen, however, you will
be able to move toward whatever is best for you without
being trapped because of money. And if your relationship
continues to be healthy, this is probably in part because
you and your husband both know that you are capable of
paying your own way in the relationship. You are not just
staying together because he is your meal ticket.

HARRIET

Twenty years ago, when my children were growing up, working mothers were few and far between in the suburban area that we lived in. It was kind of assumed that they had to do this because they needed the money. Women's lib was not a big thing--no one was trying to show that they had an identity of their own and they could go out and earn money and have a career--even those who were college-educated and had experience. If someone did work, it looked like her husband couldn't support her. Or if someone whose husband divorced her did go into a career, then that was understandable, that was acceptable-- you could do it even though you had children of school age.

If you already have a significant income of your own, take a look at the ways in which you and your husband share money. Most couples put money into a common pool; most husbands also make more than their wives. That can lead to friction, with the husband feeling he should have a greater voice in how the money is spent because he is bringing in more. We know some couples who keep their money separate, prorating their contribution to expenses based on what they are earning and adjusted for contributions to the marriage that don't bring in income, such as childrearing. They report that this eases tension considerably. If you are among the small but increasing number of women who earn more than their husbands, you know already that you have special problems to contend with, depending on the extent to which your husband's feelings about himself are tied up with the amount of money he earns. Again we would suggest prorating or some similar system as a way of reducing the tensions that arise around joint decisions about expenditures.

Does that advice sound cold and calculating? Are you afraid your husband will think you don't love and respect him because you want to be financially self-sufficient? Some men are very threatened by wives who work. Men know very well the independence that money brings and can fear it in their wives. They may also worry that others will think them not capable of supporting their families. You will have to decide whether your growing independence is worth his anger and disapproval. But after working with more than five thousand women, many of whom stayed in their marriages and improved the relationships, we are

convinced that economic independence is the first step in
building a truly egalitarian, mutually fulfilling marriage.

LEARN TO COPE--AND SHARE THE COPING

Learning to do things for yourself is another important
step. Most of us have been so intimidated by carpentry,
plumbing, and mechanics that we assume we need a man
around the house to do all those things for us. Mechanical knowledge is not transmitted through the genes, nor
is cooking ability. Men learned how to be "handypeople"
and we can, too. Obviously you don't have to know how to
do a complete rewiring job on your house in order to be a
separate person. But the more manual skills you have, the
more confident you will feel about taking care of yourself
and others in concrete ways as well as with love. There
are numerous "fix-it" books for women (see Bibliography),
and there are courses on carpentry, auto mechanics, and
other skills at local Y's, night schools, and vocational-
technical schools.

By learning to do things yourself, by the way, we aren't
suggesting that you do everything that needs to be done
around the house. Many women have the mistaken idea that
the road to liberation involves becoming a superwoman:
a woman who works full-time, has an immaculate home, cooks
gourmet meals, has well-groomed children, and so on. While
that might be possible for someone with tremendous amounts
of energy, it isn't possible for most of us, and anyway,
we don't think it's healthy. Our belief is that everyone
lives in a home and benefits from it, so everyone should
share responsibility for making it run. That includes
husbands and children. Sharing responsibility has gone
on for years in poor families where everyone contributes
so that the family can survive; sharing also existed
often in our parents' and grandparents' homes. The idea
of equal responsibility is just recently being introduced
into many middle-income homes, and sometimes there is a
great deal of resistance from family members who have
benefited from being waited on.

DOTTY

*My mother had seven kids when my father died, and one
on the way, and along came another man who married
her and took care of her and took care of us like*

we were his own children. She's got this thing about me, she thinks there's a lot of men out there that are like that, and there's not, there's not that many men out there like that. My stepfather was really cool as far as I'm concerned, as a person he was really cool. She thinks a man is the answer to everything; the roof is falling down, you've got to have a man around the house, that type of thing. Right now she's a widow, and she underestimates her abilities. She's got twelve kids, and she really underestimates herself. She doesn't think that she can make it. She might be coming around some now, but I can remember a few months ago she was trying to buy a house, which was hard for her because she's alone. She had to depend on my brothers since they're doctors, so the name would be good on the deed. So I can see why she's like that, because she has had to depend on men a lot. She thinks they're the answer to everything.

EMOTIONAL INDEPENDENCE

Probably the trickiest part of being a separate person in an intimate relationship is developing some emotional independence. Moving in this direction *surely* goes against the grain of what traditional marriage is supposed to be. One of the clearest messages we all get, men and women, is that your partner is supposed to fulfill all or most of your emotional needs. There is something wrong with your relationship if you need close friends or other lovers to share important events of your life. One psychologist has developed the theory that the American idea of romantic love is actually an addiction.* Many couples, he says, arrange to spend most of their time together, excluding other friends and failing to develop separate interests. Rather than developing ways in which they can grow as individuals within the partnership, what they are doing is becoming "hooked" on each other, using the other person as an object for their love. While such closeness may sound idyllic, the problem is that it may not stand up over time because the partners are not secure, well-developed people, sharing freely with each other and open to growth. They are only there to get their own needs met, not to give to the other. When anything interrupts the

---

*Stanton Peele, in *Love and Addiction*. See Bibliography.

closeness, such as having to be apart for a time, one of the partners may easily find someone else who meets his or her needs better. Understandably, this kind of relationship is usually characterized by jealousy and possessiveness. We agree with that analysis. We think that arrangement puts an incredible burden on the other person. It's almost as if someone tried to figure out the conditions under which two people would be most likely to suffocate each other and then called it marriage. In the days when extended families were more common than they are now, especially in middle-class communities, husbands and wives did not have to depend on each other so much for companionship, advice, and support. It was also easier for children, who had aunts, uncles, and grandparents to turn to and learn from. But in today's mobile, isolated nuclear family, too much is expected of partners who must meet each other's needs and their children's needs, often without the support of relatives and close friends.

Once again the issue is how to be interdependent without being dependent. If you bring all or most of your needs for love, closeness, honest feedback, dependency, sex, fun, and challenge to one other person and expect that person to meet all those needs, we think you are asking the impossible.

There are a number of issues connected with emotional independence, and we point out a few of them here. Thinking about those issues yourself and discussing them with your partner is part of the process of developing an equal relationship. You and he will have to decide which issues you can compromise on, which each of you feels comfortable with as they are now, and which are areas for future struggle and growth.

HARRIET

I think this happens to a lot of wives who are married to men who have white-collar jobs at more or less the executive level. The men get into the drinking bit and the entertaining the people from out of town and so on and so forth. When the wife is home and keeping the home fire burning and taking care of the children and Poppa is out having a helluva time and comes in three, four, and five in the morning--having been out and the wife worries about him in the first place--this is a very common thing, and the husband doesn't call home to tell the wife where he is--those are the things you live through and you get awfully mad. I think the young people who get married today, if this happens in the first year or two of marriage they don't give it a chance to simmer down and talk it out--right away they have to get a divorce. Things have a way of working out, and I am pretty vocal and made myself heard and it worked out for us.

You could start by thinking about your name. Did you take (are you taking) your husband's name at the time of your marriage, or did you retain your maiden name, your birth name, *your* name? The custom of a woman taking her husband's name is an old one. It indicated a woman's civil death upon marriage; that is, a woman became the property of her husband and ceased to exist legally as a separate person. While women today are gaining more legal rights within marriage, taking your husband's name still suggests that you are an extension of him, if not in your own eyes, certainly in the eyes of the community. There are realistic reasons why women take their husband's names: many women want to be identified with their husbands in that way; it does get complicated to explain your situation, especially when there are children; and people are often hostile to women who keep their names. We are not saying that you must have your own name in order to have a healthy marriage. We are suggesting that you think about your own situation and what your name means to you. Chapter 3 explains how to retain your own name, or retake it after marriage, should you decide to do that.

Another issue connected with independence concerns pursuing separate interests. Some women find strength and enjoyment through hobbies or religion or their work and yet often feel uneasy about being away from home. Other women simply enjoy being alone but feel that they are not entitled to privacy. This uneasiness may come from their own feelings of having stepped out of line or may result from their husbands' actual disapproval. Yet it is much more acceptable and often admired for men to be "married to their work" or deeply involved in a hobby. Our feeling is that external interests and supports, whatever form they take, are important for a strong sense of self. Both men and women are entitled to their own psychological and, if possible, physical space. Learning to accept your partner's separateness is difficult for many people who grew up with the idea that lovers should be inseparable, but learning to accept that separateness is part of what becoming your own person is about. You will have to decide for yourself how extensively you want to pursue your interests, based on the amount of resistance you encounter versus how much enjoyment they bring you.

SARAH

I think it's very difficult to have a monogamous relationship and to work that out, so it's not threatening for two people to have various needs met by other people. My experience is that friends who get married tend to be further apart from me than they were before they got married, and I sometimes feel that as a real loss. One friend and his wife really try to allow for diverse relationships separate from each other, but I think it's difficult to do. You only have so much energy and a whole sense of commitment to that person that changes. If I got involved in a long-term relationship I would like to do that. I think initially your involvement with that other person becomes pretty total, like any new thing in your life, and later that tapers off and you go back to putting energy in a more balanced way into many more things. I'd really have to work at it. I think it would be easy for me to get blinders and discover later that the relationship wasn't enough.

The separate-interests issue often comes to a head at vacation time. Many women complain, for example, that for years they have been forced to go where their husbands want because the men are the major breadwinners and deserve to relax where they want to. The idea of separate vacations is frightening to many couples. One partner may assume that the other wants to be free for sexual involvement with someone else; one partner may worry that the other simply doesn't need her or him to have a good time; a woman may worry that her husband, when left alone to take care of himself, can do it very well. What does that say about her role in the marriage? Couples who choose to take separate vacations invariably are criticized or ridiculed by friends and relatives. Yet taking separate vacations makes much more sense than one partner imposing his or her will on the other. Couples who do vacation separately, either alone or with friends, report they get

a new and healthy perspective on their marriages and have
a good time as well. Taking separate vacations doesn't
guarantee a good marriage, but the discussion of whether
or not to do so can open up an important dialogue.

Perhaps the most sensitive issue for couples where the
wife is moving toward a more independent life is the one
of separate friendships. Going to needlepoint class once
a week or joining a bowling league is one thing; having
one or several intimate friends is something else.
Husbands fear that their wives may leave them, psychologically or physically. Wives may also fear being
left by their husbands, but since men are usually working
and have greater opportunity for contact with others,
their independence is usually taken for granted in a
marriage. Despite the risks involved, we feel it is
worthwhile to develop, however slowly, friendships in
which you can truly share important experiences and
feelings. For different women this can take different
forms: family, close women friends, close men friends,
co-workers, lovers. Later in this chapter we discuss
women as friends and supports. Some of the other options
are discussed in Chapter 6 on alternatives to marriage.
Whatever ways you choose to develop supports for yourself,
it is worth the effort. There is always the risk, of
course, that you will find someone who is more important
to you than your husband, and that is a frightening
prospect. But by developing many facets of yourself you
will probably find that you have more to contribute to
making your relationship strong. Knowing that you are
capable of closeness with others, you may not be quite as
devastated if the relationship ends. If the relationship
doesn't end, it may be that the two of you don't have
expectations of each other that are so unrealistic
they can't possibly be met.

Making It Work

Perhaps it sounds as if we are being simplistic. You say
you can't expect someone who has had a traditional marriage
for a number of years to develop outside interests or to
start spending more and more time with friends without
causing incredible shock waves in the relationship. You
are absolutely right. We don't want in any way to suggest

that it will be easy. Moves toward independence are
very threatening to children, families, friends, and
especially husbands. We need to warn you that your attempts
to become a separate person may not work. Some husbands
are so threatened by any signs of change in their wives
that the backlash is terrible. The struggle of dealing
with your husband's anger and hostility may not seem
worth it to you. On the other hand, you should not assume
that the aspects of your marriage which you are dissatisfied with can't be changed. There *are* men who have
responded favorably to their wives' moves toward independence. Only you know how your husband is likely to
respond. The ideas we share here can be a foundation for
your own growth. You need to find what is right for you,
learning to walk the line carefully between developing
yourself and totally upsetting your marriage. We suggest
that you go slowly, test out new ideas, think carefully
about what you are doing, and get support from sympathetic
friends and family.

CATHERINE

*I see the main strength in our marriage as the fact
that we saw each other at our best right before we
were married. We weren't clouded by romantic
feelings, by competition with anyone else. . . .
It was very real, no question about it. We couldn't
kid each other about anything. It was clear. For
one thing, if John was dating me, he was making
some commitment to me, because you don't just date
pregnant girls for kicks. And I really allowed him
into my life. In letting him share that, I was
really saying something to him about how I saw him
as being a good person for me then, and since it was
such an important time, I was saying a lot. I was
really letting him into a very private, personal,
intimate place for me. When we got married it was
very bad for several years, and part of that, and
maybe all of it, was our falling into roles we
felt were part of marriage. John became his father,
I probably became my mother. But it was like we no
longer saw each other as people. It was very confusing to me. I didn't understand what was going on.
It took me a long time to work my way out of that.
But even with that happening, even with John becoming
what I felt was not aware of me as a person or
thinking about me or listening to me as a person,*

just thinking of me as a wife, we never destroyed that first year we had of each other. We never went back to that part and said, "I wish I'd never met you then," or "You never really were a big help to me then," or "I just needed you, it wasn't that I loved you."

There are ways in which the threats associated with change can be minimized, however, so that you and your husband can feel that the changes in your relationship are benefiting both of you. Honesty is an important ingredient. As tempting as it might be to play down your anger or the extent of your dissatisfaction with the relationship because of the negative response you might get, your feelings will become apparent in the long run. It is much more useful to try to recognize them in yourself and share them with your husband. For many women this goes counter to a lifelong habit of telling others what they want to hear. Whenever a relationship is in flux, the partner who has not initiated the change is likely to be more frightened of where it is all going. Your husband's fears about what you will do may be worse than the reality. Reassure him whenever you can that you still love and care for him; when you are feeling confused or negative about him, be honest without being punitive. You can't guarantee each other that the relationship will continue to be satisfying to both of you; many relationships have ended when the partners realized that their individual growth was taking them in different directions. But talking about your changing feelings as you go along is preferable to one or the other suddenly walking out because the pressure of change has strained the relationship to the breaking point.

It is also important for you to keep in mind what your husband must be feeling. He, like most men, has probably grown up with the idea that women are there to meet his needs, since that has undoubtedly been his experience with his mother, his women relatives, his secretary (if he has one), and you. Now he is being asked not only to do without some of those comforts but also to provide them for you and perhaps your children. Maybe he has never cooked or washed dishes or spent long periods of time alone with the children or helped you cope with the problems in your life. Without compromising what you feel is right for you, you can be appreciative of his efforts to change, however minimal they might seem to you. And allow him to do what you are asking of him. Many women

want their husbands to take more responsibility for
household chores and child care but are also reluctant to
let go of their control in those areas. Most men have had
little experience in taking care of others and need time to
develop their skills, which includes making mistakes.

Mother-in-Law

With a critical eye
Faster than a speeding bullet,
You graciously grasp my hand.

Dripping perfection,
Head to toe,
You illuminate my flaws.

Muscles sag,
Defensively,
As I squirm before your scrutiny.

Saccharine words
Spill from your mouth,
Jangling against the drums of my ears.

My mouth moves
As if programmed
By some long-forgotten script.

For three days
We're locked in a duel
Of endurance of roles.

Your rules are tougher--
I wearily withdraw,
Waiting for him to return.

> *Anonymous*
> *November 30, 1975*

ROBERTA

Throughout the early years in my marriage I was the
one who nurtured the relationship between my mother-
in-law and her son, and between my mother-in-law
and me and her grandson, and between my mother-in-law
and my parents. This took the form of sending

little gifts at holiday time, sending pictures of the family, reminding my husband to call on Mother's Day--what shall we get for her birthday? It was all my thinking and my thoughtfulness, and I felt like I was really working hard in the face of adversity. The adversity was that I felt I had to work hard to make her like me, and that my husband didn't like his own mother.

At some point I made a big announcement to my husband that I was resigning from that role. He knew when her birthday was and if he wanted to send her a card or a present, he could take himself to the store and see to it. He knew her phone number, and if he wanted to call her, he could pick up the phone and call her. I was not going to suggest it to him any more.

Over the years I guess she did develop her own brand of love for me, although she never really did know my name or what my occupation was. She called me by the name of her other son's ex-wife, which always endeared her to me. Once she even sent me a gift, direct from her to me. It was some sexy negligée. I think that my husband developed a much better relationship with his mother without my help than had I hung in there.

Look realistically at how each of you is responding to the changes in your relationship. Different men respond to their wives' pressure for change in different ways. Some men are openly resentful and refuse to do what is asked of them. Others feel hurt and show it by withdrawing. Others talk about being open to change and growth but resist in subtle ways. Still others genuinely appreciate their wives' efforts to change patterns that have been unsatisfying to both of them. Women behave differently, too, in their quest for growth. Some women realize immediately how angry they are about having sacrificed themselves for many years and express that anger directly. Other women, unused to expressing feelings openly, still find themselves being manipulative and controlling even when they want to stop behaving in that way. Recognizing your own and your partner's behavior and discussing how you perceive each other can go a long way toward eliminating mistrust.

Talk about goals and expectations for yourselves and

whether you are moving toward or away from those goals.
Discuss what each of you will have to give up in order for
the relationship to change; also, think through what each
of you can gain. Are you willing to compromise? Is he?
Chapter 9 describes some of the costs and benefits for men
in responding favorably to their wives' pressure for
change. In general, despite having to give up some
privileges, most men have found that supporting their
wives' desire for a more equal marriage has resulted in
unexpected benefits for them. The role of husband, while
it usually carries with it more options than the role of
wife, often locks men as well as women into limiting
behavior patterns.

Above all, recognize that what you are trying to achieve
is difficult. There are few supports in this society
for couples who want to depart from a traditional marriage,
and even fewer supports for men than for women. When you
have tied your happiness and security to one other person,
changing the dynamics of that relationship can be
frightening indeed.

CATHERINE

*I always have been committed to my marriage. It
feels like if I left John or he left me, there would
be good things about not being married. I could also
find somebody else. But it's clear to me that I
couldn't find somebody better for me than John, in
spite of all the bad things, in spite of all the
things that get in our way. I know what he's really
like. Things would get in the way in any relationship. And because I know what he's like, strong and
sensitive and caring, if I could get through my
pregnancy with anybody, it would be with John.
Even when recently he feels we have nothing in common,
and our marriage isn't working, I feel like he
really loves me. It's like he can't see it right
now, but I'm so sure of it that that's enough. And
at other times in our marriage, he's been that sure
of it when I wasn't. When one of us falls apart and
becomes completely despairing, the other one becomes
the strength. We do it unconsciously, but it's
almost too coincidental to think that we don't
realize that it's our turn. It just seems to me that
one of these days we're going to be exactly together
on it. That will be nice.*

Recognize, also, that you can probably expect resistance
from yourself, since it is much more comfortable for all
of us to stand still and hope for the best. Taking risks
is painful, and experiments sometimes don't work. Choosing
among different options can be painful, too; sometimes it
seems to us that life was much simpler when we weren't
asking any questions. Maybe you don't want to branch out.
You feel your marriage isn't perfect, but making major
changes seems too threatening. Economic independence,
an extensive network of friends, and a variety of interests
do not *guarantee* happiness.

Our experiences at Women in Transition have taught us that
most women can't afford to stand still and hope for the
best. Happiness doesn't drop into our laps like they
told us it would. We have to work for it. And marriages
that are built on the foundation of women's subordination
are in trouble from the beginning unless the wives are
willing to sacrifice themselves forever to keep the marriage together. Even women who sacrifice in that way
are not always able to achieve the marriages they want.
Husbands die or find younger women, children move away or
run away from home, houses burn down, money evaporates.
Life is unpredictable, and the best insurance is your
ability to rely on yourself.

So don't expect growth to happen without pain, and don't
expect changes overnight. Most of us who are struggling
for separateness have been doing so for quite a while and
see that struggle as a never-ending process. Sometimes
we wish we could stop and go back to the peaceful life we
thought we had before. Sometimes we just get stuck.
But most of the time it feels so good to be trying honestly
to figure out what we want and how to get it that to stop
would be even more painful.

What are the joys? They vary according to each woman's
situation. Many women say they are able to be more honest
than ever before in their marriages. They don't have to
lie or manipulate to get what they want; they can ask
directly and negotiate from a position of strength.
They and their partners openly share feelings, ideas,
fears, and questions in a new way, and the relationship
takes on a new richness. Some women say they nag less, are
less grouchy, scared, martyred. They feel a new respect
coming from husbands, children, friends. They are less
worried about their husbands outgrowing them and consequently finding the marriage limiting. Because

(like it or not) in this society people's worth is often
measured by the money they earn, women who are starting to
earn money feel a new sense of self-confidence and power.
In general, despite the difficulties involved, women who
are struggling to become separate people feel as if they
are taking control of their lives. It's a good feeling.

Women As Friends and Supports

One of the greatest joys of developing separateness can
be the discovery that we don't have to mistrust other
women or compete with them. Most of us grew up with mixed
feelings about our girl friends or sisters. On the one
hand, they were the people we shared our lives with. We
giggled, gossiped, comforted each other, learned from
each other. On the other hand, especially as we got
older, every close friend was a potential boy-friend
snatcher. Even if she wouldn't go that far, the hint of
competition was always there. Is she prettier than I?
Thinner? Is her fiancé more handsome than mine? Smarter?
Richer? After we married we sometimes let our old friends
slip away--our husbands were more important to us. Our
husbands, however, still went out with "the boys." Other
times we used our friends as people to complain to,
shoulders to cry on when things went badly. But we were
reluctant to talk too honestly because it seemed disloyal
to our husbands and shameful to admit that all was not
perfect.

> *The Impossible Dream*
>
> *Perched like a displaced toad*
> *On an ancient bicycle,*
> *The woman struggles, panting,*
> *Trying to drive the fat from her body.*
>
> *She pedals frantically,*
> *Looking foolish*
> *In the rush hour traffic,*
> *Her face strained and discouraged.*
>
> *Standing beside the bike for a breath,*
> *Her face shows warmth and character,*
> *Lovely in its fullness,*
> *Hair pulled into a graceful chignon.*

Her body is thick and solid
From many years of nurturing
Others and herself,
Life a series of unsatiated hungers.

Was it a doctor's warning
That drove her to the bike,
Or a feeling of lost youth
And lost attractiveness?

I want to yell to her
Walk tall and proud.
But I am silent,
Sharing, vicariously, her shame.

Judith Bondy Brigham
June 10, 1975

Some of us in the women's movement first learned that we
didn't have to feel this way about women when we joined
a consciousness-raising group. A consciousness-raising
group is a small group, usually between six and ten
women, which meets without a leader to discuss things that
are important to its members: their sexuality, feelings
about their children, feelings about men, self-confidence,
anger, and so on. Consciousness-raising groups have been
the starting point for many women who now consider
themselves part of the women's movement. Through a small-
group experience many of us developed a sense of our
own self-worth. We discovered that our problems with
husbands, children, friends, bosses, and co-workers were
not unique personal problems but were shared by many other
women as well. We shared practical advice as well as
ideas and feelings. We learned we did not have to be
isolated.

This *political* dimension of the consciousness-raising
experience has been its most significant aspect for many
of us. It was through consciousness-raising that we
learned about sexism as a system and ideology that
oppresses women, developed an analysis of institutions
that oppress women specifically and people generally,
and began to channel the anger that welled up as a result
of these discoveries.

It was with the support of the women in our consciousness-
raising groups that many of us first began to push
for changes in our marriages. Some of us had to end

those marriages because there was only so much pushing
our husbands would stand for (or they ended the marriage
for us). Others of us were able to make changes in our
marriages without destroying them. But it was a struggle.
The support and encouragement of the women in our groups
are often what kept us going during rough times.

For those of us who were often hostile and suspicious of
other women it was a new and exciting experience. Many
of us carried over the good feelings we had for the women
in our groups into the rest of our lives. We developed
a new caring and respect for friends, neighbors, co-
workers, family, and often our mothers. We believe
strongly that a small group is an important support for a
woman thinking about entering into an intimate relationship or making changes within an existing one. We don't
feel, however, that other women should be used to improve
your relationship with your husband. Relating to women
is separate and apart from the husband-wife relationship
and is fulfilling simply on the basis of women being
together. If you are interested in joining a group,
investigate whether there are any run by a local women's
center or the NOW (National Organization for Women)
chapter in your area. If there is no group near you or
if you think you would not feel comfortable in such a
group, we would still suggest you think about ways you
can get support from other women if you are not doing
so now.

   ANN

   Lou is not your typical man, and I respect that.
   When I was in a women's group, all of us came home
   and acted out the problem of the week, got mad,
   the whole business. Lou flinched and fought like
   everybody, but when I look back I can see movement
   in one direction. Just look at everybody else's
   trouble making changes like this. These things
   about him I deeply respect. The greatest part is
   not so much where the changes ended up, but the
   process of being able to fight about it and then step
   back--both of us letting things settle out and
   starting at a better place and not letting hostil-
   ities build up. He doesn't like bad feelings lying
   around, so he does what he can so that they dissi-
   pate--and not by sweeping them under the rug. He gets
   stormier than people who know him would ever imagine,

but he just hangs in there through that process.
It's just fantastic, and that's the source of the
stability. He completely respects me as another
human being regarding work and everything. I think
he admires me, and it's not condescending.

Professional Support

Many women, especially those whose friends think that
psychotherapy is an accepted way of dealing with problems,
feel that therapy is the best way of coping with painful
feelings they have about themselves and their marriages.
In an excellent article called "Marriage and Psychotherapy"
(see Bibliography) psychologist Phyllis Chesler points out
that psychotherapy and marriage are "the two major
socially approved institutions for women, especially
middle-class women." She details the ways in which
therapists often encourage women to adjust to limiting
marriages rather than help them develop the strength to
change the marriages or end them. We couldn't agree more
with her article. At Women in Transition, for every
woman we met who felt her therapist had helped her become
a stronger person, we met two others who felt their
therapists discouraged attempts to grow and encouraged
dependency on their husbands and on the therapy itself.

We are not opposed to therapy for women who are struggling
with conflicts in their lives. On the contrary, we know
that in many cases therapy can enable you to cope with
problems, understand your internal tensions, and develop
a feeling of confidence and comfortableness with yourself.
It is also a chance to try out new kinds of behavior.
But in order to make therapy work for you, it is important
to become a careful consumer of mental health services.
Women in Transition has published a "Therapy Information
Packet for Women" (see Bibliography), which contains
articles on deciding if you need and want therapy, what
a therapist is and how to choose one, where therapy is
done, and how to evaluate a therapy experience. The
following paragraphs are excerpts from that packet
about our views on women and therapy.

> Often when we see ourselves, or others see us, as
> unfulfilled, depressed or unable to function, we
> feel crazy and think that something is wrong with

us. There is, of course, something wrong. It
can be our health, our fears dominating us, the
pressures of the outside world or an unhappy
marriage. Usually prolonged anxiety caused by something outside us comes to be something inside us.
We may not be "crazy" at all to begin with, but years
of fearing that we are can drive us to something
close to it. Many women face the same kinds of
problems trying to adjust to roles which are not
healthy and not fulfilling. For so many different
women to demonstrate the same emotional problems
suggests some similarities in cause. We feel that
in many cases, although not all, the suffering may
be caused by the warped and destructive cultural
expectations we live with rather than by an un-
changeable sickness within. And one of the strongest
cultural expectations is that women should flourish
in the institution of marriage, which requires that
many of us deny huge parts of ourselves.

The mental health field has been criticized both
from within and by the women's movement for tending to
mold women into traditional patterns rather than
encouraging us to change and grow. There are, of
course, sensitive, socially and politically aware
members of the mental health professions (psychiatry,
psychology, social work, counseling), but many women
have been victimized by therapists who have been, at
best, ineffectual and, at worst, destructive.

If you are feeling depressed, anxious or frightened,
you should not assume that you need therapy but
should look at all aspects of your life. You may be
better off trying to make some changes, such as
getting a job or job training, leaving an unhealthy
relationship or challenging your partner about its
destructive aspects, finding a new neighborhood,
etc., rather than attempting to adapt yourself to
an unsatisfying (but conventionally accepted) way
of life.

The positive effects of therapy, such as an understanding of self-destructive patterns in your life,
insights into your reasons for behaving as you do,
and the increased ability to deal with difficulties,
are valuable for anyone. They need not be obtained
only through therapy. Women have found them in a
variety of sources: intense friendships, religion,

women's groups, Yoga and meditation are a few of
these. You may want to utilize one of these other
methods of self-discovery at the same time you are
in therapy. You may prefer group therapy to individual therapy. Different women have different needs
at different times. Choosing what type of help you
want depends on which of your problems you want to
work on and how.

Types of therapy for people concerned with relationship
issues include premarital counseling, marriage counseling,
and divorce counseling as well as individual growth
counseling. In recent years there has been general recognition within the mental health professions that the
traditional one-to-one method of counseling is not always
the most useful. A number of pioneering therapists are
developing knowledge and techniques for helping couples
and families work on problems that are common to all of
them and that result from their interaction. The biggest
drawback of family and couple counselors is that they are
trained and do their work in the same kinds of institutions
as other therapists--institutions that have been created
and maintained for the most part by white, upper-middle-
class, academically oriented men. Those institutions are
steeped in traditional notions about the way the world is,
notions about what the family is and what women's role in
it should be, how poor people behave, why black people
are the way they are, why homosexuality is considered a
sickness, and so on. The "Therapy Information Packet for
Women" can give you guidelines for finding a family or
couple therapist who is trying to free herself/himself from
stereotyped ideas.

    ANNA

    Don and I went into counseling at the Marriage
    Council together and that was the first time I ever
    started dealing with the whole reason for our being
    married. I had never looked closely into or tried
    to understand the reasons for my behavior and my
    decisions. I always had some complex set of ratio-
    nalizations. If I hadn't gotten married, for ex-
    ample, or hadn't lived with anyone with such a
    commitment, I don't think I would ever have reached
    that point of really closely looking at myself.
    And for that I'm really grateful. The result of
    that experience is that I am somewhat different

than I was five years ago, and would probably make different decisions. I probably have somewhat the same needs and desires but my attitudes as to how to solve them would be more rational.

BEA WEIDENER / PHILA., PA.

EVA SHADEROWFSKY

EMIKO TONOOKA

3

JANICE

One of the things that I think is special about black women is that we are not raised to expect very much out of marriage, or at least my generation wasn't. We wanted marriage, and we kind of expected it, but we knew that it would not be the kind of thing where we would be the protected, pampered, dependent kind of woman.

I was very much in favor of marriage and wanted desperately to get married. I married Tom in my last semester of my senior year in college. My mother wanted me to finish college and go on to graduate school and start to work before marriage. She was also opposed to him because he was of a different class, she said, than I was. By that she meant that he hadn't graduated from college. He was from Louisiana which was out of my mother's world, and therefore she couldn't check out his family connections. He had not finished college, and he was not a professional man. Her dream for her daughters was that each one of us would marry a professional man. It turned out that none of us did. I think maybe that's what pushed me into becoming a professional woman . . . the notion that that determined one's worth—if one made a lot of money and was a professional.

For me marriage defined my identity. If I couldn't find a man to marry me, I was therefore less of a woman. And having children was part of that. That was what I needed in 1952 to be complete. I wasn't at all aware of what it took to have a child. I literally did not know how one got pregnant. Birth control was not a part of my knowledge base. I was very stupid about a lot of things. Like, getting undressed in front of my husband was not part of what I did; I got dressed in the closet.

On the one hand, marriage was very much what I wanted to do because it was accepted and expected. On the other hand, I was terrified about what it meant. I didn't understand the responsibilities of marriage, I wasn't prepared for the sexual aspects of marriage, I wasn't prepared for the two different types of personalities coming together and having to make some kind of rapprochement about what marriage meant. So there I was, out in Oklahoma on an army base trying to understand all these issues. I didn't really have anybody to talk to. There was some vague idea in my head that if you had problems, you talked about them and worked them out. Well, my husband didn't come from that same background, so we didn't talk, and there were times when I literally stopped speaking to him for two or three weeks with the hope that he would say, "What's the matter, honey? Let's talk about it." But that never happened, and I didn't want to have to give in.

My marriage was pretty frightening; it was horrendous. The sexual part of it was the most difficult for me to understand. I was very, very naïve, and very inexperienced sexually. Intellectually I knew sex was supposed to be enjoyable, but I didn't know what that meant, and so it always hurt. But I felt a very deep sense of responsibility to have intercourse with my husband whenever he wanted it. It never occurred to me that I had any rights or that he had any responsibility to me. That was just not a part of my thinking.

An army base is not quite the place to develop a good marriage. It's a stultifying, boring life which depends on almost total obedience and dependence from the soldier, the male. But I wasn't in the army, so I wasn't into being dependent, and certainly not obedient. So I went over to apply for a librarian job on the army post and was offered the job. I came home excited and ecstatic about the whole thing, and my husband said to me, "You cannot work.

66

You cannot take the job." Well, that was a little beyond my belief. I couldn't believe he was telling me this, but I pushed him, and the reason was because there would be men coming into the library, and they would flirt with me. It was not a safe place for a woman to be. Well, I guess we fought for six weeks on that one, but I had to go back to the man and tell him that I could not take the job. My husband had ordered me not to.

The next several months were spent in this constant bickering about who would cut the grass, and the goddamn grass grew to be three feet tall until I couldn't stand it any more and I cut it. Or who was going to do the shopping, but I couldn't shop because I didn't know how to drive. I asked him if he would teach me how to drive, but he felt that wasn't anything a woman needed to know. So I got my girl friend to teach me how to drive.

I got pregnant as a way of reconciling the marriage. For a month or so after that things seemed to be getting a little bit better. I didn't know I was pregnant until three months later when I was really showing. I tried to abort the child by all kinds of home remedies, none of which worked.

Poor little Willie had colic for three months, and I'm sure it was a direct result of how I was feeling and my own emotional condition. Meanwhile my husband moved out of the bedroom and slept in a separate room, and we had no sex for maybe six months, three months before the birth and three months after. By the time we left the base to come home it was quite clear that the marriage was not going to survive. So finally we separated, and it had mostly to do with my being more independent, more assertive, more motivated to do things with my life.

Fortunately, in all this, there was my family. I lived with my family for about nine years after the separation. The good part about that was I could do what I wanted to do and needed to do while having a child, because there were a number of built-in babysitters. It was very much the extended family where the children were well taken care of and nurtured by everybody. So that freed me to work, which I had to do anyway. I didn't have any choice about working. Part of that money was to take care of the whole extended family: my parents didn't have any income. And also to take care of myself and Will.

I see lots of black families where it's perfectly acceptable for either the daughter or the son to go back home. My brother came back home. The extended family is more than just a figure of speech or a myth. It's still very much a part of middle-class as well as lower-income black families. My mother's role was to take care of her grandchildren, and she saw that very clearly. The extended family goes in both directions, though. The role for the three of us who had incomes was to help take care of my parents and my grandmother. My sisters and I lived at home for a very important reason, and that was to take care of them. I think the way black families treat their elderly is different from the way white families treat their elderly, although maybe not. But certainly my mother feels very, very useful at seventy-seven and is seen by her children as being a useful person.

Anyway, the first fifteen years of my single life after marriage I never wanted to get married, I was very happy being a separated, single woman, and certainly very self-sufficient. But I did date. I have dated the same man for twenty-one years. In a way that's like marriage. I don't want to duck that issue. It's like marriage but not having the responsibilities of marriage for either one of us. I don't have to cook meals regularly, I don't have to houseclean, I don't have to be at home. But I have the companionship of a man, I have some kind of relationship with a man. But I'm also free to do exactly what I want to do. And that's the thing that I am unwilling to give up.

He wanted to marry me years and years ago. I'd say for ten years he really pressured me, and I resisted. The freedom was a big issue, and I was afraid to get back into a marriage because my experience with marriage, both my parents' and my own, was so unsatisfactory I just couldn't see that as a viable alternative unless the person was a very open one who was willing to talk about it and work on the marriage. But this person is not very emotionally open, not a complete person emotionally. Intellectually he's incredible, but emotionally he's rather atrophied. And I know that marriage sometimes seems attractive, but on the other hand I'm not willing to prostitute myself (that's how I look at it) to a person who can't offer me the emotional stability and openness and completeness that I want. I would remarry if I could find a person who allows me the freedom to be what I want to be. The likelihood of that ever happening, I think, is about 15 percent.

The problem I think I have with being a single woman has nothing to do with money, it has nothing to do with being professionally competent and excited and stimulated. It has to do with personal loneliness, and for that reason I would like to get married again. I feel very complete as a woman, I feel very complete as a person. Maybe one of the reasons I have been able to manage my singleness as well as I have is because black women are socialized differently from white women. We are socialized, as part of the black middle-class culture, to be independent and to be self-sufficient and to expect to work and to take care of ourselves. Not a single black middle-class woman of my age that I know of has ever thought that her life would be different. That isn't to say that she might not be taken care of by a man and not have to work. My mother, for instance, worked very little of her life, but she was prepared to go out and work if she had to. And there was a short time in her life when she had to provide the family with food, clothing, and shelter, which she did with no hassle at all. She went out and got a job, a menial job, and she worked. For a couple more years she ran three or four restaurants because that was something she knew how to do, and it produced money, and she did it. My father wasn't earning much money at that time.

In addition to black women being socialized differently, to be independent but also to be assertive and go after what we want, I think we are also influenced by what happens in the wider society, so that's the double whammy. We suffer the problems of living in a sexist society the same way white women do, and so we are expected to be dependent and helpless and beautiful, but the fact of the matter is our standard of beauty is very different. The other problem is that black men are threatened by strong, independent women and tend to avoid us if we are strong and independent and intelligent, self-motivated, etcetera. But white men do not find us particularly attractive, so I think the numbers of black women who are married to white men are very small in comparison to the other way around, black men and white women. Therefore we are accepted by neither white nor black men. So we are kind of out there on our own. Some of this is historical, and some of this has to do with the way we are socialized. We are assertive people, and men feel threatened by this assertiveness. But we aren't going to behave any differently, because for our survival we have to be the way we are. Black men, historically, have not been able to get work. Black women have been able to get work, so we are in a very peculiar position. Now I'm not willing to give up that position, by the way. I'm not going to be dependent, I'm not going to be passive, because I value my intelligence and I value my skills. So I am caught between being true to myself and being what would get me a husband.

I would like to see a change in the institution of marriage and how marriage is conceived and for what purposes. I think in the past it just had to do with having children-- that was the primary function of marriage. It was a respectable way to have children. I think that marriage could become something much more important than that, but unless people are taught about how to live together as human beings, marriage is going to be a big phony scene here. It's just something people tolerate, and I think that's what it was for me and most of my peers. On those grounds I could say I support the institution of marriage, and I am basically a monogamous person anyway, so it's easy for me to support it. But I think it has to be reshaped, and I don't know that that's what our society is doing. Marriage is disintegrating as an institution.

3 / Marriage As a Legal Institution

Does Marriage Benefit Women?

After five years of working at Women in Transition, we have
been forced to come to the unfortunate conclusion that
marriage as a legal institution often does not work out well
for women. Although we are led to believe that the laws
surrounding marriage and divorce are set up to benefit and
protect women, we have found just the opposite to be true:
the marriage laws actually contain many discriminatory and
sexist provisions. In this chapter we will talk about
some of the legal disadvantages within marriage for women.
We will be saying many negative things. That doesn't mean
that we don't think that marriage can work for you. We
believe that with work and commitment it may be possible
for you and your husband to make your marriage satisfying
and fulfilling. In order to do this, however, we think it
is necessary for you to approach the marriage relationship
in ways that are contrary to the traditional concepts of
marriage and what it's all about. One of the biggest
stumbling blocks for anyone trying to work out a more equal
marriage is the legal system with its archaic notions
about husbands, wives, and their legal rights and obligations.

"Women don't need special help when it comes to marriage, separation, and divorce. The laws are stacked in favor of them. It's the man who gets a bad deal." We had heard these sentiments expressed so often by so many people, both male and female, that we were inclined to believe them ourselves when we first opened Women in Transition. However, we got so many calls from women who were receiving no support from their husbands, whether they were living with them or not, from women who were being physically assaulted by their husbands, from women who had been divorced and found that they were left with nothing after putting twenty or thirty years into keeping house and raising children, that we began to question seriously whether marriage really was set up to benefit and protect women. What is the real nature of the marriage contract? we began to ask ourselves. As we started to do some research, several things quickly became apparent. First, we realized that very few people, male or female, were actually aware of what the marriage contract was all about.

. AURELIA

> Do I know what the law says about me as a wife? It says I'm as equal as my husband. Anything his is mine, anything mine is his. If you do get a divorce, this house has to be split in half. I have the children and I'm going to stay in it. Unless he catches me doing wrong.

Most people think of marriage as a sacred institution based on love and commitment, a partnership, a fifty-fifty proposition. The marriage laws, however, bear little relation to that image. The laws we live under today have their roots in a society in which women's status was quite low, so in order to understand where marriage is today we need to understand how the institution has evolved. Let's look at the marriage institution from a historical perspective.

THE HISTORY OF OUR MARRIAGE LAWS

"By marriage, the husband and wife are one person in law: that is, the very being or legal existence of the woman is suspended during the marriage, or at least is incorporated and consolidated into that of the husband: under

whose wing, protection and cover she performs every thing"
(Chitty, L. *Blackstone's Commentaries*, 1826, p. 422). The
marriage laws in this country are based on English common
law, which held that women were the property of their
husbands. Women were permitted no legal existence other
than as extensions of their husbands. A married woman was
not permitted to own property in her own name, she was
permitted no activity that her husband did not approve,
she was legally bound to follow and obey her husband at
all times. An illustration of the historical powerlessness of women within marriage is the concept of *consortium*,
the husband's right to the sex, services, and society
of his wife. Under the theory of consortium the husband
can sue a third party for loss of his wife's consortium.
If a wife is injured in an automobile accident, for
example, and can no longer render sexual services to her
husband, he can sue the responsible party for the loss
of his wife's services. Until very recently, however, the
wife had no such right under the law.

> The Court's refusal to extend the right to consortium
> to women is founded upon the common law rationale
> that a woman spouse was her husband's property. She
> owed him duties much the same as did a servant his
> master. If he by injury to her suffered a loss of
> some feudal service owing to him by her, he and he
> alone--for she was too inferior a subject to have
> such a right, much less the privilege to assert it--
> was allowed to sue to recover, just as he would sue
> for injuries done to his cattle. He, for all
> technical purposes, owned her at common law.
> [*Neuberg* v. *Bobwicz*, 401 Pa. 146 A. 2nd 662 (1962)]

The doctrine of *coverture* was also basic to the institution
of marriage. That doctrine holds that the husband has the
legal right to control all the property owned by the
parties and, indeed, the right to control his wife and
punish her if she disobeys him. In the past that meant, in
addition to the inability of the wife to own anything or
to enter into contracts, that she had no right to keep the
wages paid to her for work outside the home, she had no
right to sue her husband, she had no right to refuse sexual
intercourse. The doctrine was recently upheld by the
North Carolina courts (*Koob* v. *Koob*, 288 N.C. 129, 195 S.E.
2nd 552 [1973]), although it has been disavowed in most
other states. The coverture concept continues to influence
many areas of marriage law.

"To have and to hold" and "to love, honor, and obey" are two of the phrases that all of us are familiar with as part of the marriage ceremony. Where do these phrases come from? What do they mean? While they sound very romantic, their origins are not romantic at all but rather reflect the "natural superiority of the male" that is assumed to be inherent in the marriage relationship. Originally the "have and hold" phrase was a legal expression that was used when two people wanted to transfer possession of a piece of land. "To have and to hold" described possession. Once the purchaser "had and held" the piece of land, he owned it. This is why the father "gives away" or transfers possession of his daughter. The "to obey" phrase applies only to the wife, not to the husband. Obedience is one of the wifely "duties" that are part of every marriage contract. Unfortunately, the modern marriage ceremony is a reflection and extension of the age-old concept of women as the property of their husbands. Today, however, many couples are changing the wording of the ceremony to reflect more equal expectations of both spouses within the marriage. We heartily endorse this practice.

Fortunately, there have been important changes within the marriage laws since they were originally enacted, and many of them eliminate some of the inequality and power-lessness of women as wives. These changes have been slow in coming; many discriminatory provisions remain. Changes first began to occur during the period just before the Civil War. Many of the women working within the abolitionist movement began to make connections between the lot of slaves and the lot of married women. The law treated both as pieces of property, and neither had any political or civil rights, including the right to own property or vote. But beginning in Mississippi in 1848, married women's property acts began to be passed. Those acts protected certain types of property belonging to women from the absolute control of the husband. As a result of those laws women were, for example, allowed to sell any property they held separately in their own names, or to buy property for themselves with money from their separate accounts. The catch is, of course, that most women did not, and still do not, have property or incomes that are separate and independent from their husbands'. (See page 91 for more information on current property laws.) Consequently most women are still vulnerable when it comes to property ownership.

In addition to changes in the property laws, husbands lost
the right, around the turn of the century, to punish their
wives physically. Those changes came about as divorce
laws were changed and modified. The catch here is that
the wife's right to protection was and is virtually unenforceable (more on this later).

THE LAW TODAY

Although black people can now vote and own property, there
is still a great deal of discrimination for the black
minority to contend with, and even though married women
can now own property and vote, they still face a legal
system which continues to reinforce their submission and
subservience to their husbands. The modern marriage
contract still obliges the husband to render to his
wife the basic necessities of food, clothing, and shelter,
just as slaveowners had to render those necessities to
their slaves under the southern "Slave Codes." The wife
is still required to render unpaid labor and sexual services
much as the slaves were required to do. Should a husband
choose to ignore his duty, most courts will do nothing so
long as the parties are living together. In 1953 Mrs. Ruth
McGuire petitioned a Nebraska court because she was living
in a house with no toilet, no hot water, and no kitchen
sink. The court refused to require her well-to-do husband
to give her the fifty-dollar-a-month allowance she re-
quested on the grounds that, since the couple had been
married thirty-three years and Mrs. McGuire had never
petitioned the court before, there was no problem.

> The living standards of a family are a matter of
> concern to the household, and not for the courts to
> determine, even though the husband's attitude towards
> his wife according to his wealth and circumstances,
> leaves little to be said on his behalf. As long as
> the home is maintained it may be said that the
> husband is legally supporting his wife and the pur-
> pose of the marriage relation is being carried out.
> [*McGuire* v. *McGuire*, Neb. 226, 59 N.W. 2nd 336
> (1953)]

The rule is, you live with him, take what he gives you,
and don't complain. If the marriage becomes a disaster,
you are free to move out, assuming you have the means to do
so and are not going to depend on him to support you
during the separation.

Another form of discrimination under the marriage laws
centers around the definition of place of residence.
Although married and single men and unmarried women have
the right to establish domicile anywhere, married women
do not have that right. A married woman is bound by
law to reside with her husband. If she chooses not to do
so, she can be charged with desertion. Consider the case
of a woman who has been married for twenty-five years to
a minister. When he was transferred to a new locality she
refused to go with him. Her husband was granted a divorce
on the grounds of desertion. The court quoted the Old
Testament as an accurate interpretation of Pennsylvania
law: "For where you go, I go." The court recited, "It is
the duty of the wife to live with her husband in a home
provided by him. . . . Where there is a failure to comply
with this duty, she is guilty of desertion" (*Sachs* v.
Sachs, 200 Pa. Super. 223, 225). The fact that this particular wife had twenty years of service with the government
and would lose all pension benefits if she went with the
husband was irrelevant to the court. (See also *Yohey* v.
Yohey, 208 A. 2nd 902, 205 Pa. Super. 32 [1965].)

In some states, a woman still cannot sue her husband if
he breaches a contract to pay her for work she does in his
business, nor can she sue him to enforce a partnership
agreement. The assumption is that the wife owes her husband certain labor and is not entitled to financial compensation for that labor even if it goes above and beyond
the call of duty.

> It is not the intention of the legislature to de-
> prive the husband of his common law right to the
> earnings or services of his wife, rendered as wife,
> by her in or about either their domestic matters or
> his business affairs. For such services she has not
> legal recourse against him or his estate. [*Standen*
> v. *Pennsylvania R. Co.*, 214 Pa. 189, 63 A. 467 (1906)]

Another interesting discrepancy occurs within the provisions regarding the age of consent to marry. In some
states women are allowed to marry without parental consent
two to three years earlier than men. One of the underlying presumptions at work here is that since marriage is
the most important goal of women, females should be
encouraged to marry at an early age, while men should be
encouraged to engage in more important pursuits such
as a career.

More damaging to many women is the assumption that rape
does not exist within marriage. That, of course, stems
from the tradition that the wife is the property of the
husband and it is his prerogative to do with her as he
pleases. Within marriages that are physically abusive to
the woman, rape usually occurs, and the abused wife finds that
there is little, if any, recourse. (See Chapter 8, "Violence
within Marriage.") (Note: Some states are considering
legislation that would recognize the possibility of rape
between spouses, especially if they are separated.)

Another holdover from the coverture doctrine is the question of how much control a wife has over her body. Although a U.S. Supreme Court decision clearly states that
whether or not to have an abortion is up to the woman and
her physician during the first three months, many hospitals
and doctors will insist on having the husband's signature,
fearing the possibility of suit. Some states now say
consent of the spouse may not be required.

Most of the marriage laws are based on the presumption
that the husband is the breadwinner and that the wife performs the support functions necessary to keep the family
alive and well, such as cooking and cleaning. In fact,
the law says that no matter how much labor is performed by
the wife, she is entitled only to bed and board, and as
we have seen, the law stipulates that it is of no consequence what kind of bed and board; she is entitled to a
roof over her head and subsistence-level food and clothing,
nothing more. There are no protections under the law for
a woman who has put all of her energy into working in the
home as she was encouraged and expected to do, only to
find twenty or thirty years later that she can be discarded
by her husband for a younger, sexier model and left without
income, job skills, security, or any means to pay the
mortgage or bills. Her labor has gone unrecognized and
uncompensated, in spite of the fact that recent studies
indicate that it would cost the average family $13,391.56
per year to replace the average housewife.* Once again
we see the ancient marriage myth at work, this time de-
priving women of the economic value of their work at home.
The resulting economic dependence on the husband leaves
many women incapable of providing for themselves or for
their children should the husband desert or refuse to pay.

*Margaret A. Sanborn and Caroline Bird, "The Big Giveaway:
What Volunteer Work Is Worth," *Ms.*, vol. 3, no.8 (February
1975), p. 88.

If the marriage turns sour and the dependent wife decides
to leave because her husband refuses to do so, she had
better have an independent source of income to accomplish
the move, or she becomes trapped with no resources to find
a way out. She can't just pick up and move with three
children. Where would she live? How would she pay the
rent? What would she do with the children while she worked?
What kind of job could she get?

The protections that many of us think exist within marriage
simply are not there. There are thousands, maybe millions,
of women who believe that they would be protected by the
law if their marriages didn't work and their husbands
became abusive or hostile. Unfortunately, they are sadly
mistaken. It has been a heartbreaking experience to
answer the telephones at Women in Transition and listen
to woman after woman describe the hopelessly unfair
situations in which they find themselves. Of course,
there are many women whose husbands would not take undue
advantage of the heavily weighted legal system, but no
woman's survival should be based on that assumption. For
the economically dependent woman who wakes up one morning
to discover that her husband has cleaned out the bank account, refuses to give her any money, or refuses to leave
the house while ordering her to leave if she doesn't like
it, there is little or nothing that she can do. If you
are a woman to whom this could happen, or if you are a
woman who would like to make sure that this never could
happen, we strongly urge you to develop and ensure your
own economic independence. We talk about this in greater
depth in Chapter 4.

MARTHA

*I had an agreement with him about support, but this
was also Art's second marriage and divorce, and he
had three children from his first marriage. I had
seen from that relationship what to expect. He is a
pretty shrewd person, and what he does is pay a portion
of what was ordered, because that shows his good intentions. It means he can be quite far behind in
child support and no one will do anything because
he's paying regularly. But the fact that he would
pay one-third of what he was supposed to pay has
little relevance. So we had an agreement, and for
the first three months I did not work at all. I was
not capable of it. If I didn't actually go through*

a nervous breakdown, I probably came pretty close to it. I could not bear to stay in the house. I made a very foolish move, which was to sell the house. We split the proceeds exactly evenly. There wasn't much, because he had taken out a second mortgage on the house, which I was not aware of, but a man can do that in this state without his wife's knowledge. So we each wound up with less than a thousand dollars. By that time I needed that for living expenses. I was already going in the hole.

While many feminist groups are urging women to become economically independent, they are also pushing for more equitable marriage and divorce laws, insisting that the state begin to recognize the sexist nature of the laws and take steps to create a more fair and just system. The state has always played a major role in marriage. In fact, the state is a third party to every marriage contract.

> Marriage is not only a contract, but a kind of fealty to the state as well. [*Bove* v. *Pinicotti*, 45 Pa. & D.C. (1942)]

Marriage, in other words, is too valuable an institution to leave in the hands of the people who are involved in it. Marriages are not made in heaven, but in the legislatures, as explained by the U.S. Supreme Court:

> Marriage, as creating the most important relation in life, as having more to do with morals and civilization . . . than any other institution, has always been subject to the control of the legislature. [*Maynard* v. *Hill*, 125 U.S. 190, 205 (1888)]

One may still wonder, all the same, why the state is so concerned with the marriage relation. Love does not appear at first glance to be an item that would concern senators, congresspersons, and judges. The roots of the state's great concern with marital and family relationships go deep into history.

Centuries ago in Europe a woman deserted by her husband was considered a terrible drain on the community--all the more so if she had children--because it became a community obligation to support her with public money. Fatherless children presented a similar problem. In order to plug up the rather serious drain on the community "welfare" sources, laws were passed giving the local government the

right to sue the husband so that the community could be
reimbursed for supporting his wife and children. These
laws were related to "poor laws"--early antecedents of our
welfare laws. Poor laws made it a crime not to work,
or for unemployed people to move to an area where they did
not have a job, and established the principle that only
the "worthy poor" should get welfare.

In many states today "desertion and nonsupport" by a husband or father is still a crime. It was from this practice
of the state suing the husband for the support of his wife
that the theory that a husband had a legal duty to support
her was first developed. But note that the duty was owed
to the state so that the wife would not become a drain
on the public treasury. We feel that a healthier way to
organize society would be for the responsibility for
women, children, old people, sick people, and any dependent
person to be considered the responsibility of everyone,
not just the individual family. A society that has a
sense of community rather than a dog-eat-dog mentality
would certainly be a better place for most people, especially those most handicapped by the nuclear family:
namely, women and children. The state's concern with
children it labeled "illegitimate" sprang from similar
roots. Thus, the state had a vested economic interest in
keeping married couples together. That is one reason why
no-fault divorce legislation has been so long in coming.
The view is that it becomes too easy to get divorced. Of
course, in our opinion, if it were a lot harder to get
married, and a lot easier to get divorced, marriages
would be entered into in a more rational manner, and
divorce would be readily available to those who came to
need it.

We have found that the state has such an investment in the
institution of marriage that it refuses to recognize any
marriage contract that does not reflect the concept of
marriage as the state defines it. We have talked with
couples who have tried to write marriage contracts that
eliminate the inequalities and role assumptions inherent
in the traditional state-approved contract. These couples
have found that although they are free to write, sign, and
abide by such contracts, the state will in no way act to
enforce them and will not permit either spouse to sue
for breach of contract if the agreement is violated. Their
reasoning: equal marriage contracts run contrary to the
"nature" of marriage. (More on marriage contracts later
in the chapter.)

In addition to feminist attempts to persuade the state to enact fair and equal marriage and divorce laws, there is a large-scale campaign underway to ratify the federal Equal Rights Amendment which would prohibit discrimination based on sex. How this legislation would affect marriage and divorce laws is not quite clear, but some states have passed state ERAs, and the limited litigation that has developed so far on the state level indicates that ERA can be both a blessing and a curse. On the one hand, ERA legislation could eliminate discriminatory laws by extending to men some of the benefits currently given only women (alimony, for example, which has been granted to men in only a few states). On the other hand, some judges and courts are using ERA legislation to punish women. One example of this is burdening women with equal support responsibilities. This seems fine in theory, but until women are given equal pay for equal work, and equal educational and job opportunities, their earning capacity will remain much lower than that of men and they will be unable to assume equal financial obligations. We are hopeful, however, that ERA legislation will eventually remove the legal presumption that the wife is subservient to and dependent upon the husband and will guarantee her adequate economic protection within marriage.

THE LAW IN THE FUTURE

In order for marriage to become the fifty-fifty proposition that we would like it to be, several things have to happen. First, ways must be found to compensate a wife for her contribution to the family's well-being and for her lack of marketable skills, if such is the case. Also, discriminatory forms of ownership and control of property must be done away with. It is clear that nothing short of a radical restructuring of the legal aspects of marriage can solve these problems. The historical assumptions about the nature of women and their obligations to provide servant labor to the family must be buried. Second, the judiciary must relinquish its pose of objective detachment and dirty its hands in domestic affairs when necessary to protect the rights of wives who are not given an equal say in the management of family resources, or who claim they or their children are not adequately supported by a husband with whom they live. More drastic steps are necessary in the area of property law. Property ownership should be structured so that each spouse owns his or her share and can dispose of it at will. The presumption

that any property purchased solely in the husband's name
out of his earnings belongs to him alone (not applicable
in community property states) must be abolished until men
and women have equal access to equally remunerative work,
and equal responsibilities for housekeeping and child care.
As long as those circumstances do not exist, women must be
specially compensated for the work they do in the home,
either by a salary paid by the husband during the marriage
or out of an escrow fund established by the husband to be
used for the wife's benefit should the marriage dissolve
or the husband die before her. Strong community property
laws should give whichever spouse is working in the home
one-half of the income brought in by the employed spouse.
Until such measures are routinely established, women must
have the right, upon separation or divorce, to be compensated for work previously performed in the home in the
form of payments extending over a period of time to be
determined by the husband and wife after consideration of
the following factors: the length of the marriage,
the time spent by each party doing housework and child
care, and the educational and salary levels of the parties.
If the husband is unable to compensate the wife adequately
(or vice versa if the husband has been the homemaker),
then ideally the state should provide the compensation,
possibly through the Social Security system. Whatever
the method, the goal should be economic independence
for the dependent spouse.

Wives who left college, discontinued job training, or
otherwise interrupted an educational career in order to
support their husbands' academic or professional training
must be given the right to receive similar support from
their husbands. Until housework becomes recognized as
economically productive work which contributes both to
the wealth of the individual family and to the gross
national product, most married women will not be compensated for their labor either during or after marriage.
And until they are so compensated, married, separated,
divorced, and widowed women will remain on the margins of
the economy.

Until our society realizes that men and women are created
equal human beings, we will continue to see laws that are
based on the assumption of women's innate inferiority, laws
that relegate women to a second-class position within the
home and in society at large. When those laws are changed
to reflect that child care, housekeeping, and careers must
be shared responsibilities depending on the needs,

abilities, and inclinations of the spouses rather than
their sex, we will have gone a long way toward ensuring for
women their inalienable rights to life, liberty, and the
pursuit of happiness.

What You Can Do Yourself

It is not our intention in this chapter to tell you not to
get married. We know that almost everything that we have
said so far is negative. We wish we could say that the
marriage laws were based on equality rather than inequality,
but we can't. What we can do now is give you some useful
information on making an institution that was not designed
for your benefit into one that works for you, rather than
against you. In our opinion, the key to success within
marriage for women is emotional and economic independence.
Emotional and economic dependency are often intertwined,
but economic dependency is the real crippler for the
married woman. It can lead to feelings of resentment,
insecurity, and possessiveness in an intact marriage, and
it leaves a woman vulnerable and helpless should the marriage fail. In some ways economic dependency may actually
contribute to a marriage's breakdown in that it imposes
unfair burdens on the husband and locks the wife into a
housekeeping role, a role that many women do not find as
fulfilling as they would like. In Chapter 2 we talk about
ways that you can be a separate, independent person within
an intimate relationship. In Chapter 4 we describe in
depth how to attain or maintain your economic independence.
Credit in your own name, job skills, education, and pursuing your own interests are necessary for your emotional
and economic well-being.

MAKE A CONTRACT

Whether you are married or living together, we suggest that
you and your husband or lover sit down and think about the
terms of your relationship. Once you have agreed upon the
major terms, we think that it is a good idea to spell them
out in a contract.

Historically, upper-class families often saw to it that no
daughter married out of the family without a written
"ante- (before) nuptial contract." This contract was in
many ways like our modern separation agreements. Basically

it spelled out what items (usually land and intangibles such as stocks, bonds, certificates, and valuable personal property [sometimes including slaves and servants]) were to be held as the separate property of the wife. Some of that property was then subject to the husband's power to manage, encumber, or dispose of "marital property." The daughter's dower (the price paid to the husband for marrying her) was specifically described so that the husband could not later claim a portion of her separate property as his dower. The distribution of marital property, intestate rights of the parties, and other items now included in separation agreements were also spelled out contingent upon the marriage being terminated by divorce or death (or interrupted by separation).

Modern **marriage** contracts serve a much less practical purpose, although ante-nuptial agreements are still entered into among wealthy families. But today's more popular contracts serve primarily as a written reminder to the parties of their mutual intentions and respective obligations taken on at the commencement of the marriage. For persons entering into nonceremonial marriages, they may provide important documentation of the marriage itself, especially if witnessed by third parties.

As a practical matter these contracts *cannot* supplant the state-imposed terms of the marriage contract. As private individuals you may enter into a contract to do whatever you can agree to--even if it's prohibited by law. But the courts will *not* enforce any contract that is contrary to "public policy." Thus, if there is any conflict between the terms of your homemade marriage contract and state-imposed terms, you cannot enforce the terms of your contract by going to court (technically asking the court to enforce the terms of your contract through "specific performance" or "injunction"). Terms in your contract that are additional, but not in any way contrary to either the state-imposed terms or "public policy," *may* be enforceable in courts.

The purpose and value of these marriage contracts is not in their legal enforceability but in getting two marriage partners to think and decide ahead of time just what would go into an equitable marriage between them: Wages for housework? Keeping separate bank accounts? Equal child care responsibilities? Separate vacations?

Many of us know women who supported husbands through
graduate or professional school with the "understanding"
or agreement that the husbands would later do the same.
Then came the push to pay off his ten thousand dollars in
loans, then children . . . and she is still waiting to
complete her B.A. Or, he skipped out of the marriage the
day he finally graduated from law school. Of course,
no contract is going to prevent disappointments or even
a jagged breakup, but we can't help thinking that some
disappointments and inequalities could be prevented by some
thought ahead of time and a written record of what the
parties intended.

A typical contract should include the following standard
items, as well as those of particular concern to you:

1. *The phrase "intending to be legally [and/or "morally"]
    bound hereby, do agree to the following terms."* That
    phrase may be prefaced by the words "now, therefore,
    in consideration of the mutual promises contained
    herein and other valuable consideration." That legal
    mumbo jumbo is a technical requirement for legally
    enforceable contracts, but the words themselves are not
    magic. It's not a bad idea to include them if you want
    the possibility of legal enforcement, on the theory
    that the more your agreement looks like an orthodox
    contract, the less disgruntled a judge may be by your
    request for enforcement.
2. *A recital of the names, ages or dates of birth, date
    and place of marriage of the parties.* It is important
    to make it obvious that you are already married or
    planning to be married--a contract that says, in
    essence, "If you will do something for me, then I will
    marry you," will probably be considered void as being
    against public policy. See the sample for appropriate
    wording of a contract entered into before marriage.
3. *Statement of purpose.* What principles guide your
    drawing up the contract? Why are you doing it? This
    is not a legal requirement, but it seems like a good
    way to begin looking at specific obligations.
4. *Specific terms.* These are up to you, but remember that
    any that are contrary to state-imposed terms will not
    be enforceable in court: e.g., a commitment to plural
    sexual relationships. An agreement that requires the
    husband to be in the home doing housework and/or
    child care may not be enforceable. The more it looks
    like he will be doing 50 percent or more, the slimmer
    your chances for enforcement (yes, Virginia, the

courts do enforce sex-role stereotypes as well as laws).
You might want to consider drafting terms concerning:

> *Income:* How shared, managed, spent, invested.
> What kind of decision-making?
>
> *Employment:* How to decide whose is more important
> if there is a conflict (for example, if her
> job demands a transfer, he is earning more . . .
> but next year is his year to stay home with
> the kids). Who works outside the home and
> when and why? Does the one who works inside
> get paid? How much and when?
>
> *Children:* Decisions to have them, how many,
> effect on employment of both parties, princi-
> ples of childrearing (communal or nuclear).
> Other life-style questions: what effect on
> children, what conflicts between partners now
> would have to be worked out if there are
> children, relationship to grandparents or to
> siblings from other marriages, what impact on
> income/employment plans, religion?
>
> *Vacation:* Separate time, separate space, if either
> or both of you feel this is important. What
> will you do to maintain/respect each other's?
> What about after children are born?
>
> *Name change:* Will the wife keep her own? Why?
> How to name children (surnames)?
>
> *Principles on decision-making and managing:* In-
> volving children in decision-making, children's
> education (public, private, college). Who
> decides, who pays?
>
> *Disputes:* How to resolve within and without the
> contract? Strongly advised: a panel of
> three arbitrators, one selected by each party
> and one mutually agreeable, to resolve dis-
> putes under contract. What to do in the event
> one party feels the marriage is in trouble?
> Trial separation? Counseling? Discussions
> between parties? With or without arbitrators?

5. *Clause declaring all promises in the contract* <u>*severable*</u>*,*
   so that if one is void or otherwise unenforceable or
   broken the rest remain intact.
6. *Contingencies.* What is the effect of separation,
   divorce, death on specific terms of the contract? Do
   you want to sketch out property/income and custody terms
   in the event of a breakup within the next one, three,
   or five years?

7. *Modifications*. You should provide that any term may be modified by mutual written agreement of the parties at any time unless you want to make specific items not subject to change.

8. *Enforcement*. Recommended is a team of three impartial arbitrators who will read the agreement, hear from both parties separately, and render a decision in writing that reflects the spirit and terms of the agreement as presented to them. This mechanism is to be invoked by either party after the parties fail to resolve a problem in meaning, application, or enforcement of any term of the agreement.

9. *Review and adaptations*. The parties agree to review the terms and evaluate compliance annually on a date specified. New terms or modifications of old ones may be added as the parties desire at this or any other mutually agreeable time.

10. *Date of parties signing the agreement and signature of one witness for each party*.

If you know at the beginning who your arbitrators are going to be, you may want to make a copy for each of them. There should be at least two copies, if not three, all with original signatures, and a phrase in the agreement specifying the number of signed copies, "each of which shall constitute an original."

SAMPLE MARRIAGE AGREEMENT

(Standard items only are written out in full. Supply your own terms in language you feel comfortable with. It doesn't need to sound like gibberish to be legally effective. Just make sure your own phrases say what you want them to. It might help to have a third person read them and tell you what s/he thinks they mean.)

Virginia B. Scott, born on the 1st day of May, 1950, in Cleveland, Ohio, and Thomas J. Watkins, Jr., born on the 19th day of April, 1952, in Queens, New York, have been married this 8th day of January, 1977, and intending to reside in the state of Ohio, now wish to enter into an agreement regarding our mutual promises and respective rights and duties throughout the marriage (and with respect to our future roles as parents of any children that may be born to us).

Virginia and Thomas enter into this Agreement out of
a deep respect for one another and a commitment on the part
of each to preserve, support, and continue to respect the
individuality of the other. We desire not to avoid the
responsibilities inherent in the commitment to marriage
but wish to accept those responsibilities as two equal
adults.

We also bind ourselves to this contract in protest against
the traditionally unwritten marriage contract by the terms
of which women, upon marriage, lose the right to act as
free and responsibile beings. [Ad lib here. Describe if
you wish particular things about the traditional contract
that disturb you.]

It is in this spirit that Virginia and Thomas, in consideration of the mutual promises and obligations undertaken,
intending to be legally [and morally] bound, thereby do
now, this 8th day of January, 1977, each promise and agree
as follows:

Surnames

Virginia B. Scott, wife of Thomas J. Watkins, Jr.,
will continue to use the name by which she has been known
throughout her life. The parties agree that this is most
appropriate in light of the tradition of a wife's taking
her husband's surname as representing her civil death and
the merger or obliteration of her personality in his,
and in light of the common-law right of any person to use
any name suitable to her or him.

The parties desire that any children born to both of them
carry the surnames of both. Recognizing, however, that
theirs remains a patriarchal society which stigmatizes
children bearing the names of their mothers, they agree the
children shall be surnamed Scott-Watkins.

Individual terms

[Write your own according to our previous suggestions.]

Severability

Each and every clause and promise of this agreement is
separate and independent of all others unless otherwise
specified in individual paragraphs hereof, and should any
clause or promise be found void or otherwise unenforceable,
the remainder shall continue in full force and effect.

Dispute resolution

The parties agree that in the event a dispute should arise
between them as to the application, interpretation, or
modification of the terms hereof, they shall submit such
dispute to a team of three impartial lay arbitrators, one
to be chosen by each party and a third to be mutually agreed
upon. These arbitrators shall, after having been furnished
with copies of this Agreement and having heard from each
of the parties separately about a particular dispute,
render a written decision on the question before them,
which decision shall be attached to this Agreement and
become a part hereof.

Modification

Unless otherwise specified herein, any term of this contract may be modified in writing upon the mutual agreement of the parties, but not otherwise.

Review

The parties agree that on the anniversary of this day
each year they shall meet to evaluate this agreement as
it then stands and make any appropriate revisions.

If you want an agreement to accomplish many of the same
things frequently accomplished through ante-nuptial contracts, you should look at samples in your nearest law
library (look under "marriage" or "husband and wife"
headings in the form books for your state).

One last thought: as a private alternative to divorce
insurance, some parties may want to agree to put one
thousand dollars in an escrow fund (where it will earn
interest) to be used to cover legal fees in the event
of a separation and/or divorce.

KNOW THE LAW

You should know the laws in your state concerning marriage
and divorce. Just what does the law say about your role as
wife? About the role of your husband? Are they blatantly
discriminatory? Chances are they are, and you should

be aware of this before you marry. Knowing what the law
says can help you take the proper steps to ensure your
well-being should the marriage fail. We realize that the
last thing you want to be thinking about as you approach
the altar is the possible breakup of your marriage.
Ignoring this possibility, however, can leave you unprepared
and unable to survive on your own should the necessity
arise. Don't think that we are saying that you shouldn't
love and trust your husband; it's just that there's no
telling where you will be ten years from now. People change
and grow. If your marriage were to break up some time in
the future, it would not necessarily have to be because you
were a terrible person or because he was a terrible person.
It is possible that you could just outgrow each other or
change and develop in different directions. Whatever the
case, you should know in advance what the separation and
divorce laws are about so that you won't be legally
vulnerable if the marriage doesn't work out. Some states
(New York is one) are seriously investigating the possibility of an insurance policy to be taken out by couples
at the time they marry which matures at the time of divorce
and provides a minimal level of support for the children
of a broken marriage. If there are no children, the wife
would be able to use the proceeds to continue her education
or receive job training. Happily married couples could
convert the policy to education, retirement, or other
benefits, or cash it in after a certain period of time.
To be completely effective, such a policy would have to be
mandatory. Most people refuse to think of divorce at the
time they marry, despite the fact that 455 out of every
1,000 marriages end in divorce. The purpose of divorce
insurance would be primarily to put an end to the national
scandal that child support and alimony payments are becoming and to stop penalizing children financially for
their parents' mistakes.

Divorce is not the only way marriages end. Widowhood is
always a possibility. Even if you are sure that your
marriage will be a success, or if you are in a marriage
that has little chance of ending, you are still vulnerable
should you become a widow. Life insurance will not solve
all the financial problems that you will face. Once again,
taking steps to minimize your economic dependence should
be a priority. The last thing you need, regardless of
your age, is to fall into the "helpless widow" category.
It can be devastating.

Property

Although property law is confusing, we think that it is important for you to know your status, whether you are married or living with someone.

The legal definition of *property* includes your home, any other real estate, stocks and bonds, bank accounts, debts, and household appliances. The laws concerning ownership of property by married people are archaic, confusing, and sexist. Joint ownership of property is determined by laws rooted in the feudal system. For a starting point, we have the maxim "In marriage two become one, and that one is the husband." Because of the fictional "unity" of the husband and the wife, neither has clear title to any property held as marital property ("community" property in some states). Because "that one is the husband," wives usually have little or no independent basis for credit, no liquid assets, virtually no independent financial power. Before she can sell or mortgage the house she lives in, a deserted wife must either locate her husband to obtain his signature or obtain a judicial decree permitting her to sell the house only upon a finding that the husband has abandoned her. In that event the court will also protect his interest in the house; she is not entitled to all the proceeds even though she may have completed mortgage payments and paid for insurance, taxes, and repairs for ten years.

It is impossible to make any further generalizations about the nature of marital property and the effect of separation or divorce on property holdings of married people. The laws vary from state to state and are still evolving. The best we can do is suggest some ways to avoid the confusion.

The major question is, What property is considered marital or community property? Usually it includes the house in which the parties live. Income property--rental units and real property--are also usually considered marital or community property, assuming both names are on the deed, finance agreement, or mortgage. Investments other than real estate--stocks, bonds, and so on--are often marital property, depending on state law and what the certificate of ownership indicates. Cars, other valuable property, and household appliances and goods are often, but not always, marital property.

What are the consequences of something being determined
marital property? The answer to this question depends on
state law. In states with a modified common-law system,
marital property is the only kind of property that can be
held as what's known as "tenancy by the entirety." What
this often means is that neither party can sell, lease,
or mortgage the property held by the entirety without the
signature of the other, and a creditor of either party
cannot touch such property to satisfy a default. The
principle is that property so owned is owned *entirely* by
both parties. Thus, the whole thing belongs to the wife
and cannot be used to satisfy the husband's creditors if
he owes money for *purely personal* debts (golf clubs).
But since he also owns the whole thing she will have a
hard time getting credit or loans based on her interest
in the property, because a creditor of hers could not
touch the property to satisfy her *personal* debts.

Except for the consequences described above, marital
property held as a tenancy by the entirety is just like
a "joint tenancy"--a form of property ownership available
to unmarried or unrelated persons who wish to own property
together and ensure that the entire property ends up being
owned by whichever party lives longer. (Upon death of
one of the joint tenants the entire property goes to
the survivor, with no inheritance tax consequences since
in theory both parties owned the whole thing.)

One major difference between joint tenancy and tenancy by
the entirety is that it is easy to dissolve a "joint"
tenancy or convert it into a "tenancy in common,"
whereby the parties own separate portions of the property.
Tenancy in common is the common-sense way you think of
owning property together. Each person owns an identi-
fiable share of the property and may do whatever she or
he wishes with it. Her individual interest serves as a
basis for credit and may be rented, sold, or bequeathed
to third parties without the involvement or consent of
co-owners.

In some states tenancies by the entirety have been abolished
or converted to joint tenancies. It is possible, in most
states, for married persons to own property as tenants in
common, but they must be very careful and explicit when
acquiring title to ensure that the deed and other instruments of transfer clearly indicate their intent to own the
property as tenants in common and not as tenants by the
entirety or joint tenants. The disadvantage to this form

of ownership is that there is no automatic passing of the whole property to the surviving spouse--there are tax consequences if the spouse's portion of the property is inherited.

Married persons may also own property as joint tenants rather than by the entirety. Joint tenancy avoids the inheritance problem--the spouse's interest passes automatically to the survivor. Should you not want that to happen (say you're separated and would want your children, but not your spouse, to get the property), you have problems if the property is owned jointly or by the entirety. Also, in many states you have no right to compel your joint tenant to account to you for profits received from jointly owned property, so long as you have not been ousted from it, and you both have an equal right to live in the property. That can be a real disadvantage.

In many western and some southern states another system of marital property is in effect. The community property system, in theory, has some advantages for married women. However, many states have destroyed that advantage by either implicitly or explicitly decreeing that the husband has the sole right to manage and control community property, funds, and so forth. The basic idea behind the community theory is that any property acquired by the husband or wife during the marriage is considered community property belonging to both. This is supposed to protect wives by giving them an interest in property acquired by their husbands and giving them a right to share as equal partners in his income and investments. The theory doesn't hold up because men are given the right to "control" the community property--at least until recently. States that have enacted the Equal Rights Amendment and have a community property system, and others, by recent judicial decision, are modifying the rule that the husband alone has the right to control community property.

Here are some issues to keep in mind when trying to figure out what property you have a legal interest in:

1. Property acquired by either party separately before the marriage belongs to that person and not to the spouse.
2. In some states "gift statutes" have the effect of giving a spouse legal interest in property acquired by the other spouse during the marriage.
3. Even without a gift statute, you as a wife have a legal interest in property acquired during the marriage and

for which your name is included in the deed, mortgage, lease, or other instrument of transfer. Whose money went into the property does *not* determine who owns it. Whose name is on the deed does.

4. If you want to acquire real property separately, without your spouse, during the marriage, you will probably be told, at least initially, that it is impossible. You will have to be very clear and state your intention to own such property as a single person, that it was purchased from your separate funds, and that you wish to create no interest for your spouse. You may have to consult an imaginative feminist attorney to accomplish this in some states. (See the information on the Equal Credit Opportunity Act in Chapter 4.)

5. If you are separated but not divorced, mortgage companies or banks can be trusted to give you a hard time about acquiring property without your husband. It can be done, and the federal Fair Housing and Equal Credit Opportunity acts should be brandished when you are threatened with not being able to obtain a mortgage without your husband's signature. There are clever ways of getting around the rules and practices of mortgage companies. You are not advised to make any attempts on your own, however. You should have qualified legal counsel. Banks and real estate agents will tell you that the only way to get separate property is to obtain a divorce. If you are not ready or are unable to do that, you may obtain a form in which your husband releases all claim to own any property with you, including future property. Or such a clause may be written into a separation agreement. If the agreement is incorporated in a divorce decree, you're on solid ground and should have absolutely no problem.

Property ownership is a complicated area of the law, and the consequences of a mistake can cost you thousands of dollars, your house, and hours of frustration and anguish They can also be felt for generations, so before you act in this area, consult someone (or several people) who knows this area of the law for the proper state (where the property is located, as well as where you live) before attempting to buy or sell.

Housing

While litigation concerning sex discrimination in housing is in its early stages, federal laws, and some state and

local laws, provide protection for both buyers and renters.
A federal fair housing statute prohibits discrimination
based on race, sex, and national origin in both sales
and rental housing. Additionally, the Equal Credit
Opportunity Act provides remedies for those persons who
have been discriminated against on the basis of sex in the
financing of home purchases. Finally, federal regulations
concerning Housing and Urban Development (HUD) federally
subsidized or financed housing prohibit "automatic" discrimination based on marital status. Federal law, however,
does not protect buyers or renters who are denied housing
opportunities because they have children.

The laws at the state and local levels are widely divergent.
Fair housing or human relations statutes that prohibit sex
discrimination may exist in your state. Some states have
equal rights amendments to their constitutions which may,
if the courts have interpreted them favorably, offer
protection to women seeking housing. Very few states have
or are considering legislation prohibiting discrimination
against adults with children, and no courts have yet
found that such discrimination, because of its dispro-
portionate impact on women, is sex-based.

Since we are only beginning to see the development of the
law with respect to sex-based discrimination in housing,
the fullest possible protection for women will develop as
more and more complaints are received in the appropriate
federal and state agencies and in the courts. If you
think you have been discriminated against, contact your
municipal or state human relations commission and the fair
housing division of the HUD area office in your region.
For assistance in pursuing your claim, contact a private
lawyer through a lawyers' reference service or, if you are
eligible for their services, the local legal aid society
or legal services. In addition, most cities have active
housing groups and organizations that can provide both
legal and practical counseling.

Social Security

In this section we discuss ways in which the Social Security
system discriminates against women and what is being done
to remedy the discrimination.

In November 1975 hearings were held on discrimination within the Social Security system. As a result of those hearings, Social Security commissioners issued a statement

agreeing that the Social Security Administration penalizes departures from the stereotype that men are the bread-winners in any family unit and that the accepted role of women is that of housewife and mother. Recently two provisions of the Social Security law were found unconsti-tutional. One presumed that the wife is the dependent of the husband, but that a husband must prove he is in fact dependent on his wage-earning wife in order to benefit from her Social Security insurance. The second provided that widows but not widowers can collect survivor's bene-fits to care for minor children. That means that now if the mother dies, the father can collect benefits to help support the children just as a mother would if the father died.

One example of current discrimination that may be fairly simple to rectify is the regulation specifying that when both husband and wife get special age-seventy-two-and-over payments, the husband gets full benefits, whereas the wife receives only half of what he gets.

Former Representative Bella Abzug introduced two bills to cure some of the inequities of the present system. H.R. 4539 would reduce the length of time a woman had to remain married in order to share the benefits of her husband's Social Security from the present requirement of twenty years to five. H.R. 4357 would seek to end the present discrimination against families with two wage-earners by allowing a working married couple to combine their work records in order to let them draw on the total income base of the two. A further, more far-reaching, proposal is to allow women working at home without pay to earn Social Security credits in their own names regardless of separa-tion, divorce, death, or remarriage of a former spouse.

All those legislative proposals are a long way from being made into law.

Marriage and Taxes

In this section we discuss federal income taxes only.
Local property taxes, state income or other taxes, and in-heritance taxes vary too widely to make generalizations.
The federal income tax system codifies most of the glaring inequalities in our social and economic system. Discrimi-nation against poor people and people who are not part of traditional nuclear-family living arrangements is partic-ularly striking. While the federal income tax system

allows people who own their own homes to deduct certain
items related to the expense of buying their homes from
their gross income, renters may deduct nothing. Investors,
of course, get the best treatment, with special deductions
for depreciation of expensive equipment and special tax
rates for capital gains.

Of particular interest to women, however, is the increasing
deduction allowed for child care expenses. But you must
check the regulations carefully to see that your child
care arrangements qualify. And, of course, you may not
take any deduction unless you are going to itemize your
deductions rather than take the standard deduction.

The federal tax regulations defining "head of household,"
"dependents," and "exemptions" all reinforce the traditional stereotypes about married couples. The most
favorable tax rate is often available only to married
couples in which one party earns significantly more than
the other. That high earner is rarely the wife. If the
husband and the wife are both earning a salary and the
salaries are approximately equal, it is often economically
advantageous to file separate returns, each itemizing his
or her own expenses and deductions.

In order to qualify for "head of household" status you must
have a biological relationship with other people living
in the same house. In order to get the dependent deduction from your gross income, you must be related to the
person dependent upon you and provide over half of his or
her total support. People living in anything other than
traditional nuclear families rarely qualify for any of
the advantages to be gained from having "head of household"
or "dependent" status, despite the fact that they may
actually be providing support for unrelated persons.
Couples who do not have a legal marriage, or roommates
believe in income sharing, may not take advantage of the
joint income tax option.

On the other hand, married women may be held liable for
their husband's income tax fraud and receive both criminal
and civil penalities, as well as being held liable for the
entire amount due and unpaid on the couple's income tax
bill and being charged interest for late payments. Although those provisions seem grossly unfair, they have yet
to be successfully challenged, and married women must take
extreme care before signing a joint income tax return. It
is important that you understand not just what you are

signing, but what went into filing the return as well. You may be held liable for any false statements or tax cheating contained in the return, despite the fact that you signed a blank return or have no income of your own.

Children

What the law has to say about children depends a lot on whether or not they are considered "legitimate." If the parents of the children are married to each other, then the children are considered "legitimate" and are entitled to inherit property. If the parents are not married to each other, however, things can get confusing. In the next few pages we try to provide some details regarding the status of "illegitimate" children. You need this information if you already have children and are not married to the father, if you are living with someone and decide that you want to have children without getting married, or if you are living alone and decide that you want to have a child without marrying or living with the father. More and more single women are deciding to have children and remain single. If you are considering that, you should definitely inform yourself about the laws in your state. If you are living with someone and decide to have a child without getting married, you may be able to avoid having the child labeled "illegitimate" by claiming you have a common-law marriage when you arrive at the hospital. Of course, this is possible only in states that recognize common-law marriages (see page 398). It also assumes you want to be married in the eyes of the community, which some women do not.

Q: Why are children born to unmarried women called "illegitimate"?

A: Of course, it's ridiculous to label a child "illegitimate." *There is no such thing as an "illegitimate" child,* which is why we always write "illegitimate" in quotations in this book. Most states and government agencies believe that children whose parents are not married are "illegitimate" and discriminate against those children in a variety of ways.

Q: Are there any states in which there is no "illegitimate" status for children born to unmarried parents?

A: Yes. North Dakota, Arizona, Oregon, and Minnesota
       have all recently adopted laws abolishing the status
       or the discrimination generally associated with
       "illegitimacy." In all other states the status and
       the discrimination persist, although that is changing.
       Some states will not even release the birth certif-
       icate of "illegitimate" children to their mothers--
       although they will to school boards, the armed forces,
       and other official agencies.

Q: How does the problem of "illegitimacy" affect single-
       parent women?

A: There are several ways. First, if you're separated
       and thinking about an annulment instead of a divorce
       (for religious or other reasons), you should find out
       what your state says about children of annulled
       marriages. Some states declare these children retro-
       actively illegitimate because an annulment declares
       that you have never been married. Some states have
       specific laws saying that the children of annulled
       marriages are *not* illegitimate, but you should check
       carefully before filing for an annulment or allowing
       one to be granted.

       The second way the problem affects single-parent
       women is in a situation where you either don't care
       all that much about a divorce, or you don't have the
       money to get one. Any children born to you for the
       rest of your life (or at least until a divorce has
       been granted) will be presumed to be the children
       of your husband. This is to "spare" them the
       stigma of "illegitimacy." However, if their real
       father would ever want custody, or if you should ever
       want to sue him for their support, problems would
       arise. Legally, those children would be the children
       of your husband, and anyone else wanting to assert
       his rights or responsibilities would be incapable
       of doing so until you (or he) proved his paternity.

       People who don't "bother" to get a divorce and then
       enter into what they consider either a common-law mar-
       riage or an official marriage are treading on very
       thin ice should the undivorced spouse from marriage
       number 1 ever care to assert himself. That spouse
       could have your second "marriage" annulled, and the
       children of that marriage could become "illegitimate."

Finally, if you're divorced and you've decided you never want to get married again, you might want to think it over if you're planning to have any more children. Children born to unmarried mothers are "illegitimate" under the law.

Q: In what ways does the law discriminate against "illegitimate" children?

A: Traditionally, there have been four major areas of discrimination against "illegitimate" children: support, inheritance, benefits (such as Social Security, insurance, welfare, worker's compensation), and custody. Mothers who apply for welfare or public housing have also been discriminated against on the basis of their having "illegitimate" children. Let's see what discrimination has meant in each area. The additional issue of names is discussed in "Children's Names" on page 111.

The first, and certainly the most important, is that of *support*. Here the usual rule is reversed. The mother has always been obligated to support her "illegitimate" child, while the father, traditionally, has had no such duty. This rule hardly encouraged unmarried fathers to take the institution of marriage (or fatherhood) more seriously! In 1973 that rule was reversed, and all children now have a right to be supported by their father, whether or not he is married to their mother. A husband is *not* legally obligated to support the children of another father-- regardless of whether their mother was married to the father or not.

Another important area is that of *inheritance*. Until at least 1967 both New York and Louisiana declared that "illegitimate" children had no right to inherit property from their mother! The problem today is usually whether or not they can inherit from their father or their father's relatives. Most states say that the word *children* in a will means "legitimate" children, unless it is clear from the will that the person making it intended benefits to go to the "illegitimate" children as well. This can be shown by using the full names of the children when writing a will.

Most of the problems come when there is no will.
Every state has laws that declare how property
should be divided when the property owner dies without a will. Several states give equal rights to
"legitimate" and "illegitimate" children; others
give full rights to "acknowledged illegitimate"
children. Several states have declared that under no
circumstances can "illegitimate" children inherit
from their fathers without a will naming them specifically, and still other states have no clear position
on the question.

If you are the mother of an "illegitimate" child and
are concerned about inheritance, the best thing to
do is to have the person from whom the child might
inherit write a will that names the child specifically
by full name.

In the area of *benefits* major progress has been made
toward doing away with legal discrimination against
"illegitimate" children. It has been ruled that the
word *children* in insurance policies means both
"legitimate" and "illegitimate" children, and that
"illegitimate" children have rights to Social Security
survivors' benefits and other benefits under certain
conditions--usually that their father supported the
children during his lifetime. Paternity does *not*
have to be proved for "illegitimate" children to
share in their father's Social Security benefits.
"Illegitimate" children have equal rights to medical
and dental care under the Armed Services Dependents'
Medical Care Act of 1972.

In that area the law varies a great deal from state to
state and is in the process of change. If you feel
your child is being discriminated against on the basis
of her or his status as "illegitimate," consult an
attorney immediately. Many local and state agencies
and businesses are not well informed about the state
of the law or continue to have clearly unconstitutional practices because they have not been faced with
a legal challenge. Remember: You don't have to be
rich to bring this kind of action. Legal service
lawyers are there to do it for free.

Until 1967 many housing authorities used the fact that
a mother had "illegitimate" children as a basis for
excluding her from public housing. In December 1968

the Department of Housing and Urban Development
sent a circular to all public housing authorities
stating that having one or more "illegitimate" children may *not* be used as a basis for keeping women and
children out of public housing. It is not illegal,
however, for housing authorities to be concerned with
the "morality" of tenants and prospective tenants.
It is not hard to imagine that mothers of "illegitimate" children may often receive unfavorable treatment for this reason.

If you suspect that you have been discriminated
against by public housing officials because you have
"illegitimate" children, consult an attorney at once.
Chances are the discrimination was illegal. Discrimination against "illegitimate" children in federal
welfare programs is also clearly illegal today.

> Most illegitimate children . . . are the result
> of a mistake. . . . The second time around we
> think represents a lack of judgment and demon-
> strates an unstable moral attitude on the part
> of the mother . . . that is inconsistent with
> the minimum moral standards the community
> requires.

Those words were taken from the opinion of a Maryland
court decision, *In re Cager,* which was reversed by the
Maryland Court of Appeals. That decision illustrates
the lengths to which overenthusiastic law men (a state
attorney in this case) may go to use the law to enforce what they consider to be "morality" in determining the matter of *custody.* In the above-mentioned
case, the state attorney had a suit brought to remove
an "illegitimate" child from its mother's custody on
the ground that she had "neglected" her child by
giving birth to a second "illegitimate" child! The
confidential information was obtained from cooperative welfare officials.

The traditional rule has been that mothers had a
right to custody of their "illegitimate" children,
while fathers did not. Some states exclude such
fathers from adoption proceedings when the mother has
decided to surrender the child. It is clear that in
almost every state the fathers of "illegitimate"
children do not have the same rights as the fathers of
"legitimate" children, although in most states today

the father of "illegitimate" children can get custody if the mother dies. In many states these fathers have a right to custody of their children secondary only to that of the mother.

Some states have laws providing that if the father chooses to live with his "illegitimate" child, that child becomes "legitimate," and that the father has full rights to custody and visitation as if he and the child's mother were married.

Q: Is there any way to change the status of a child who was registered as "illegitimate" at birth?

A: Yes, there are several ways, depending on the state you live in. In all states the child becomes "legitimate" when you marry the father. In some states marrying the father is the *only* way to make the child "legitimate."

Q: Suppose I am not married when my child is born. Is there any way I can prevent its being registered as "illegitimate"?

A: It depends. As mentioned before, you may want to assert a common-law marriage. The fact that you do not use the father's last name should not determine whether your child is "legitimate" or "illegitimate." In some states a child becomes "legitimate" as soon as it is "acknowledged" by the father. If he is willing to take legal responsibility for the child and have his name on the birth certificate, the child is "legitimate" in those states.

In some states the status of "illegitimate" has been abolished, and in others hospitals and state bureaus of vital statistics or other agencies are no longer allowed to classify children as "legitimate" and "illegitimate." Your local legal services attorney should be able to tell you what is true for your state. Or you can write to the attorney general of your state asking for an opinion about the legality of branding some children as "illegitimate."

Q: Is there any way to do away with this problem once and for all?

A: Sure. Abolish the status of "illegitimate." Several
      countries, including New Zealand, have done this
      without any noticeable ill effects. This could be
      accomplished in America on either a national or a
      state-by-state basis. The United States Supreme
      Court has resisted several opportunities to declare
      that all discrimination based on this status is un-
      constitutional and illegal, but it might still come
      to this conclusion. Another possibility is that this
      kind of discrimination will continue to be abolished
      on the state level, either by means of legislation or
      by suits brought by "illegitimate" children and their
      parents in local courts.

Common-Law Marriage

If you are a single woman who lives with someone or has
lived with someone, you may be interested in whether or not
you have a common-law marriage. If there are children, it
may be important, since your marital status can influence
such questions as support, benefits, and inheritance.
Even if there are no children, you should know exactly what
your legal status is, especially if you are in a long-term
living-together relationship. It is possible that you may
want to establish a common-law marriage for the purposes
of collecting Social Security or other benefits.

In order to have a common-law marriage, you must have a
present-tense agreement or understanding that you will
live together as wife and husband until death (or divorce)
separates you. Promises to get married in the future don't
count. "Sure, honey, I want to get married" is not a
good substitute for an exchange of vows. Neither is "Don't
I treat you just like you were my wife?" On the other
hand, acting as if you are married, when it is not done to
mislead, is good legal evidence that you consider yourself
married. The essence of common-law marriage is that both
parties consider themselves married to each other, and so
do their neighbors, friends, and families. Of course,
a requirement for common-law marriage is also that both
parties be legally free and capable of getting married.
That means that common-law marriages entered into by minors
or people who are already married to someone else (even
though they're separated) do not count--in fact, they are
illegal.

States that have decided not to recognize such marriages
base their decisions on the fact that common-law marriages
are usually claimed when one of the parties has died and
the other wishes to collect certain benefits that would
normally go to a legitimate spouse: Social Security,
worker's compensation, death benefits, life insurance, or
inheritance. Since one of the parties to the alleged
marriage is dead, it is difficult to prove. The surviving
spouse must show enough evidence to convince a judge or
jury that the parties had indeed intended to be married
and not just "living together." Exactly what you must do
to prove a common-law marriage differs from state to state.

States that have decided to recognize common-law marriages
base their decisions on the importance of families and of
keeping children off welfare rolls. Another consideration
frequently raised is the state's reluctance to "bastardize"
children. There is strong feeling that the stigma of
"illegitimacy" is a terrible burden to place on a child.
It certainly is--but that concern has led very few states
to take the logical step of abolishing the status of "illegitimate" altogether. The Appendix lists which states
currently recognize common-law marriage.

People involved in a valid common-law marriage are just as
legally and permanently married as those who have a license.
The same duties and rights arise from common-law and official marriage, and the children of common-law marriages
are as officially "legitimate" as those of formal marriages. Common-law wives are entitled to support from
their husbands and may sue for support if they are separated. Finally, it is just as hard to get out of a common-
law marriage as an official marriage. You can't end a
common-law marriage by walking out the door. If you want
to be free to get legally married again, you must get
a divorce.

RUTH

*Larry and I talk about getting married occasionally,
but we consider ourselves married, so it's just a
question of satsifying forms and other people.
We're both legally divorced, and Pennsylvania recognizes common-law marriage, so when we apply for
food stamps and other things, my name is his name
on all the papers. I haven't attempted to change my
driver's license and that type of thing, so I don't*

know how that will work, whether we'll have to have a marriage certificate for that. But our car insurance--the car's in my name, my old name, and I have to get a single person's rate. It would be much lower to have a married person's rate, but we would have to show a certificate for that.

If you want to establish a common-law marriage, the Appendix lists the ways to go about it, as well as some legal advantages and disadvantages. Many couples who live together have no desire for a common-law marriage--in fact are opposed to marriage in any form. Even though you may be trying to avoid all of these legal complications by simply living together, we suggest you check the Appendix to make sure exactly what your legal status is.

Lesbian Marriage

Legally, there is no such thing as gay marriage. A recent Washington, D.C., divorce reform bill included a provision legalizing gay marriage. It caused such a furor that it was dropped by the bill's sponsor so that the rest of the no-fault divorce provisions would be enacted.

Other attempts have been made to legalize gay marriage, but so far these have led the courts to deny gay people the right to marry. Their decisions are often based on myths and misunderstandings about the nature of homosexuality and marriage itself. Often they refer to dictionary and what they call "common-sense" definitions of marriage as an institution requiring one man and one woman. Some courts have also based their rejection of gay marriage on the premise that marriage is for the purpose of procreation and since procreation (they insist) is not part of gay marriage, the marriage is impossible.

State laws, however, almost never *say* that applicants for marriage licenses must belong to opposite sexes. In states where both parties must appear to obtain the license or the sex of the applicants is obvious (stereotyped female or male names), the request for an application is usually rejected. In some states where it is not necessary for both applicants to appear and where the names of the parties are not obviously both male or both female, it may be possible to acquire marriage licenses and certificates, although it is questionable whether these marriages would withstand any legal challenge.

When gay people are denied marriage licenses, they may try
to sue in federal or state courts in what is called a
mandamus action. Often local civil liberties lawyers are
willing to provide free or subsidized legal support for
such challenges, although the track record of those cases
so far may cause many a conscientious lawyer to hesitate
to file such a suit. The theory behind the mandamus
suit is that the marriage license bureau has an absolute
duty to issue licenses to people who follow the procedures
set out in the state marriage laws. Since these laws say
nothing about being of opposite sex as a requirement for
getting a license, the bureau is failing to perform its
duty when a clerk balks at issuing one to gay applicants.
In theory, you are just asking a court to order a public
servant to do his or her duty.

One case that followed that theory was appealed all the
way to the Supreme Court (*Baker* v. *Nelson*, 191 N.W. 2d
185, Minn.[1971]). The Supreme Court dismissed that case
for lack of a "substantial federal question," rejecting
a wide array of constitutional arguments based on the
right to privacy, freedom of religion and association,
and denial of equal protection of the laws. Since the
Supreme Court did not think these questions were serious
enough to warrant its attention, there is little hope of
getting judicial recognition of gay marriage in the
near future.

Some states have also used the existence of laws making
certain sexual acts criminal as a justification for
refusing to allow gay marriages. The trend in the area of
criminal law is somewhat confused right now because of
the recent refusal of the Supreme Court to consider the
constitutionality of certain criminal laws used against
homosexuals. In the late sixties and early seventies it
appeared that the trend was toward "decriminalizing" all
forms of sexual activity that were performed in private by
consenting adults; Colorado, Delaware, Hawaii, Illinois,
North Dakota, Ohio, and Oregon did so. (The definition
of *adult* remains a problem, however, as does the definition
of places in which one is considered to have a "reasonable
expectation of privacy.") In states that have removed
all criminal sanctions against sexual acts between people
of the same sex there is less legal justification for
refusing to issue marriage licenses. Refusals to recognize gay marriage might also be more successfully attacked in cities that have enacted gay rights bills which
prohibit discrimination based on sexual preference.

These cities include Alfred, New York; Ann Arbor, Michigan; Berkeley, California; Columbus, Ohio; Detroit, Michigan; East Lansing, Michigan; Minneapolis, Minnesota; San Francisco, California; Seattle, Washington; and Washington, D.C. A book that covers the topic more thoroughly is *The Rights of Gay People* by Marilyn Haft et al., which is listed in the Bibliography.

Although gay marriage is not legally recognized, there are many gay churches and gay ministers with gay ministries and congregations. Often gay marriages are performed within that context.

Reproductive Freedom and Health Care Rights

The United States Supreme Court has declared that a woman has a right to obtain an abortion and that the decision to do so is based on her constitutional right to *privacy*; the right is superior to any right a father may assert to the fruit of his genetic matter. And a woman's right to privacy is superior to any right asserted by her parents to control her or their genetic matter. Minors also have a right to abortion, without requiring their parents' consent. Some states have passed statutes that require a husband, or the parents or legal guardians of a minor, to consent before a woman can obtain an abortion. Those statutes are pretty clearly unconstitutional and have been so declared, or repealed, in many states. Similarly, state laws that prohibit advertising or in other ways prohibit the sale of nonprescription contraceptives to minors without parental consent are unconstitutional.

Laws prohibiting unlicensed doctors from performing abortions are now being challenged in several states. This may have important effects on the cost of abortion and other gynecological procedures and could affect the quality of health care available to women as well. Contact the women's health groups in your area for developments. It is now illegal in most states for people who are not physicians to perform abortions.

If you believe your rights to privacy and reproductive freedom are being denied, call the nearest legal aid or other legal services office or women's counseling center. If you can't figure out whom to call, try the local Civil Liberties Union. Check under either American Civil Liberties Union (ACLU) or the name of your city or state, followed by *Civil Liberties Union*.

CATHERINE

When I went into labor, I called John and he took me to the hospital. We had planned for John to be with me during labor. But I hadn't made that clear to anybody in particular, and I got a lot of grief about that at the hospital. They knew that John wasn't my husband, and I had put on the application for a room that I was not married. They were expecting me, and it was like there was a special negative reaction to me. I was really amazed at that. I somehow hadn't expected it, naïve as I was.

So the nurse wouldn't let John in, and I refused to go into the hospital unless he was allowed there. The nurse told him to go down and fill out some papers, which he did, and she told me to come along with her, and we both realized at the same time that he was not going to be allowed back up. So I stopped and said, "Is he going to be allowed back up?" and she said, "Well, no, why should he?" and I said, "We've taken natural childbirth courses together and I expect him to be up here. I need him." And he realized it at the same time and just turned around and came right back up. It's like I prevented myself from being taken prisoner. And he supported me in that. So we just sat together, but then he had to go to another room and I had to talk to the head nurse about it--I was in labor, right?--Anyway, I just insisted and called my doctor and he was supportive of me. He didn't take me particularly seriously, but he was nice to me. He thought I was cute or something. So he said that was all right and the hospital had to agree. So John was allowed in.

Also currently being litigated in several places is the issue of a father (or any other person chosen by the mother) to be present in the delivery room at the time of delivery. At least one court has upheld a regulation banning fathers from the delivery room. The parties in that case apparently made the mistake of admitting that the presence of the father was not *medically* necessary, and that they were deferring to the judgment of medical authorities on what was best for mother and child at the time of birth. In future cases parents should emphasize that the presence of the father or other "coach" is *medically* necessary--part of a planned program for the birth, the result of training, as in the Lamaze or other method.

<u>Names</u>

"My name is the symbol of my identity, which must not be
lost," declared Lucy Stone, who in 1855 became the first
American woman to keep her own name after getting married.
In 1921 the Lucy Stone League, a group whose goal was
to establish the legal right of a married woman to use her
own name, was established. The league was important in
winning many early victories for women who wanted to use
their birth names. However, the right of a woman to use
that name after marriage remains a complex issue today.
Married women who wish to use their birth names are
still faced with many bureaucratic and social obstacles.

ANNA

*Those decisions about keeping my own name, my own
money, not wearing a wedding ring, were pretty much
a function of how I felt about being independent
and being free, quite apart from any of the rhetoric
of the women's movement. The women's movement just
gave support for that kind of decision. It really
is not more complicated than that. I think I have a
pretty strong reluctance to get very committed to
people and to a relationship, and that was one way
of avoiding that. Also an ineffectual way. Whether
I keep my own name for me has little to do with
the dynamics of my relationship with Don as a person.
It serves more as a symbol or label for the outside
world than anything else. As for keeping my own
money, that's just my security.*

Most states now recognize the right of a woman to retake
her birth name after a divorce. Some states put conditions
on this right--for example, women with children may not
retake their birth names in Arkansas, Michigan, South
Dakota, West Virginia, and Wisconsin. In Kentucky, New
Hampshire, and Oklahoma name changes are granted only to
women who are not *"at fault"* in the divorce!

Recently some of the obstacles that face a woman who wants
to retain or regain her birth name have been removed or
reduced by court decisions and state attorneys general's
opinions. Most of these are based on the common-law right
of any person to use any name she or he chooses so long as
she or he is not doing so to defraud creditors or others.
Hawaii is the only state in the United States requiring

a woman to take her husband's name. In all other states
a woman need not *ever* use her husband's name. In all other
states a woman is able--in theory--to change back to her
birth name after using that of her husband, without going
to court. In reality it is much harder to retake your
birth name than it is to keep it.

If a married woman has taken her husband's name and wishes
to regain her birth name or take another name, she has two
options in most states. The first is to change her name
through the common-law process, which consists of simply
adopting and using her new name. In many states this
procedure will be complicated by opposition from state
officials--voting registrars, departments of motor
vehicles, and the like. A woman who decides to change her
name by this method should try to collect as much identi-
fication (Social Security card, driver's license, credit
cards) as possible in her new name, in order to prove to
stubborn officials that she is now identified by this name.

A second option is the formal name-change procedure in
effect in your state. Although a formal court proceeding
may eliminate many problems in dealing with officials,
the procedure often has its own difficulties. In a few
states it may be easy, does not require a lawyer, and is
inexpensive; in others a lawyer is customary and court
costs amount to several hundred dollars. In addition,
a judge may require an explanation of why you want your
name changed. If he or she is not satisfied, he or she
may deny your request. Name changes that have been denied
can be appealed.

For further information we suggest you contact the Center
for a Woman's Own Name, 261 Kimberly, Barrington, Illinois
60010. The center publishes a booklet dealing with applicable law and personal experiences of women who have
changed their names. See the Bibliography for further
information.

Children's Names

The best way to be sure about what the law says about
children's names is to check with the state bureau of
vital statistics, a local feminist attorney, or your state
attorney general for the specifics. Here is some general
information.

The old common-law rule is that children whose parents are
married receive their father's name; "illegitimate"

children are considered the children of no father and so are given their mother's surname. This is still the prevailing rule, although Ohio seems to represent a different trend. Children born "out of wedlock" there are given the mother's surname, but there is no longer any special notation for "illegitimate" children. However, if both parents agree, the child can have the name of its biological father, so long as mother and father sign a form at the hospital before filing the birth certificate.

It's easier to give your child a name other than that of the father (or mother, if the child is "illegitimate") at birth than to change a name the child has used for some time. Massachusetts has just ruled that a child can be given any name at birth, that the state has no interest whatsoever in the name given a child at birth. Few states have been so clear in their rulings or practices.

GAIL

When John and I decided to have a baby, we were absolutely clear that we didn't want to get married. We were also clear that we wanted our baby to have a hyphenated last name, mine and his. It was important to John to have his name second, and the two names sounded better that way anyway. Our strategy was to try to fill out the birth certificate as if this were the most common thing in the world. The day before we were to leave the hospital after the baby was born, the nurse gave me a pink form to fill out, and I nonchalantly wrote down the hyphenated last name in the space where it says "Baby's Name." The medical records clerk came scurrying into my room almost immediately. "You can't do this," she said. "The baby of an unmarried mother has to have her last name. Period."

"I don't want it that way," I said. "Take it back and see what you can do."

Several minutes later she came marching back with her superior, and both of them insisted it couldn't be done. This went on until the next day when it was time to leave. By this time John and I were getting pretty anxious because they were threatening either not to let us take the baby or not giving us a birth certificate unless we signed the form the right way.

I am enough of a law-abiding citizen that I was sufficiently intimidated by this time (not to mention tense and anxious from coping with a new baby) and agreed to sign a paper saying we considered ourselves to have a common-law marriage (which we don't) so that John's name could go last and the baby could be registered as "legitimate." I feel like I sold out. And even at that the baby's name didn't get hyphenated on the birth certificate.

One real problem is name changes for children after their mother's divorce. The question is being argued back and forth in courts these days, and the answer varies from state to state. Normally, if the divorced father (who does not have custody) does not object to his ex-wife's changing the name of her children to her maiden name, the name change will stick. If the father does object--if he goes to court to get an injunction against school officials' registering them in a new name, for example--the outcome is unclear. At least one court recently refused to allow a divorced mother to hyphenate the children's name, adding hers to his (*Laks* [*Eliot*] v. *Laks*, 2 F.L.R. 2022, Arizona Ct. App. 10/8/75).

It is even harder to change the name of a child from the surname of an ex-husband to that of a new husband (stepfather). The biological father's objection is almost certain to win the day. The only general rule is that if the father does not object, the name change is acceptable. If the father does object, the court will try to decide what is in the best interest of the child but will usually inject no small amount of respect for the patriarchal traditions: "The natural and appropriate desire of a father to have his children bear and perpetuate his name is significant," one court recently declared (*Robinson* v. *Hansel*, Minn. S. Ct. 11/1/74). The rule of that case is that names of children will be changed with court approval in the face of the father's objections only when there is "clear and compelling evidence that the substantial welfare of the child necessitates." Massachusetts, Ohio, Arkansas, New York, and Minnesota now adhere to the rule that after a divorce the children must keep their father's name. Other states are less clear.

Hyphenated surnames do not look like the wave of the future the United States. Bureaucracy doesn't have room for them. The first of the two inevitably gets dropped. IBM cards, standardized tests, and computer printouts don't have room for long names.

Wisconsin specifically allows parties to name infants with the surname of either the mother or the father.

The Legal Aspects of Wife Abuse

The traditional remedy for wife abuse is divorce on grounds of "cruel and barbarous treatment" or its closest equivalent. "Constructive desertion" as a cause for divorce is another traditional remedy: if a husband beats his wife, she has a right to move out and get a divorce on the grounds of desertion. Even though she moved out, his treatment of her made her "desertion" necessary for her health and well-being. The problem, of course, is that divorces take months, if not years, and offer no help to women who are terrorized by their husband's physical assaults and threats.

The criminal courts are reluctant to "interfere" in what they see as "marital problems." Police usually refuse to arrest and district attorneys are reluctant to prosecute for assault and battery when the complaining witness is the wife. If the D.A. refuses to prosecute, the abused wife may file a private criminal complaint. Both criminal procedures require that you go to the district attorney as soon as possible after the incident. Many cities have an intermediate step between your initial complaint to the D.A. and the trial itself: arbitration or conciliation. If you think talking things over with third parties might be useful, the step may be worth going through. The power of the arbitrators varies from place to place. The general experience of those who have been through the court procedure is that it is woefully inadequate and rarely deals with the problem in a satisfactory way. The outcome of a trial initiated upon your private complaint will probably be probation or a bond posted by your husband, which will be forfeited if he violates an order not to molest you again. In large cities, however, the whole process is often designed to get you to withdraw your complaint. If you aren't sure you want to go ahead with the complaint, think before you file it. Once you start the process, don't back down or be talked out of it. Technically, the district attorney is your attorney, and you do not need to be separately represented. However, a sympathetic lawyer might help you by talking over the facts, helping with your testimony, or just guiding you through the bureaucracy. Chapter 8 explores the problem of wife abuse more fully.

Rape within Marriage

The new Michigan revisions of the sex crimes law defines
rape (which is not called *rape* any more, but some degree
of criminal sexual conduct) as, among other things, "sexual intercourse with a non-consenting wife who has filed
for divorce or separate maintenance." Other states that
are in the process of revising criminal codes or specifically "sex crimes acts" may have similar developments.
Local antirape groups may be pushing legislators for the
inclusion of wives (even those not instituting divorce or
separation proceedings) in the rape statute.

Of Interest to Men

There has been great concern expressed lately about how
changes in domestic relations laws (those concerning
marriage, divorce, support, child custody, and wife abuse)
will or will not keep pace with women's demands for more
equality. Our feelings about the Equal Rights Amendment
and ERA-related legislation are mixed, but in the next
few paragraphs we want to explore some of the probable
effects of that legislation on men.

Many men may be surprised to learn that they are inci-
dental beneficiaries of the new state or national equal
rights amendments, or judicial interpretations of other
"equal rights" laws or constitutional amendments. The
thrust of those developments is not preferential treatment for women but the elimination of any category or
stereotype based on sex. One effect of this trend toward
"sex-neutral" interpretation of the laws has been that
many statutes that formerly provided special advantages to
women have been declared either invalid or equally applicable to men.

Most typical are statutes providing alimony, child support,
and counsel fees and costs to separated or divorcing
women. Some states have simply decided (either by statute
or by judicial interpretation) that the benefits formerly
available only to women are now available to either needy
spouse. Thus, if a husband interrupted his educational
career in order to support a wife who was obtaining a
professional degree, he may now be able to receive alimony,
assuming her income is considerably greater than his. A
wife who earns more than her husband is rarely (any more)
allowed to force her husband to pay for the cost of the
divorce, and most states hold that an "employable" wife is

not eligible for any substantial support in the form of
alimony after several years of separation. Of course, the
question of what makes a wife "employable" may be the subject of widely varying interpretation. We would hope that
the number of years the wife has been out of the labor
market as a result of her uncompensated service in the
home is taken into consideration by judges trying to decide
whether a wife is "employable."

At the very least, the old myth of wives who live off huge
alimony payments for the rest of their lives can no longer
be supported by reference to laws that compel husbands to
support their wives after divorce. In deciding on peti-
tions for alimony, courts will consider the length of the
marriage, the education and marketable skills of the wife,
and the availability of jobs for a person of her age,
experience, and ability. If anything, courts tend to err
in favor of the husband (assuming, for example, that a
fifty-five-year-old woman who has not worked in thirty
years could get a job as a secretary because she held
such a position before the marriage). In many states wives
who apply for permanent alimony must show that they are
unemployable because of a physical impairment or other
permanent condition. Courts are more lenient when it
comes to "temporary" alimony, especially for the duration
of any separation before divorce (sometimes called
pendente lite, "during litigation"), and it is still assumed
in most states that a husband will pay his wife's counsel
fees and litigation expenses, although courts in several
states have specifically ruled that statutes requiring
a husband to meet these expenses are unconstitutional.
Statutes that require the partner with the greater income
to pay for the legal expenses of the other are *not* unconstitutional. The assumption that a husband should pay
his wife's legal expenses is just a shorthand way of
generalizing about the fact that husbands' incomes are,
as a rule, superior to those of wives.

In other words, the trend under either state or federal
equal rights amendments and some judicial decisions would
seem to remove women from the position of being automatically protected because of their sex and supposedly
inferior abilities to support themselves, and to place men
and women on an equal basis before the law, by requiring
an investigation into the facts of each specific case to
determine whether one party is in fact economically dependent on the other. If one party is dependent, the
trend is to require the party with the economic advantage

to support and compensate the disadvantaged party for at least a limited period of time. However, the courts are not interested in precise equality. As a rule the only people eligible for any form of alimony are women who have been married a substantial number of years, have not worked much outside the home during the marriage, and have raised several minor children. The occasional househusband may also be compensated if he has had a career comparable to the average housewife. Young couples who have approximately equal education and no children are usually allowed to separate without further obligations to each other for support or compensation.

The trend that might disconcert husbands is the idea subscribed to by an increasing number of courts that wives who have sacrificed their educations for the sake of a husband's career should be somehow "made whole." That most often involves a wife who put her husband through college or professional school at the price of her own career. Several courts recently have ordered husbands who benefited in this way to pay their wives' tuitions and continue to support their wives through higher education. This is part of the new concept of "rehabilitative alimony" under which payments to wives after marriage are aimed at helping her gain financial independence.

Courts are also taking a much closer look at the present earnings and work ability of wives who ask for child support payments. It appears that those changes will ultimately benefit men as well as women. Under the traditional attitude that women are innately inferior, and therefore dependent, men are locked into unfair "caretaker" roles. This has led many courts in many states to fail to take into account women's earning power and therefore to burden men unfairly with support obligations. Although men who don't want to support their ex-families can get away, those who do want to meet their obligations are often penalized by having to support two households, especially when their ex-wives get preyed upon by unscrupulous lawyers who convince them to gouge.

As far as child custody is concerned, men who want to stay close to their children often have to battle "clutching" mothers who want to deny them custody or adequate visitation. Of course, that problem would be significantly reduced if women were not conditioned to see motherhood as their primary source of gratification. Too often the courts have failed to recognize the problem and deal with

it effectively. Added to all of this is the adversary
nature of the legal process itself, which pits separating
and divorcing spouses against each other and makes it
difficult for either to behave fairly, even when they are
so inclined.

So men have it rough, too, and our basic position is that
once women are freed from economic and social discrimination and are no longer programmed for dependence and
subservience, men will be freed from the unfair burdens
that the stereotyped "breadwinner" role places upon them.

Conclusion

The legal system that purports to govern marriage and
parenthood does not in fact solve the many conflicts
that frequently arise out of those relationships. Even
if the laws were changed to create equal expectations of
men and women, we still would question the right of the
state to govern those relationships. We believe that
people should be free to determine the nature of their
relationships without interference from the state. Such
is not the case, however, and for the present we must
struggle along within the existing system as best we
can. We hope that this chapter will be helpful as you
work to establish your own personhood, whether you are
married, single, or living with someone. The legal
system can be turned around and made to work in your be-
half if you know your rights and how to get them implemented. That knowledge can go a long way toward ensuring
your ability to live your life as *you* see fit. Although
the law presumes that you are dependent, you *can* see to
it that you live an independent, productive life either
on your own, or within an emotionally and economically
equal relationship with another person.

EMIKO TONOOKA

FEMINIST RESOURCES   FEMINIST RESOURCES

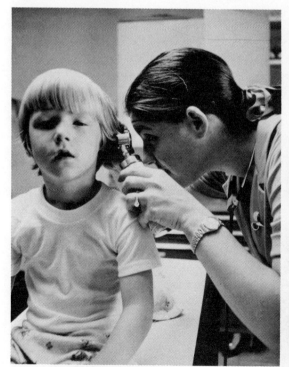

EVA SHADEROWFSKY

FEMINIST RESOURCES   FEMINIST RESOURCES

4

MARYANNE

Dennis knows how I feel. When I first started work, he had to stay with the children all day because he was laid off. Every day when I came home he'd say, "I don't know how you keep the house so clean. How do you keep the kids so clean? I never realized what a job it was." Now he is realizing that not only is it a responsibility to keep the house clean and to plan everything that has to be done, but also to take the time with the children to sit down and draw or listen to everything they come in to tell you. It really has worked good for us. For me, I realize that I'm independent, I'm helping out, I have something more to bring home to our relationship than just "Well, today I changed Eric" or "I washed the dishes." Now I can talk about other things and interesting people I've met.

Dennis is happy for me. He enjoys the fact that I'm happy working and also because it's helping us out. What's nice about it is I don't feel guilty, because he is with the kids. I'm not leaving them with someone else, they're not sharing their time with some other person, because I think I'd be jealous. Dennis is getting to see more of the children, which a father should.

I think fathers should have maternity leave, too, so that they can be here when the mommy gets home with the baby instead of leaving two children and then bringing home another baby, and then the husband comes home and he wants dinner. That's not my idea of a relationship. My idea is halfway. He's fantastic anyway. If the wash has to be done and I'm tired, he sneaks out with the kids and goes to the laundromat and does it. He does the shopping. He does anything. So it really works out good for us.

When I'd come home from work he would say, "These damn kids have been harassing me all day long!" and I'd say to him, "Really?" All those times before I was working when I'd be in a bad mood, he'd say, "Aw, hon, come on, get out of your bad mood. The kids are in bed now." And now he realizes that it wasn't something in my mind, I'm not going nuts because I'm a housewife. The kids do get on your nerves. They're your own kids but you can actually hate them sometimes. And I never felt like I had time for myself. There were always a lot of things I wanted to do that I'd put off. I couldn't sew because the children were around, I didn't want them near the sewing machine. I couldn't write poetry because I couldn't concentrate. Now I get to do that stuff, plus working, and it really feels good. I enjoy it.

My father was a piece worker, he worked in a factory making grinding wheels, and my Mom didn't work until I was just going into high school, and then she got a job because my Mom and Dad's relationship was not the best. My father, he was the big macho, head of the family chauvinist thing and my Mom wasn't into that. I looked at all men as being like my father because I had no other men to compare to. I knew when Dennis and I first met that I had a lot of feelings about my father. Even when he didn't say something, I assumed that he meant what my father's reaction would have been. It took a long time for me to adjust to a person being honest with me, because I knew my Dad wasn't.

I took a secretarial course in high school because I also was into being a secretary. Sitting behind a desk, taking notes, meeting nice people, and all that. But I was always involved in theater. Even now Dennis will mention that I should get involved in one of these adult theater groups, but I think my acting ambition was more because in my family it was usually an act--when my Dad was around you put on an act. With my Mom we could be totally honest,

120

and I was more like a friend with my mother than a mother and daughter relationship. When my Mom died, it messed me up. It took a long while to get straightened out.

Then I met Dennis, and my ideas about marriage and men changed. I think mainly at first with Dennis it was that he was replacing my Dad, because that's how our relationship started out. I looked to him as somebody that would understand me. He was replacing my parents, really. But then it grew into more of a man-woman relationship after we were married. But even for the three years that we went together it was really like Mommy-Daddy stuff. I don't know what Dennis thought, because I never really asked him. I think that even he was getting a little bored with that. I was running to him with every little problem. I was just really messed up. I was very dependent on him.

Then I got married, and I realized that there were times, especially because Dennis's Mom had died too, that he needed somebody that he could talk to on an adult level, not someone he had to talk down to all the time. There was no set time that it happened, but suddenly he would turn to me and say, "You know, I feel like I'm really communicating with you. I'm really getting through to you. You're understanding my feelings, too." And that's when I realized that all those years I depended on him to be there for me, but I didn't always necessarily have to be there for him. Our relationship completely changed, and it was more two adults communicating instead of a father and child. And it's worked out ever since then. I feel we have a very good relationship. It's very fair and understanding. He doesn't talk down to me. He understands that I'm a person.

For both of us there's only two things in marriage that really matter the most, outside of the fact that initially you're usually in love with each other. But after all that starry-eyed "It's always going to be roses and candlelight dinners," it came down to two things: first and foremost for me and Dennis, that you can respect and be considerate of each other's feelings. But secondly, compromise is a big part of marriage. You both have to give and take a little bit. I'm not saying you have to compromise basic principles or something you really believe in.

I think people that just live together are copping out. Not that a paper makes any difference to me, but I felt like when I was getting married to Dennis, this was a commitment, this was my way of saying,"I want to live within a relationship. I'm going to try to make it stick. I'm going to go a little further than somebody that's just saying, Look I love you and I want to live with you and I want to sleep with you, and if it doesn't work out I can just leave." For us, we have to try just a little bit harder, and now with children--although I don't believe if you have a bad relationship you should stay together for children, because I think that hurts more than helps them. But even now with the children, that itself was something for us to cope with and grow together with, because having children really puts a lot of pressures on in a way I didn't realize before.

Dennis plays the guitar and I don't. There are times when he'll sit for three or four hours just playing the guitar and teaching himself songs, writing music. And then there are times when I have to be alone and write poetry, and he's not into that. Or sew. Or knit. Or whatever. On that level, we do have different interests, but as far as sports or going out anywhere socially, almost all the time we go together. We find that most of our friends are people that we both like anyway, so that's why we spend time together.

If Dennis and I weren't together for some reason, I'd be lost. That's very hard to say, because when you have someone with you, you can't imagine when they're not going to be with you. If I had to cope on my own, I would be able to do it more now than when I first got married six years ago. Just everything about me has changed--I've matured, I have changed a lot of my ideas. I have my own money, and there's no questions asked about what I do with it. I can write out a check, I can do whatever I want. I feel that if I had to, I'd be able to cope on my own after some amount of time.

At one time we had had a joint account with a bank, and I applied for a checking account myself, and they really didn't want to hear about me. All they did was give me a hard time and ask me about my husband. I would look on getting my own credit as another goal reached, or an accomplishment. For me personally I would feel a little more independent and a little more able to cope with things.

I know my ideas are a little different from most of the people around me. I have an advantage, because I have one sister-in-law who's into women's lib, so I know there must be women out there that feel the way that I do. My other sisters-in-law definitely don't, most people in my family don't. My sister and my sisters-in-law are all into the husband being the head of the household--which I don't put someone down for because I can understand it, it's just that I think I've gone a little bit past them.

I really think Dennis supports me in being an independent person. He doesn't suppress my ideas. There are times when he doesn't agree with me, but that's his prerogative not to agree. But if it was something I really felt and really wanted, he would say he didn't agree with it, but I'm sure he wouldn't stop me. He really didn't like the idea of the wife working. He thought the husband had to be the provider. Then when he realized that there was no alternative but for me to go to work, he had to give in a little or compromise. And now like I say it has helped our relationship, not hurt it; he looks at me with a completely different view, and it's helped us.

4 / Who Controls
the Pursestrings?

Money may not be the root of all evil, but it certainly
is the root of a lot of marital, premarital, and post-
marital conflict. Getting money, making it stretch
further, and learning how to make wise decisions about
spending it (and they become joint decisions when you
marry) are tasks that most of us encounter at some time in
our lives. Some of us develop by trial and error the
skills of acquiring and managing money; others of us are
totally mystified if we have to do much more than cash a
check at the supermarket. Our attitudes and habits about
money vary widely, ranging from excessive pennypinching to
reckless generosity. Our potential for earning money also
varies; those with professional degrees or specialized
skills can realistically expect to earn more than those
of us with little formal training or education. While each
woman's relationship to money is influenced by factors such
as her personality, her parents' ways of handling money,
and her current marital situation, our experiences with
and values about money depend, probably more than anything
else, on whether we come from upper-income, middle-income,
or low-income families. In addition to having access to
different amounts of money, families from different class
backgrounds vary in how they view and spend money.

Despite our differences, however, we as women have one
important thing in common: *we become, to a greater or*

124

lesser degree, economically handicapped the minute we say,
"I do." In Chapter 3 we explored the ways in which the
unwritten marriage contract handicaps women legally and
financially, since the two areas are intertwined. We have
found that without a doubt, the term of the unwritten
marriage contract that cripples the largest number of women
is the absolute economic power most husbands have over
their wives. Unless the wife is independently wealthy and
manages her own money, she is essentially dependent on her
husband's generosity. As long as the marriage is congenial
and the husband generous, many women don't mind this arrangement. But if the marriage goes sour, or if the husband turns out to be unusually frugal, the wife becomes
a beggar. In couples that stay together over the years,
many husbands willingly provide love and money in appreciation for the devotion of their wives. Most of these
women feel, on the one hand, that they are happy to serve
their husbands and children for love. On the other hand,
however, they often experience feelings of uneasiness
about their present financial dependency and worry about
what the future might bring, whether it be death of the
spouse, separation, layoff, or other hard times for the
family.

Many women are shocked to discover how few economic protections they have under the law when their marriages
dissolve. While in some states alimony and support laws
are written to provide for financially dependent wives and
children upon the breakup of a marriage, in reality,
enforcement mechanisms are usually inadequate. Women who
have not worked outside the home for many years are the
most disadvantaged because they do not have job skills or
seniority to enable them to become partially or totally
self-supporting. But even women who have jobs or job
skills find it difficult to maintain the standard of living
they and their children have become used to. Without the
voluntary support of their husbands, they find no effective
legal way to obtain what they feel is due them for their
years of service in the home. Many other women, whose
marriages are intact, face discrimination in such areas as
credit, insurance, Social Security, and employment because
of their married status.

AVOID ECONOMIC DEPENDENCY IN MARRIAGE! That is the most
important message we can share with you from our experiences at the Women in Transition program. Those of you
who are happily married or planning to be married are probably reluctant to think about what would happen if your

marriage were to break up. But more and more marriages are
ending through separation, and older women should prepare
themselves for the reality that their husbands may die
first. Knowing how you would provide for yourself in
either event can only be to your advantage. One important
way to contribute to the viability of a marriage is for
the wife actually to be supporting herself or to be capable
of it. Staying in a marriage because it is the most
appealing emotional option to you is, in our opinion, far
preferable to staying in a marriage because you are financially dependent on your husband. That kind of dependency
can breed resentment and mistrust in both of you, regardless of how much love you feel for each other.

CHARLOTTE

*When my husband and I were first married we both
assumed he would manage the money, even though I was
working and had always handled my own money up until
then. What happened is that things got very tense
between us. We didn't have a lot of money (he was
a student), and he got very critical of whatever I
spent. He used to get angry if I brought home more
than two bags of groceries, so I would bring them
home when he wasn't there and put them away real
quick. This didn't really help, though, because he
always asked to see the sales slip. But that uproar
was nothing compared to what happened when I bought
a new dress.*

ROBERTA

*I remember in our women's group when Joyce talked
about having a five-thousand-dollar inheritance from
her aunt that she kept in her own name, to the great
annoyance of her husband. I could never understand
why she wouldn't want that money in a joint account.
Then they ended up separating, and she still had her
five thousand dollars. Now that I've separated, I
sure wish that I had done that with the one thousand
dollars I had gotten from my mother.*

In this chapter we focus on how to become financially self-
sufficient within a marriage. If you must depend on your
husband for support, either in the short run or the long
run, see Chapter 3 about your rights and options under the law.

We assume in this chapter that you either are not working now or have a volunteer, part-time, or low-paying full-time job which pays you less than enough to live on if you were on your own. Basically we believe that the long-range solution to the financial problems we have seen in American marriages is for women to have equal access to paid work, for men to share fully in child care responsibilities, and for high-quality, low-cost (or free) child care to be readily available. Obviously these changes are a long way off, both because our society is structured to make it almost impossible and because many people are skeptical of altering roles that they have been encouraged to believe are natural and fulfilling. In this chapter we focus on some of the shorter-range individual solutions you can put into practice now, but we draw your attention to suggested readings in the Bibliography. Many people have been thinking seriously about ways to improve the quality of life for women and men in this country, and their ideas are not as far-fetched as you might expect. The experiences of thousands of women have taught us that *the importance of women's economic independence within marriage cannot be stressed too much.* We want to prevent some of the heartaches and tragedies we have seen.

ELLEN

Initially, in theory, I thought supporting my husband was a good thing to do. I thought we had what was a fair arrangement. He was finishing his Ph.D. so he would have the credentials he needed for his profession; he then would be capable of supporting me for a while when I went to art school. However, it just turned out to be a huge drag, and the pressures increased about being THE person who seemed to be constantly responsible for supporting the whole household. With increases in costs of everything, I just felt really trapped. The initial arrangement was a one-year thing, and that dragged on two and a half years. Even though now he has a job, he still hasn't finished his doctorate. So I just don't see the point at which it's going to be reciprocal, even yet.

I really got the feeling that if I were a man, I would never want to be in a situation of supporting a woman all the time. It's probably harder for women to do that anyway because of our socialization.

But I just got to be very resentful that there was another adult in the house who had skills at least equal to mine and yet he wasn't earning any money. I felt that instead of living with an adult I was living with a child. I just thought if I were a man living with a woman, even if she had children, I wouldn't want to be in that position of being responsible for all the income myself.

The First Step: How Do You Feel about Money?

One of the first steps toward taking charge of your financial situation is to look at your attitudes and behavior in relation to money. Many of us fall into spending patterns we are unaware of or, if we are aware of them, feel powerless to change habits we don't like. Many of us feel powerless about money anyway, because there never seems to be enough of it. We are never able to feel totally secure or to buy all the things we want. The feeling of never having enough seems to exist in people at all economic levels, even among the rich. There are no "shoulds" about handling your money, and we don't believe anyone can tell you how to do it except to provide some suggestions for budgeting. Living in this society has created in most of us complex, irrational, and often self-destructive attitudes about money which are usually difficult to change because there is so little support for alternatives to a wasteful, competitive, and consumption-oriented definition of happiness, success, and self-respect. A first step in learning to make money serve you rather than the other way around is to understand your feelings and behavior with money so that you do not feel you are pushed and pulled by forces beyond your control.

There are a number of factors that influence how you feel about money and what you do with it. Your personality is one factor. Do you tend to be tight with your money (and maybe your time, your affection) because you feel you will be taken advantage of if you aren't careful? Or do you spend money easily, too easily perhaps, on friends and family, often because you want their approval? Do you fall somewhere in the middle? Are you comfortable with how careful or loose you are with money?

Another factor is how your parents felt about money as you
were growing up. Do you find yourself duplicating their
patterns or behaving in a different way, perhaps exactly
the opposite from theirs? How does your husband's attitude
about money affect you? Do the two of you work well together, making joint decisions about spending, or do you
find yourself spending in ways he disapproves of? Does
he do that to you?

Probably the factor that shapes our attitudes and behavior
about money more than any other is our class background.
At Women in Transition we noticed some major differences
in women from low-income, middle-income, and upper-income
backgrounds. Those differences fall into two areas: how
much there actually is to spend, and how the women feel
about what there is to spend. For low-income women the
reality is that there is often not enough money coming in
to meet basic survival needs, or that if there is enough,
it can't be counted on in a regular way. This can lead
to the stereotyped behavior of the welfare recipient who
receives her check and blows it immediately on liquor
and steaks. Some behave in this way but many, of course,
do not. The point is that there are understandable reasons
for this behavior when it occurs. Poor people do not have
much money to work with, so they have little incentive
and opportunity to acquire money management skills, although many low-income women are wizards at stretching
incredibly small amounts of money to meet their families'
needs. More important, since financial security always
seems to be beyond their grasp, many poor people have even
less incentive to try to shape the future through thrift.
When you've been without money for a long time and can't
predict that you will be getting any with regularity,
then spending it on things that will bring pleasure now
makes all the sense in the world. That is one concrete way
to treat yourself when you have been feeling deprived,
since it is psychologically easier to feel rich and
satisfied one day and starved the next three than just
scraping by for four. Underlying all of these psychological factors are the economic and social realities: the
lack of alternatives to high-priced goods, the cost of
credit, and the societal pressure to define ourselves
through spending.

Blue-collar middle-income people are one step up from this
sense of powerlessness and actually have more dollars to
work with, so many middle-income people, women especially,
are very thrifty. They often feel that more money is

the way to solve all the problems of life, and having tasted
some of the power that comes along with money, they are
hungry for more. In blue-collar families the wives often
take charge of the finances, spending carefully and saving
when they can. Concerned that their husbands get ahead,
concerned perhaps that their children have a better life
than they have had, blue-collar wives often see their
future happiness tied up in how much their husbands can
increase the family's earnings and sometimes put a lot of
pressure on their husbands to get ahead.

In upper-income middle-class families the husbands often
make the major money decisions, perhaps because the stakes
are higher (that is, there is more money to be managed)
and they are concerned that it be done correctly. Managing
a complicated investment program is usually considered the
husband's province. Because many upper-income people have
learned to like their relatively affluent life-styles,
they are often fearful of losing what they have and become
anxious about spending money too loosely.

Of course, we are generalizing about these class differences
and talking about the extremes. There are upper-income
people who spend lavishly, just as there are low-income
people who are stingy. There is also a continuum of behavior in relation to money, so that some people cannot
be described by any one classification. For example, some
families have an income that puts them in an upper-middle-
class bracket but still have spending habits shaped by
their working-class upbringing or their parents' working-
class upbringing. The archetypal millionaire in books and
movies remembers what it was like to be poor and pinches
his pennies accordingly. Also, in any given family the role
of women in relation to money varies greatly. In some
upper-income families the wives are more sophisticated
investors than their husbands; in others the wives are
totally helpless when it comes to budgeting or going over
the month's expenditures. In some working-class families
the wives take over the paycheck as soon as it comes and
parcel it out as needed; in others the husbands give their
wives an allowance to run the household and carefully audit
the expenditures.

There are some attitudes and habits that cut across class
lines, however. This is a country that attaches great
importance to material wealth and tends to measure individual worth by the amount of wealth a person has accumu-
lated. We think this is destructive. This value system

locks people into lives of producing and consuming, which
blinds them to other options for fulfilling lives. That
is, if most people believe that happiness can be found
through buying a new car or eating in an expensive restau-
rant rather than walking through the (uncrowded, unpol-
luted) woods or sharing an evening with a close friend,
then they will be under great pressure to earn more money
themselves. They will probably also support economic
policies that favor increased production of consumer goods
rather than the development of human services or recreation
facilities. We are encouraged to believe that a society
organized for profit will benefit those who work hard and
have a will to succeed, but that does not take into
account that the benefits of this system go not to those
who work and save but to those who accumulate capital and
invest it. And, of course, large segments of the population are systematically denied access to the tools of
success. Consider also that this society does not really
take responsibility for protecting people against social
calamities (long-term illness, birth of a handicapped
child, a debilitating old age) but insists that each of us
somehow build our own security. That leaves most people
with a fundamental sense of uneasiness about their lives
and confusion about how best to achieve satisfaction.

We are bombarded regularly with messages that money will
do the trick for us, so many of us spend our lives agonizing
about how much we have, how much we want to get, and what
to do with it. Some women are even one step removed from
this and must push their husbands into making more money
to achieve their own happiness and security. Women who
do not work outside the home bring in no money, and most
women who do work make less than their husbands, so that it
is often even more difficult for a woman to be clear about
her relationship to money. Many women feel consciously or
unconsciously inadequate because they are not contributing
a substantial portion of the family's income. Often their
husbands aggravate that feeling of inadequacy. Some women
only feel good when they are buying things for themselves,
their families, and their homes, even when they can't
afford to; they are caught in the grip of compulsive spending patterns which they feel they can't overcome. For many
women it is difficult to draw the line between reasonable
and compulsive spending, because being a consumer is part
of their role as wife and mother. In many families the
woman is expected to dress nicely and have a beautifully
furnished home as a reflection of her husband's success.
For some women "keeping up with the Joneses" is a major

preoccupation because they have no other way to measure
their own worth.

RUTH

*We have not too many problems as far as dealing with
money. He gives it to me and I pay the bills; he's
a generous person. I would like him to have a better
job, and he could care less. So we have a problem
there, because we have different values about an
important thing. He doesn't have a job right now--
he's still collecting unemployment, and I don't know
how long he will be on for. I would like us to have
a house, and I don't want to freeload off his
mother or my mother. My mother I'm sure has enough
money to buy us a house that we could all live in,
and she would probably do it if I asked her. But
I don't want it like that. We're still barely just
making it. We have zilch savings. But he doesn't
seem to care too much about it. He's willing to
just let it go. If a job comes by, fine; if not,
fine. "We'll get by" is his attitude, I guess.*

We aren't attaching any judgments to our descriptions of
people's relationship to money, nor are we saying that
one person's habits are preferable to another's. We *are*
saying that in this society it is very difficult to develop a healthy, self-affirming approach to money because it
is so often connected with how much we value ourselves.
Married women operate under some special handicaps in this
regard because it is the exceptional woman who earns a
sizable income. We aren't laying down rules here about
handling your money but are offering some basic suggestions
that can help you begin to understand yourself in relation
to money and to take charge of your financial situation.

1.   Think about your own earning and spending habits and
      those of your husband. Sort out which of your
      habits you think are productive and which aren't.
      Do the same for his. Think about ways to change
      the habits you don't like.

2.   Insist on knowing about your family's financial ar-
      rangements if you don't already. That includes how
      much your husband earns, what investments there are,
      insurance policies, safe deposit box, and so on. At
      Women in Transition we were amazed at the number of
      women who, for example, signed joint income tax

returns without even looking at them. You never
know when you may be handling the money by yourself.
(As signer of a joint return you can also be held
liable for both civil and criminal penalties for any
false information, or for the entire amount unpaid,
plus interest and costs.)

3.   Have the confidence to know that you *can* learn money
       management skills. Most of us got the message at
       an early age that math is too difficult for us.
       Not so. Learn from books, friends, family money
       management courses. Handling figures well is more
       difficult for some women than others, but all of us
       have the power to do it. The Bibliography lists
       useful articles and books about money management.

4.   Get credit in your own name if you do not have it.
       See the section on credit later in this chapter for
       information on why and how to do this.

5.   Recognize that you don't have to define yourself by
       the things you buy. Most people like to own nice
       things, which is perfectly reasonable. But ask
       yourself whether the things you acquire really make
       you happy. Do you shop because you have few other
       positive activities or relationships in your life?
       Or do you buy things because you truly enjoy them?
       Would you be happier with a life-style less oriented
       toward possessions?

6.   Think through the extent to which you have been
       pushing your husband to advance on his job as a way
       of meeting your needs for success. If this is
       causing friction between you, start to think about
       ways you can acquire recognition and money on your own.

Supporting Yourself

Many women feel that the only way to survive is to live on
the income of a man through marriage. However, many women
have been the major or sole support of themselves and their
children. Most women support themselves in one of three
ways or in some combination of them:

1.   Support from a spouse
2.   Support from the state (for example, public assis-
       tance, unemployment compensation, Social Security)
3.   Paid employment inside or outside the home

Women are disadvantaged in each of these areas for one
reason or another, and in this section we explore the ways
in which you can maximize the benefits from whichever
arrangement is most suitable for you at the present time.
Our strong suggestion is that your long-range goal be paid
employment or the potential for it because of all the
liabilities mentioned earlier connected with women's
economic dependence in marriage. We recognize that being
self-supporting may not ever be a realistic option for
many women because of their age, lack of skills, physical
handicaps, or other obstacles. If that is the case for you,
however, you should know your legal and financial position
so that you can maximize your options. Chapter 3 and the
next section of this chapter explore these options.

Whichever of the three support arrangements (or combinations
of them) you are living under now, it is important for you
and your husband to work out an agreement about how money
will be handled which you are both comfortable with and
which is not destructive to either of you. Women who are
entirely dependent on their husbands' income are the most
likely to feel limited in negotiations of this kind. Read
the next section for a discussion of how your contribution
in the home is really crucial for the functioning of your
family. Your work is economically essential, and even
though there is no monetary compensation attached to it,
recognizing its worth is important in any discussion about
money between you and your husband.

If you and your husband both have incomes, whether from a
public program or from paid employment, think about
alternatives to whatever money-sharing arrangement you
currently have if it is not satisfying to both of you.
Probably the most common arrangement is for a couple
to put their incomes in a joint fund and meet expenses
from the common pool. That works well for some couples,
but for others friction results. Sometimes one partner
is critical of the other's spending habits. Sometimes the
partners are dissatisfied with the relationship for other
reasons and use money to hurt each other, either by with-
holding it or by spending it in a way that is guaranteed
to infuriate the other. Some couples with individual
incomes (or with only one income to divide) keep separate
accounts. If the incomes are roughly equal, the expenses
are split in half. Other couples, in which one partner
makes considerably more than the other, also keep separate
accounts but prorate their expenses on a percentage basis
according to the difference in their incomes. That means

that if John makes $15,000 a year and Mary makes $10,000, their combined income is $25,000, of which his contribution is 60 percent and hers 40 percent. Through prorating, John contributes 60 percent of the rent, utilities, medical coverage, entertainment, and so on, and Mary pays 40 percent. Another possibility is to keep some money separate for personal expenditures but have a joint fund for common expenses.

That may sound peculiar to you, since for most couples the notion of a marriage partnership automatically includes sharing money. Many couples assume that if their marriage is good, the money matters will work out. We think that is unrealistic, given everyone's differences about money. Deviating from the standard arrangement of pooling all your money does not mean that the two of you don't love or trust each other but recognizes that you may have entirely different values and are taking steps to eliminate unnecessary friction. Try it.

ANN

Last year, after a conversation with you, I went home and said to Lou, "It's time for me to have a separate account." First he went through how we make mutual decisions about how to spend, and you've never denied yourself what you wanted because of my opinion. His back was up, but the conversation ended with, "So open a bank account and put in whatever you want." It came down to the fact that I couldn't pinpoint expenditures that he disagreed with, and I couldn't pinpoint harassment by him. So I said that I thought the problem was that I had some feelings about wanting my own separate pot. I make a lot of money, and I feel that some of it should be mine and not ours. I want to make separate decisions, go places with other people. I didn't feel he had done anything wrong, but I knew I would feel more independent if I had separate money. So Lou says, "Have separate money." Then we discussed how much, and let's figure out a proportion. He asked me to figure out what would make me feel comfortable.

It's so hard to do. The sad thing is that if you complain about the finances it sounds like you don't trust the other, and in the present that's probably unfounded. We went through this whole thing about wills. Was that painful! For instance, if I inherit money from my parents and I die, currently the will says Lou is the recipient and he decides what to do with it. I don't particularly want Lou to get a wad of money from my parents and then remarry and spend it on some other woman. Now that just happens to gall me. So, in the present that hurts his feelings, because he wouldn't do that. But if I die, what's he going to do? Sit around looking at a pot of money? He's going to find other people and keep living his life. So a long-term look can be tricky. One thing I did do was build in other people. My friend Vivian, the family that takes care of my daughter Becky, some cousins that are important to me. Still, fifty percent will go to Lou. You can also leave trust funds. I don't want Becky to be denied anything. I hope there would be other adults around to help with her. It's not like I want him or her to be alone the rest of their lives. But he'll say, "Of course Becky will be well taken care of. Why do you have to specify that the money be spent on Becky?" I want the best for her. I'll make sure she's not denied anything. But then my sister who is a lawyer and does a lot of wills says, "Yeah, but things happen." It raises a lot of interesting questions about who are the most important people and how long in the future can you make decisions about now.

Developing an alternative money arrangement, however, will not automatically solve all your money problems. Money will always be an emotionally charged issue for most of us and can be a handy weapon to use against someone else. Friction can result, for example, if one partner chooses an interesting but low-paying job when she or he could be earning more, consequently lowering her or his share of the joint income. The other partner may feel trapped in a less interesting job and forced to subsidize the other. There can also be tension if the wife earns more than the husband; although some men are able to handle this situation with relatively little stress, others are surprised to discover how their self-image suffers when they are not in the role of the major provider. The wife may also feel martyred. Finally, if one partner does not really respect the other's right to make choices about money, then no mechanical arrangement is going to make life easier. Those are all situations where the dynamics between the partners in nonmoney areas need to be taken into account.

In order for any alternative money arrangement to succeed, the partners must work together to develop a genuine respect for each other's capacity to make judgments that are right for them. Creating an alternative money arrangement is only the first step.

SUPPORT FROM A SPOUSE

In most marriages, especially those with children, the husband is the major breadwinner. While the wife may work part-time or full-time outside the home, especially in these times of economic stress, she is still basically dependent on his income. It is difficult enough for two people with different tastes and quirks about money to come to spending decisions that are agreeable to both. It can become terribly strained when a partner feels misunderstood or at a disadvantage. Those stresses take different forms. The husband may feel he should have more say in money decisions because he is bringing in all or most of the cash. The wife may feel she cannot do her job of managing the household on the amount of money coming in. Some men want total control of the money and are highly critical of how their wives spend it; other men don't make direct comments on the spending but undermine their frazzled wives with comments such as "Well, what did you do all day?" Sometimes women feel inadequate because they are not paid "workers" which this society values. Yet, this is confusing because these women are fulfilling the housewife/mother role which they expected would bring them happiness and security. They sometimes become manipulative of their husbands, pushing them to get ahead on the job so there will be more money to spend on clothes, furnishings, and entertainment.

> Housework is invisible work. No one notices it until it isn't done--we notice the unmade bed, not the scrubbed and polished floor. Housework is maintenance and restoration; the daily restocking of the shelves and return of each cleaned and repaired object to its starting point in the family game of disorder. After a day's work, no matter how tiring, the housewife has produced no tangible object-- except, perhaps, dinner; and that will disappear in less than half the time it took to prepare. She is not supposed to make anything, but to buy, and then to prepare or conserve what has been bought, dispelling dirt and depreciation as they creep up.

And each housewife works alone. No companion workers,
no other housewives, not even other members of her
family (unless they are pre-school age) are around
during her workday. Housework has been politically
invisible, too. Unpaid, unorganized "women's work,"
it has been dismissed and ignored, as if housework
were something as biologically determined as childbirth, an ancient and changeless form of female
labor. [Barbara Ehrenreich and Deirdre English,
"The Manufacture of Housework"]

In our opinion, one reason so many couples struggle over
money is because the work that women do in the home is not
compensated. Many feminists have begun to organize around
this "wages for housework" issue, viewing it as the key to
understanding women's oppression inside and outside marriage. There are disagreements among feminists about how
to remedy the problem, but most agree on the basic concept
that women who work inside the home (usually wives) should
be paid for their labor. When asked what they do, many
housewives reply, with some embarrassment, "Oh, I'm just
a housewife." They are acknowledging that this society
values the unpaid work of women very little, despite the
rhetoric that making a home and raising children are a
woman's most important job. In fact, these *are* valuable
contributions to the national economy as well as to an
individual family. In 1972 a study showed that more than
28 million women remained in the home and worked a total
of at least 145 billion hours a year, which was worth
one-third of the gross national product that year, or
$375 billion. In addition to performing services for other
family members for which the husband would have to pay,
the contribution of the wife/mother/houseworker frees one
or more of the other family members to devote their energies
to full-time wage-earning. In 1970 the Chase Manhattan
Bank estimated that the average housewife works 99 hours
a week; her labor at that time was worth at least $13,391.56
per year (44.5 hours weekly as a nursemaid at $2.00 an
hour, 17.5 hours as housekeeper at $3.25 an hour, 13.1
hours as cook for $3.25 an hour, and dishwasher at $2.00
an hour for 6.2 hours weekly),* and twice that amount would
be reasonable compensation. Without that division of
labor, the family's earnings, under the present economic

*Margaret A. Sanborn and Caroline Bird, "The Big Giveaway:
What Volunteer Work Is Worth," *Ms.*, vol. 3, no. 8, (February 1975), p. 88.

structure, might diminish considerably. Obviously the
national economy benefits also.

RUTH

*Larry sees the housework as my job, that and a lot
of other things. Like feeding our dog, and doing
our wash, plus housework--all those things. They're
my job, he calls it. I try to argue with him about
that, but he has me as long as he can argue, "I
work for X number of hours, and I come home, and now
I'm tired, and you don't have a job to go to during
the day." And I try to say, "Well, I went out and
did this and that," and he says, "Well, there we are
back in that again. That's your job. That's what
you're supposed to do. And you probably sat in
front of the TV all day." Sometimes I don't think
he knows me at all. I wouldn't sit down in front of
the TV all day unless I was sick. But he really
thinks that's my job. Every now and then he'll pitch
in and do something, but he is the type of man, a
male chauvinist--he would never change a child's
diaper. He has done clothes washing, and he has
vacuumed, but he would never wash a dish. Now it's
at the point where he would tell the kids to do it
rather than him doing it. I don't like it, but I'm
willing to put up with it. I try to change it, but
how can you change something that was ingrained in
him as a child? I think a lot of his problems are
from when he was a child, because his mother did
practically everything for him.*

It is our belief that the time has come to recognize the
economic value of the wageless work performed at home by
women. It will probably be a long time, however, before
some of the proposals for remedying the situation will be
implemented, and in the meantime millions of American
women are faced with finding a satisfactory arrangement
for the present. Chances are your husband will not be
enthusiastic about paying you for your work out of his
own income, although more and more men are recognizing the
fairness of that arrangement. You might want to suggest
that his income be divided in half; you can treat your
half as your own, to be negotiated with as if you had
earned it on the paid job market. However, individual
solutions are not the long-range answer to this problem.
State and nationwide programs need to be developed.

Again, we suggest you think about ways to become employable
or employed (see the section on work, which follows) if
you are not employable now. In situations where that is
not feasible, such as if you are caring for young children,
and where your husband resists acknowledging your work
in the home as worthy of compensation, see Chapter 3 for
information about how much your contribution to the home
is recognized under the law. And continue to point out
to your husband the value of the work you are doing for
him personally and for the whole family. Remember,
you are not "just a housewife," you are a fully contributing half of the partnership, and you deserve to be
treated as such.

The Housework Poem

Even before the women's movement, I hated housework;
that was no big deal.
I laughed as I cooked the noodles right in the
chicken soup, which then became completely absorbed
by the former.
I compared notes with my new-bride friends who also
didn't bother to dry dishes, make beds, or sweep
dust under rugs more than once a week.
Once a month we'd get together and lug our duffle-
bags of delayed wash to the local launderette,
flippantly flipping all the colors together.
It was no big deal.

"Dissent is the prelude to revolution."

I never mended socks--Yock! I'd throw them away and
buy others in Macy's basement.
Jeff taught me how to make that slimy red blob look
like a steak.
I took all the shortcuts the La Leche League Manual
tells you to take when you're nursing twins.
No, I was nothing like Jeff's cousins, who talked of
silverware patterns and early American decor, and
I told my mother, "Housework? Nothing to it!"
But?

I felt guilty, really, I was apologetic, just a little.
For, when you came right down to it, I was in so many
words
A bad housekeeper,
Wasn't I?

I simply wasn't doing my job very well.
Peg Bracken wrote the I Hate to Housekeep Book,
*   made a living out of not doing her job very well.*
She made it her job not to do her job very well.
(A man could never have pulled it off.)
But I--I had to settle for being a bad housekeeper,
Not a professional bad housekeeper.
Just a plain ol' bad housekeeper.

And that's where the women's movement comes in.
The women's movement says dissent is the prelude to
*   revolution.*
The women's movement says I am not personally a bad
*   housekeeper; I am politically a bad housekeeper.*
I am making a statement by being a bad housekeeper.
In fact, I am not a bad housekeeper; I am not a
*   housekeeper at all.*

Marion D. Cohen

WAGES FOR HOUSEWORK

In 1898, long before women won the right to vote in elections, Charlotte Perkins Gilman observed in her book *Women and Economics*, "Whatever the economic value of the domestic industry of women is, they do not get it." Little progress has been made since then toward establishing the right of women who work inside the home to be paid for their labor. Many observers have pointed out, however, that compulsory work without wages amounts to slavery or peonage, which was outlawed by the Thirteenth Amendment to the Constitution.

One of the most difficult questions in the wages-for-housework discussion is not "Do women deserve to be paid for their labor at home?" but rather "How should women be compensated for their labor?" The answers must be worked out in some detail once there is general agreement on the first question. Several suggestions that require relatively minor alterations in present legal and economic systems include introducing federal legislation to provide Social Security and insurance benefits to houseworkers and modification of state property laws so that husbands and wives have equal (and equally enforceable) rights to control the joint property of the marriage.

Such state or nationwide reforms are preferable to individual solutions, although premarriage contracts in which
husbands agree to compensate their wives for work performed at home are good consciousness-raisers. In most
states those contracts are not legally enforceable should
the husband later change his mind or default. One suggestion that we view as potentially dangerous is that
houseworkers be compensated from additional tax revenues
obtained from individual income taxes. Such a suggestion
hardly deserves the name *solution*. Given the present
inequitable structure of the tax system (single people,
old people, poor and middle-class people being taxed disproportionately to the very rich, the corporations, and
the generally more well-off), using income taxes to pay
houseworkers would be taking from the poor to give to
the poor.

The effect of removing the more archaic forms of marital
property (tenancies by the entirety, which prohibit
either party from selling or renting without the written
consent of the other--see Chapter 3) and truly equlaizing
the right to control "community" property would go a long
way toward compensating women for the work they now do
for free. The struggle of houseworkers for recognition as
income-producers must also be seen in the context of the
exploitation of women workers generally, especially those
who do what has been traditionally considered "women's
work." Domestic workers, maids, waitresses, nurses'
aides, and women who work in food processing and packaging
industries and other related areas receive minimal wages
for work performed outside the home and then return to
their unpaid domestic duties.

Some of the present forms of oppression due to wagelessness
may be abolished under the better interpretations of the
state or federal equal rights amendments (see the section
in Chapter 3 on the ERA). One radical departure from
current law and tradition which would improve the status
and economic security of women married to middle-class men
and working at home would involve changing the laws on marriage and family so that housework became a job rather than
a "duty" or a "role" in exchange for which the wife was
entitled to "support." Right now most states will not
uphold any employer-employee relationship which a couple
has established. Husbands are entitled to their wives'
"sex, services, and society" without having to pay for them;
in exchange the husbands assume responsibility for supporting their wives and children. Most judges, however,

are reluctant to set any standards about the quality of
that support. Hence, another progressive innovation
would be to persuade family court judges that it is not
meddling in a domestic budgetary quarrel to take steps
against a husband living in the same house as his wife
but squandering his assets and forcing the family to live
well below his means. Legislation must also be passed
allowing a judge to order husbands from the home when they
have physically abused their wives or deserted or refused
to support their families.

All of these proposed changes must be evaluated in light
of the concept that housework is not a job for which
women are biologically more suited but one that should be
shared among family members. Any proposal that further
reinforces the idea that men automatically deserve to be
taken care of by women and that women's place is only in
the home, regardless of how well they are paid to stay
there, undermines women's potential to be independent
and economically self-sufficient people.

THE STATE

Some women support themselves totally or partially by
public subsidy programs through which they receive money
from government funds if they are living on less income
than a certain standard. The programs which affect the
greatest numbers of women are public assistance (welfare),
unemployment compensation, and Social Security. In general,
being dependent on institutions is frustrating and exhausting. Regulations are complicated, the amounts given
to recipients are generally low, and you are often subject
to annoying and perhaps insulting invasions of privacy
by agency workers. Over time you can begin to feel you
will never have control over your life again. About the
most positive thing that can be said for married women
about living on a publicly supported program is that you
minimize the potentially destructive interpersonal dynamics
that sometimes arise when you are financially dependent
on one other individual. In this section we point out some
of the key issues for women related to these programs,
share information about new developments of importance,
and list referrals for further information.

Welfare

> The truth is that A.F.D.C. is like a super-sexist
> marriage. You trade in *a* man for *the* man. But you
> can't divorce him if he treats you bad. He can
> divorce you, of course, cut you off any time he
> wants. . . . *The* man, the welfare system, controls
> your money. He tells you what to buy, what not to
> buy, where to buy it, and how much things cost. If
> things--rent, for instance--really cost more than
> he says they do, it's just too bad for you. He's
> always right. Everything is budgeted down to the
> last penny and you've got to make your money stretch.
> [Johnnie Tillmon, "Welfare Is a Women's Issue," *Ms.*,
> Spring 1972]

The general policy of welfare has been to help only families
that are not intact. At present the AFDC--U (Aid to Families with Dependent Children--Unemployed) plans to provide
assistance for intact families in some states, but it
provides no assistance to needy families with incomes near
or below the poverty line as a result of part-time or
seasonal work or substandard wages. Thus, as a result of
the present tax structure, the working poor may actually
be financially in better shape if they are on welfare and
eligible for food stamps, medical assistance, and other
special allowances such as for housekeepers or child
care. This is not to imply that being on welfare solves
anyone's problems or makes it possible to live in any
security but only to emphasize that while the welfare
system leaves much to be desired, the working poor (part-
time and seasonal workers, domestic workers, and others
not covered by the minimum wage, and persons who receive
the minimum wage but have to support large families or
unrelated people) are often financially in worse shape
than the classic single mother with children on welfare.

Our previous book, *Women in Transition: A Feminist Handbook
on Separation and Divorce*, explains who is eligible for
welfare, what you are entitled to receive in terms of money
and other benefits, and what rights you have if you think
you are being treated unfairly. We include here a few
recent developments in welfare procedures.

The name-the-father, sue-the-father rules

In order to get federal money, states must now require
that applicants cooperate in establishing the paternity

of their children. They are also required to transfer to
welfare their rights to child support from the fathers.
A welfare applicant who refuses to name the father of
her children (unless she doesn't know it) can be denied
welfare; so can one who refuses to do everything she can
to assist welfare in locating the absent father. But in
the usual Alice-in-Wonderland way of welfare, if the
welfare recipient lives with the father of her children
(and he is employed--in some states) she and the children
also become ineligible. AFDC--U programs, available in
some states, provide assistance to eligible families in
which both parents are present but there is need due to
the unemployment of the father (only, in some states) or
both parents.

Food Stamps

Food stamp recipients have a right to a "nutritionally
adequate diet." Several suits have challenged the basis
on which the amount of food stamps available to a family
is calculated, the point being that the amounts do not
enable people to get the legally required "nutritionally
adequate diet." If your allotment is cut back, see the
local legal services offices.

Medicaid

Many states have tried to limit coverage for abortions to
those deemed "medically necessary." These efforts are
illegal under a number of recent federal decisions. So
are the efforts of a public hospital to perform only
"medically necessary" abortions.

Unemployment Compensation

The Unemployment Compensation system discriminates against
women in a variety of ways that are rarely counted as
illegal forms of sex discrimination. For example, all
applicants for unemployment benefits must be ready, willing,
and able to work at any suitable job. They must have "good
cause" for voluntarily leaving their jobs. Women who
leave their jobs because of family obligations (so they
can care for four children, so they don't have to try to
sleep during the day and work at night, so they can see
their husbands) are not considered to have "good cause"
for leaving. Women who move with their husbands from an
area in which jobs were available to them into an area of
"high persistent unemployment" are considered to have made

themselves "unavailable" for work and are thus not
eligible for compensation. An interpretation of "suitable
work" does not allow women to be flexible in their sched-
ules or available to their children. You must agree to
take almost any job offered (often at substantially less
then you made on your last job, or less than you could
make if you waited a little longer) or be considered as
having made yourself unavailable for work and thus no
longer eligible for unemployment compensation.

The most active battle for women's rights in the area of
unemployment today centers around how the system treats
pregnancy. Many states have laws which presume that
every pregnant worker is "unfit for gainful employment"
and therefore ineligible for unemployment compensation for
fixed periods of time (from end of second trimester
through first six weeks after childbirth, for example).
Many of these laws have been struck down. The best
approach is to consider the *individual circumstances* and
factual ability to work of each pregnant woman or new
mother. The laws of Rhode Island, Washington, Michigan,
Maryland, Ohio, Connecticut, Texas, Maine, and New
Hampshire are changing in this respect. Other states may
also be changing. But remember: in order to get unemployment benefits you must also meet all the other requirements and tests--be available for any suitable work;
be ready, willing, and able to work; have been terminated
from the previous job through no fault of your own or
for "good cause." In many metropolitan areas there are
now independent unemployment counseling programs maintained by groups working for social change. If you are
confused about your benefits or feel you are being treated
unfairly, call your local women's center or activist group
to find out if such counseling exists near you.

Supplemental Security Income

SSI--Supplemental Security Income--is available to needy,
blind, aged, or disabled individuals. Like most other
governmental programs, it is riddled with sexist assumptions
about the "natural" and "proper" spheres and roles of women.
For example, it is much harder for a woman to prove she is
disabled, because the work she is presumed to be qualified
for is housework--regardless of the kind of work she performed before the disability--and it is, in the eyes of
government economists, almost impossible for a woman to be
incapable of doing housework.

At least one court has recently ruled that it is all right
to maintain a double standard of SSI--one for separate individuals and one for married couples. Individuals who
receive SSI but are part of a "married couple" receive less
than they would if they were living apart. But the law
presumes (and does not allow proof to the contrary) that
married couples stay married for at least six months after
separating. So they continue to split a "married couple"
allotment rather than each receiving the full amount due
an unmarried individual. The reasoning behind the courts'
approving this kind of discrimination against people in
transition is that although the rule doesn't make sense,
it doesn't have to. What's involved, in the court's eyes,
is not the right of an individual to get a certain amount
of money from the government, but a "bonus" handed out
from the government's largesse, which the courts are
loath to police in any way.

Social Security

More women currently receive benefits from the Social
Security system than from any other public source. Since
many women are both workers and dependents (or dependent
survivors), determining eligibility for benefits can be
complicated. The Social Security Administration provides
pamphlets giving a general description of the program as
well as information for individual situations:

> Social Security Administration
> Department of Health, Education and Welfare
> Washington, D.C. 20201

The traditional assumption throughout the Social Security
system has been that "men are the principal wage earners
in any family unit and that the 'normal' role of women
is that of housewife and mother"; those who depart from
those roles have been penalized by reduced benefits. Recent decisions, however, have challenged that assumption.
Chapter 3 details the traditional discrimination and
what is being done about it.

WOMEN'S WORK

We are assuming in this section that you want or need to
work. There are several issues that you need to take into
account at the beginning. Many women who have not worked
outside the home since their marriage or who have only

worked at volunteer or part-time jobs are frightened at
the prospect of full-time, demanding work. Be assured
that this is a reasonable fear on your part. Many community
agencies, such as YWCAs, and community colleges are now
offering "life option" courses for women which not only
explore how to go about getting a job or job training but
also provide a supportive setting for women to express
their fears and hopes about moving out beyond the home.
By all means take advantage of such a class if one is
offered near you; if not, some of the readings listed in
the Bibliography can be helpful.

A FEW STATISTICS ABOUT WOMEN IN THE LABOR FORCE

- In 1974 nearly 36 million women were in the labor
  force; this was 46 percent of all women 16 years
  of age and over.
- As of March 1974 married women (husband present) ac-
  counted for nearly 58 percent of all women workers.
- Of all married women (husband present) 43 percent were
  in the labor force as of March 1974.
- More than half (54 percent) of the 6.8 million women
  family heads were in the labor force. One out of 10
  women workers was head of a family (March 1974).
- About 13.6 million mothers with children under 18
  years of age were in the labor force, of whom 5.1
  million had children under 6 years. Children of
  working mothers numbered 26.8 million (March 1974).
- The 1974 unemployment rate for women was 6.7 percent,
  compared with 4.8 percent for men.
- In 1974 about 35 percent of all employed women were in
  clerical jobs. They included more than 4 million
  secretaries, stenographers, and typists. More than
  21 percent were service workers. About 15 percent were
  professional and technical workers, and about 13 percent were operatives, chiefly in factories.
- The earnings gap between women and men continues to
  widen. The median 1973 annual income for all women
  was $2,796, or about one-third the $8,056 income for
  men in 1973. Women employed full-time, year-round, had
  a median income of $6,488, or 57 percent of the $11,468
  received by men. In 1956 fully employed women's
  earnings were 63 percent of men's earnings; in 1970
  they were 59 percent.
- In 1973 the median wage or salary income of minority
  race women who worked year-round, full-time, was $5,772,

or 88 percent of the $6,544 income of white women. In
1963 their median income was less than 64 percent of
that of white women.
- Among all the working-wife families, the contribution
  of wives' earnings was about one-fourth of family income
  in 1973. When the wife was a year-round, full-time
  worker, her contribution was nearly two-fifths--38
  percent.

[From the *1975 Handbook on Women Workers,*
Women's Bureau, U.S. Department of Labor]

Another issue for many women when they first venture again
into the paid work world is the resistance of husband,
children, parents, and friends. Many men are threatened
by their wives' ability to earn and handle their own money
and are resentful that their wives are no longer as available to them as they once were. Children, especially those
who have had their mother's full-time attention, naturally
miss something which they have grown used to and which makes
their lives easier and more pleasant. Parents and friends
are often critical of a woman who deviates from what they
consider to be the norm; sometimes this is a cover-up
for envy because you are doing something they didn't or
can't do themselves. Chapters 2 and 5 explore ways to
handle this resistance. Chapter 5 in particular discusses
fears you may have about putting your children in day care
centers if they have been at home with you since birth
and explores ways to share household chores so that you
are not performing two jobs while only getting paid for one.

Finally, so that you don't think we are naïvely advocating
paid work as the answer to all of life's problems, let us
say that we don't. Most work in this country is tedious,
frustrating, and underpaid. Some jobs, of course, are
exciting, creative, and lucrative, but generally these are
jobs in the professional, managerial, or artistic fields.
Most women work at jobs that are fairly routine, not at
all glamorous, and hardly well paid. The average income
in this country received from employment is greatest for
white men, followed by black men, white women, and black
women. This is not a society that places high priority on
developing meaningful work for its people. Nonetheless,
work is a crucial component of self-esteem, not to mention
economic survival, and women who want and need to work
should have the encouragement and opportunity to do so.

KATHLEEN

It was miserable working at the noodle company. I was a packer and machine operator, and my husband was a machine operator. He cut spaghetti, and I packed noodles and macaroni. There was a lot of pressure there to speed up. We got paid by the hour, but they wanted us to work faster. Like piecework—turn out more and more but get paid by the hour. They would come by and say you had to have it done by the afternoon. They'd really be on your back about getting it out. The foreman and the boss. The boss would be standing right behind you. If you didn't get it done, they would have a fit. They would tell you they would fire you. Sometimes they would fire people. Mostly they just said that to keep the pressure on you.

Volunteering

American women volunteer almost $14.2 billion worth of their work every year for charitable causes, not counting the $499 billion worth of labor performed for free for their families. For a number of years feminists have been arguing over the pros and cons of volunteerism. Those in favor of it say that volunteering enables women to develop skills and a sense of self-worth, to get out of the house and meet new people, to give them more to share with their husbands, to have more flexibility and control over their time than in a paid job, and to support needed services that might not otherwise be available. Many women volunteer in a particular field as a way of coming to terms with a personal or family affliction. Women with handicapped children, for example, work with organizations concerned with public awareness of the problems of the handicapped. Those opposed to volunteering argue that volunteer work is simply an extension of women's unpaid work in the home, is low-status because it is done primarily by women and because it is not paid, reinforces the idea that women should be self-sacrificing, and takes some of the pressure off government agencies and corporations to provide necessary social services. In addition, volunteers are almost always upper-middle-class or wealthy women, because lower-income women don't have the time and/or can't afford the out-of-pocket expenses usually involved. Some feminist groups distinguish between traditional volunteer activity, which shores up the charity establishment, and political or change-oriented volunteer activity, which

they favor. They also call for reforms that would upgrade
the image of volunteers, such as tax and Social Security
credits, insurance coverage, and reimbursement for expenses, such as child care and travel.

While we agree that women's labor has been abused in the
volunteer work force as well as in the home, we recognize
that volunteering is a logical way for a woman to begin to
develop her skills and self-confidence if she has been in
the home for a number of years. We suggest that if you
do volunteer, think of the work you are doing in the
context of a long-range plan for developing your economic
independence. Try to volunteer in a situation where you
can develop skills which will get you a job later on or
where you will meet people whose contacts and ideas can
be useful to you.

As you are thinking about what kind of volunteer work you
would like to do, ask yourself the same questions about
skills and areas of interest which appear later in this
chapter in connection with paid work. Do some research
about the kinds of organizations you are interested in by
talking to volunteers or paid staff who are already working
in the field. As you narrow down the choices, interview
the organizations about what will be expected of you; try
to find out what kind of reputation for utilizing volunteers these organizations have in the community. Your time
and skills are valuable, and you don't want to waste them
on a group that is inefficiently run or whose practices
differ from their stated goals. And as you work as a
volunteer, enjoy what you are doing, the people you are
meeting, and the control you have over your work time.
In your paid-work life you will probably never again be
as free to try out something new, risk failure, and tell
off the boss if you are dissatisfied.

Working out of Your Home

Providing a product or service from your home can be a
good way to ease back into the income-producing world.
There are even a number of now-classic stories about how
women parlayed their part-time work at home into multi-
million-dollar enterprises, although it is more likely that
you will just break even or earn a small addition to the
family's resources. The advantages of working out of
your home are that you can provide a service or product
that you are familiar with rather than having to fit yourself into a job interviewer's requirements for an employee;

you have control over the amount of time you want to work;
and you can spend more time at home with your children and
husband. The disadvantages are that you may not earn
enough money to make the whole project worthwhile; you
may get bored with seeing the same four walls every day;
and if your business grows you may find yourself subject
to unpleasant pressures because the responsibility is all
on your shoulders.

The first thing to do, obviously, is to figure out what
you are good at and whether or not you need to brush up
or get more extensive training to make your skill salable.
Typing, tutoring, telephone sales, babysitting, catering,
and dressmaking are skills that women often have or can
easily acquire. Some women with professional or technical
expertise can also work on a part-time or full-time basis
from home; counseling, legal research, and writing are
just a few examples of these. You need to assess if there
is a need for your skill in the area where you live and
then figure out ways to advertise your existence. After
the work starts to come in, it is a good idea to evaluate
realistically if you are bringing in enough to make it
worth your time. If not, you may want to raise your
prices. If that is not feasible, you may decide to continue at your present rates because you are getting
valuable training or because you enjoy the contact with
other people and the sense of accomplishment. The key is
not to delude yourself about how lucrative your work is.

If your work is going well, you may want to return to an
established business or agency rather than continue on
your own, or you may want to expand into a full-fledged
business operation yourself. The following section describes how to begin to look for a job, and the Bibliography
gives references for information on starting your own
business. Weight Watchers International is now a multi-
million-dollar organization which started in one woman's
living room. That kind of success is not out of the
question for you. Good luck!

Paid Outside Employment

Women have always worked. If you have been married for a
number of years, all during your marriage you have worked.
What else would you call lifting babies and carting piles
of dirty clothes to the washer or the laundromat? Cooking
and cleaning, scrubbing and polishing, mopping and dusting
. . . shopping, making clothes, paying bills, pinching

pennies . . . nursing sick children, waiting on your hus-
band--what else but work?

But when you sit down to write that job application or
résumé, when you are interviewed for a job, what can you
say about your previous employment? How does your employer rate you? What was your most recent pay level?
You've acquired many skills and considerable education
in a variety of fields including nutrition, early childhood development, child psychology, and probably some
sociology and economics. You have physical skill and
stamina for which men are well rewarded on the job market.
So what are you qualified for? If you are younger and
recently out of school, you may feel that you have few
skills and few life experiences that would interest a
prospective employer.

You'd probably be able to do any number of jobs for which
you couldn't possibly be hired. Special training, education, or experience are often prerequisites to many jobs
you could do well if you were only given the chance. But
there's no use complaining. There is absolutely no reason
why "women's work" shouldn't be anything a woman wants and
is trained to do. The next section of this chapter should
help you think about the kind of work you want to do and
how to adapt your life to it; also, we'll discuss the
possibility of delaying working until you have acquired
further training.

How to find and apply for jobs is a complex subject which
we can't cover adequately here. There are a number of
helpful books on the subject listed in the Bibliography.
They cover such issues as where to look for a job, how to
write a résumé, and how to use a job interview to your
advantage. You may also want to locate one of the specialized employment agencies or career counseling programs for
women which have been created in different communities
throughout the country. These programs take into account
women's special needs and problems in the job market.
Some are for profit, some are nonprofit, so you would do
well to check into fees and reputation in the community.
Call the women's center nearest you, the women's studies
department of a local college, or YWCA to find out if
there is such a program in your area.

RUTH

In the beginning of our relationship he said, "No wife of mine will ever work." I didn't mind too much, because I had been working and trying to take care of a young child. It's hard--working out a baby-sitter, paying a babysitter. What have you got left? Practically nothing after that. And I had had it with that, so I felt grateful to be able to stay home. The kids were still young enough that they were only going to school half a day. Now I'm thinking seriously about getting a job, but only part-time because I would like to have some time to myself without the kids. Full-time work plus cooking, washing, cleaning, shopping, and everything with them--it's too much. The job I have in mind would be at the school, but it would be school hours, so any day they have off, I have off, and I would never have a chance to be without them. But the pay rate is really crummy--two dollars and twenty cents an hour, which I think is minimum wage. So if I did take it, I would want more money. I don't know if they would give it to me, but I would ask for it. This is as a teacher's aide. I did substituting. I think I'm the only substitute they have, so I would be first on the list for next year if there's a vacancy.

Questions to Ask Yourself:

What jobs might I qualify for?
> Start by making a list of education, previous job training, experience at home or through volunteer work. Consider all your skills and experience and don't forget to include skills you have acquired as a wife and mother, or as a result of hobbies or other interests.

Do I have any skills which could be developed into a job possibility?
> Have you worked on your own car, done electrical work, carpentry, or plumbing in your own home? If you did things like these and enjoyed them, you might consider attending a vocational school or finding a training program to enable you to receive certification in these fields. Or you might be able to get a job at a local gas station or with a car-penter you know, or take courses from the local Y

or women's center in the areas of your interest.
Look into apprenticeship programs as well. In other
words, consider the possibility of *not* working in
order to develop long-range goals and possibilities.
A job that offers a chance for growth and development in the future is probably better than one that
starts off at a higher pay rate but offers little
hope of advancement.

Am I confused about my skills?
Think back--what areas interested you in high school,
before marriage? If you can't think of anything,
you might consider taking aptitude tests, available
through career development agencies, among other
places. But beware--those tests can be quite expensive (and sometimes a little ridiculous). Your
best guides are your own feelings and your own
memory.

What jobs have I held?
What did I enjoy about those jobs? What did I
dislike? Are there situations or jobs which make
me feel uncomfortable, incapable? Why? Should I
avoid them?

What kind of job do I want?
Involving numbers and money, travel, meeting people,
sales? Do I prefer working alone, or with people?
How important is flexible scheduling, independence,
freedom to move around?

How much would I like to earn?
How much will I contribute to the family's budget?
Will my income cover the additional cost of child
care? If it doesn't, is that all right until my
income increases? Can I find good child care?

How many hours a week can I work?
During what part of the day?

What kinds of resistance am I likely to encounter?
Does my husband feel that he will be less of a man
if I work? Will my children be resentful? Will my
mother complain that I am neglecting my duty?
Think through ways to handle these situations; get
support from friends who are working.

There are a number of helpful books on job-hunting: where
to look, writing a resume, interviewing. They are listed
in the Bibliography.

SARAH

*I knew that a college degree wouldn't get me any-
where, and I also knew that I had a lot of trouble
working for people in what I call a "shit down system"
which is, I found out, all systems. All hierarchies
are "shit down systems." It was the same thing I
felt about "belonging." If you wear the right
clothes, you'll be O.K. If you become a professional,
you'll be O.K. Those people know, they understand.
I came from essentially a working-class world with
aspirations and called myself an upward striver for
a long time. Part of it was to get out of the muck
of my own depression, and the fears of living an
empty, isolated life, and part a sense of the sunlight
is out there where those people are. And a desire
to use my skills and capabilities. I realized at
the job I was in that I couldn't go anywhere there,
and I really didn't want to. I didn't like the
place, I didn't like the values; I didn't have alternatives to it, but I really hated it. I was bored
and disgruntled, and I knew there was a real positive
element of wanting something more for myself. This
was my job at the airlines, but it wouldn't have
made any difference. The airlines was little better
than ticket sorting or the accounting department at
the bus company. All those kinds of places are real
dead ends to me.*

A Few Words about Discrimination

It is almost impossible to escape some form of employment
discrimination once you decide to get a paying job. There,
as elsewhere, you will run into many sexist attitudes and
false assumptions about the true nature and proper role of
women in society. Women active in the most recent wave of
feminism, which began in the late 1960s, have done an im-
pressive job in documenting and combating the many forms
of discrimination against women which exist in this country.
But no laws are going to change the prevalent antiwoman

attitudes or the more subtle forms of discrimination you
are likely to experience. Your best defenses are to be
well informed about your job rights and to join together
with other women to fight discrimination when you encounter
it. This section is not a comprehensive manual for dealing
with employment discrimination but points out in general
what you can expect. We suggest you check into the
readings in the Bibliography which explain in more detail
your job rights and how to proceed if you feel you have
been discriminated against.

MARTHA

*I worked for a small trade magazine that was housed
in an old condemned building and had a staff of
nine women. The publisher was a man, and he used
and exploited all of us. He paid us very little--
that's why it was all women. The staff of nine did
the work of a staff of twenty. We would think
nothing of staying until ten at night or midnight
because we were all loyal. He hired people who were
not totally qualified, let us learn as we went,
built an unbelievable commitment to the magazine,
so that we all had a personal interest in it. He was
very shrewd. The other side of it was that it gave
me an incredible chance to do all kinds of things
that I was not qualified for. It was learn as you go.*

Many women who reenter the job market after an absence are
surprised when a prospective employer asks them sensitive
questions about their marital status and family situation.
Because of the current tight employment situation, employers are often looking for ways to exclude women and
minority applicants. There are certain questions that
employers are legally allowed to ask and others that leave
them open to censure by the Equal Employment Opportunity
Commission (EEOC).

These "sensitive areas" have to do with, among other things,
marital status, living situation, number of children, birth
control, criminal record, and age. The situation is complicated because some questions on these topics are permissible and others are not. The situation is further
complicated because employers are legally allowed to ask
some of these questions as long as they are asked of men
and women both. The problem for women is that the prospective employer will probably be listening to their

answers about birth control, for example, much more carefully than to those of male applicants. And you can be
certain that employers know more thoroughly than most
applicants which questions they can get away with.

It is important, then, to know what your rights are in
that situation. This includes being familiar with what
questions you are required to answer and those you are not.
You should also know some of the myths about working women
(such as "Women's raging hormones interfere with performance on the job") and the facts which refute them. You
might also want to familiarize yourself with the current
discussion about the "fear of success" syndrome in women
and think through where you stand on such issues as
competition on the job or the strains of job versus family
obligations.

HARRIET

I did have a business school education and I wanted
to go back to work after my youngest left home.
Nobody wanted me really--I had some skills and I
passed tests.

I was a great typist and secretarial skills I could
have brushed up on if somebody wanted me but I found
that they do not want you in a big company when you
are forty-eight or forty-nine.

They don't tell you that to your face, but they don't
want you because you are going to upset their pension
plan, their benefit plans, and their health program.
One company I interviewed with my job would have been
a part-time job. I would have been working in the
personnel department administering the same tests
that I helped design--not helped design, but I worked
for the man who made up the test in the first place
and marketed it. I had done the testing and I knew
how to do it. I was told that my skills were terrific when they tested me, but they said, "You have
a couple of daughters in college and you probably
want more time off than we can give you. . . ." They
backed out of it very discreetly but all the time I
had the feeling that it was because of my age.

I accepted this, because when I first started in the
business world it was when you could not get a job.

This was back in 1935 when we were coming out of the Depression.

But knowing your rights and thinking through the issues will only prepare you for what to expect, not solve the problem. You don't want to antagonize your prospective employer by insisting on your right not to answer. It is important to work out for yourself answers to these questions, if they arise, that you feel comfortable with. Some employment counselors suggest answering a tricky question by saying you are not sure how the question relates to your qualifications for the job; you might want to turn the question back on the interviewer by asking if he or she thinks it's relevant, or if other applicants are asked that question. How you handle ticklish questions also depends on your style--some people respond with humor, others more directly. The trick is to avoid a hostile response, as difficult as that may be, especially if you want the job. Given the attempts to discourage you, you might reconsider whether you even want the job, although finding the perfect employer when you are vulnerable and un- (or under-) employed is not that easy to do. If you don't get the job and suspect that it is because of your sex, you have the option of filing a complaint with the EEOC.

The discrimination against you will probably not end once you are on the job, however. Despite the rapidly changing legal protections for women and minorities, discrimination is still rampant. In brief, you have a right to file a complaint of discrimination if:

- an employer's advertisement for employees carries a sex label
- an employer refuses to let you file an application but accepts others
- a union or an employment agency refuses to refer you to job openings
- a union refuses to accept you into membership
- you are fired or laid off without cause
- you are passed over for promotion for which you are qualified
- you are paid less than others for comparable work
- you are placed in a segregated seniority line
- you are left out of training or apprenticeship programs

And . . .

- the reason for any of these acts is your sex, race, color, religion, or national origin

Also if . . .
   • your employer provides racially segregated lunchrooms,
     locker rooms, restrooms, or recreation facilities.

> [*A Working Woman's Guide to Her*
> *Job Rights*, Women's Bureau,
> U.S. Department of Labor, Revised 1975]

Filing a complaint of discrimination takes a lot of time
and energy, and the decision to do so should be considered
carefully. Here are some issues to think about: (1) There
is no way to file a secret complaint against your employer,
so if you are still working or want to return to work
there, you have to evaluate how furious this is likely to
make him or her. If you have been discharged, the choice
is easier. (2) Filing a complaint will take a long time.
Speed is essential in making up your mind to file a complaint and following through on it, since the faster you
move the faster you will get results, and you lose your
right to file a complaint with EEOC if you wait longer
than 180 days. It is also possible that quick action on
your part will force your employer to back down without
your even having to file a complaint, as an employer's
only tactic in many discrimination cases is delay. (3) Your
employer will undoubtedly dredge up humiliating things to
say about you in rebuttal. This strain is somewhat les-
sened if you join in a class action suit with other people
who have been discriminated against in the same way. Organizing with others is important even if you don't file
a complaint. Many employee rights do not exist under the
law; the power to fire an employee arbitrarily (except in
the above situations) still lies in the hands of the employer. In the past the way working people have secured
most job rights for themselves has been through organizing,
whether to use the legal tools available to them or to
pressure for rights not covered by the law. (4) Historically
the EEOC has shown more interest in cases of race discrimination than sex discrimination, evidently not believing
that the latter is all that important. Private attorneys
are more likely to be interested in sex discrimination
cases, which they feel are often easier to prove because
the discrimination is so blatant. EEOC is often slow to
process discrimination cases, so that it is important to
have a private attorney (if you can afford one) or other
advocate pushing your case. (5) Bearing all this in mind,
try to make your decision of whether or not to file with
the support of friends. It may be a long-drawn-out
process, but every successful complaint benefits not only

the women who brought the complaint but many of her sisters as well.

One court has held that a height requirement of five feet, eight inches for hiring onto the police force was permissible, although it clearly cut out more women than men, while a weight requirement of 150 pounds was not permissible.

The Seventh Circuit (federal appeals court covering Wisconsin, Illinois, and Indiana) has declared that women who work in bars are no more likely to be promiscuous than men similarly employed, so it is unconstitutional to have a rule forbidding female but not male bartenders from "fraternizing" with the customers.

INSURANCE AND INCOME PROTECTION PLANS

Informing yourself about your rights in the area of insurance and income protection plans is especially important. Blue Cross-Blue Shield, private insurers, and company insurance plans routinely discriminate against women, single mothers, and anyone living in nontraditional arrangements. The state of California recently adopted regulations designed to curb some of this. The new regulations prohibit the following standard insurance practices:

- canceling insurance coverage for women living with anyone other than spouse or relative
- giving higher benefit levels to men
- denying coverage that is available to married women to single or divorced women
- giving better benefits (or some, as opposed to no benefits at all) to dependents of male employees (wives, daughters) than to those of female employees
- refusing to cover childbirth, pregnancy, and related expenses for daughters of covered employees.

The forms of such discrimination are too common and various to enumerate; many are illegal. If you run into discrimination or other insurance problems, call your state insurance commissioner's office; check with your local commission on the status of women (in many state capitals), complain to consumer advocates in and outside of government; consider bringing the matter to the attention of the state attorney general. Seek legal advice to see if you have grounds for a sex discrimination suit or if the particular form of discrimination being practiced against you has been ruled illegal.

The basic principle should be no different treatment for women or men, dependents or employees, pregnancy or other "disabilities."

However, there is one troublesome Supreme Court decision that is confusing a lot of these issues: *Geduldig* v. *Aiello*, 417 U.S. 484, which says that the California rule excluding pregnancy from disability insurance for state employees is not a violation of the equal protection clause of the Fourteenth Amendment of the U.S. Constitution. Disability insurance provides for a person's income when he or she is actually disabled; it is different from medical insurance, which covers hospital and doctor expenses.

More recent decisions indicate that the *Geduldig* decision will not be extended beyond the "insurance" context: it should not cover rights to medical assistance, unemployment, and the like. *Geduldig* is a real mistake and many lower courts may find ways around it.

Many courts have ruled that, for employees of private employers not covered by the Fourteenth Amendment but subject to Title VII, pregnancy may *not* be excluded from sick leave plans set up by employers or joint employer-union trust funds. It must be treated as any other non-work-related disability. Nor may the time period during which such benefits are available be shorter for pregnancy-related disabilities than for any other non-work-related disability. One thing to remember, though--you must be *disabled* from working to benefit from a sick leave or disability insurance program under these rulings. In a normal pregnancy, that means about two weeks before birth and six weeks after. Women employees who choose to take a leave of absence beyond their period of actual disability must be treated by their employer in the same way that other employees who choose to take leaves of absence are treated.

MEG

I was working for an organization which didn't have any insurance to cover its employees, so I dutifully paid my Blue Cross-Blue Shield premiums every quarter for several years. I thought the premiums were outrageously expensive, but my parents had insisted I have some sort of coverage in case I had an accident or serious illness. When I got pregnant, I blithely assumed that maternity benefits were included in my policy. I thought I had better check on it, however, and was promptly informed that Blue Cross would not cover single mothers on that type of policy and would not let me switch to any other type. I went around and around with them for several months with no luck, so I figured I'd better do something to cover the cost of having the baby. I had quit my job and was planning to live off my savings for a while until I went back to work. Fortunately, I was able to get on medical assistance, and the total cost of the birth was a dollar and twenty cents (for Kleenex and phone bills). The way I figure, medical assistance can go after Blue Cross if they think I ripped them off. I certainly think I was entitled to what I got.

Education and Reeducation

STARTING FROM THE BOTTOM

Women have been deprived of educational opportunities for a variety of reasons. Sometimes, if there is limited money in the family, the sons may be sent to school rather than the daughters. Often women are simply excluded from certain schools or specialized training programs. Probably the most widespread form of educational discrimination is the message most girls get as they are growing up: "Plan for your man" rather than "Plan for your own financial future." If you experienced such pressures and discriminations, you probably do not relish the thought of returning to something you may not have enjoyed the first time around. But remember, fear of failure and lack of self-confidence may be keeping you from a new job and a

more fulfilling life. Education is important, not because
it shows how smart you are, but because it can open doors
for you. If you have not especially enjoyed your experiences in school before, you should consider continuing
education anyway. It is an investment to help you achieve
economic security. And you may discover that once you go
to school with a definite purpose, you enjoy learning.

Additional education may open up new job opportunities for
you. You don't have to be a nurse or a secretary if you
don't want to. The difference between traditionally
"female" jobs and jobs that are more rewarding and well
paid is often education or training.

Getting a college degree won't necessarily enable you to
find a job that you like, unless you are able to continue
your education beyond a bachelor's degree, and that, of
course, takes more time and money. Academic credentials
aren't the only way to find a good job. Vocational training
in specific skills may be even more valuable on the job
market, depending, of course, on what kind of job you
want to do. This is becoming increasingly true in today's
tight job market, where more and more college-educated
people cannot get jobs because they are "overqualified."

When considering further education of any kind, ask yourself the same questions you did when you were thinking
about finding a job. Before you left school, got married,
stopped working, what were you interested in or good at
doing? When was the last time you did anything connected
with that area of interest? What caused you to stop? Are
you still interested in it, or have you found other things
which excite you more? What are the first steps to take
in order to get back in this field?

ANNA

*I decided to become a lawyer out of some very roman-
tic notions that I could create social change out
of it. When I was at the American Friends Service
Committee I was doing community organizing work and
foreign affairs issues, war-peace issues. That was
very thankless work, as far as seeing any kind of
success. So I decided I needed a tool, a very specific, narrow tool, and skill that I could offer.   That
would be my best contribution to the world. So I
decided to go to law school because I have the kind*

*of analytical mind that enjoys manipulating problems
and problem solving. And that just seemed like a
natural for me.*

A few more questions to consider: Can you arrange for
child care while you are in school? How much will this
cost? How much time and money can you afford to spend
getting your education? Are you going to have to work
during the day and go to school at night? Or are you
taking a course that will last only eight or ten months?
What schools are close enough to be convenient? What
kind of transportation will you need to reach them? Are
you qualified for entrance into the program of your
choice? You can get a high school diploma by taking an
examination called the "general equivalency diploma"
examination, given periodically in your area. Call a local
high school for information. In some areas there are pre-
paratory classes for the test. Correspondence schools
are another way of getting a high school diploma, and
sometimes you can receive credit for high school graduation
by taking courses at a local community college.

Are there scholarships, sliding-scale payment plans, deferred payment plans, or other financial opportunities you
could take advantage of?

Ask yourself those questions, and give yourself credit for
being a person who is capable of doing anything you are
seriously determined to do. Since you are probably going
to work anyway, it might as well be at something you
enjoy doing and are rewarded for.

JOB TRAINING RESOURCES

Job training programs can be a great beginning for a woman
who has few marketable skills or who is interested in
getting into a field she has had no previous experience in.
Learning a trade that is considered "masculine"--such as
electricity, plumbing, or carpentry--has both advantages
and disadvantages. The pay is usually much higher in
these fields than in traditionally "female" ones. On the
other hand, you may find it very difficult to get jobs in
these "male" areas, even with sufficient skill and training.
But the skilled trades do not have to be considered an end
in themselves. After going to school and becoming licensed
(usually this means taking a city or state qualifying test),
you might want to open your own business or go on to take
college courses to become an engineer or contractor.

The availability of training programs designed for, geared
to, or including women will vary according to area. Throughout the country the National Urban League and R-T-P Associates, Inc., operate programs which recruit and train
minorities for the skilled trades and apprenticeable
occupations. A significant number of these programs have
components for the placement of women in nontraditional
occupations. Contact these organizations to get a list
of programs in your area:

> National Urban League
> Labor Affairs Program
> Gwendolyn Poole, Coordinator
> Women's Component
> 500 East 62nd Street
> New York, N.Y. 10021
> (212) 644-6701
>
> R-T-P Associates, Inc.
> Ernest G. Green, Executive Director
> 162 Fifth Avenue
> New York, N.Y. 10010
> (212) 691-0660

There are different types of job training programs:
federally funded, private vocational or trade schools, and
on-the-job training (which may also be government-funded).

Federally Funded

Comprehensive Employment and Training Act (CETA). The
purpose of the act of 1973 is to decentralize the design
and delivery of employment and training services to the
state and local government levels. CETA, in effect,
transfers control over a large portion of federal revenues
to state and local jurisdictions and replaces a variety
of federal employment and training programs. Each local
CETA program operator, usually a unit of government, then
determines what needs exist, what kinds of programs are
planned and funded, who is to be served, and so on. The
programs developed are then operated by the "prime sponsor"
itself or by community or governmental agencies so des-
ignated.

Basic eligibility requirements include unemployment or
underemployment (working below your possible skill level
or for less than poverty wages). For some programs and
services, additional criteria could include limited

income or being a member of a special target group (for
example, women, minorities, veterans, heads of household,
high school dropouts, handicapped persons, or any combination of these). These criteria will vary depending on
your jurisdiction. For an unemployed or underemployed
woman, depending on her economic status, various services
and programs are available, including job placement (in
the private sector or in public service employment),
training, transportation assistance, child care subsidy,
and on-the-job training.

It cannot be stressed enough that what services are offered
and available depends entirely on how a jurisdiction has
structured its programs and how it plans to spend its funds.
For more information about the CETA program in your area,
contact the CETA State Manpower Services Council in your
state (see the Resources section at the back of the book).
For CETA to work more effectively, it is essential that
key labor market participants, including women and women's
organizations, become involved in all aspects of CETA,
from the planning stages through the delivery of services.

Work Incentive Program. This combined program of the U.S.
Departments of Labor and Health, Education and Welfare is
operated in most states through the state departments of
social services or welfare in conjunction with the state
Employment Security agencies. In the WIN program participants can receive both grants from welfare and trainee
allowances. You must be on public assistance when you
apply for the WIN program, and there is usually a waiting
list; ask your caseworker for information. It should be
mentioned that in recent years the original emphasis on
training has declined and placement of WIN participants in
jobs has been the primary program goal. This has often
short-circuited attempts of many women on public assistance
to receive training in nontraditional, often higher-paying,
occupations.

KATHLEEN

*My husband and I are both on welfare. He is in the
WIN program, and they are supposed to be finding him
a job. If he doesn't have money to go to a job
interview, he'll ask them for a bus ticket. But his
worker says, "We don't give out bus tickets." R.L.
says, "How am I supposed to get there?" and the guy
says, "Walk." So then he reports R.L. upstairs, to
the higher-up, that he wasn't cooperating.*

State Employment Security Agency. The SESA (in your area
it may be called the Bureau of Employment Security or
State Employment Service) can be used for either direct
referral to jobs through the Job Bank system or as an
information source regarding training and other programs
in your area. Remember that all referrals must be made
on a nonsexist, non-racial-stereotyped basis. Ask to be
informed of all jobs available in your skill range, not
only those traditional (probably low-paying) ones. Surveys
have shown that when a man and a woman (equally unskilled)
are interviewed, somehow more openings at higher pay are
available to the unskilled man! *Ask questions!*

Opportunities Industrialization Centers (OIC) exist in most
states. They receive government funding. OIC is available
to all low-income people at no cost, offers training in
trades and business skills, and grants high school equivalency diplomas as well. People under eighteen are sometimes referred to other programs.

GERTRUDE

I was trained as an auto mechanic at OIC [Opportuni-
ties Industrialization Center]. Before I went there
I was just doing it on the street on my own, watching
other people and messing with the car myself. I love
the OIC program because I like mechanics and because
they gave me my big break. I learned how to take
starters apart and tune up cars, about brakes, about
materials in a car, how to treat the customers. It
was a beautiful experience dealing with a group of
men in their field. A couple of men gave me a hard
time at the beginning, but after that everything
cooled down. I felt like I had to try harder because
I was a woman, but the good thing about this is that
I have got a little farther than the men. Some of
the men take it for granted that they will get ahead,
but you'd be surprised at how many doors will open
when you try harder.

The hardest part was my family. I'm married and
have three children. The children were not used to
me being away from home, and when I got home I had
to stay outside taking cars apart. The most hassle
was with my husband. He's African and women there
don't do this. I was determined I was going to show
him this is how American women are--life doesn't

stop when you get married. He didn't tell me to stop, but he threw screws at me mentally. But I wasn't about to give it up, so in time everybody got to where they accepted it.

I went to work for Sears as a tire buster, changing oil, lubrication. I don't like tire busting because it's heavier than anything I've done. When you're a woman, they throw the hardest part on you first. But I was determined to stick it out. Then I got laid off and went to work for a trucking company, where I learned a lot. I have seen enough places of business to know how to run one. I'm ready to own my own shop--that's my dream.

Better Jobs for Women is sponsored by the YMCA of metropolitan Denver and funded by the U.S. Department of Labor. This program is using a sixty-thousand-dollar grant to help women who want to apply for apprenticeship programs and nontraditional jobs offering training in skilled trades. It may be able to direct you to one of these in your area. Call or write Better Jobs for Women, 1545 Tremount Place, Denver, Colorado 80202, (303) 893-3534.

Private Training Schools

These can be expensive, time-consuming, and fraudulent. Before you sign any contract with a private training school, get an evaluation of it from your local Better Business Bureau and conduct your own investigation.

1. Determine that the field of study you are interested in is one that will leave you with marketable skills.
2. Write or call schools which offer the courses you need. Compare brochures to determine costs, subjects offered, length of program, and availability of financial aid. Check to determine whether the same or a similar program may be offered at lower or no cost at community colleges, area vocational-technical schools, or adult education courses. (These are also often of higher quality.)
3. After studying the material and deciding which courses and costs meet your needs, make an appointment with a counselor at the school. Check the classroom equipment available to you. Talk to other students. Ask for names and addresses of employers who have hired graduates from the program. Ask about the possibility of a tuition refund if you decide to drop the course.

4.   Do not, at this time, give a registration fee or
     deposit. If possible, take home a blank copy of the
     contract and reread it. Find out if the school is
     affiliated with a national association. Make sure
     the school has a placement service to ensure they
     will get you a job.

Some schools listed in the Yellow Pages, such as computer
schools, can be a good source of job training. But be sure
to find out whether the training offered by the program is
sufficient to get a job, or whether there are additional
requirements as well. Most computer-programming jobs,
for instance, require a college degree in addition to the
training.

Many schools and libraries subscribe to the *American Trade
Schools Directory*, published by Croner Publications. It
lists all the trade schools in the United States and is
updated every month; it does not evaluate the schools listed.

The Urban League maintains a "skills bank" in many cities
which has referrals to jobs and training.

Other Programs

JOBS, or Job Opportunities in the Business Sector, tries
to interest private business in training low-income people.
It is available in most cities and is sponsored by the
National Alliance of Businessmen.

You might check with community social service agencies and
your city's Community Development Agency. Many of these
agencies employ nonprofessional members of the community.
The available jobs are usually related to social work.
You might also contact local public schools and ask them
if they know of programs or businesses offering on-the-job
training. In professions such as law and health, on-the-job
training is a relatively new idea. Nonprofessional workers
in these fields are sometimes called "paralegal" or "paramedical" workers. As with most social service agencies,
jobs tend to be in the community served and are usually
open to residents of the neighborhood. These jobs are
most worthwhile for women with little or no experience in
the field. If you have done work in the area of tenants'
rights, welfare rights, or volunteer work in a community
health clinic, you have a better chance of getting a paying
job in these areas. Contact your city and state departments
of health or community legal service agencies if you are

interested in job training in these areas. Be aware that
with recent program cutbacks and eliminations many degreed
professionals are unemployed or underemployed, so jobs
without training and experience are rare and competition
is tough.

There are also private on-the-job training programs in
industry. Companies like General Electric and Bell Telephone have been training their employees in their own
schools for years. Many department stores train their own
employees for managerial positions. Usually these programs
are open only to those who are already employed by the
firm that offers the training program. Think about the
skills you already have that may lead to a job with additional training available. The Xerox Corporation, for
example, trains people with some background in electronics
or mechanics to repair its equipment.

Apprenticeship

Apprenticeship is a major vehicle for training skilled
workers in the labor force. Apprenticeship fits into two
categories: construction and industrial. The advantage
of apprenticeship is that the trainee is a *paid* member
of a production force while training on the job and in
the classroom.

The apprenticeship agreement sets out the work processes
to be taught and the hours and wages for each training
period. At the end of the apprenticeship the trainee is
awarded a certificate of completion. Apprenticeable trades
cover a wide range of occupations: bricklayer, carpenter,
sheet metal workers, printer, tool and die maker, drafter,
and many more.

For many years tradition and discrimination have combined
to exclude women from apprenticeships. As a result, women
have been greatly underrepresented in these occupations,
although many women may have the necessary aptitudes and
potential skills. Pressure for change is increasing,
primarily because of the activities of women's organizations. Women are beginning to consider nontraditional jobs
as an occupational option. More young women and girls are
seeking out vocational training at elementary and secondary
levels.

Here are some suggestions if you are considering making a
nontraditional occupational choice:

1. Think "skilled trades" and include them among your
    range of job possibilities.
2. Know employment laws, including provisions for equal
    opportunity in employee training and education
    programs.
3. Indicate your willingness to perform a job using
    your mechanical ability as well as your intelligence.
4. Be aware of resources in your community which can
    assist in locating apprenticeship opportunities.
    They include:

    a. Bureau of Apprenticeship and Training
        U.S. Department of Labor
        (Regional and area offices; consult U.S. govern-
        ment listings)

    b. Women's Bureau
        U.S. Department of Labor
        (Regional offices; consult U.S. government
        listings)

    c. State Apprenticeship and Training Councils
        (Consult state government listings)

    d. Apprenticeship Information Centers
        Operated in key labor market areas by state
        Employment Security agencies to provide infor-
        mation and counseling about local availability
        of apprenticeship opportunities. Also, appli-
        cants often prescreened for referral. (Consult
        state listings)

    e. Apprenticeship Outreach Programs
        Originally intended to recruit minority males
        for apprenticeship, many have recently amended
        work plans to recruit, counsel, and tutor young
        women.

    f. Building and construction trades councils and
        employers' association in your vicinity.
        (They may not be overly enthusiastic or receptive,
        but they should be made aware of your interest.
        One of the chief excuses for exclusion is "women
        and minorities are not interested in apprentice-
        ship.")

    g. Special programs underway to help women enter
        skilled trades:

Advocates for Women
Women in Apprenticeship Program
256 Sutter Street
San Francisco, Calif. 94108
(415) 391-4870

Better Jobs for Women
1545 Tremount Place
Denver, Colo. 80202
(303) 893-3534

Lady Carpenters' Institute
20 St. Mark's Place
New York, N.Y. 10003
(212) 982-7166

Wider Opportunities for Women
1649 K Street, N.W.
Washington, D.C. 20006
(202) 638-4868
(They publish the magazine *Women's Work*, with
excellent information for job-hunters--well worth the
five dollars a year.)

Women in Skilled Trades
Women's Resource and Policy Development Center
1501 Neil Avenue
Columbus, Ohio 43201
(614) 421-1315

Women Working in Construction
1854 Wyoming Avenue, N.W.
Washington, D.C. 20009
(202) 387-5261

The woman electing apprenticeship, or other male-dominated
fields, will receive many benefits: high wages, a chance
to develop a previously unknown capability within herself,
new job frontiers. She may at the same time encounter
resistance, hostility, even harassment. If you know this
is the job you want and you sense your capability, don't
give up in the face of hardships. Your persistence will
benefit not only yourself but also countless women to follow.

GOING (BACK) TO COLLEGE

Before you rush to enroll in a four-year academic program
from which you will emerge with a bachelor's degree and

swell the ranks of unemployed college graduates, ask yourself, "What do I expect this degree to accomplish?" It is
unfortunately no longer true that a college degree is a
guarantee of a decent-paying, maybe even interesting job.
In many areas you are better off with a particular skill
than a general liberal arts education. So if you are
interested in the college degree mostly because you assume
it will help you land a good job, think about it some more.

Perhaps a more realistic possibility is one of the specialized programs offered by many junior colleges, community
colleges, specialized schools, and business schools. The
two-year degree or one-year certificate program may be a
shorter path to decent paid employment. They offer training
in a variety of fields, many of them in the human services
(such as child care, paramedical, mental health) but also in
more technical fields (drafting, business-related). A two-
year program is a smaller investment of time and money and
is designed to make you employable at the end of that time,
which is not always the case with a liberal arts degree.
This degree may limit you to certain jobs, but once you are
working it may be possible to advance, either through on-
the-job training or by enrolling full-time or part-time in
a four-year program. Often, advancement in your chosen
field will require additional study toward a bachelor's
degree, but you may be in a better position to pay for
further study after working for a few years (or your employer may help pay tuition).

Two-year certificate programs do not necessarily make you
employable. Some are in obsolete areas or meet faculty
teaching needs more than job market needs. Investigate the
marketability of the skill you want to acquire. One good
way to decide whether you want to train for a particular
occupation is to talk to someone who has the job you want.
The person herself is often pleased to talk to you. If you
don't know anyone who has the position you are interested
in, the college placement office may be able to recommend
a contact.

If you want to enter one of the professions--teaching,
medicine, law--you must get a four-year college degree. It
is a prerequisite to other aspects of your professional
training. Of course, if you have the time and money and
want to go to college but don't have a specific occupational
goal in mind, that's all right, too. If you have the financial resources, by all means take advantage of the opportunity. But remember there are costs beyond tuition--fees,
books, child care, transportation.

JORDAN

I started thinking I wanted to be a dentist right
before I went to college. I thought about being
a dentist or a doctor. I liked my dentist real well,
so I thought that would be a good thing to do. Ex-
cept I think I'm too selfish to be a doctor. It
takes too much time. I can't give up all my time.
My teachers always encouraged me, and my parents did.
It's strange at school sometimes. I really miss
having girls to talk to about the little things that
you talk about that you never would mention to a
guy. Sometimes I feel real lonely. Not very often,
but just once in a while. There are a few professors
who make it very easy for you because they like girls
or they think they have a chance with you. They're
nice to you and tell you you look nice and give you
a good grade. There are other ones who almost make
it rough on you. I don't know if they don't think
you have the stamina or what it is. They definitely
don't think that women belong in dental school. So
it seems like they're either to one extreme or the
other.

I don't think it's going to be hard when I get out
because there are so few dentists for the number of
people needing them. A lot of people would rather
go to a woman, I'm sure, even if they had some res-
ervations. It would be a lot better than putting
up with a toothache or waiting for a long time for
their dentist. I think there are some people who
would rather go to a woman anyway. I think a lot of
it would depend on if you treated them well and they
liked you. It's just like any other dentist, if you
don't cause them much pain they're going to be glad
to go back. And if you aren't too expensive. Or
if they don't have to wait a long time in the office.
Dentists aren't the only people who are busy; every-
body else has something to do, too. But they don't
tell you that in dental school.

Once you've decided a college degree is definitely what you
want, you should begin to think about what kind of education
you are looking for. This will become clearer if you ask
yourself these questions:

1. Is your primary motive to use your degree as a step-
    pingstone to further education, for personal growth

or achievement, or to increase your earning potential?

2. How much time can you devote to this educational
    project? Are you able to go to school full-time or
    part-time? During the day or at night?

3. What kinds of support will you need (child care, as-
    sistance with cooking, cleaning) and where will you
    get it? Is child care available to you in your com-
    munity or at the school you plan to attend? Can you
    count on help from your family for chores and respon-
    sibilities that used to be yours?

4. Would a program which includes work experience (for
    credit) as well as academic subjects be more valuable
    to you?

5. Do you need a highly structured program with assign-
    ments and lots of direction from professors, or would
    you prefer a program which allows for a great deal of
    independent study, research, and writing?

6. Would taking a few courses over an extended period of
    time meet your needs as well as going immediately into
    a full-time schedule? When are you free to attend:
    day, evening, summer, all year round?

7. What areas do you most want to learn about? What sub-
    jects are most difficult for you? Should you take
    a refresher course in these areas?

8. With what kind of student population would you feel
    most comfortable: an all-woman college, a coeduca-
    tional college, a commuter college with day students,
    or a residential college? Is it important to you to
    be around older, more experienced students?

9. What will you have to give up to return to school?
    Church, volunteer commitments, leisure time, special
    attention to the needs of friends and relatives may
    have to be reduced.

Many women who have been out of school for some time are
not eager to compete (and let's face it, most of American
education demands competition) with younger students.
You may feel your learning skills and study habits have
rusted. Younger students are probably more adept at test-
taking, writing papers, and memorizing. But this is only
because they have used these skills more recently than you
have. They are not inborn gifts, but learned habits. They
demand little more than use and discipline. You should
remember that although you may not have been in school for
many years, you have not stopped learning. Your life experiences have given you insight, judgment, and discipline
that most younger students lack.

Many colleges and universities are developing special programs tailored to the needs of women entering college after careers as wives and mothers, or returning to an interrupted education. These are generally called "Continuing Education Programs for Women" (CEW). To see if there are such programs at universities and colleges in your area call the local institutions, or ask at the local branch of the American Association of University Women or at the local women's center.

Some colleges and universities (including those with CEW programs) accept results from the College Level Examination Program (CLEP) in lieu of college credit. Depending on your score on these examinations, you can receive college credit for knowledge you have gained outside a formal academic setting. CLEP offers two types of tests: general examinations and subject examinations. The general examinations cover English composition, humanities, mathematics, natural sciences, and social sciences and history; they measure knowledge usually covered in the first two years of college. The subject examinations test for achievement in specific college courses and can be used to obtain credit for or exemption from such courses. Inquire about whether the college or university you want to apply to accepts CLEP scores for academic credit. Further information about CLEP is available from: College Entrance Examination Board, Box 1824, Princeton, New Jersey 08540.

More and more colleges are making arrangements to give credit for previous learning you have had outside of an academic setting. The procedure varies at each institution but usually includes writing a description of what and how you learned and petitioning the faculty for a certain number of credits. Past work such as writing, art, music, or other accomplishments may be submitted as evidence of your learning. Where these arrangements exist, however, the provisions are never exactly what the potential student might want, and it usually requires great perseverance to get such credit. Inquire whether the school you are considering offers life- or work-experience credit. Some institutions which give large amounts of credit for prior learning are called "Universities without Walls" and belong to the Union for Experimenting Colleges and Universities. You may find out more about these programs by writing to: Union for Experimenting Colleges and Universities, c/o Antioch College, Yellow Springs, Ohio 45387.

Check into entrance requirements before applying. Many
four-year institutions require certain high school entrance
units. Two-year schools tend to be more flexible. Some
schools will waive the entrance examination (SAT or ACT)
required of younger, in-sequence students. Most will
transfer credit earned at other universities with some
variations, depending on the length of time elapsed and
the applicability of the courses to your current choice of
major, and your grades.

Inquire at each institution you are considering about all
special provisions for women returning to college or entering after a long absence from formal education. In
addition to flexible entrance requirements there may be
a special orientation program for older students and
other support services to ease your transition into college.

A Few Words about Survival on the College Campus

The number of contemporaries you will find in your classes
depends on several factors: whether the school has a program of continuing education for women, whether it is a
commuter or community college, and, to some extent, the
field you are studying. Ivy League, residential, and
liberal arts colleges are most likely to have only small
numbers of women who have not been in school continuously.

A woman who is isolated from campus life by family or job
responsibilities may be able to find or form a group of
other people attending school under similar conditions.
Many schools are beginning to have women's groups that
may be helpful. Often those groups sponsor day care programs for the children of students, faculty, and community
residents. If the school you attend seems oblivious to
the need for child care, perhaps the first step is to seek
out other women with the same problem and work out sharing
day care arrangements. You might also try to find sympathetic women at the school and organize student support
for a university-supported day care center on campus.

Finally, you should be prepared to change the ways in which
you spend your time. When you are facing finals, time
becomes precious. You would never consider baking that
birthday cake from scratch; you feel lucky to be able to
dash into a bakery and pick one up. Friends will complain
that they don't see you as often, even if you have much
more to talk about when you do get together. Your family
may be irritated or hostile when you are not as available

to them as you used to be. Thinking those things through and learning to let go of your previous patterns and expectations for yourself can prevent the "superwoman collapse syndrome" which hits many women who return to college.

JACKIE

I went back to school for several reasons. First, I went back for the obvious reasons--to get credentials, to secure a position in the job market-- but more important, I went back because I had quit, and it was something I had always felt bad about. I quit at eighteen for the traditional reasons-- to get married and raise a family. I felt it was unfinished business in my life.

My kids were nine and ten at the time. It was very difficult because I was not used to the academic way of life, disciplining myself in an academic way. I was used to making sacrifices for my kids and to run my household, but not for myself. I was basically an undisciplined person, and I went into an academic setting which was very nontraditional and required a large amount of self-discipline. Nobody was standing over my head, whipping me into shape. Many times I wanted to quit, but I kept thinking about how bad I would feel if I quit for the second time, if I failed twice. I knew I would be unhappy for the rest of my life if I didn't stick it out and see it through. So I gritted my teeth and forced myself to do what was required. There was constant conflict between trying to fulfill my educational responsibilities and my household responsibilities and my mother responsibilities. My kids would often interrupt me when I would try to write, for example. But I made it, and my diploma is now sitting on the mantel. It's a great feeling.

Women's Studies

One possible way of making your college studies more meaningful to you is to investigate whether your school has a women's studies department, interdisciplinary courses in women's studies, or courses about women within traditional disciplines. In recent years individual women and women's groups on campuses have pressured schools to widen

the traditional curriculum to include the study of women.
Women's studies courses tend to be primarily in literature
and history but are also in such varied disciplines as
anthropology, biology, linguistics, and film. Learning
about the history of women and putting your experiences
and the experiences of other contemporary women into a
wider perspective can be tremendously exciting. Participating in a women's studies experience can also help bridge
the gap between the formality of academic study--which for
so many women seems intimidating and "out there"--and what
is real and important in your life.

Financing Your Education

Up until now, few institutions have recognized the financial
needs of older students. You can count yourself fortunate
if you have a nest egg saved to cover your education or if
your husband is willing to finance all or part of it. If
this is not the case, you may find yourself caught in the
same situation that has kept many willing potential
students from low-income families out of college. By and
large, there are few financial aid programs designed specifically for adult women students.

Some of your options include government grants and scholarships and work-study programs, state grants and scholarships, subsidy by business and industry for their employees,
individual college scholarships and work-study programs,
and foundation and other special grants such as the Upper
Division Scholarship Competition. To determine if any of
these sources are available to you, inquire at the school
to which you are applying or in which you are enrolled.

Government grants and scholarships include a program of
guaranteed loans. Students accepted for enrollment in
approved colleges, vocational schools, business schools,
or universities may apply to banks, credit unions, savings
and loan associations, insurance companies, or colleges.
Undergraduate students may borrow as much as $2,000 a year
up to a maximum of $7,500 ($10,000 including graduate
studies) from these institutions with a state agency, private nonprofit agency, or sometimes the federal government
guaranteeing the loan. The interest on the loan will be
paid by the government for students with an adjusted
family income of less the $15,000 a year. Repayment does
not begin until nine to twelve months after graduation and
may be further deferred if the student serves in the Peace
Corps, VISTA, or the armed forces.

Financial aid for students in areas of special study such
as teaching, counseling, library work, health fields,
social work, guidance, and vocational rehabilitation is
available from the U.S. Department of Health, Education and
Welfare. Write for further information.

Other programs include educational opportunity grants in
which half your grant is supplied by the institution you
attend and half is matched by the federal government (from
two hundred dollars to one thousand dollars a year).
Recipients of these grants are named by the institution
they attend. National defense student loans offer long-
term, low-interest loans. Undergraduate students may borrow up to two thousand dollars a year to a total of
five thousand dollars. Interest is 3 percent and repay-
ment begins ten months after graduation.

Michigan and Iowa give grants to adult students who wish
to attend their state universities. Some other states also
follow this policy. There are some states, however,
such as Massachusetts, in which continuing education programs must by law be self-supporting, which means you must
contribute your tuition costs.

Some businesses encourage their employees to return to
school and agree to undertake payment of their fees. Some
businesses are reasonable about giving their employees time
off from their jobs to attend school. Frequently this may
involve taking night courses or courses specifically related
to your job.

Many colleges and universities offer scholarships or work-
study programs or a combination of the two for their low-
income students. "Work-study" usually refers to federally
supported employment where the employer, usually the
college, pays only 20 percent of the wages. Usually those
jobs are low-paying and on-campus, although there are ex-
ceptions. The maximum hourly wage under federal guidelines
is $3.50 per hour. "Cooperative education" is usually
paid and supervised work which counts for academic credit.
The pay for this work is also usually low, sometimes
barely equaling the tuition you must pay to get the college
credit for the experience. There are also practicum work
experiences, which are often volunteer-supervised work
situations required by particular majors (social work, for
example). In some majors, practicums are offered but not
required. The point of these jobs may not often be the
money, although the money helps, but the experience--and

in a tight job market experience counts a lot. Work also develops valuable contacts for use after graduation. These work experiences are useful not only for a younger, inexperienced student, but also for an older woman who has many life experiences but little or no experience in the work world.

The Upper Division Scholarship Competition awards sizable grants to students nominated by their college. It requires its recipients to be graduates of a community or junior college.

Many college placement offices maintain a listing of part-time jobs for students.

When determining if any of these options are available to you, consult the financial aid office at the school you are interested in attending. Inquire about the specific scholarships they offer, how much, to whom, and under what conditions.

Credit

Discrimination against women in financial institutions has in the past taken many forms. The first aspect of discrimination is that creditors often deny a married women credit in her own name unless she is the sole or major source of support for the family. Even then she has to petition to get her own credit recognized.

We strongly believe that married women should take advantage of the opportunity to establish separate credit, even though quite happily married. Death as well as separation or divorce could wipe out your credit rating altogether. If a wife has never had credit in her own name, she may establish such credit even though all bills, loans, or mortgages are joint (in the name of husband and wife). Even if you expect to want only joint credit for the rest of your joint lives, it makes sense to insist on a credit rating in your own name, based on your joint credit history.

As of November 1, 1976, when the final provisions of the federal Equal Credit Opportunity Act (P.L. 93-495) took effect (see box), married people must be informed of their

rights to separate credit accounts and separate credit
ratings. Until now, women have been stuck with their
husband's lousy credit ratings; there was virtually no way
they could demonstrate their financial independence and
gain good ratings for themselves in anticipation of a
separation or divorce. A woman who wanted a good credit
rating and was divorced had to pay her husband's bills to
get this rating, and once she separated, "his" credit was
no longer relevant to her creditworthiness. Her record was
wiped out and she had to start all over again and be considered a bad risk because of her (marital) "instability"
to boot. The new Equal Credit Opportunity Act should end
this. Wives may now establish their own credit during
the marriage and need not suffer from their husbands'
financial derelictions.

EQUAL CREDIT OPPORTUNITY ACT--FEDERAL LAW (P.L. 93-495)

Effective: October 28, 1975, although some regulations
             go into effect later. All regulations of this
             act will be in effect by November 1, 1976.

Purpose: "To make credit equally available to all
             creditworthy customers without regard to sex
             or marital status"

This act prohibits *discrimination* based on sex or marital
status. It does not prohibit requiring information as to
sex or marital status, since that information may be
relevant to risk and liability of creditors, security of
debt, and so on. It does not prohibit requiring both
parties in marriage to sign for loan or credit. Basically,
the act just provides that sex and marital status can't
be used to determine creditworthiness.

Applies to: federally regulated banks and mortgage com-
             panies, and any other credit-granting insti-
             tution under federal control

Remember: You do not have a right to be granted credit;
             you must prove your "creditworthiness." You
             do, however, have a right not to be dis-
             criminated against in the granting of credit:
             if you have the same financial status and credit
             history as another applicant, you may not be

denied credit simply on the basis of your
sex or marital status.

Wives who want to establish separate credit based on their
own incomes have a right to do so and may not be discouraged
merely because they are married. You have a right to be
given a credit rating purely on the basis of your own
income, without regard to your husband's. If you intend
to use *only your own income or property* to repay the loan,
creditors may not even inquire into your husband's earnings
or assets. However, if you plan to use as security for the
loan any property which, under the law of your state, is
jointly held (most commonly, the house you live in--but
also any property held as "tenants by the entirety" in some
states or as part of the "community property" in others),
then your husband's income and assets are relevant and
you must disclose them.

CLARE

*I went to the manager of the bank and asked could I
have a two-thousand-dollar loan to pay off some of
my daughter's debts. He said my husband's name had
to be on the loan, two signatures are better than
one. I said, "How can it be, since my husband is
retired and I'm bringing in most of the money from
my babysitting business?" I have money in my own
account and we have money in a joint account, but as
long as we are married, both names have to be on the
loan. It would be different if I were single. I
asked the manager how this affects my credit, if Joe
and I got separated or divorced. He said my credit
would be nil. I would have to start all over again
from rock bottom to get the credit rating.*

Contrary to popular practice, creditors may no longer even
ask what kind of birth control you use, how many children
you expect to have and when, and so on. If you are single,
your plans to marry or not, any use of birth control, and
other personal questions are likewise irrelevant and should
not be part of any information you are required to give in
order to obtain credit.

If you are relying on court-ordered support, alimony, or
voluntary payments from your ex-husband as part of your

"income," his income assets and credit rating are relevant and will be considered in determining your creditworthiness. They may be skeptical about the regularity
of support or alimony payments from your husband, and
your best hope here is to be able to demonstrate a record
of prompt and regular full payments. Creditors must
consider and may not at all discount income you earn from
part-time work.

You are entitled to a written statement of the reasons for
which your credit application is denied. *Insist on this
statement*. Often when the reason for the denial is
discrimination and nothing more, insisting on the statement
will yield the desired credit. If you still think there
is discrimination, check various state and local offices
of consumer affairs, or credit bureaus. Your state or
local human relations commission should also help.

If you are pretty sure you've been discriminated against,
you may sue the parties who denied you credit. You will
probably want the help of a lawyer to do this. You may
recover both what the loss of credit (or denial of credit)
actually cost you, plus up to ten thousand dollars for
deliberate and malicious denials and discrimination.

Some states have equal credit opportunity acts similar to
the federal law, and some state human relations acts
specifically prohibit discrimination based on sex or marital status in credit and mortgages. Some prohibit sex-
based but not marital-status discrimination. In many
states discrimination in credit is not specifically prohibited, although it is more likely that mortgages or
other housing-related areas will be mentioned. If discrimination in credit is not mentioned in your state or
city human relations act, a competent lawyer may be able
to make a good argument that such discrimination is
covered anyway. It depends on how the act has been interpreted in your area, who the judges are, and other factors.

A last word on credit--under the federal Fair Credit Reporting Act you have a right to see your credit file and to
challenge inaccurate and untrue statements therein. You
have a right to file a statement denying or explaining any
material in your file that is inaccurate, misleading, or
false. Under the Equal Credit Opportunity Act you may also
demand and get access to your spouse's credit file if it
reflects on your ability to pay debts--for example, if you
have had credit together and you are applying for joint
credit, but in your own name.

Check better business bureaus and consumer protection
programs locally and in your state for more information
on establishing a good credit record and remedying viola-
tions of your rights as a credit applicant or holder.

An excellent book called *Borrowing Basics for Women* is
available free. It explains what you need to know initially about establishing and maintaining credit, taking
into account the new Equal Credit Opportunity Act.
Write:

> First National City Bank
> Public Affairs Department
> P.O. Box 939
> Church Street Station
> New York, N.Y. 10008

MIRIAM GALPER

CAROLYN KOTT WASHBURNE

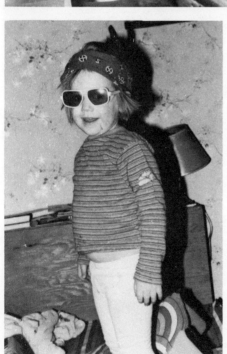

MIRIAM GALPER

IAN M. HARRIS

5

ALICE

When the time came that I began to give serious thought to
having a baby, I felt sure that I was making my decision
on the most rational, sensible grounds. I was a living
example, or so I thought, of planned parenthood. I was
twenty-seven years old and had been married seven years.
My husband and I had purposely avoided having a baby before
that time in order to, as the saying goes, build and develop our relationship. We had all kinds of interesting
experiences together including a stint in the Peace Corps.
He was working in a job he liked as a civil rights attorney
and I had just completed a masters degree in social work.
I knew enough about myself to appreciate that I was not
a person who would be content to be at home devoted to
family. I thought I had prepared myself to integrate
work and family life in a realistic way. I planned to
devote some months to full-time mothering and then at a
later time, look for a job, part-time at first.

I have come to understand that no one ever decides to have
a baby for rational reasons. One may concoct seemingly
coherent reasons to explain behavior, but a decision as
deep and as basic as deciding to become pregnant comes
from very deep inside. And no matter how much you think
you are prepared, the reality of the situation sooner or

later bowls you over. I had been used to a life in which I was active and involved in work and relationships and had probably defined myself too greatly by external factors. To be thrust suddenly into a situation in which I was at home all the time, just the baby and me, without outside supports and stimulation, produced frustrations and anxieties that I scarcely could have imagined.

This is not to say that it was all a heavy, burdensome existence. There were clearly warm and pleasant times as well. I liked stepping off the treadmill for a while, turning inward and devoting myself to the baby. Holding and nurturing a child inside me for nine months, seeing my belly grow, experiencing the incredible high of the delivery, breastfeeding, the entire range of very direct and intense giving and receiving of love that takes place-- these experiences added depth and fullness to my life. It was as if in becoming a mother a part of me was tapped that had never been touched before.

Nevertheless, when the baby was six months old, I became restless and began to look for a part-time job. I quickly realized how few positions existed that required anything less than a full-time commitment. My baby needed me less and I, in turn, began to feel bored and trapped since mothering was now my only identity. Although some of the problems of staying home with a baby were beginning to gnaw at me before, I now keenly felt the drawbacks. Certainly there was always some drudgery in mothering, but the boring, mundane tasks were intensified by the fact that there was little else in my life. Other women I know also say they were unprepared and genuinely shocked at how narrow their lives suddenly became.

You exist in a kind of distinct subculture when all you are doing is taking care of a baby. Generally, you are either alone or relating to other mothers. As I look back, it was not the actual responsibilities of mothering a small baby that were hard, it was my total immersion in this subculture and the way of life it represented.

I remember reading Philip Slater's The Pursuit of Loneliness which says that mothers are taught to believe they hold the power to make or break their children. The extent to which a child will be more or less intelligent, well adjusted, socially acceptable, all depend on the quality of care given by the mother. This assumption in the back of my mind made my interactions with my baby more burdensome than

188

was necessary. Since I was responsible for the major part of his care, I felt alone and unsupported in what was probably an unrealistic goal. There should have been other supports to rely upon--husband, friends, family, social resources.

Every day when my baby was little I took him to a nearby park, as much so I could be with other adults as for him to be around other children. What could have been a chance for all of us to get together, share experiences, and make some personal connections too often turned into a competitive struggle, more open on the part of the children, more subtle but nonetheless real on the mothers' parts. The mothers engaged in endless discussions about the accomplishments of their individual children--whose child had talked first or walked first, whose child had made one or another developmental leap or was performing well. Rarely did we talk about our anxieties about childrearing, let alone our inadequacies or our failures. I spent hours sitting with women and their children in the park and on the street, but we still remain individualistic and isolated from each other. We raise our children with the vague notion that they should be "happy" but we build in loneliness, privacy, and possessiveness.

Suddenly people were asking me to run errands and perform tasks that they never would have asked before because they saw me as having time on my hands. Previously, my husband and I had shared all household tasks and responsibilities. Now because I had more time and fewer outside demands, most of the household tasks fell to me. It became very hard for me to hold onto myself, to give priority to my own needs and goals. Feminist literature talks a lot about the woman as "the eternal nurturer," her identity so tied up with taking care of other people that she loses herself in the process. For the first time in my life I felt that was happening to me. I had a recurrent fantasy of an office somewhere designed just for mothers, a place outside the home where I belonged and where I could not be interrupted.

At the time I was involved in a number of different projects and activities, some that were quite important to me. Often I would hire babysitters so that I could be free to do the work that was required. Yet every day it seemed as if I had to structure my day anew. The lack of outside demands or pressures, so little direction produced a feeling of aimlessness. It killed my enthusiasm and I found it harder and harder to motivate myself to be active and engaged on a daily basis.

As the mother of a small baby, I found, whether I liked it or not, conversation with other adults invariably gravitated toward discussing children. Since raising a child was a good part of my life at that time, it was important to me to talk about what I was going through. I often found myself waiting for other people to comment on my child and how they saw him doing. I soon realized that I was experiencing a compliment or criticism of his behavior as a compliment or criticism of me.

Some of my eagerness for comments from other people was understandable. As the mother of a first child I had no previous experience to rely on, and lack of confidence made me hesitant to trust myself and my own perceptions. I also discovered that there was very little external validation for the job I was doing as a mother, and I became keenly aware of my own need for it. There were times when I got pleasure just from the day-to-day tasks and interactions with my son and had a sense inside of me that things were going right. But, there really is no concrete way of evaluating how you are as a mother. Perhaps, because we live in such a product-oriented culture, we judge how good a mother is by the performance of her child. Yet, for a child to carry this burden seems sad and dangerous to me; not only must the child justify his own existence, but his mother's as well.

I have encountered a peculiarly dualistic attitude toward mothering. On the one hand, there is the sentiment that motherhood is the most important role a woman undertakes. Mothers still must bear their own guilt and the criticism of others if they leave their children to go to work. On the other hand, motherhood is terribly devalued. It is an unpaid position in a society that places enormous value on money, and most people seem to feel that it is a task almost anyone can perform.

I always winced at having to respond to "What do you do?" Too much importance is placed on determining a person's worth by the job he holds, but it is still difficult for a woman not to define herself that way too. If motherhood were seen as valid and meaningful work and rewarded accordingly and if ways were developed to perform the tasks of mothering in more satisfying ways, in union with others, then other women would not have to encounter the depth of discouragement that I did.

190

Probably some of my unhappy feelings can be attributed to factors in my own psychology. But as I look back, I was not alone in seeing the limitations to the role I had assumed. However, few women I knew found it easy to admit to any negative or even ambivalent feelings toward their children. After all, we have all been socialized to believe that motherhood will be a joyful time and much of the psychological childrearing literature reinforces this notion. When mothers did talk about their unhappiness, they saw it as some sort of personal deficiency. It seems to me that although every woman must go through her own personal adjustment to being a mother, the process is made more difficult by a society that stresses the importance of each of us making it on our own, that does not encourage sharing of our struggles or our resources, and that continues to see the best mother as the one who stays at home and completely devotes herself to her child.

In our society it is not easy for a woman who happens also to be a mother to live an integrated life. It is extremely difficult to affirm both parts of yourself--the part that truly wants to raise a child and that which needs to be part of the larger world. The unavailability of decent part-time jobs, the lack of adequate social supports like day care, the fact that often for purely economic reasons fathers must be away from the home so much of the time-- these factors all contribute to placing an unfair burden on the woman who suddenly finds herself with a baby of her own and is not quite sure what hit her. I remember thinking to myself, "Why didn't somebody tell me?" Nobody ever does seem to tell us what is in store. The old myths are still supported so that we do not prepare ourselves adequately and are more shocked than we need be.

My life has become a great deal fuller and more pleasurable since the early days when I was home alone with my baby. I went back to work, my child got older and more independent, child care resources became more accessible, and I gradually began to regain my sense of self once more. But from my own experience I now know that women must begin sharing their experiences honestly so that we know what to expect and can plan accordingly. I also know that motherhood should be viewed as only one avenue of a woman's life, an important one certainly, but not the only one.

5 / Motherhood

DOTTY

Before I went to the hospital to have my first baby, I would create fantasies about what it was going to be like to be a mother. I would think about cute baby clothes, bassinets, and doting grandparents and relatives. I imagined my baby as this sweet smiling bundle of joy. It never occurred to me to think of motherhood as a lifelong commitment and responsibility from which there was no escape. It wasn't until I came home from the hospital that I had the overwhelming realization that I wouldn't be able to go out of the house without a babysitter for something like ten or twelve years. It was then that I began to realize that the realities were a far cry from my fantasies and I wondered why I hadn't thought about these things beforehand. Why hadn't I thought through all that motherhood entails and made some sort of choice about it instead of just falling into it as if it were the only natural order of things? Maybe I still would have decided to have my baby, but at least I would have known what I was getting into.

Redefining Motherhood

Women have always assumed that they'd have children, just
as they've always assumed they would get married. In this
chapter, along with motherhood, we would like to explore
other choices and options which may not be the traditional,
socially acceptable ones. If you are a woman who hasn't
yet decided whether or not to have children, we hope to be
able to provide you with some tools for making a clear,
intelligent decision based on your own life, rather than
on the many myths that surround motherhood. We are not
going to encourage you *not* to have children, although we
will reinforce your right to make such a choice. Instead,
we want to present a view of motherhood as it really is.
It is our feeling that young women are encouraged to think
of the motherhood experience in very romantic ways that
often leave them unprepared to deal with the enormous
responsibility that it actually entails. So in this chapter
we speak not only of the joy and satisfaction, but of the
frustration and disappointment as well. In so doing we
hope to provide you with reinforcement and support if you
choose *not* to become a mother, and with helpful information
and insight if you choose *to* become a mother. If you have
decided that you definitely want children, this chapter
will help you implement that decision in the most positive
manner possible. And if you already have children, we
hope that this chapter will serve as a useful resource and
coping guide as you live your life as a mother and as a
person.

We know from talking to many women that motherhood almost
always turned out to be something different from what they
were led to believe. Although almost every woman we talked
to has found great happiness in being a mother, it has not
been clear whether that happiness outweighs the intense
strain that motherhood brings. The unfair division of
labor and the confines of the nuclear family (biological
parents and offspring) often leave women feeling more
trapped and harassed than satisfied and fulfilled. We do
believe, however, that with a lot of hard work and re-
thinking of the mother role it is possible to lessen the
amount of self-sacrifice that is required, and to be fulfilled not only as a mother but as a person as well.

The experience can vary immensely from woman to woman.
The working mother, the low-income mother, the middle-

class suburban mother all have different experiences, but
all share the responsibility that motherhood imposes and
all share the need for a better, fairer definition of
motherhood and the mother role.

Thinking about Motherhood?

Let's begin this discussion with a look at the prevailing
attitudes, beliefs, and traditions that surround the
institution of motherhood. Our society tells us several
things: all women want children, all women must have
children if they are to act in accordance with nature.
Women will find their fulfillment and happiness through
the motherhood experience. Women were created to have and
mother children. The essence of womanhood is motherhood.
To fail to have children is to fail as a person. To decide
not to have children is to be cold, unwomanly, and abnormal.
To be childless is to be pathetic. Motherhood is blissful
and exciting. Whatever other ideas a woman may have, she
is first and foremost a wife and mother.

First and foremost a wife and mother--a concept that many
of us have never questioned, a concept that is just now
beginning to be challenged. What do the prevailing attitudes toward motherhood reflect about society's view
of women? To assume that women must have children to
act in accordance with nature is to reduce us to a biological function. If it were biologically necessary for
women to have children, we would die if we didn't do it.
Women have childbearing equipment. Men have big muscles.
Nobody says that men are going against nature if they don't
develop and use those muscles. A woman who chooses not
to use her childbearing equipment is not blocking what
is instinctive; she is simply making a choice.

The fact that women are biologically equipped to bear
children does not necessarily mean that they are better
equipped mentally and emotionally to rear them. The belief that women were created simply to bear and mother
children denies them the right to develop their own resources and creativity, a right that is automatically
accorded to men. To assume that women are failures if
they don't have children is to believe that they are
nothing more than sets of reproductive organs. To tell a

woman that motherhood is blissful and glorious, without
telling her it is also boring and frustrating, is to tell
her a lie.

We do not accept the notion that the maternal wish and the
activity of mothering are instinctive or biologically pre-
destined. Often women think that they need to be mothers,
crave to be mothers from within. Actually these feelings
are psychological, not biological. Many of them stem from
the way we are taught to equate our womanhood with motherhood. Of course women are going to have these feelings
when they have been conditioned to believe that their
purpose in life is to mother. Some women do find their
happiness and fulfillment in life in their role as mother.
Many other women want a broader role, or a completely different one.

DOTTY

> I just wanted to have a child. Babies are so pure,
> you know. At this time in my life I need somebody
> who can't mess over me. I can give him real good
> love. I can't give it to nobody else. If I give it
> to my man, he just screws right over me. It's my
> baby.

Many women are, in fact, deciding not to have children at
all. We think that a woman has the right to make such a
choice and be supported in it--and that it is possible for
women to be happy and fulfilled without children. In fact,
it is quite possible that the existence of children actually
serves to rob many women of the happiness and fulfillment
they seek. A recent study by sociologist Jessie Bernard
demonstrated that single women without children turned out
to be substantially less stressed and overtly more happy
than married mothers. Along these same lines, further
studies have demonstrated that married couples without
children have a higher level of marital satisfaction than
those with children--interesting information, considering
that so many women believe that having children will cement
or improve their marriage relationship. Some women have
decided that having children would place such burdens and
responsibilities upon them that they would be unable to
pursue their own interests satisfactorily. Other women
feel that the relationship they currently have is very
meaningful and are concerned that having children would

detract from rather than add to that enjoyment. The
nuclear family, they feel, can box women in to the extent
that motherhood becomes so much of a strain that a truly
healthy, productive mother-child relationship is almost
impossible to develop. Some women decide not to have
children because they feel that there are already too
many children in the world who are unwanted or unloved and
that if they ever did have children it would be through
adoption. And some women decide against motherhood simply
because they find their nonmother state satisfying and
rewarding and have no desire to change it.

LIANNE

If you are considering motherhood, do you like the
idea of being a mother as opposed to the actual
doing of mothering? As I recall the thinking that
led up to my becoming pregnant ten years ago, it
went something like this: We have been married five
years. Of course, we're going to have children;
why not now? We had both just completed our education, my husband had a good-paying job, why not take
some time out from working now to start a family?

What I did not realize was that up to that point I
had mainly invested my interests in intellectual pursuits. Basically, I had always found child care
boring and had little if any contact, by my own
choice, with families with children. I had disdained
babysitting as a teen-ager, except if the children
were asleep, so as to pursue more "interesting"
activities such as reading or studying. I must have
thought my interests would automatically change once
I had a baby, if I thought about it at all. Or
that I would simply add mothering to all my other
interests.

I think I pictured myself moving gracefully into my
professional work and back again by sharing child
care responsibilities with my husband. Share them
we did, up to a point. Who was to judge whose work
was the more important, and often I found myself
bowing to my husband's work needs, if only because
I did not feel he was as competent a parent as me in
caring for a young child. However, we both had a
major problem in shifting from work to child care
and back again. This is because the demands of

building a career are almost diametrically opposed
to the demands of child care. Professional work
requires an aggressive intellectual dynamic; child
care requires patience, the ability to fill out the
days and nights with empathy, intuitive and sensual
gratifications. Caring for a child for most of us
means slowing down--as opposed to speeding up to
meet the demands of a competitive work market.

ANNA

Generally I do not think about children. At all.
I was pretty firm when we got married that I would
not want to have children. Don was not really of
that mind, and I think secretly he thought that he
would win me over, and that he could get a family
out of me. But as it happened, I won him over, and
at least at this time he is pretty much a committed
nonparent. Apart from me giving him my rhetoric
about that over the last four or five years, as we
got older we associated more and more with people
who have children, and I think he became aware of
how limiting that can be and started to assess more
closely whether he wanted that kind of limitation.
And I don't think he does at this point. I certainly
don't. I have an overdeveloped sense of responsibility, which may be another name for an overdeveloped sense of guilt. I think if we had children I
have a fear of becoming a slave to them, and given
what I know about myself, I think that's not an
entirely unjustified fear. I would feel just so
totally responsible, even if it were understood that
we were sharing the responsibility, and even if in
fact we objectively did share the responsibility, I
would still feel that they're my kids. Who knows
where that comes from? I think I want to avoid that.

We aren't getting pressure from friends about this.
My parents occasionally, like once a year, will
mention it. They used to mention it more frequently,
but I think the writing has been on the wall for a
long while that we don't seem to be headed in that
direction. I think when I went to law school it
started to sink in. And Don's parents are totally
supportive. They think it's fine. Of course, they
have four other kids, one of whom is pregnant, whereas
I'm an only child. The name stops here.

*I like kids. I sometimes get annoyed with the
dynamics of couples who have children--the dynamics
of the couple with each other and with the children.
In more traditional relationships, it's very hard to
watch the mother assume all the responsibility, be
it either in very mechanical or physically supportive
ways or emotional. I resent that. It makes me feel
more resentful toward both of them. I resent the
women as well as the men for permitting that. I
can't think of anyone offhand who has anything different, as a matter of fact, except for one couple.
They are an exception to the rule as far as my
experience goes.*

From childhood on, a little girl is taught that her future
consists of motherhood and wifehood. She is given dolls
to play with as preparation for the day when she will be
"a real mommy." Her teachers curb her adventurousness and
her parents downplay her tomboyishness until she has been
scolded and molded and shaped into the little lady that
everyone finds acceptable. By adolescence she has learned
that her success and status in life will depend not on
what she accomplishes in the world as an individual but on
how well she meets society's expectations of her as a
female. And the biggest and most important of these
expectations is motherhood. Small wonder that she can't
wait for all the joy and fulfillment that she has been told
will come her way through the simple act of giving birth.
She looks forward to pregnancy as a time when she will
receive the pampering and attention that she may never
otherwise get. She is told that childbirth will be an
uplifting experience and that motherhood will be blissful,
rewarding, and fulfilling. She believes that babies are
cute, cuddly, and lovable. Small children are fun to play
with, sweet, innocent, and angelic. Older children are
respectful, helpful, well behaved, and well mannered.
Grown children are grateful, considerate, and committed to
taking care of you in your old age. Life as a mother will
be as they describe in the baby magazines: pleasant
outings with your children, lots of help from doting grandparents, a warm, loving family atmosphere.

What are the realities? How do they measure up to what she
has been led to believe? Starting with pregnancy, we find
that her experiences fall far short of the fantasies that
have been created for her. Pregnancy can, in fact, include
periods of extreme physical discomfort. Nausea, backache,
heartburn, swollen legs and feet, inordinate weight gain,

and general discomfort all serve to detract from the
radiant glow she expected she would acquire. Although she
may, in fact, find the pampering that she anticipated,
often it becomes so overbearing that it is simply an interference and a nuisance.

Childbirth turns out, in many cases, to be a process over
which she has little or no control. Insensitive doctors
and nurses, lack of information, pain, fear, and isolation
generally turn childbirth into something far less than
uplifting.

Babies turn out to be demanding, exhausting, messy, and
whining, as well as cute and cuddly. A mother's world is
turned upside down by the arrival of a newborn. Suddenly
her life revolves around one thing: the baby. She may
feel overwhelmed, unprepared, and depressed as she realizes
the irreversibility of her actions. It begins to dawn
on her that a significant part of her being has been cut
out and earmarked for this other person, a part of her
being that she can never reclaim, no matter how much she
may want to. Such realizations are often responsible for
the "postpartum depression" that many mothers experience
right after childbirth. If she has never had any responsibility for the care of an infant in the past, she is likely
to be more or less ignorant about how to cope on a technical as well as an emotional level. Well-meaning parents
and in-laws can serve to increase her confusion by bom-
barding her with conflicting advice.

Small children turn out to be boring, demanding, totally
selfish, easily frustrated, and fidgety, as well as sweet
and innocent. During the toddler stage many mothers feel
as if they absolutely cannot tolerate the constant need
for attention. It is usually during this period that young
mothers realize that, even if they are at home all day,
they face an unending battle against piles of dirty diapers,
rooms that are messed up by the children five minutes after
they've been cleaned, mounds of dirty dishes, and there is
never any way to be *finished*. For the mother who works
outside the home things are twice as chaotic. For the
low-income mother or welfare mother the lack of sufficient
money makes life incredibly difficult and frustrating.
Women at this stage of childrearing often consider themselves lucky if they can get out long enough to buy a loaf
of bread, much less find the time for an outing or other
enjoyable activity. And taking small children out sounds
good but is often impractical. By the time she has gone

through all of the preparations to take her children with her somewhere, she may find that she is too tired to go. If she does go, their demands and the necessity for constant supervision make it impossible for her to relax and enjoy herself. In addition, how many places exist where a mother can feel comfortable taking young children along?

Older children misbehave, disobey, and fight with each other as much as they are respectful and responsive. Many mothers feel frustrated by their inability to control their children adequately at that stage. Although they are now in school and she has more free time, new demands fill the gap left by the old ones.

JUNE

I babysit other children when my kids are all in school. It's funny--they're all littler kids and I always liked little kids so much that this is how I'm spending my time now. I do find myself looking back to when they were littler. This may seem funny too. I don't know whether I'm looking back in regret that I wish my kids were still little when you had more control. It's a different kind of thing when you were changing their diapers and they'd come with you by the hand. Now they're doing things where you can't take them by the hand and you're hoping that they've learned enough since they were little that they will go the right way.

No matter how much she has devoted herself to her family, she may find that everyone (including herself) will think that it wasn't enough. If she is struggling to create a life of her own separate from the children, she may be doubly blamed. Rarely is the children's father held accountable in such a manner. If she tries to demand that her children and husband respect her need for her own time, space, and identity, she may find that she is fighting an uphill battle. If she tries to recruit their help in sharing household responsibilities, she may face another uphill battle. In fact, she may feel that life has become an uphill battle, period!

Grown children can be as uncaring, neglectful, inconsiderate, and ungrateful as they can be caring and concerned. A mother may feel deserted as her children turn from her to live their lives, often without much more than a

backward glance, leaving her confused and sad. She did it
all just like they told her to. She gave her all, she
worked and worked to make sure that her children were
loved and cared for and provided for, she devoted herself
to them and to her home, she always put them first and
herself last, no sacrifice was too great. Why is it
turning out that she has nothing left? Why is it that she
didn't get a Mother's Day card or a holiday phone call?
What did she do wrong?

Of course motherhood is not all hard work, sacrifice, and
frustration. Children do bring much joy and happiness
through the years. Small children can indeed be delightful
little people, fun to play with, fun to teach. Older
children certainly can make a mother proud as they grow
and develop and learn to cope with the world. And grown
children often do return the love and consideration that
their mothers provided as they grew up.

Motherhood can be fulfilling in many ways. Learning to
love and cherish your children and receiving their love in
return is an important part of mothering for many women.
Having children around can be a blessing to the many
women who find themselves basically alone in the world.
For many women, having children to depend on in time of
crisis helps them to cope satisfactorily with whatever
problems they face. And some mothers function better on a
day-to-day basis when dealing with the necessities of
mothering and child care than they would if they had to
rely on their own initiative.

So children *can* be a joy and a comfort. We would never
say otherwise. We also feel that it is important that
these positive aspects of motherhood not be overromanticized
and glorified.

Think about your reasons for having children. Are they
tied up in your own ego needs? Do you want to have something cute to cuddle, to love? Do you want to have a baby
to see what he or she would look like? Are you "curious"
about pregnancy and childbirth? Do you want to cement your
relationship with your husband or lover? Are you getting
family pressure to produce a grandchild? None of these is
a good reason for bringing life into the world. Do you
want to have a baby because you feel that you will not be
carrying out your role as a woman if you don't? Do you
want someone who will take care of you in your old age?
All of these needs and feelings are natural, but we hope

that you will take the time to read on and become as
knowledgeable as possible about motherhood before you
enter into it. In this way you can assess where you are,
talk it over with the prospective father carefully, weigh
the pros and cons, and make an informed decision based on
what you really need and want.

Some positive factors to consider in deciding about
motherhood are the prospect of watching your children grow
and develop, getting a sense of connection with the experience of parenting, recognizing that children are fun
and filled with warmth and playfulness, and the opportunity
that parenting provides for you to get in better touch
with your own childhood.

CHOICE OR CHANCE

We are assuming here that you indeed have a choice to make
regarding motherhood. Some women are unable to have
children. Often, women in this position feel inadequate
and incomplete. If that applies to you, we urge you to
seek out women who are child-free by choice in order to
get positive reinforcement. We do not feel that being
without children is necessarily a negative thing, but if
you feel strongly about wanting children, then of course
adoption and foster care are possible. If you do become
an adoptive or foster parent, remember that you are no
less a parent than the biological one; it is the care,
love, and nurture that define parenthood, not the biological process.

Many women, through lack of adequate knowledge about birth
control, are not fortunate enough to be able to decide
whether or not they want to get pregnant. Low-income
women in particular are denied sufficient access to safe,
effective birth control methods or are sterilized without
their consent. We would hazard a guess that most of those
pregnancies that occur do so by accident, not by design.
We believe that all women should have control over their
bodies and should know about the birth control options that
are available to them.

We're not necessarily saying that all women should use
birth control; there are women who do not, for religious
or other reasons. We do feel strongly, however, that
every woman should have the option to use it or not.

Having a baby by design rather than by accident can do much
to help a woman adjust to motherhood. Having babies by
accident or by default can be devastating both emotionally
and physically--even more so if it's the second, third, or
fourth pregnancy, and especially if the pregnancies are
coming one right after the other. Many women in that
position find themselves overwhelmed by the burdens of
small children and pregnancy. If you are in that situation,
we urge you to find ways to break out of the pattern, and
we hope that even with the odds so stacked against you,
you will find it possible to create some space and time for
yourself. No matter how many children you may have, you
are still entitled to a life of your own. As difficult as
it may seem, try not simply to resign yourself to your
situation. Try to structure your life so that you exist
for yourself as well as for others. If you are a low-
income woman for whom that is true, we know that you at
times feel desperate and hopeless, especially if you are
a single parent. We know that you face immense struggles
as you try to find happiness in life. That happiness is
there, though, and there are ways to find it. Later in
the chapter we discuss coping and survival techniques for
all mothers with some special suggestions for low-income
mothers.

Once You've Decided

If you have carefully thought things through and have decided that you want to have children, you are in a position
to plan ahead and do it in a way that will be the most
rewarding for you. First, we urge you to inform yourself
about pregnancy and childbirth. There are some important
books available. *Our Bodies, Ourselves* is an excellent
feminist health book which tells you everything you need to
know about your body and how it works. Birth control,
abortion, pregnancy, and childbirth are all covered. No
woman, mother or not, should be without this book. Another
good book that a prospective mother will find useful is
What Now? which provides helpful information on how to deal
with the arrival of a baby.

Most women are mystified by pregnancy and childbirth. The
only information that many of us have is what we've picked

up from our mothers and other women. Rarely do we know
what to expect. Our impressions of pregnancy range from
being frail and sickly to glowing with radiant health.
Childbirth is either horrible or uplifting, depending on
whom you listen to, one of those experiences women have to
suffer through to discover the joy. Any woman who is going
to have children should make it a point to educate herself
about those experiences so that she can know what to expect
and so that she can control what happens to her. There are
different medical approaches to prenatal care and childbirth. Prospective mothers should know what kind of procedures they want and how to get the kind of care that they
want. Childbirth can be a brutal experience in the wrong
place and under the wrong circumstances. Check with local
women's health groups, talk to your mother and other women
about their experiences, pick and choose carefully.

JANICE

*I went into labor at something like five in the
afternoon, waited for Tom to come home, knew I was in
labor. When he got home he said, "No, you're not in
labor, don't worry. When you're ready to deliver
we'll get you to the hospital." He took it rather
lightly. At about eight the pains were excruciating,
and I knew I'd better get to the hospital. So we
got ready and he took me to the hospital. They put
me in a little tiny room on a table, closed the door,
and left me. I never had a needle, an aspirin,
nothing else. I was in labor until three thirty the
next day with no help of any kind. It was a breech
birth. I went to the bathroom and sat on the toilet,
because I didn't know you weren't supposed to do
those kinds of things. The baby might have been born
in the toilet bowl. I screamed and cried--it was
the most horrendous experience I have ever had in
my life. I was alone the entire time. In those days
in the army hospital there was no nursing care, so
that mothers had to take care of their newborn babies.
I had to diaper him, feed him; he stayed in my room
with me. I breastfed him for about a month.*

*When I came home the episiotomy was sewn improperly,
so I was in excruciating pain. It was lapped over
in a way--I don't know what was the matter, but it
was horrible. My blood pressure went down to sixty.
I was terribly anemic. Tom took me back to the*

hospital to see the doctor, who said I was acting
like a child, and that I needed to grow up, and that
I was now a mother who had a child, and he didn't
want to see me again. I continued to get sicker and
sicker, and my mother came out to Oklahoma to take
care of the baby. I couldn't get out of bed, I was
so weak. Finally after six weeks my mother pre-
vailed upon my husband to take me to a private
doctor who found that I was terribly anemic and that
the episiotomy was incorrectly sewn, and he corrected
that and the anemia.

LIANNE

Childbirth is a ritual and like other rituals--such
as a marriage ceremony or graduation from school--
serves to aid a transition from one life-style to
another, with a concomitant change in responsibilities. Imagine being knocked out just before your
wedding and waking up sometime later to find that
you are now married. Or sedated so that you are
aware of what's happening but don't care; deadened
from the emotional involvement, which is the effect
of many of the drugs that are given to "aid" childbirth. All those feelings one has--of fear, doubt,
and high expectations--are better experienced fully
within the circle of supportive persons, including
"wise" ones (experienced doctors, midwives, nurses)
and trusted friends (your husband or other close
friends). In this ritual, like others, how you
handle your feelings will have a lasting effect on
how competent you feel to handle mothering. Wide
awake, if you come to terms with the experience, you
will have mastered your fears and self-doubts.

The Second Time Around

Well, love the second time around may not be quite as
   innocent, or as guilty,
But pregnancy the second time around is just as jilty.
I'm not referring to morning sickness (although I
   probably will be soon).
I'm simply referring to the feelings I feel, which are
   as sentimental as the moon in June.
Not only are they sentimental, but I've also found
That I can't seem to keep them on the ground.

Yep, the art of anticipating (as well as that of
  remembering) is something I've always been good at,
And containing myself I'm hard put at.
My mind leaps ahead at all the great things for
  which I'm in store;
I know, because I've done them before.
Yep, when I think about once again going through it,
When I think about informing our relatives and
  friends, and the various ways we could do it,
When I think about finding a doctor and going for
  visits and later going to the Lamaze classes,
Why, I feel as happy as a lark and as rich as Onassis.
And when I think about how this time I'm gonna
Buy at least one maternity dress at Lady Madonna,
Why, my excitement proceeds in leaps and bounds,
And I think in terms of interjections, not adjectives
  or even abstract nouns;
When I think about how my complexion will improve
  again,
And how I'll feel the baby move again,
And how I'll walk around feeling pleased as punch,
And eat lunches for breakfast and suppers for lunch,
Why, it simply is too much to take,
To be able to both eat and have your cake.
To think that I'll have the fun, all over again, of
  watching the due date come and go
And being the chief concern of all those who know
And then of that "joy ride" to the hospital which
  is so unreal--
When I think of all that, you can imagine how I feel.

I don't dare think of the actual birth.
It'd move the earth.
Or of the baby born, be it Kerry Suzanne or Daaren
  Scot.
I'd melt away on the spot.
To overanticipate would be our ruin,
But I can't help doin'.

                              Marion D. Cohen

Once you have carefully planned your pregnancy and childbirth you should think about what your life will be like
once the baby arrives. Be realistic about how much your
life will change. You will *not*, repeat *not*, be able
simply to pick up where you left off. The arrival of a
new baby will create a complete upheaval in your life. If
you think that the baby will fit into your life, you

will discover that it's the other way around. Babies are
demanding. You will be tired, maybe exhausted, maybe
depressed. If you are living with the baby's father,
discuss how you will share your new joint responsibility.
Know ahead of time about child care, even if you'll only
need it to go shopping. Learn ahead of time about the
technical aspects of caring for an infant so that you
won't be overwhelmed or frightened by the responsibility.
Talk at length with the prospective father. Often men
become jealous when their wives or lovers are suddenly
giving all their time and energy to the baby instead of to
them. Have help on hand when you get home from the hospital! Think through whether or not you will want to work or
return to work. Make provisions. It is possible to minimize the most draining aspects of becoming a new mother
so that you can relax enough to enjoy your new baby and
your new life.

MIRNA

When I first had Lisa you know I was all excited when
I was about to have her. But when I had her I was
so depressed. I don't know if that is very common
but I was so depressed in the hospital--I didn't
want her with me--I felt she was safer with nurses
than with me. Before I had her, I used to go with
Fil if he would say let's go somewhere. Even if I
was cooking I would turn everything off and just
leave. But then when I came home, oh my God, I really
regretted it because I had to stay home with her. You
know, I really regretted having Lisa then and not
going out. It eventually worked out, but at first
I was really depressed.

The Mother Role

Remember the old song that goes, "M is for the many things
she gave me . . ."? They still play it on the radio once
a year when Mother's Day comes around. The song, of course,
is a tribute to mothers everywhere, an expression of the
gratitude and respect that is supposed to come naturally
from the mother-child relationship. It certainly would be
nice if all parent-child relationships were healthy and
productive. Unfortunately we have to say that we see a

tremendous amount of conflict between parents and their
children. This is not to say that we don't see joy and
love and satisfaction; it is to say that all of the
glorifying and romanticizing that we have been talking
about has robbed us of a realistic approach to childrearing and robbed our children of being raised in a
clear-thinking, common-sense way. There are literally
hundreds of books on the market that deal with raising
children. What we would like to discuss instead are some
of the issues that involve your perception of yourself
as a mother.

PRESSURES

Many so-called experts tell us how a mother either makes
or breaks her child, how her child needs her constant love
and attention. This puts us in a "no win" situation. If
we lavish all the love and affection on our children that
they imply we should, then we are guilty of being over-
protective and clutching. If we refrain from too much
lavishing of love and affection, then we are guilty of
neglect. Any woman who can wade through all this and find
the ground where she feels really comfortable about her
interactions with her child is indeed fortunate. Most
of us just feel confused and inadequate.

MARION

*Society is constantly trying to lay guilt trips on
mothers. Articles on children seem to be against
mothers, somehow. It's only a vague feeling I have,
but between the lines I always detect the accusing
finger pointing at the mother. In particular,
society seems to be constantly blaming mothers for
its shortcomings. "Imagine how frightening it must
be to a child," reads a typical pro-child article,
"to live in a world where everything is designed for
people twice his size. Imagine trying to get up
on a chair that is as high as your waist, and eating
from plates that are bigger than your head . . .,"
etcetera, etcetera. Well, first of all, these
article writers are seeing the situation from adult
eyes, and I don't believe children are petrified of
our furniture. (On the contrary, if psychologists
would only stop and look at children for a minute or
two, they'd notice how siblings are always fighting*

over who gets "the big chair," and they'd see how
Arin wants to eat his cereal with the soup ladle!)
Sitting on big chairs up to your waist seems weird
only after you're used to sitting on chairs up to
your knees--a situation which doesn't apply to
children. Anyway, when I read articles like this,
articles which tend to pity children and make them
passive, I sense, once again, the accusing finger
pointing at none other than Mother. It's just a
feeling. . . . I can't really prove it. . . . Cer-
tainly the article doesn't state that it's blaming
the mother. Nevertheless, after reading it, I always
wind up thinking indignantly, "So? It's not my fault."

In addition to the conflicting messages that abound in
popular childrearing literature, we find that the child-
centered value system that pervades this literature is
particularly damaging to the low-income or minority woman.
Due to the survival dynamics that are prevalent within the
low-income family, those women have been less inclined to
adopt that child-centered attitude. The low-income woman
has been more likely to insist that her chidren see her
as a separate person. Often her children more readily
accept the fact that their mother works since they know
that the well-being of the family unit depends on her
income-producing capabilities as well as those of the father.
Popular childrearing literature could make low-income women
feel guilty about their approach to raising children. We
feel that women who have adopted the child-centered approach
could learn much from the more realistic ways that low-
income women have dealt with their children, and we encourage low-income women to maintain the value system that
they have found works best for them. We all need to think
about raising children who can deal with their parents'
emotions, and who can experience all those emotions themselves as well.

We find that the nuclear family contributes to the difficulties women encounter as mothers. In other cultures, in
past generations, and even today to some extent within our
minority cultures, the extended family exists or did exist
as the framework for childrearing. By extended family we
mean a family consisting of members other than just the
biological parents and their offspring. Often these families include grandparents or other relatives. We see these
families as providing a somewhat more healthy environment
because child care responsibilities can be shared. Since
there are more people, whatever unhealthy or negative

behavior patterns exist are more likely to be spread out
with less impact on each individual family member. The
emotional well-being of each member does not rely so
completely on each other member. As a result, the extended
family can be a more positive experience for those within
it, particularly the children. With some of the burden
taken off the mother, she may be able to feel less ex-
asperated by her children and enjoy them more. With other
adults to relate to, the children may feel less ordered
around and less bored.

HARRIET

*There were bad times in having several young children
around because my husband traveled when they were
young. It was boring and the money wasn't coming
in too fast. You couldn't just have sitters, where
today if you want to go shopping in a shopping center
you take your child along and take a little cart and
you stick the kid in the cart and you can have a
great day out by yourself. You couldn't do that
then—they didn't have that kind of shopping center
and you didn't get out. And, for a long while, I
didn't have a car I could use, and it makes a
difference when you are stuck in with three little
children in the winter months. It is awful.
That I remember as being grim. When summertime
came and they could be outside and I could go outside, that was fun.*

For those within the nuclear family, life can be intensely
pressured and stressful. We are not saying that no one
can be happy within the nuclear family. We want to point
out the limitations that it imposes as a way of understanding how to offset some of its negative effects. Even
the best of people with the best of intentions can feel
trapped within that setup, and we hope to be able to make
some suggestions about how to cope.

One of the common dilemmas that we see is the inability of
everyone within the nuclear family to get their needs met.
It seems as if someone must always be sacrificing her
needs to someone else's needs. A mother who works not
so much for money, but rather for her own satisfaction,
may have to send her children to a babysitter they don't
like. She tries to find another sitter and can't. She
is then faced with the dilemma of sacrificing her well-being

by staying home, or sacrificing her children's well-being
by leaving them with a babysitter they don't like. Either
way, someone loses. Which choice she will make varies from
woman to woman. We have found some interesting differences
along lines of class and race. We find that middle-class
mothers tend to be more passive and self-sacrificing. On
the other hand, they have had the time and space to develop more equal relationships with their children. The low-
income mother is likely to take a more hard-line position,
since she has less choice about whether she works or not.

In addition to the competition that family members are
forced into, there are other power struggles going on.
Children, for example, are basically powerless within the
nuclear setup, and as a result much of the parent-child
relationship is filled with conflict around the child's
need to be assertive and the parent's need to control.
Sibling rivalry is caused by the child's need for parental
approval within the nuclear family. How successfully a
child gets his or her needs met depends not on what action
he or she takes, but on what action his or her parents take.
Little Johnny, therefore, is investing large amounts of
energy into getting his parents' approval. To the extent
that he does that at the expense of his sister, Kathy, is
often relevant to the extent of sibling rivalry that goes
on. Johnny and Kathy are placed in an adversary position
from the beginning by the need to compete for parental
approval. As Johnny gets older, the rebellion that char-
acterizes his adolescent years is not only an effort to
establish his own identity; it also represents the first
taste of power that he acquires. It is only natural that
he indulges in overkill.

The nuclear family also serves to reinforce and lock in
women's dependence on men. By relegating many women to
the home front, the family ensures that they will turn
primarily, if not solely, to their men for their economic
and emotional survival. The existence of children reinforces this by further ensuring that women will invest most
of their time and energy in the home.

Staying together "for the sake of the children" is another
manifestation of the nuclear family that we consider basically unhealthy. People often mistakenly believe that a
"broken home" is automatically bad for children. It is our
feeling that all family members are better off going
through the pain of a separation than they are if two
people stay together who shouldn't. A divorce *can* be

handled in a creative, nontraumatizing manner. (See our first book, *Women in Transition*.) Much greater damage to children and adults can occur from living in an unhappy home, the inevitable result of an unhappy marriage.

Another of our criticisms of the nuclear family is that it perpetuates and reinforces sex-role stereotyping. If the mother and father are living in the traditional male-female patterns--dominance and submission, division of labor according to sex, with assumptions that boys are supposed to be strong and girls are supposed to be weak-- then the children will undoubtedly grow up with these negative and unhealthy patterns themselves. Even for those who try to do it differently it is quite a struggle. The dynamics of the nuclear family are such that, as with marriage, it becomes exceedingly difficult not to buy the value system that comes with the institution, so acute is the pressure to conform.

MARYANNE

If I had a daughter I would not raise her differently from my sons. Absolutely not. When I was a little girl, there were a lot of things I did and afterward I was told little girls don't do that. I missed out on a lot of fun. I always had the worry that my mom was going to say, "Your dress is dirty, Maryanne." But my brothers could run outside in their suits, and if they fell down she would say, "Isn't that just like a boy?" But if I didn't sit right, I wasn't like a girl, I was like a slob. I wasn't even considered a boy, I was an in-between nothing. I think if I had a daughter she would have the advantages and disadvantages equally.

IDENTITY PROBLEMS

Do you live for your kids? To some of you that may seem like a silly question. To others it may be right on the mark. We have found at Women in Transition that many, many women have been led to believe that in order to be a good mother one has to be all-sacrificing, totally devoted to her children.

What are some of the patterns that develop when a woman tries to find her identity solely through motherhood?

Often, she finds that she can become enslaved by the constant demands of children, and often children can begin to
feel that their mother exists solely to meet their needs.
As a result, many mothers find themselves falling into a
martyr role, as they begin to exist more and more for their
children rather than for themselves. Instead of trying
to find ways to minimize the self-sacrificing, many mothers
see it as a necessary part of motherhood and spend a good
deal of time complaining about it. Much criticism has
been made of the "martyr" mother, but very little has been
said about the way that the prevailing societal views create
the syndrome. In the first place, women are told that they
should fulfill themselves through motherhood--that they
should be willing to give their all. Those mothers who do
give their all can end up feeling resentful because of the
inherent unfairness of such a requirement, especially if
they feel that their children are not appreciative enough
of all the sacrificing they've done. And usually the
children aren't all that appreciative since they've been
taught that it's mother's "job" to sacrifice. Instead of
the gratitude and respect that they were led to believe
would be the result, they find that their children have
taken them for granted and have been unable to treat them
with the consideration they need. Naturally they feel
cheated.

Connected to this pattern is the "nagging mother," the
mother who lives vicariously through her children. Since
the world around her will measure a mother's worth not by
what she accomplishes in the world as an individual but
by how well her children behave or "turn out," some mothers
tend to become too wrapped up in the lives of their
children. That happens because they believe that the more
they can control and direct the lives of their children,
the greater the chances are that the children will meet
society's expectations. The more "successful" they have
been with their kids, they feel, the more approval they
as mothers will receive from those around them. Many
mothers feel that if their children don't turn out "well,"
they are failures as parents and consequently as people.
In addition, many mothers live through their children
because they don't have lives of their own. That is
clearly one of the more negative results of women defining
themselves solely through motherhood and wifehood. The
father who has a successful career can feel better about the
fruits of his years of labor even if he's not too happy
with the way his kids are. He can still feel good about
himself and his accomplishments. The mother who has

nothing but motherhood is much more dependent on her
children's being what she wants them to be. That is why
it is usually the mother, not the father, who is a "nag."

The "clutching mother," the mother who cannot let go of
her children, is another product of the motherhood
conditioning process. If she had been given another
identity to hold on to, perhaps she would find it easier
to let go of her "mother" one.

Changing the Goals

Motherhood has been so sanctified that many women, both
middle-class and low-income, feel guilty about wanting
a life of their own or going out to work. Guilt is a
major factor operating in the motherhood syndrome.

Our society has created artificial and unrealistic expectations that no woman can really live up to. That
creates a feeling of insecurity that allows a mother to be
controlled by accusations or insinuations, either her own
or someone else's, that she isn't doing enough, isn't
caring enough, isn't trying enough. Many women have a
nagging feeling that says, "You can never be a good enough
mother."

In fact, the "perfect mother" ideal is an impossible and
useless goal. The nuclear family and sex-role stereotyping have placed an unfair amount of responsibility on
the shoulders of the mother. With greater sharing of
child care responsibilities, women would be substantially
freed from the day-to-day drudgery of child care. Yes,
we did say *drudgery*. It is time that we as women declare
openly that there are aspects of the childrearing experience that are boring and frustrating. We have been
silent for too long. We need to realize that expressing
our negative feelings about children does not make us
criminals or unloving people, but that we are entitled
to the feelings of resentment and entrapment that motherhood produces. Talking about these feelings does not mean
that we don't love our children or find great happiness
in raising them. It simply means that we want to be able
to express the frustration that arises naturally from the
day-to-day grind without feeling guilty. There is little
that is fulfilling about wiping a runny nose. There are

times when we feel boxed in by the existence of our
children; there are times when we may even feel that we
wish we hadn't had children. It is *all right* to have
those feelings. *All* mothers have them. Of course, "good
mothers" would never go so far as to tell anyone. They
would feel much too ashamed and guilty. Well, we feel
that mothers, and all women for that matter, have been
feeling too guilty for too long. We **have** been controlled
by our guilt, and we have denied ourselves because of it.

MARION

*DON'T GIVE IN TO MOTHERGUILT. I can't emphasize
it enough. Don't simply "admit your feelings," like
a lot of the books say, and then let it go at that.
Admitting the problem is always a big step, but it
is only the first step. Take the other steps, too.
Be stubborn. Even if your heart isn't in it, do all
those little things that are guaranteed to make
child care easier, and to make you feel guiltier.
No matter how much it hurts, hire babysitters, let
your preschooler visit friends without you, let the
baby cry at night (under most circumstances), lock
yourself in a room to read, out of your children's
sight and therefore out of their minds. Repeat:
Be stubborn. Force yourself. I had to, during Elle's
first six months or so. It took me a long time to
get over the feeling that I belonged with her all
the time, that I should go to her every time she
cried (even if my going to her didn't stop her
crying), that when she cried it was my fault. It
took me a long time. But I really <u>really</u> believed
that it was better for both of us <u>not to</u> be considered as one. I really <u>really</u> wanted us independent of each other, and therefore free to love
each other. So I forced myself. I forced myself,
until I found I no longer had to. What began as a
conscious decision became subconscious as well.*

*I'm advising you to do the same. Be stubborn, until
you get the hang of it.*

What does all this mean? How can one cope with an institution that tends to lock people rigidly into artificial role-
playing and unhealthy power struggles? Since women are
likely to suffer the most from the demands of motherhood,
the demands of the husband, and the self-sacrificing servant

role they are assigned, we focus here on some concrete
suggestions for you as a mother on how to minimize the
negative aspects of the family situation.

First, and most important, is the necessity for an identity
of your own. Many of you may already be moving in that
direction and perhaps you are reading this chapter for help.
For others such a suggestion may seem inappropriate. After
all, for a mother to insist on getting her own needs met
is to go against what we have been told is the nature of
motherhood. We are not saying that as a mother you should
ignore your children's needs and focus solely on your
own. We are saying that self-sacrifice never benefits
anyone in the long run, and it is in the best interests
of all family members when the mother insists on her own
personhood. We do not mean to suggest that you rush right
out and fill your life with all kinds of activities or
job or career. You may already be working outside the
home, and we address ourselves to the particular problems
of the working mother a little later in the chapter.
The important thing is for each woman to begin to think
about herself as a person separate from her children, with
separate needs and goals. For some of you that may be
difficult to begin to do. Encouraged to think of yourself
last and to do most of the giving in the family situation,
you may encounter two main obstacles as you move to establish your independence. The first is guilt, the second is
resistance--guilt on your own part and resistance from the
other family members. As we have mentioned earlier,
mother guilt can be one of the deadliest forces working
against you. To establish your own independence, whether
through a job or not, can upset those around you who want
to maintain the status quo. If it turns out that you'll
be wanting family members to take on more household responsibilities, it is possible that you will spend many
anxious moments asking yourself whether or not you're
doing the right thing. Even though you may have come to
the conclusion that there is no reason why everyone in the
family should expect you to meet their every need, it is
another thing altogether to convince them of the validity
of your position. And it is another thing altogether to
stick to your convictions if you start to feel guilty and
once your children, if they're older, or husband start
to balk. Now we are not suggesting that all children or
all husbands will be unfair and refuse to support you.
We do think, however, that it will be difficult for them
in many ways even if they recognize the fairness of your
position. Your children probably will not feel that they

stand to gain much from taking on increased household tasks,
for example, so there may not be a whole lot of initiative
on their part. If you have very young children, we suggest that you begin at an early stage to instill respect
for your separateness. If they have not yet learned that
Mommy is supposed to exist to meet their needs, they will
be more likely to accept your attempts to create a healthier
dynamic within the household.

We should mention again a few differences along the lines
of class and race that we have found in mother-child relationships. Since there is often no choice in the low-
income family about whether or not the mother works, the
children *must* contribute their share to running the household, cooking the meals, getting the chores done. If you
are a low-income woman, you know that you have no choice
about requiring your children to contribute, and we hope
you feel positive and secure in taking this position.
In addition, we reinforce your right to demand respect
from your household. Middle-class women, we find, tend to
be more permissive in this area. Some of that probably
stems from the child-centered approach to childrearing that
we mentioned earlier. We are not advocating the other
extreme of a reactionary dictatorship which cancels out
a child's humanity, either. What we advocate is a middle-
ground position that recognizes your child's humanity but
also insists upon your own rights to separateness and a
life of your own.

MARTHA

*Part of the reason that my children are not a burden
now is that I determined I no longer had time to be
their maid, that I no longer wished to be Supermom.
That was not preparing them for what I wanted them
to be prepared for. I don't want them growing up to
feel as if they have to get married to have someone
take care of them. So we went from my being Supermom
to my being: You Will Be Independent and You Will
Love It! There still is some resistance, but on the
other hand, as I found joy in my own independence,
they are finding joy in their independence. They
realize it partially because we talk about it and
partially because it feels good to do things for
yourself. It also feels good to carry that a little
bit further--I'll not only do it for myself but I'll
sometimes do it for you. And share with you.*

And that's working out fairly naturally. There still is resistance, particularly with my oldest, who is used to this lovely life, complete with mother who provided everything for him that could be provided. But he is such a down-to-earth child that I have been able to sit down and talk with him and do some comparison with other families and children, both fatherless and intact (for lack of a better word) families, and have found a real peer respect for where he's at and what he does, which I think helps also. Oh, does he grumble to friends and to Grandma over some of the things that he has to do, but on the other hand he is just really proud. Also, because I let him do some things that are beyond his years, because in some ways he's beyond his years, he has some privileges that nobody else he knows has. But he's earned them, he deserves them, and as long as he's ready for them, I'm not going to wait until he's a certain age for him to be able to do something.

It seems that one of the built-in aspects of motherhood is that you're always on call. We strongly urge you to find ways to minimize this aspect of childrearing. It can be extremely draining and exhausting and contributes to that feeling of being unable to relax. For many, relaxation comes only when the children are in bed and asleep, and even then there's always the possibility that you will be needed during the night. One of the ways that this can be dealt with is by involving other adults as much as possible in the lives of your children. Child-free friends or relations--in fact, anyone who comes along that you can trust--can help take some of the burden off your shoulders, not only through help with child care, but also by providing other adult input into the general childrearing process.

Another area of concern is the quality of the time spent with your children. Many mothers feel that they have to "play" with their children or spend large amounts of time with them in order to meet the motherhood requirements. We think that it's important to do things with your children that you enjoy. If you have no desire or time to "play" with them, don't worry about it. What counts is that you and your children feel good being together. Your children don't stand to gain if you're doing something with them just because you think you should.

Many mothers today are beginning to question the traditional ways that children are socialized along sex-role
lines. Those mothers are exploring alternative ways to
raise their children. Usually the emphasis is on trying to
instill gentleness and tenderness as well as strength and
aggressiveness in their sons, and on instilling strength
and self-confidence instead of dependency and weakness in
their daughters. We enthusiastically support such efforts.
We urge all mothers to find ways to avoid reinforcing sex-
role stereotyping in their children. This is not always
easy, since your children will be flooded constantly at
school, in the street, and through television with the
traditional notions of what being male or female means.
We encourage you to find ways to offset this conditioning.
Children should be told that a lot of what they learn
through traditional means does not reflect accurately either
the "nature" or the role of women. History, for example,
does not inform children that there have been many women
rulers, inventors, and writers. Children's textbooks
portray girls and women as more passive, weaker, and dumber
than boys and men. Women are almost always shown in traditional women's work--cooking, cleaning, teaching, nursing--
all "service" jobs. Those portrayals reinforce the concept
that women were created to serve others. Through their
peers, children learn that only boys are supposed to play
baseball or football--that it is important for boys to
develop their bodies, but not for girls. Girls are devalued
along with things feminine. Boys consider it insulting to
be called feminine or to be accused of any behavior that
does not reinforce their "masculinity."

Through television, girls learn that their futures are
already set out for them: wifehood and motherhood. Boys,
however, have all kinds of options open to them. Children
learn that girls are "inferior" to boys and boys learn
that they are supposed to enjoy "dominating" girls.

All of this leads to the kinds of attitudes and thinking
that make it necessary for books like this to be written.
Unless parents start to break through traditional sex-role
stereotyping, equal relationships between men and women will
be difficult indeed to develop.

We need to begin talking about the unfairness of a system
that relegates women to a child care role and gives all
the "important" work to men. We aren't saying that childrearing isn't important; what we are saying is that women
have been told on the one hand how important childrearing is,

while on the other have found that the status of mothers
can be very low indeed. If society really considered
childrearing as important as all that, then men would be
doing it also and on an equal basis with women. After all,
it takes two to make a child; why is it always assumed
that the woman should shoulder the responsibility? The
father, too, should be encouraged to take an equal share
in the raising of his children. He should be encouraged
to nurture and love his children as well. The artificial
division of roles within the family is in many ways as
unfair to men as it is to women. Being locked into the
breadwinner role often denies fathers the opportunity to
be with their children, really to participate in the
childrearing process. Unaccustomed to thinking of themselves in a caretaker role, fathers often feel uncomfortable caring for children, especially when they're small.
Often, they have to wait until the child is older to be
able to relate. Having been raised with the notion that
others exist to meet their needs, men often have a hard
time when called upon to meet the needs of others, especially children. Many men avoid adjusting to parenthood
by leaving it all up to the woman. Everyone loses in this
kind of situation, including the father. In addition,
having been trained to be unemotional has left many men
out of touch with their feelings and unable to extend
themselves emotionally to others, including children.

JUNE

*I can get confused sometimes--Is this the right
thing to do? Am I being too easy with my children?
Am I being too strict? I question myself an awful
lot about that. My husband is more sure of himself.
I worry more, which is natural for a woman, about
the children's feelings: Do they need this at a
certain time? Maybe that will upset them too much.
I think women being more emotional and more sensitive
than men do think of these things more.*

*I've had more of the responsibility of raising the
children. And there are things that I don't think
their father even realizes have happened. Since the
time they were born we went through years when he
did work a lot at second jobs and wasn't home at
night and weekends, so I guess I really have had
most of the responsibility.*

We think that women should encourage fathers to participate
as much as possible in the rearing of their children. That
may be difficult to accomplish if your husband got married with the traditional assumptions about child care.
Rather than confronting him angrily with this issue, we
suggest that you point out the advantages that he will
experience through greater intimacy with his children.

Sometimes women find that they have difficulty letting go
enough to give the father a chance to develop his own
skills. For women who have found most of their fulfillment
through mothering, it can be quite difficult. We urge all
mothers, though, to encourage the father to develop his
own style, make his own mistakes, and go his own way. It
is also important to break unconscious habits such as
always being the one who gets up in the middle of the
night. Ideally, the father will recognize the unfairness
of the traditional arrangement and will cooperate in an
effort to create a more equitable childrearing process.

JUNE

*I was saying that sometimes I'm a little resentful
of my husband, because when I'm standing out here
washing dishes at night, and the kids are busy doing
homework, and the oldest one is babysitting or has
somewhere else to go, I feel that it would be nice
if my husband came out and said, Can I help you with
the dishes? But he won't, because he feels if you
have four children they should be responsible enough
to come out and do the dishes themselves. They
don't, they get away as quick as they can, and I
haven't put enough force behind them myself to get
them to do these things. But then I feel, well,
he's their father. Maybe he should be the one to
tell them to go out and help your mother. But it
would be nice if he came out himself and said he'd
help me.*

Fathers' sharing the load more equally is one step toward
the creation of a more just response to the demands of
parenthood. There are other contributing factors to the
problems of motherhood: the confines of the nuclear family,
inadequate child care, lack of sound economic supports--
particularly for the low-income woman--and the lack of a
feeling of community experienced by the majority of people
in this country. Under other, more ideal, conditions, it

is clear that the motherhood experience would be far more
positive. Without doubt, it has its times of love, joy,
fulfillment, and inspiration. But as it now stands,
motherhood can also lock a woman into a caretaker, servant
role which can often leave her wondering whatever happened
to the best years of her life. Yes, it is rewarding. Yes,
it is fulfilling. But great struggles are necessary to
maximize the positives and minimize the negatives. We're
not saying that it can't be done. What we are saying is
that as long as women continue to be defined primarily by
motherhood and wifehood, and as long as there are not
enough adequate supports for the childrearing process,
women will find that all that love and sacrifice and hard
work will not automatically bring them the rewards that
they deserve.

Mothers are people. For many of them, child care is not
the be-all and end-all of their existence. They want
something more, they have the right to something more.
Motherhood must ultimately be restructured to ensure that
right.

International Women's Day Poem

For my mother:

1.
We came together
as strangers
reading movements
of our oppressions
and rebirths
singing one song
          for all

2.
In celebration
We look into
      the lives of women
and see spring coming
but we also
know how and why we struggle
because
We're women

                    Robin Christie
                    March 1975

The Mother Who Works outside the Home

For years people have been arguing about whether or not
mothers who work outside the home are harming their children by not staying at home and being full-time mothers.
We wish that we could see this controversy laid to rest.
Study after study has demonstrated that not only are the
children of working mothers relatively unscathed; in many
ways they are better off than the children of mothers who
work only in the home. Greater and earlier independence is
found in the children of mothers who don't stay at home.
Often these children have healthier relationships with
their mothers. Children who have their mothers home with
them all day do not necessarily benefit unless their mothers
are truly happy and content in that situation. Although
many mothers who stay at home are content with the arrangement, many are not. Children do not benefit from having
their mothers around all day if the mothers are not really
happy to be there and are consequently resentful, bored,
or frustrated. Some full-time mothers take those negative
feelings out on their children.

AURELIA

*I think if a woman's working, her husband should come
in and help with the housework, if they have children.
If they don't have no children, the wife's place is
to keep the house up. But if they have children like
we had, my husband and I, my husband on his day off
put the clothes on the line, he would pull them up
and iron them. He did his part of the work. He
would bathe my children, comb their hair. If I had
to leave early, he would plait their hair. Yes, I
think that a man, if he has children and the wife is
trying to help him accumulate some, he should split
down even with her. But if she don't have no children,
the man don't have no right doing her housework
because it's her place to do the work. She don't have
nothing to occupy her. Idle hands gets in mischief.
Why does the man have to come in and work when there's
no children there? What is she going to be doing?
Sittin' down?*

Although greater support and reinforcement exist today for
the working mother than twenty or thirty years ago, women
still tend to feel guilty about not being home with their

children on a full-time basis. Even if her children are
well cared for while she is away from home, a mother will
always manage to find something to worry about, part of
that feeling of always being "on call" that we have talked
about. It is important, of course, not to let that guilt
control you if you are working. It can lead only to
frustration and resentment. Remember, quality is of much
greater importance in the mother-child relationship than
the actual amount of time spent together. Your responsibility is to see to it that your children are cared for
to the best of your ability. Having fulfilled that obligation, you should do your best not to let guilt feelings
interfere with the rest of your life. Sometimes this is
not easy, especially if your immediate family is not too
overjoyed with the fact that you work outside the home.
Other relatives, neighbors, and friends can be critical
as well. Once again, do not let them make you feel as if
you are not meeting the motherhood requirements. You *are*
doing the best that you can. Nobody ever criticizes
fathers for going out to work. Women should have the same
opportunities as men to define themselves by work outside
as well as inside the home. Of course, the majority of
women who have jobs do so out of necessity. Even then,
though, the mother-guilt factor still exists. We hope
the support that you may get from other women who think
and live in a similar way will offset the negative feedback
you may get elsewhere. Some mothers who don't work outside
the home feel threatened by those who do and may not be
particularly supportive. If the support that you need
does not now exist, we again urge you to seek it out.

As we have already mentioned, lack of adequate child care
is always a problem, not only because mothers need time off
from mothering, but because children benefit from spending
time with their peers, learning and playing and becoming
independent in a pleasant environment. The problem becomes
even more acute if you are the only adult responsible for
the children most of the time. In the past few years
there has been much interest on the part of federal and
state governments in developing day care facilities for
women on welfare. The rationale behind this interest
involves "breaking the poverty cycle" from generation to
generation by training welfare recipients into "desirable"
occupations (usually traditional, low-paying "women's"
jobs like clerks, hairdressers, household workers).
These programs, however, serve the state better than they
serve the women and children who use them. They are often

designed primarily to get women off welfare and are not
intended to help either the children or their mothers.

There has been less interest in establishing day care for
middle-class mothers, who are still encouraged to believe
that mothers and young children belong at home together.
There is a small but growing force exerted by the women's
movement which is demanding that low-cost child care be
available to all who need it. Finally, a number of corporations are also investigating the profit-making possibilities of day care and may soon sponsor some on a
profit-making basis.

The result is a hodgepodge of options, most of which are
inadequate, overcrowded, or expensive. Women who can
afford the price of private child care (babysitters,
housekeepers, nursery schools, women in the neighborhood
who take in children) often, although not always, can
work out something satisfactory. Women with the time and
energy can participate in parent cooperatives where they
can have some say over the kind of experience their children are having. Sometimes it is possible to find a warm,
loving person who enjoys being with children or a child
care center that provides a meaningful social or educational
experience.

Women who can't afford private child care often have to
leave their children with people they don't trust because
they simply don't have other options. You may not like
how your grandmother gets along with your son, but since
she's free and close, you feel you can't complain.

It is important that we have a say in what happens at the
child care centers our children attend. But with the
pressures of work and taking care of our houses and children, that is out of the question for most of us. You may
find yourself in conflict with the atmosphere and teaching
methods at the center where your child goes but feel too
tired and powerless to do anything about it. Perhaps you
will be able to make arrangements elsewhere, or work with
other parents who feel the way you do to change things.

There is still some federal money available to start day
care centers for the children of low-income families. One-
quarter of this money must be raised through state, county,
or local sources, including contributions from government,
businesses, industry, large institutions like universities

and hospitals, and private foundations and individuals.
If there is no Head Start or other free day care program
in your neighborhood, you might find other mothers who
would be interested in meeting with local agencies and
organizations to get funds for a day care center in your
area. Organizations like the Urban League, the N.A.A.C.P.,
child welfare agencies, or local day care councils may
provide help in writing proposals and finding local
sources of money.

Women in several housing projects have started their own
day care programs in the meeting rooms and playgrounds
of the projects. Social service workers, community
action programs, or the local Office of Economic Opportunity might be able to help you organize your own
day care center or get funds for a full-scale developmental program with professional teachers.

Finally, don't overlook colleges and universities that
may be in your neighborhood as excellent locations for
day care centers. Often women's groups on campus are
pushing to get day care for students and community people
provided by the university. This is an especially good
idea if the university has departments of education,
early childhood development, or psychology. Locate
the women's group on campus and find out if they are
working on university-supported day care.

You may have already considered many of the following
child care options, but we want to list them here to
cover any you may have overlooked.

1.   Relatives: paid or in exchange for housing and food;
     not paid, in your home or theirs
2.   Unrelated babysitters: paid or in exchange for
     housing and food; not paid, in your home or theirs
3.   Employee day care at work
4.   Nursery schools or play groups
5.   Exchange babysitting or co-ops
6.   After school: neighbors, friends, activities at
     school or elsewhere
7.   Federally funded programs such as Head Start

You can find out about most of these through word of
mouth (such as through friends, neighbors, doctors,
hairdressers) or advertisements (newspaper, bulletin boards
at church, food co-ops, local stores).

Other options you might want to think of include:

1. Working at home (tutoring, typing, telephone sales,
    babysitting, dressmaking)
2. Taking your child to work with you
3. Sharing your home with another family, single woman,
    student, or older person in exchange for babysitting
4. A live-in housekeeper if you can afford one

Bear in mind that day care centers can be good places to
seek out other mothers with outside jobs for help and
support. Whatever your day care hassles, it is important
to maintain the attitude that you can work out some sort
of satisfactory arrangements. It may take some time and
a lot of work. You may have to change your child care
arrangements more often than you would like, but it is
important not to feel overwhelmed by the lack of adequate
resources. (Recent economic cutbacks have made day care
even less available.) Remember that most women who want
to work or who have to work eventually find a way.

A FEW STATISTICS ABOUT WORKING WOMEN AND THEIR CHILDREN

(March 1974 figures)

- About 13.6 million mothers with children under 18 years
  of age were in the labor force, of whom 5.1 million had
  children under 6 years.
- The labor force participation rate of mothers (with
  children under 18) was slightly higher than that for
  all women. In 1940 the rate for mothers was less than
  one-third as high as for all women.
- More than half of the mothers of children 6 to 17 years
  of age (none under 6) were in the labor force--54 per-
  cent--compared with 49 percent in 1967. Nearly 37
  percent of the mothers of children under 6 were in the
  labor force, compared with 29 percent in 1967.
- Children of working mothers numbered 26.8 million. Of
  these children, 20.7 million were 6 to 17 years of age
  and 6.1 million were under the age of 6.
- Among the children of working mothers, 4.6 million had
  mothers who were heads of families; 913,000 of these
  children were under the age of 6.
- Day care is still vitally needed. The estimated number
  of licensed day care slots is only 1 million for the

6.1 million children of working mothers who are under the age of 6.

From the *1975 Handbook on Women Workers*, Women's Bureau, U.S. Department of Labor

Another problem common to almost all mothers working outside the home is the exhaustion that is the inevitable result of coming home from one job only to face another. It can be compounded by the fact that usually working mothers have to save their sick days for their children's sick days, so they can't take an occasional day off when they're feeling extra tired. If your job is not a particularly fulfilling one, the exhaustion can be intensified because there are no exciting rewards to reap as the result of your hard work. We don't have many concrete suggestions regarding ways to get out of feeling tired all the time. Of course, if the children are older than three or four, they should be expected to contribute to the work of running the house. If you are married or living with someone, he or she should help out as much as possible. Assuming that you don't run into too much resistance, sharing the tasks of running the household should help considerably. We have found, though, that even with help two jobs are a very heavy load, especially if you are a single mother. There just never seems to be enough time. Try to make sure that you do not burden yourself more than necessary by taking on extra responsibilities-- volunteer work, for example. Occasionally you may be able to trade off some help with friends, doing favors for each other such as cooking or babysitting. One important survival technique consists of lowering your standards of cleanliness. We are not suggesting that you go to the other extreme, but we do think that women are trained never to feel content about how clean the house is, how well the meals are cooked, how often the beds are made. If you have set high standards for yourself, it may be impossible both to work and to keep house according to your standards. We suggest that you work on letting go of some of the expectations that you have placed upon yourself. You may be surprised to find that you can accept some lowering of standards more easily than you think.

Children can be resentful of working mothers. Often that can contribute to whatever guilt you may be feeling about not being at home full-time. Children have been known to

play upon a mother's guilt feelings to try to keep her home.
If that doesn't work, sometimes they will resort to things
like getting sick in the morning. In many ways, of course,
it is understandable that children may not want their
mothers to work. Often they will feel that they are not
getting enough attention. If they are young, it may be
very difficult to get them to understand that it is necessary for you to leave them. The most important thing
in dealing with these problems is to keep a good perspective. While it is undoubtedly true that there are some
ways that your child loses out by your working, it is also
true that there are ways in which he or she gains from
the experience, as we have pointed out.

In spite of the hardships, there are many rewards for the
woman who works outside the home. These, of course, vary
in degree and scope. The rewards for the career woman can
be greater than those for the woman without credentials
or a college education. That is not to say that it is
impossible to find fulfilling work without an advanced
education. It is true, however, that the most rewarding
jobs are generally reserved for those with the most credentials. But even for women in less exciting jobs there
are advantages and benefits. Financial independence is
one. It can be a good feeling to know that you can command
a salary, even if that salary is not enough. Knowing that
you are not totally dependent on someone else for your own
or your children's survival can be very reassuring. In
addition, your own feelings of self-worth can increase as
you become more and more self-reliant. Moving out of the
home and into the work force can also provide you with a
good push toward establishing your own identity. Just
being in the outside world, making new friends and contacts,
can serve to make you less dependent emotionally as well
as economically on the home front. Working can often
serve as the impetus for developing your own interests and
activities, as well. New horizons and opportunities can
open up once you have moved away from defining yourself
totally in terms of the home. All in all, we find that for
many, many women, working outside the home can be well
worth the difficulties and obstacles.

If you are currently working and are about to have a baby,
it is important that you make realistic assessments about
how much you will be able to continue your life-style
once the baby arrives. You won't be able to do everything
you did before you became a mother. Of course, you will be
able to go back to work if you want to, but even with

adequate child care, you will feel tired, frustrated, and burdened. Be prepared. You can minimize those negatives, but it will take careful planning and arranging.

The Single Mother

Many mothers do not live within the traditional nuclear setup of one man and one woman plus their children. In fact, 13 percent of all families are now headed by women. They have to deal with an even greater sense of responsibility; there is no one to share the load with. If you are raising children alone, you may have feelings of isolation and insecurity about your ability to raise them successfully on your own. What are some of the ways that you can cope?

First of all, if the children's father is in the picture, and the amount of hostility between the two of you is under control, we suggest that you try to involve him as much as possible in the childrearing process. The concept of shared custody, where separated or divorced parents try to share child care responsibilities equally, is something that we advocate because we feel that children should not be seen as the property of one parent or the other. Shared custody allows both parents to share more equally in the responsibilities and pleasures of their children. It also provides more opportunity for the children to know both of their parents as real people. Of course, there are problems that arise from any kind of custody arrangement, particularly from the more traditional ones. Something that we call "glorification of the absent parent," for example, can be a particular problem when the mother has the children during the week. She is responsible for all of the daily aspects of their care, such as homework, chores, discipline. The child is around her during the times when she is at her worst, tired after a day's work, irritable, or out of sorts. Then comes the weekend with the father. Instead of being a drag, Daddy takes them out for a good time. Often he has more money than Mother and can buy the child presents that she can't. In effect, Daddy can become a Santa Claus in the eyes of the child. Many women feel very angry and frustrated when this occurs. If the children end up acting as though they would prefer to be with Daddy, many mothers can become extremely depressed. Sometimes children will even use that issue, if they know that their mother is feeling insecure about it,

to get their way. If you are going through some form
of that problem, we feel that it is important for you to
realize that it, too, will pass. The key is to stick
it out, maintaining your confidence in yourself, and
nine times out of ten, your children will come to recognize
the situation for what it is. Sometimes talking it out
with your children or ex-husband can help.

MARTHA

*In the beginning, when Art and I first separated, he
was Superdad. Far more so than he ever was in the
marriage. He insisted on even having it written
into the divorce documents that he was to have the
children every other Thursday from five to eight the
following morning, and every other weekend from
five on Friday to eight on Sunday night. Even if
it meant sitting in front of my house for five minutes,
at five minutes to eight, he did it. He totally
spoiled them, encouraged their dependence on him, and
this lasted for about a year. At that time he was
about to get into his third marriage, and he went
from being a constantly devoted, attentive father
who had been fostering dependence in these two
children, including constantly feeding them with
"It's because of your Mom that we can't all live
together. You know that I love you and her and want
to get back together. She is the one who wants to
do this." And it was very confusing to them. At
the same time I'm trying to foster their independence
out of necessity and because I can see the larger
implications of life.*

*So he went from seeing them constantly and fostering
their dependence on him to a total cutoff. No ex-
planations, no nothing. He just all of a sudden
didn't show up. So the first time he just didn't
show up and the children were packed and ready to go,
I called him and said, "What's happening?" And he
said I just didn't have to bother to get them ready
any more. And that was the end of the conversation.
So I had no choice but to let it go, with constant
inquiries from the children about "Why don't I get
to see my Daddy any more?" or looking at me out of
the side of their eyes like, I know you must have something to do with this. My only thing to do was to
give them love. You can't explain that your father*

doesn't want to see you any more. You can't ex-
plain that some people have a greater capacity
for love than others, you can't explain that people
change, because in those ways children just simply
don't understand. You can't hurt their hearts that
way. So I kept their time busy, the time that they
normally would have spent with him. I tried to do
something special with them, but not to the degree
that they could all of a sudden start manipulating
me because of a situation that I had no control over.
That started happening about six months ago, and we
all went through that. Now I am just a parent, I'm
not their mother, and that probably would not have
happened if Art had not decided not to see them
any more. And I consider that to be fairly positive,
not only for them because it has adjusted my thinking
in that direction. We now are such a firmly estab-
lished family unit that maybe we're overcocky or
something, but at this point it seems that there's
nothing we can't do.

Another issue that many women are unclear about is the
concern about a "lack of a male image" that is frequently
raised during discussion of female-headed households. We
feel that the thinking behind this concern makes the assumption that women are incapable of demonstrating certain
qualities to their children such as assertiveness, self-
confidence, athletic ability. Women are in fact capable of
demonstrating these qualities, and rather than worrying
about having a man around, single-parent women need to
focus more on seeing to it that their children understand
that everyone needs to develop these qualities and that
anyone, male or female, is capable of demonstrating them
to others. Of course, if there are caring and concerned men
in your life who want to spend time with your children,
then so much the better. It's just that it's important
not to let yourself feel guilty or inadequate if such is
not the case.

As a single mother, it is even more important for you to
involve other adults in the caring and rearing of your
children, since you are carrying the full load on your
shoulders. Cooperative nurseries or day care, shared
babysitting or car pools, can help you get some free time
alone. Day care and free lunches are available to the
children of low-income families at local Get Set centers
in the neighborhood, free of charge. Many churches and
community groups sponsor child care centers for young

children. Women in some neighborhoods have organized
cooperative play groups or babysitting co-ops in which
mothers take turns babysitting for their own and each
other's children.

Today more and more mothers are choosing single parenthood,
or ignoring the stigma traditionally attached to it.
Often single mothers are women who decided from the beginning that they would be raising the child alone. Even
single-parent adoption is becoming more accepted by social
welfare agencies. People are beginning to realize that
the traditional nuclear family is not necessarily the
healthiest environment for childrearing. It is important
for you to feel positive about raising your children alone
and not to let others downgrade your life-style.

Stepfamilies

If you are in a stepfamily situation, you may be feeling
insecure about a number of things--your role as a stepmother if such is the case, the role of the stepfather,
the relationship between siblings, negative attitudes
toward stepfamilies on the part of the psychiatric establishment (although single parenthood is not reinforced as
a positive life-style either).

We see many positive experiences coming from the stepfamily situation. Often, children develop new and important relationships with stepparents, relationships that
can often offset some of the negative aspects of relationships between biological parents and offspring. Although
parents and stepchildren can get into resentful and
defensive behavior patterns, these patterns are often the
result of common misconceptions about what one or the
other is feeling. Some children may resent the intrusion
of another adult into the parent-child relationship,
but once they are reassured that their relationship with
the biological parent will continue, resentment most
likely abates. In its place, warm feelings and mutual
interests may develop. Some stepparents may be insecure
and unsure about the stepparent role. Sometimes the natural
parent may be ambivalent about the role of the stepparent.
These issues need to be talked out and resolved so that
unproductive behavior patterns don't develop.

PETER

I fell in love with Judy and thought that she was
the greatest thing I had ever encountered, and her
four kids were simply a part of her. I didn't have
that much experience with a family myself (I had no
father after age four), so in some way I was looking
for the kind of family and father-son relationship
that I had not had myself. In some funny way going
in as a stepfather gave me the best of both worlds.
If the kids encountered problems and messed up, they
weren't my kids, it wasn't my fault. If the kids
did well, that was the result of my wonderful influence on them.

I think initially there was an unreal expectation on
both our parts that I could move in and be the complete father, bind up all the wounds, be "better"
than the previous father. That was the only image
I had, that of being the perfect father, because
there really is no clear image of the stepparent in
our culture. What images there are are very superficial and unreal, and they're almost at two poles--
the cruel, uncaring stepmother or stepfather and
the isn't-it-wonderful, the hero or heroine, healer
of all wounds. Between those two poles there isn't
much to go on.

One day about two or three years after we were married we were visiting some friends and somehow the
crisis of the week with the kids came up for discussion. I found myself for the first time saying,
"You know, I'm not their father, I'm only their
stepfather." That meant two things. On the one
hand, I was admitting that my feelings weren't as
strong and as powerful. I was neither as upset by
their problems and failures nor as overjoyed at
their successes as a real parent, nor could I really
be expected to have as powerful an influence on
steering them in the so-called right direction. I'm
sure that was only a point on a continuum, but in
my own consciousness from that day on I felt more
at ease in my stepparent role, no longer chastising
myself with guilt over any misstep that any of the
children made.

Stepfamilies give members the opportunity to extend trust
and love to children and adults who are not related by blood.

Children's lives are often enriched by the broader exposure to the various life-styles that the stepfamily provides; they often develop new nonnuclear concepts of "family." Children within the stepfamily situation frequently find it productive to be able to turn to other adults for emotional support and guidance. Sometimes the natural parents are threatened by this; often they are secure enough within themselves and in their own relationship with their children to encourage it.

We are not saying that the role of the stepparent should be exactly the same as the role of the natural parent. How much the stepparent becomes involved depends on the individual situation and on how the children feel. Often the stepparent can play an auxiliary role that is different from, but no less important than, that of the natural parent.

We are all familiar with the "evil stepmother" image portrayed in children's fairy tales. Sometimes the negative connotations applied to stepparents, stepmothers in particular, can contribute to whatever insecurity a stepparent may be feeling about his or her role. Children also can react toward stepparents with negative assumptions and expectations. Stepfamily members need to work consciously toward adopting a positive mind-set with positive expectations.

By the same token, there are assumptions that stepsiblings will naturally resent and compete with each other. Our experience has been, however, that many lifelong friendships are formed through these relationships. Often, the existence of stepfamilies cuts down on sibling rivalry. When children are encouraged to broaden their perspectives about family life, they can often react enthusiastically to new children coming to live with them.

In general, we see the stepfamily experience as a plus rather than a minus. We do not believe that family members must be biologically related to provide love, affection, and emotional support for one another. The stepfamily chapter in the book *The Courage to Divorce* by Susan Gettleman and Janet Markowitz provides an excellent perspective on the stepfamily and the relationships within it.

Economics

How do economic factors affect the motherhood experience?
We have talked briefly about some of the class and race
differences we have observed. If you live anywhere near
the welfare eligibility level, you face all of the pressures that we have been discussing along with the additional problems posed by poverty or racial discrimination.
The welfare system, for example, serves to humiliate and
degrade women who are forced to turn to the state for
financial assistance. It also encourages the breakup of
the low-income family by refusing to provide assistance
to the "intact" family. This encourages low-income men
to abandon their families so that they will become eligible
for assistance. It was only recently that the United
States Supreme Court decided that midnight raids to see
if there was a man in the house were illegal invasions of
a welfare mother's privacy.

Poverty is one of the most destructive forces that a
woman can encounter as she raises her children. Faced
with a constant struggle for survival, many low-income
women feel overwhelmed by the seemingly insurmountable
obstacles facing them. The poor mother finds that she
does not even have the luxury of *thinking* about her own
needs, much less going about trying to get them met. The
heartbreak experienced by the poor mother as she finds
herself unable to meet her children's needs is devastating.
Often she must sit back and watch while her children
attend inferior schools and experience discrimination in
the outside world. In addition, women in the ghetto must
contend with the second-class status to which their
neighborhoods have been relegated. Many low-income women
find themselves competing with the pull of the streets
in their day-to-day dealings with their children. No
matter how hard she may try, for example, there is no way
to protect her children from street violence. The lack of
adequate birth control and abortion information often
makes women into very young mothers. With children locking
them into the home, there is not much that can be done to
increase education or to obtain job skills. The lack of
adequate day care is even more pronounced in low-income
communities.

If you are a low-income woman, we urge you to think about
whatever resources may be available that you could use to

your advantage. Employment counseling, economic development programs, new housing for low-income people, special
welfare supplements for pregnant or nursing women, and
medical clinics do exist. Information about what's available is often slow in getting around. Often caseworkers
know about different programs but won't volunteer the
information. You have to ask. (Our first book has an
extensive section on dealing with the welfare system.)
Awareness of the forces working against you can make you
feel powerless--powerless to combat the pressures of the
outside world, and sometimes powerless to prevent those
pressures from seriously affecting your relationship with
your children. Part of the psychological effect of poverty
is to create such a state of mental as well as physical
powerlessness that poor people will think that any attempt
to change things is hopeless and that they are doomed before
they start. This ensures that poor people will stay "in
their place," and it serves to maintain the status quo.
While it is too true that you face a steep uphill battle,
it is also true that you *can* make it. It takes strength
and perseverance, but it *is* possible to obtain some degree
of control over your life. Poverty does not have to be a
perpetual state. Learning how to manipulate the system is
a skill that will serve you well in your struggles to
become financially independent. Although being poor is
dehumanizing in many ways, the skills that you have acquired as a poor woman struggling to survive are just as
valuable and useful as the education acquired by many
middle-income people. We feel that low-income women have
always been strong and independent in many ways, and we
believe that your strength is your greatest asset as you
move to obtain a satisfying and rewarding life. There are
ways to overcome the devastating effects of being poor and
female in a world that is controlled by rich men. An
essential ingredient of this process is the development of
a positive self-image, the ability to believe truly in
yourself as a person. This is not easy for many middle-
class women; it is even more difficult for low-income
women. It is important that you think about the ways that
you have been taught *not* to value yourself and begin to
reverse the process.

In dealing with your children you may feel incredibly
trapped. Crowded living conditions, lack of child care,
lack of decent medical care can make you feel that you
want to give up. It is important at those times that you
try not to take too much of it out on the children, a

natural reaction to the stress and tension created by
trying to survive. If possible, try to find some sort of
child care. Even if it's just for a few hours a week,
the breathing space can make a big difference. If you are
working, you have already been through this struggle. If
not, make it a priority. Once you have managed to create
enough space for yourself really to think and plan, you
can begin to think about other directions in which you can
move, whether that would mean going back to school, getting
a job, or just picking out some sort of activity that you
really want to do. Even if you think that you are not
in a position to do something that would benefit only you,
such as learning to play the guitar, or signing up for a
dance, carpentry, yoga, or self-defense class, see if you
can't do it anyway. We think it may be helpful if you can
feel that you don't *always* have to be sacrificing your
own emotional needs because of the need to survive.
Once again, your children must respect your right to your
own time and space and it may be beneficial if you can
structure quiet, private times for them as well. There
are many, many forces working against you. We do not mean
to make a bunch of smart suggestions that fail to take
into account the immense struggle you face, but we know
that it is possible for you and your children to find
happiness.

Child Abuse

The abuse of children by their mothers stems from the
fact that motherhood can become a prison for many women.
The feelings of being trapped that come when you have
responsibility for children can lead some women to take
their anger and frustration out on the children. One
reason is the lack of any other target. Society as a
whole is responsible for locking women into the caretaker
role. It is impossible to vent one's anger and resentment
on the total society, so the most likely target becomes
the child who seems to be standing between the mother and
freedom. In reality, it's lack of paternal responsibility,
the nuclear family, the welfare system, and inadequate
child care that deny the woman her freedom. That is not
always easy to see, however, and sometimes the child suffers
for what society has done. There are many groups working
to help parents who think they are or may be abusing

their children. If you have fears along these lines, we
urge you to give one of these groups a call. They will be
understanding and sympathetic and will deal with you on
a confidential basis. See our Resources list.

Women As Support

For all mothers there is one resource that we haven't
mentioned yet. This is because we wanted to give it a
special section of its own, we consider it so important.
We strongly urge you as a mother to begin to turn to other
mothers for help and support during the childrearing
process. We urge this for *all* women--middle-class, low-
income, whatever. We feel that by sharing your frustrations, your anger, your joys and rewards, your survival
techniques, and your ways of coping, you will be infinitely
more capable of meeting the challenge. You are involved in
a process that has been so filled with myth, so rigidly
and unfairly defined and structured, that it is almost
impossible to feel really secure about what you're doing
and why. That applies whether you are a housewife, a
career woman, or a welfare mother struggling to survive.
Women are beginning to see that they have been given the
short end of the stick when it comes to parenting, and by
talking and sharing with each other, mothers can find much
of the encouragement and reinforcement they need to make
it. This can happen in groups structured to deal with
the various issues confronting mothers, or it can happen
more informally. The important thing is that women experience the love and concern of others who are in similar
life situations.

MARTHA

*Would I have children again? That's a hard one. I
really like my children as people. They're an unbelievable joy in my life, they're a marvelous
stabilizer in my life, they are also an unbelievable
responsibility, and I realize that as many skills as
I have now or the potential for, I will not be able
to really pursue them until my children are grown,
and that's a real heavy one for me. I'm talking about
career kinds of things and other things that are
important to me, like being able to travel. I would*

be one of those people who would up and move to
another country, join the Peace Corps for three years
if I were on my own, because I would truly enjoy
something like that. I don't require that much myself, but your whole life-style changes when you have
children. You have to provide certain things. You
can't move every year or two. The implications are
incredible. But when I weigh those kinds of things
that are important to me against what I have with
my children, it's a toss-up. I'm glad I'm not faced
with that choice. I have a friend who did give up
her children, and having lived with them for so many
years, she did become the very successful, competent
businesswoman, but she's also pathetically morose
periodically about being torn from them. I guess you
have to make the choice, either never to be a mother
or to be a mother, at some point in your life earlier
than most of us even want to think about it, because
it's not anything you can change. If you get it
into your head that you're going to be a mother, you
will always feel empty if you don't have children,
and if you determine at an early enough age that
you're never going to have them, you might be able to
fill your life up in other ways easily and naturally.
For me I guess I have no choice at this point. I do
know that when I talk with younger women, I encourage
them not to have children until their late twenties,
no matter what. This is a real hard thing for me to
even think about, maybe because I don't have that
choice. But I'm happy and satisfied now with having
them.

In the End

We've provided a lot of information so far in this chapter
which deals with the negative aspects of motherhood and how
you can cope. But motherhood isn't all coping. Motherhood
is loving as well. Motherhood isn't just putting up with
kids; it's enjoying them, too. Sharing good times and
experiences, feeling you are doing well by your kids, hug-
ging and kissing and squeezing, are all part of motherhood,
and although we do feel that motherhood's been overromanticized we see no greater love anywhere than the love experienced through the mother-child relationship. We have

seen many mothers sacrifice beyond belief for their children, not only because it's their obligation but also because they experience joy and happiness with their children.

What we hope we've done in this chapter is provide you with enough insight and information to enable you to find as much pleasure as possible in the motherhood experience. That pleasure, we feel, will come not through denial of your own identity, but through the creation of it. Fulfillment within motherhood will come not through self-sacrifice but through your own fulfillment as an individual and the sharing of that individuality with your children. Only when you have a self of your own will you be able to give that self to others, including your children. Your children stand only to gain. Whether you are a working mother, a single mother, or a mother living in a nuclear family, you are first and foremost a *person*. You are *not* a person who is first and foremost a mother. You were created to live your life, fulfill your potential, and develop your sense of self, not just to make babies.

If you are child-free and *choose* to include motherhood, you are free to do so not because society dictates that you must, but because you can think it over and make a carefully considered decision. If you choose not to do so, we reinforce your right to that choice. You are not abnormal or acting contrary to nature.

Motherhood should be, first, a matter of choice, and second, an institution that does not stifle and confine those women within it.

There are no easy answers or solutions. The struggles that you face are enough to overwhelm almost anyone. But we believe that you are capable of demanding the right to your own person, and we believe that you are capable of becoming that person whether you are child-free or a mother. Life is *not* one long sacrifice. Life is a celebration. We have the right to enjoy it.

Airport Farewell

The phallus nose
Of the silver bird
Greedily mounts the air,
Gobbling up the clouds.

Inside its delicate ribs
You sit,
Gazing across space,
Thoughts anchored to the ground.

My nose presses the cold glass
Of the concrete and steel nest.
My fingers still tingle
From our farewell embrace.

Like a fresh death,
Implosions of memories
Burst into my head
And drip from my eyes.

The infant you
Has been wrenched from my heart
By a young soldier in uniform.
My job is done.

Judith Bondy Brigham
September 9, 1975
For Doug

EVA SHADEROWFSKY

EMIKO TONOOKA

IAN M. HARRIS

EMIKO TONOOKA

FEMINIST RESOURCES   MIRIAM GALPER

6

SARAH

Being single once made me feel like an oddity, a nonmember of the world of "normals," forever an outsider. Now I feel that staying single has had a lot to do with growing whole, with being me and free to be with and without a person. Intellectually I haven't figured a reason why legal marriage makes sense (except possibly for children and in the past two or three years I've grown to question that reason as more of my friends have children without legal bonds). Somehow it seems more a commitment if people are choosing from within to be together. The legalities in the entanglement seem only to fan hatred (and do little to protect financially dependent women anyway, although in some places that's changing).

But feeling O.K. about being "single" hasn't been easy. Single meant being alone with a capital <u>A</u> at times. I didn't have the filled weekends of some women, had never learned how to get men to call (and "women don't call!"). It meant not seeing and doing lots of things--movies, restaurants, places. Friends were available at times, but "being with the girls" intensified being alone/single. Anyway, our thoughts were about men and the lack of, so we were hardly really with each other.

I suppose two things made a difference for me: my desire, deeply personal, to grow and be my own person and, with the women's movement, the knowledge that I wasn't alone.

Being my own person meant expressing myself to not be a carbon copy--to feel O.K., to create strong, self-reflecting environments for myself, to have things (pots, pans, dishes, TV, stereo) for myself now and not to do without till I was married, to learn skills such as carpentry and build stuff 'cause I liked to do it, I liked being self-sufficient, liked feeling the strength in my back and arms. To be able to have sex when I wanted to, one-night stands, ongoing relationships, whatever. To be able to say <u>yes</u> and no. To have friends I liked for themselves, to go to a bar 'cause I wanted to have a drink with a friend and not 'cause I was looking for a man. To not need to look for a man.

Until about two years ago, sex meant with a man. Masturbation was something to do when no man was available or guiltily and silently after unsatisfactory sex with a man. About six years ago I tried sex with a couple and realized I wanted sex with a woman. But what's important here was the discovery that sexual need was the one thing where I remained non-self-sufficient. About two years ago I began to experience giving myself all the sexual pleasure I wanted. And I was amazed how it reduced my dependency on men as sexual partners or for sexual satisfaction. This does not change the fact that at times when I am not with a man I long for a penis inside me or at other times for arms other than my own to nurture and cuddle me, or for a warm body to press against in the middle of the night. But I don't feel deprived.

I had always valued women and had always had an easier time with women than men. The movement lifted a weight from my shoulders. I no longer felt weird and alone. I still had to become aware of and work through a lot in therapy and in my consciousness-raising group, but it felt less like moving from "mental illness to mental health" than learning and relearning. It just carried a less heavy judgment of personal inadequacy. And it gave me women. People like myself to grow with, struggle with, learn from, think with, join with, hug and share, feel warm and wanted and valued. It was like a supportive family that expects you to grow and develop and cheers and supports your efforts. This was both in contact with persons and in contact with women's writings.

244

Now my automomy, independence, self-sufficiency were also a defensive posture as well as a positive position of strength. If you can meet all your own needs then you won't get hurt or destroyed if the other person leaves, or be trapped by being too scared or ill-prepared to leave. This autonomy camouflaged a lot of dependency needs and my fear of contact and being hurt.

My process now is one of being/growing more truly alone. A basic _living_ philosophy of mine is that I want to live in a way that if I die tomorrow I can say all is O.K.-- no unfinished business, no regrets, that whatever has happened up to now is as far as I could go at this point.

I can remember when I first discovered the difference between alone and lonely. That alone is essential to being human and lonely is a transient quality to life and relationships, painful at times, real and essential to living, but transient.

I don't seem to feel _scared_ about being single. It seems to me that my life has gotten fuller and richer, that I have found people like myself, people I can share with, so I assume this will continue into the future. I have anxieties about the future, like old age, though less about being alone than about being dependent for physical care, about being senile. I have anxieties each step of the way. Forty is my next big one even though I have very positive women models who are over forty. It feels like a cutoff point for having a child (though I know rationally and given my health probably isn't). Thirty-five was my last anxious step, a midlife, top-of-the-mountain point for me (my father died that year so death was a very present part of my experience). I began to very seriously consider (again!) how I wanted to live my life.

Though I feel ready now to have an ongoing relationship and probably would want that with a man and to have a child and share childrearing, I don't feel a sense of loss projected into a manless, childless future. Again, my living feels good now. When it doesn't I'll do what I've done before: change it. That seems to have worked out for me before so I assume it will again. I don't feel trapped. I don't know what happens with increased age, less mobility, a slowing down. Maybe change just goes slower, less broad and drastic. I know sharp, engaged, growing seventy-five-year-olds--so why not me, too? I do want now to explore all I can. I want and have worked at nonsexual friendships with men and sexual relationships with women. I've found that with age I have less desire to "sleep around." I want relationships with things and people that matter. I don't want to force people and things into some notion of what I might need. I want to be able to live with the loneliness and anxiety if that's most honest. But it's hard.

I can remember when I began acknowledging I'd rather stay home alone than have dinner with someone I didn't like. It's like I didn't want to do that to myself.

Or the time I sent a man home 'cause I realized he was not able to really be there as a person with me and I didn't want to wake up with him and start my day with the awful letdown of being alone with someone there. Alone I could wake up feeling good about it being my day.

And the ways I've hung on to men pretending to myself it was really O.K. with them/us. Thank God they often recognized the disparities and split.

I like the fact I am older. Young is rough. Experience helps with living. Having gone through different experiences--a love affair, depression, moving to a new place, lonely periods, new work, new people--more than once really helps. The ups and downs are easier. Not so high and low--but richer. You know what to expect and can be more aware, open to your experience and your environment. You can make decisions to do something different or just hang on or whatever. It's your experience now. Not something happening to you. If it's terribly painful you feel the pain and know it will pass. I've grown to appreciate and value time.

I also feel that I'm changing in the way I relate sexually. At one time it was important to be able to sleep with someone comfortably, immediately, if I wanted. If I was turned on, I could go to bed with someone I'd just met. Recently I've wanted to let things develop more slowly, to know better if I really like that person, how I like the person. It's a lot harder to get to know a person once you've slept together (used to think it was easier!). It's like having zoomed in for a close-up shot and not having any idea what the surrounding environment is like. Probably not impossible, but harder.

246

6 / Is That All There Is? Some Alternatives to Marriage

What Is an Alternative Life-Style?

Many men and women are finding, sometimes by choice and sometimes not, that traditional marriage isn't for them. Some find they can't live up to what is expected of them in a marriage relationship; the rules about faithfulness and devotion in marriage seem to have been set up by someone who had no notion of how to cope with the stresses of modern American life. Others have learned the hard way that saying, "I love you," to another person does not automatically guarantee the security and happiness they want for the rest of their lives. The search for meaningful ways to live is going on everywhere, and many people are summoning the courage to say that what is right for them falls outside the mainstream.

It is important at the outset to stress that people from different backgrounds have different opinions about what is considered a normal way to live, and therefore about what constitutes an unusual or alternative life-style. Marriage, for example, may be considered more necessary in white middle-class cultures than in black communities. While living together may be a new phenomenon for white middle-class people, many black people have been forced into that life-style for generations for different reasons.

In the days of slavery blacks were not permitted to marry. Today, marriage for many black people is not economically feasible. With high unemployment and job discrimination disproportionately affecting blacks, many low-income black men feel as if they will never be in a position to support a family adequately. Traditionally social agencies and institutions have not considered it a priority to keep black families together, which is another holdover from slavery when black families were divided up and sold to the highest bidder. The welfare system, for example, discourages marriage among low-income people by requiring that there be no man around in order for a woman and children to receive support. Until recently, when federally supported legal services were created to serve low-income communities, many people were unable to afford divorce and simply chose to live together with a new partner. Although many black people value traditional marriage and the nuclear or extended family, for some--especially low-income blacks--the middle-class ideal of a long-term, stable, married family life has become impossible.

The high divorce rate in this country indicates that people's expectations for happiness in marriage are not being met. If the marriage is not fulfilling those expectations, one or both spouses often want to find something they consider better. Recent studies show that many couples who do stay married are not satisfied with the traditional restrictions on sexual diversity. These studies have shown that three out of five men and two out of five women have engaged in extramarital sex at some time during their marriages.* What people are doing and what they are admitting to, however, are two different things since public opinion, particularly in white middle-class culture, about "adulterers" is still very negative.

The result is that individuals who deviate from the so-called norm may feel guilty, sinful, or depraved. Again, however, research contradicts the popular notion that anyone who is involved in extramarital sex is neurotic. Studies have shown that while some extramarital affairs occur because the partners are immature or destructive to each other, many affairs are enriching additions to the marriage relationship and are carried on with the knowledge and approval of the other spouse.

*Larry L. Constantine and Joan M. Constantine, *Group Marriage*, New York: Collier Books, 1973.

So much for the studies; this isn't a chapter about
research--it's a chapter about real people and their
real lives. But the studies do point out that what some
of us may have experienced on a small scale, either
in our own lives or among our friends, is in fact happening on a wider scale. Being single, "open marriage,"
marriage contracts, common-law marriage, living-together
arrangements, and communal living are all ways in which
people are stepping outside the boundaries of traditional
marriage to build love and support into their lives without compromising their need for individual growth and
freedom. We believe none of those alternatives is sick
or wrong; they represent an honest attempt to replace or
make adjustments in an institution that is increasingly
disappointing to many people. While some of these
life-styles may seem far-fetched to you, our feeling is
that they are in some ways logical extensions of the
ideas explored in Chapter 2 about becoming a separate
person within an intimate relationship.

We see those alternatives stretching along a continuum.
On the one end is traditional marriage, where the partners
are monogamous (emotionally and sexually faithful to each
other) and stay fairly close to the usual roles of "husband"
and "wife." At the other end is group marriage, where
generally the participants relate emotionally and sexually
to everyone else in the marriage. Between those extremes
is a variety of ways in which people are learning to know
themselves and know others. Because of the pressure
in this country to get married and to live up to some
idealized notion of what marriage should be, there are
few supports for people who are trying to work out something different. We feel the energy and courage it takes
to face the risks involved in exploring these alternatives
are to be admired.

Some special issues for women need to be raised when discussing alternatives to marriage. Women more often than
men are moved to work on a "bad" marriage since a woman's
identity is much more closely tied to the success or
failure of the relationship. While some alternatives to
marriage can be potentially liberating for the women involved, there are many pitfalls. The "sexual revolution"
of the 1960s, which originated mainly in white middle-
class communities but spilled over into the black community to some extent, brought incredible conflict for many
women. Women who formerly were criticized for daring to

have sex outside marriage then found themselves being
called frigid if they would not sleep with anyone and
everyone. Yet women are usually stuck with the unpleasant
consequences of sexual freedom, such as unwanted pregnancies and venereal diseases, and are often subtly criticized
for the so-called promiscuity that is supposed to make us
"liberated" and sexy. Swinging, mate-swapping, and extramarital affairs are often initiated by husbands who are
interested in having sexual variety in their lives; their
wives, who are more dependent on the marriage economically
and emotionally, go along with the idea so they won't
appear "square" and so they can hold on to what little
they may have. Women who live communally or in group marriages may find they are still the ones providing major
nurture and emotional support to the "family," which is
now a large group instead of a small one. And, women who
choose not to marry, and live either alone or with a man,
may find themselves subject to unexpected economic and
social pressures.

DEAR CHARLOTTE,

This past year has been a crazy-wonderful one that I
would never give up and would never want to go through
again. I'm emerging slowly, slowly as a real person,
but the process has been extremely painful. I am
still not divorced. I must be on the never-never
plan or something. In a way the separation of a year
has served its purpose. As positive as I was last
year than I wanted a divorce, I am thankful (I ration-
alize) for the time to be even more positive. I certainly will be glad when it is all over, though. One
good thing that has happened is that Massachusetts
has passed a no-fault divorce law which my lawyer
assures me can now apply to my case. Cruel and
abusive treatment just isn't Rudy's style.

I am still seeing Brian but not nearly on the hot and
heavy schedule I was last spring. He's a marvelous
person and I love him dearly, but in no way is
either of us ready for any kind of commitment to
anyone. I have been out with several men--mostly
losers in one way or another, but a couple of them
were really fun and have become good friends. How
nice to have male "friends."

Mostly in the last year I have gone to school. I'm on the never-never plan there, too. After a year of playing about five instruments I have decided to become strictly a keyboard player and a 90 percent harpsichord player.

I've had some not-so-pleasant experiences this year, too. For one thing, I hate being poor. What a drag! Aside from poverty, I've also been beaten up by someone I went out with. (The police have their eye on him.) He has since called and said he thought I owed it to "us" to try going out again. What an idiot. (He was extraordinarily upset because I didn't want a close, meaningful relationship with him. Of course not, he's partially deranged. But he didn't want to take no for an answer.) Thankfully I was not hurt--only frightened. (What would my mother think of that!)

My other unpleasant experience was, in the end, a rather positive one. I had to have my IUD removed in October due to recurrent infections. Thanks to insufficient counseling on the part of my doctor, I became pregnant the first month on the pill and had to have an abortion. The clinic where I went was marvelous and gave me such a positive image of myself that I have had no guilt feelings--something someone with my background of self-imposed religion most likely would have. (And what would my mother think of _that_!) I also got the most complete counseling I've ever had on birth control.

I'm sure I could think of many more soap-opera epi-sodes to relate, but you now have, for better or for worse, some idea of what's been happening to me--not all good, but oh so much better than the previous nine years.

Love,

Nancy

Choosing not to live in a traditional marriage arrangement does not guarantee that a woman will be less oppressed. The struggle for independence must continue, although the conditions may be somewhat more favorable. Alternative arrangements of any sort--extramarital affairs, communal living, living together--can offer many possibilities to

women, and on the whole we feel there are more positives
than negatives for women who are expanding on the traditional notion of marriage. Alternative life-styles offer
opportunities for financial and emotional independence
which can help women get out from under the restrictive
aspects of traditional marriage. When a woman no longer
defines herself solely or primarily in terms of another
person but begins to think about her own needs and gets
important feedback about herself from people other than
her husband, new possibilities can open up. Building close
friendships, getting in touch with one's sexuality, learning to take risks, giving up old patterns of arguing and
manipulation--all are benefits reported by women who are
choosing to develop different ways of relating to others.

We offer the same words of caution we did when we discussed
becoming a separate person within an intimate relationship.
It can be frightening and unsettling to yourself and those
around you when you begin to make changes. You need to
decide for yourself the pace and extent of those changes.
Remember that society at large as well as those close to
you have a vested interest in the status quo. Predictions
of doom abound in professional journals and popular literature. To evaluate what you are doing, rely on the feedback of like-minded friends and those feminists and sympathetic men who are writing about alternative life-styles.

It is also important to remember that change is usually
frightening, especially change which goes directly against
what most of us were taught to believe. The alternatives
may seem bewildering to you; they certainly seem bewildering
to us at times. It is usually easier to play it safe and
stick to the traditional rules, but since many of us have
found that doing so is impossible for us, we have to push
on. We know that the choices presented here can't speak
to everyone's situation, but what we are trying to do is
give a general idea of the different ways some people
have found to live their lives. The key thing when you
open yourself up to new options is to focus on your own
development. You will need constantly to define and redefine yourself as a person and think through how you want
to live. You can choose different options for particular
times in your life, not out of desperation but because
something makes sense at the time. Many people have found
that after a period of intense experimentation, such as
having an affair or living communally, they go through a
calmer period relating only to their spouse or living alone
again. This doesn't mean that the experiment failed but

that it was a time of growth and change, followed by a time
of integrating the new experiences. The important things
are to move at your own pace, try to keep in touch with
what your own needs are, and do what feels right, not
what others (or your own inner voices) tell you you should
do. A broad range of human experiences and emotions
is available to you if you choose to open yourself up to
them.

Being Single

In a society where being part of a couple is generally
considered the most natural, mentally healthy way to live,
43 million single people--almost half the adult population--
have a few problems on their hands if they want to feel
positive about their life-style. The prejudices abound.
People who have never married or lived with someone on a
long-term basis are often considered irresponsible; marriage is thought to be the true indication of adulthood
and stability, and anyone who has never married is suspect.
Separated and divorced people are sometimes regarded as
failures at relationships; the assumption is made that
they are in a brief phase between marriages, not by choice
but because they have not yet found another mate. Widowed
people are usually pitied, and it is often assumed that
they are either between pairings (if younger) or past the
age of intimate relationships and therefore sexually and
socially discounted (if older).

In the last five years, according to recently released
census figures, the number of 25- to 34-year-olds who have
never married rose 50 percent. In the same five years
the number of people in the 25-to-54 age group who have
separated or divorced and not remarried shot up 30 percent.

In addition, since 1970 the number of families headed by
women has increased by 30 percent, and the number of
children living with only one parent has consequently
increased by one-third.

The increase in unmarried Americans shows no signs of
leveling out. Today, 40 percent of all women between the
ages of 20 and 24--the median age for first marriage--are

single; in 1960, it was 28 percent. And 60 percent of
all men in that age group, 7 percent more than in 1960,
have not married.

Even the normally conservative United States Census Bureau
speculates that there may be a trend toward most people
remaining single throughout their entire lives.

Chicago Tribune, February 9, 1976, p. 11.

Single people face considerable economic and social discrimination. They pay as much as 20 percent more in income tax as married couples. Most employers believe
that in general married people are more reliable and stable
than single people, although married women are sometimes
passed over in hiring and promotion with the excuse that
they could get pregnant and leave. Credit and insurance
policies are less favorable to singles, especially single
women. Single people sometimes have difficulty buying
homes, and landlords are often reluctant to rent to single
people because of their supposed reputation for late
hours and wild parties. Discrimination in housing against
nonmarried women with children is widely documented. It
is often even difficult to find food packaged in individual
portions. While there are some citizens' groups challenging this discrimination (see Bibliography), progress
is slow.

SARAH

*I find it less difficult to be a single person in
a couples society now than I used to. But sometimes
I do a lot of stuff that's oriented toward couples.
In the group of people that I'm friends with, a lot
of them are single, some are married or with people,
but I could be the only single person or the only
noncoupled person with this group of friends and
not feel single. I can invite two couples over for
dinner and not feel that I'm single. So I think
that says something about the openness of the relationships. The reality of my world is pretty
narrow, since I'm not out there dealing with suburban America. I imagine if I lived in a small town
or a smaller area, I might feel being single more
again.*

I took a long trip alone to Canada for five weeks driving once, and I forgot I was a single woman traveling alone until people pointed it out to me, like gas station attendants who wanted to keep me warm at night. I did that trip alone because I wanted to, and I forgot it was strange until people noticed it was strange. So sometimes it feels strange to be single, but mostly it doesn't.

Single women face a particularly difficult time socially, depending on their age and their community. Single men are usually, although not always, invited to social events because an extra man is often welcomed, but single women are sometimes seen as a social liability. That can be because married women are worried about possible competition, or because the host finds it depressing to have an unmarried woman around, assuming that she must be unhappy about her situation and desperate to find a man. Not-married men and women are pressured by their friends and families to marry ("Why isn't a nice guy [girl] like you married?"), but women usually get it worse. A single man still retains some glamorous bachelor aura (although there can be insinuations that he is homosexual or has some character flaw that makes him unmarriageable), but not-married or unattached women are pitied or mistrusted. The availability of social gatherings where single women can feel comfortable varies according to locality. Single women in larger cities usually fare better than rural or suburban women simply because there are greater numbers of single people. Single women everywhere have difficulty finding places they can comfortably go alone and people they enjoy being with. In low-income and black communities, where women are often raised to be independent and not depend on men to take care of them, being single is not so terrifying. There is more acceptance of single women and more opportunities to socialize as a single person.

Will you make your own music
    learn to dance,
    listen to Bessie Smith
without your indulgent smile?
        Tolerance is no virtue--
It is a criminal impulse tightened into silence.
    I am pulled into that silent space
                        and disappear.
    Where else could I go. Alone.

                        Judith Toplin

Despite the bad press, however, singlehood for women has some definite advantages. As we pointed out in Chapter 2, research indicates that unmarried women enjoy better mental and physical health than married women--despite the pressures on them to marry and the common assumption that "spinsterhood" is barren and unfulfilling. It appears that a good number of women have been able to resist the propaganda about how they are supposed to find happiness and have sought it in other ways. Sociologists have found that single women who choose to remain that way usually do so because they are upwardly mobile and more aggressive than a marriageable woman is supposed to be. In the past, and among some mental health professionals today, this "maladjustment" was considered a problem to be cured. Fortunately, support is slowly growing to reinforce the choice of single women who are more interested in developing their own interests or jobs than they are in putting their energies into a marriage or long-term intimate relationship. Many single women feel that a bad marriage is worse than none at all, and while being single may not be a permanent choice for them, it is satsifying at this point in their lives.

SARAH

I remember in my early twenties I went around looking at relationships, and I thought, "Ah, these people seem to have a happy marriage," and then they'd get divorced. I got progressively disillusioned. I also had a strong value of wanting to know who I am, and wanting to do what I want to do--a very strong need to live a meaningful life. It sounds really trite now, but I supposed having attempted suicide and discovering that what I was doing was not meaningful made a difference in how I lived. I didn't want to live if it was going to be shitty. There was no reason to live a life that didn't feel good. I might as well be dead.

There are a number of books, articles, and organizations, some of which are listed in the Bibliography, that support being single. They stress the positive aspects of being single and explore ways to increase your enjoyment and positive self-image. Some provide techniques for dealing with loneliness--usually the biggest problem for single people. It is important to view these writings and organizations critically. Some promote a healthy understanding of singlehood, but others reinforce the idea that being single is a poor second choice and push suggestions and opportunities for meeting a potential mate. Clubs, singles organizations, and singles bars especially vary from place to place. Some are meat markets where people go to size each other up. Others provide a supportive place to meet other single people. Those which are especially for single parents can provide a structure for sharing good times with each other and their children. Trust your judgment about whether any of these activities meet your needs for companionship and fun, or whether what you are doing is basically degrading and you are justifying it in the hopes of having a good time and possibly meeting someone special.

Remember that singlehood can be either a lifetime choice for you or a temporary period when you can take stock of yourself and your situation. The negative aspects of being single, of course, are well known. Being single can mean that there is no one person in your life who cares about you and can share the good and the bad times. Along with that can come feelings of intense loneliness. Socially you may feel disoriented, excluded from some gatherings and not totally welcome at others. You may find it difficult to socialize with married friends, either because of their discomfort or your own. Your needs for physical closeness and sex may get met irregularly, if at all. The responsibility for managing your life and the lives of your children, if you have any, may weigh heavily on your shoulders. You may feel terribly alone when you are sick or think about growing older by yourself.

On the positive side, being alone can allow you the freedom to make choices about your life without having to take someone else's needs into account. You can come and go as you please, not have to apologize for your quirky habits, and develop close friendships or sexual relationships without worrying about your partner's jealousy. You can have privacy and a chance to get to know yourself better. You can be open to new experiences and travel without feeling tied down or guilty.

> ROBERTA
>
> I don't want to live communally, and I resent pressure on me to do so just because I am a single parent and it would make sense financially, child-care-wise,

etcetera. It would not make sense psychologically to me. I have worked hard, for the past two years especially, to become a separate person. Part of that for me means living alone with my child, in my own private space. Sure it's lonely sometimes, but it's also gratifying to enjoy that aloneness and look forward to coming home because it's all mine, I can do in it and with it as I please. I don't want to share my living quarters, I don't want to work on relationships with people I'd be living with. I want to work on me, enjoying eating when I want to, watching TV as I choose (except for my sons's tastes), and enjoying living by myself, for the first time in my life. And I'm thirty-five years old.

If you are a single woman with children, the positives and negatives may be somewhat different. Your feelings of loneliness can be increased when you have to take care of a sick child by yourself or make decisions alone about your children's schooling or discipline. You may also feel overwhelmed by all the responsibility you have and may have difficulty going out or traveling. You probably feel tied down and guilty more often than not. On the other hand, it may be a big relief to you not to have to share parenting with your children's father on a full-time basis. Many couples who have conflicting ideas about raising children find it much easier to be parents when they can do so separately, no longer being forced to reach agreement with each other on a daily basis. Even when the children's father is very active in their lives, many women say they are able to develop a special relationship with their children which is more honest and enjoyable than when they were living with the father.

Being single does not necessarily mean living alone. Many single women have solved some of their financial, social, and child care problems by living with family or friends. (We will talk about group living later in the chapter.) Being single also does not necessarily mean being lonely. Some women we know have over the years had a number of deeply meaningful relationships with women and men, some sexual and some nonsexual. They find that their needs for intimacy and sharing are being met, as are their needs for support and companionship, and they aren't dependent on one source for all of this support. This has required, however, that they lay to rest the deeply ingrained idea that there is one true love for every woman and her life work is to find him. They have learned to share different parts of

themselves with different friends. Some women never get
over the need for one important person in their lives but
make peace with the idea that this might not happen. The
notion of one true love has been deeply ingrained in most
of us, but many women have learned not to let that need
control them; they still have hope that such intimacy may
be theirs one day but are living their lives in ways which
are meaningful for them now.

SARAH

*One reason I'm not feeling pressured to hook up with
a man is because I can pleasure myself sexually.
I have a vibrator which I use. I don't feel I have
to be with someone just to get sexual gratification.*

These women do not belittle the difficulties of being
single, especially the loneliness and the sexual complexity
which often accompany having a number of intimate friends.
But being clear about their own needs for individuality at
this time has enabled them to experiment with relationships
in a way which has helped them to grow, sometimes pleasur-
ably and sometimes painfully. The key to whether you feel
trapped by your aloneness or enriched by it has to do with
how you feel about yourself. If you are putting all your
energies into finding a partner, whether for the first
time or to replace a relationship that did not work out,
you can enter into a relationship that can be very destructive. If you have been hurt by someone in the past, you
may be terrified of being rejected again and not open to
experiencing different kinds of relationships. If you
feel good about yourself as a person, you will be more
likely to get your needs met, either through a variety
of relationships or through a newly developing primary one.
You may find yourself less defensive about falling in love
again. If you are heterosexual, you may have less and less
need for male approval, although you may enjoy spending
time with men. You may find your needs for companionship,
affection, and love being met by other women and have
little desire to be with men. If you are an older woman
who feels that developing an intimate relationship is not
a realistic option, you may find enjoyment and stimulation
in your community, work, and family. Whatever your situation, the important thing is to focus on how your strengths
and resources can be developed to bring out the positive
aspects of being single. The books and organizations listed
in the Bibliography can give further guidelines. We hope

that someday the choice to be single will be as well accepted and reinforced as the choice to marry.

"Open Marriage"

Open marriage is a term that has become popular since the publication of a best-selling book with that title by Nena O'Neill and George O'Neill. For most people who have not read the book, the term *open marriage* has come to mean sexual freedom within marriage. That, however, is only a small part of what the book is about. Basically the authors write about couples giving each other the freedom and encouragement to grow as individuals in the marriage relationship, whatever form it takes. For some couples that includes sexual freedom, but for most it doesn't. Some people who now have what are considered highly un-orthodox interpersonal and living arrangements began by experimenting in small ways in their relationships. They found those experiments to be so positive that they con-tinued to open themselves up to new options.

One of the reasons that many couples are opening their marriages is that trying to live by the traditional rules of married life is not working for them. They feel that expectations of what a husband is supposed to be and what a wife is supposed to be are unrealistic. They reject the idea that marriage partners own each other, that they should spend a majority of their free time to-gether, and avoid outside friendships unless socializing is done in couples. They feel restricted by the notion that in order to preserve togetherness the partners must deny large parts of themselves, such as outside interests and friends; they know that married people can be lonely, too. They find that maintaining strict divisions between "masculine" and "feminine" activities and behavior is limiting. Some couples find sexual fidelity to be re-strictive also. These couples don't feel that partners should know absolutely every detail about each other's lives. They don't expect to get continual love and securi-ty from the other partner, and they don't assume that the relationship will last forever.

ANNA

Don and I have been basically monogamous. I think this will change. I have no idea when, but I think we're both feeling expansive. We're both up for the thrill and excitement of new relationships and new sexual relationships. I don't know why it hasn't happened up until now. It isn't as if we've had some taboo about it. It's just never occurred to me. I never really wanted the extra responsibility of other relationships, and I don't think he did either. But now, partly because of counseling, and because I'm on my own with a job and feel less accountable to him in some ways, I'm sure it will happen. The only thing that scares me is that I feel pretty committed to Don right now, and I know from past experiences before marriage that it's very hard to find people who can be casual or who can maintain a certain perspective on sexual relationships. That was always a problem I had in college. The prospect I don't look forward to is getting involved with people who are going to put a lot more demands on me than I'm willing to meet. When I met Don I was really ready to stop moving around. Sexually and physically, I wanted to stay in one place. I had had enough of sexual exploration at that time. Five years have passed and I'm ready for it again!

Couples who are experimenting with new forms of marriage or intimate relationships usually begin by looking at the traditional roles that husbands and wives are expected to play and then reassess what each partner wants to do and realistically can do. Thus, some couples share household tasks and child care responsibilities. They sometimes try to work this out so that each can earn an income, although it is usually difficult because part-time and flexible jobs are hard to find and women's position in the labor market is disadvantaged.

Other couples emphasize developing outside interests and friends. The partners realize they cannot have mutual interests in every area of life (for example, Susan is very interested in art but Jerry could care less; she is bored by discussions of gardening, which is his big passion). They encourage each other to form friendships with others who share those interests. They don't always socialize as couples but go to parties, activities, or meetings alone rather than force the partner to attend. They also try to allow each other time alone to sort out feelings and simply be alone. They have learned that arguing with each other does not mean that the relationship is falling apart, and they work on ways to "fight fair."

Some couples push those concepts of openness several steps further and permit each other sexual openness. However, couples who allow each other that freedom are not always experimental in other areas, such as economic self-sufficiency for the woman, or the man's taking responsibility for chores and child care. Sexual openness takes a variety of forms: one or both partners' having an extramarital affair (sometimes known, sometimes unknown to the other partner); swinging or mate-swapping (unfortunately still referred to in some circles as "wife-swapping"); group sexual encounters; multilateral or group marriage, in which three or more people consider themselves all married to each other.

DIANA

I think part of the motive for my affair was boredom. We were married six, seven years, and we were a Nice Couple the way we were supposed to be. It was a bit boring. I'm certainly much less bored now. We were very close to a couple who we had a sexual weekend with, switching and swapping. The guy couldn't have an erection with me, and that weekend I never felt close to my husband. I felt he wasn't there for me. He was pursuing something more than I was. There was something devastating to me about the whole experience, and I think I had to get back some self-esteem.

Also, I was in graduate school, and I was being intellectually stimulated. The man I had the affair with was the big mahoff there; he was dynamic, he was older, he was the idol of women. But people were also put off by him, me included. I started having a friendship with him and I asked him why he was teaching there, was it because of all the pretty young women? I don't think too many people say that to him directly. We started having this fairly open, direct relationship that was very intense. He appreciated me, he recognized me as a bright, attractive woman, which I wasn't feeling at the time. I really had the sense I could do something for him

*in the immediate interaction. With Mike, although
I know I'm important to him, when you live with
somebody you don't have all these neat encounters all
the time.*

As we said, all of these options represent different
couples' efforts to make their marriages more satisfying
for them. There is no right or wrong way to do this and
no set of guidelines to follow. Each couple needs to
work it out for themselves, and because there are so few
external supports for that kind of experimentation, couples
often find themselves feeling isolated and freaky and
wondering if they aren't destroying themselves and their
marriages. Here we want to make a few observations from
our own experiences and our work at Women in Transition.
The Bibliography lists books and articles that explore
these alternatives in more depth.

EQUALITY

The partners who announce to each other, in an honest
attempt to correct some of the previous inequalities in
their marriage, "Okay, from today on we are going to be
equal," are in for some surprises. For one thing, there
is considerable conditioning to be overcome. In *The
Future of Marriage* Jessie Bernard says:

> All right then. Take a young woman who has been
> trained for feminine dependencies, who wants to
> "look up" to the man she marries. Put her at a
> disadvantage in the labor market. Then marry her to
> a man who has a slight initial advantage over her
> in age, income, and education, shored up by an
> ideology with a male bias and an institutional
> framework tilted in his favor. Denigrate her status
> further at marriage by lowering her occupation still
> more . . . [to that of a housewife]. Then expect an
> egalitarian relationship?

If you and your partner are working to equalize your relationship, it is important to understand your own background and the previous expectations you are dealing with.
You also need to assess your own resources and skills
realistically. Otherwise you may set your goals too high
and will be disappointed if you can't reach them. It is
also important to get help in doing this, from a friend,
counselor, or third-party arbitrator if needed. Those

changes are not easy to make on your own, and you can
easily get bogged down and lose sight of the issues.
Someone with less of an investment in the relationship can
help you sort out reasonable goals and a reasonable pace
for achieving them.

For another thing, forcing fifty-fifty compromises with
your partner on every issue or insisting on total role
reversal can produce much bitterness and resistance. While
you may feel that in the past you sacrificed a lot for him
and now you are entitled to your turn, pushing equality
can cause a backlash. On the other hand, it is important
to recognize what is required of your partner. He is
being asked to give up some of his privileges, and while
that does not happen easily with some men, it must happen
if you want to develop more independence.

It will be up to you to figure out on which issues to push
for equal compromise, on which you can pull back, in
which situations you think he should give more than 50
percent, and when you want to try totally reversing roles.
Learning to share responsibility so that you can both be
open to life's opportunities takes much trial and error,
much give and take.

TOGETHERNESS

We think one of the most destructive influences on relationships is the "couple front" phenomenon. That is, couples
are expected to socialize as a couple with other couples;
suspicions are aroused when one partner goes out without
the other ("Are Harry and Barbara splitting up?"); couples
feel awkward socializing with a single person. That attitude stems largely from the idea that partners possess
each other and more specifically from the idea that a wife
is the property of her husband. The prettier she is and
the more well dressed, the better it reflects on him as a
successful man and a good provider. Chapter 2 explores in
more detail the difficulties women often have in socializing
independently of their husbands, despite the fact that it is
common for men to go out without their wives. We point this
out here as a reminder that developing separate friends and
interests is one of the first relatively nonthreatening
steps a couple can take toward creating a more flexible
relationship.

SEXUALITY AND JEALOUSY

Many of us experience considerable ambivalence about our sexuality. Single, divorced, separated, and sometimes widowed women often find they are expected to be sexually available to any man who is interested, and because of their real needs for sex and for physical intimacy they find themselves in uncomfortable situations. Saying no all the time isn't the answer, either, for many women. Married women find themselves in a variety of situations. Sometimes, even after much discussion, struggle, and perhaps psychotherapy, a married woman will find that her sexual needs are not being met by her husband, and she is faced with the choice of going unsatisfied, meeting them herself, or finding a lover, all of which usually leave her feeling inadequate or guilty. Other times the husband is unsatisfied. Some women are pressured by their husbands into tolerating his affair or joining him in mate-swapping. She may have reservations about it but feels she cannot object because she fears her husband's anger or rejection. We are not saying that the responsibility for sexual problems lies solely with men; in Chapter 9 we explore some of the ways in which men's sexuality has also been distorted. But we do feel that the legacy of the double standard is still with us, and that we as women have greater difficulties in understanding our own sexuality and finding ways to get our sexual needs met.

DIANA

My husband Mike feels that everybody has jealous feelings except him. He feels like he's always been a freak, and he's always tried to do what other people do, like playing baseball, and feel what other people feel. Everybody is telling him he should be jealous because I'm having an affair, and he told me that even his psychiatrist said that most people would be jealous, but he hasn't seen it in Mike. Since I believe that his angry or jealous feelings are not accessible to him, but have to be there, it makes me not trust him. Since that whole area is inaccessible there are other areas that are inaccessible. Mike was really in a state last night. He couldn't feel what I wanted him to and he felt inadequate. I told him that there was something I got from David that he didn't give me. My motives are not pure. I feel hurt a lot by him because of his homosexual activity and I want to hurt him back sometimes. Once he started to cry and get upset, I could be nice to him. I have to have faith sometimes that we're going to make it. I think sometimes, "What am I hanging around here for? What do I get?" I don't want to turn one guy in for another, but I'd like my own space and maybe see both of them, and other people, too.

SARAH

It wasn't that I didn't feel angry at times, because I did, but I didn't feel the need after it was over to get revenge because I had been victimized, which is often kind of a pattern. So it was a very positive experience. I think that I feel that in my life there is a desire to have an ongoing relationship, but there is also a desire to get as close to people that I care about as possible and also be able to let them go, or move on if I have to, and be clear about it, so there is no unfinished business when it's over.

While in some marriages it is the woman who initiates the extramarital sexual activity, more often than not it is the husband, since he generally has more contacts outside the home and more opportunities to act on them. Also, over the years men have been encouraged to separate sex from love more than women have, so that husbands are usually more open to such activities. Women are understandably wary of sexual experimentation. Often economically and emotionally dependent on their husbands, encouraged to think that monogamy is in women's best interests, and more aware of the dedication required to maintain a home and family, many women fear they will suffer in the end, and in some cases they do.

When couples experiment sexually, the man often gets to have his cake and eat it too, as it were. If he is having an affair, he has both a wife to provide creature comforts at home and a lover for excitement. Occasionally those affairs evolve into *ménages à trois*, where the man, his wife, and his lover all live together. They often succeed because the two women involved put considerable energy into learning to live with, tolerate, respect, and care for each other. In the few situations we know of where one woman lives with two men, those relationships succeed because most of the woman's energy goes into soothing and satisfying them.

In either situation it is the women who are virtually
making a career out of love, to the exclusion of other
friends, work, or interests. The same is often true in
group marriages, where it is the women who really cement
the families together.

DIANA

*I don't think I've really let in all the things I've
been feeling about Mike's bisexuality. I've tried
really hard not to let jealous feelings in, I run
from them. I don't think that this is the way I want
to live. I would love to live this way, it's cool,
it sounds cool. We are the pacesetters, the cutting
edge, as it were. I can't stand it--I want to get
so far away from it sometimes. This is really where
it's at, ladies and gentlemen.*

One of the biggest problems in any situation that involves
extramarital sex is sexual jealousy, which often causes
marriages to break down, affairs to end, group marriages to
dissolve. Jealousy is something that women and men who
are trying to open up their marriages feel they should be
able to take in stride. Nevertheless, it remains a problem. Observers of marriage point out that jealousy usually
stems from insecurity; when a couple's love for each other
is characterized by possessiveness and dependency, the real
or imagined threat of losing a loved one causes panic in
one or the other partner. The more the partners feel secure and self-confident about themselves and the less they
depend on each other for definition and approval, the
more resources they have to cope with their loved one's
separateness, even if that involves intimacy with someone
else.

While this argument is persuasive and while we agree that
jealousy can be an unproductive emotion which arises for
less than admirable reasons, the realities of our lives
make jealousy something that is very difficult to cope
with. Most of us were raised with the notion that if you
truly love someone, you *will* be jealous; jealousy is a
proof of love. Your husband or partner is supposed to be
your property and anyone who tries to steal your property
should be fought to the bitter end. Another common belief
is that everyone has a limited amount of love to give, and
it should be for our one-and-only. For many women the
most crucial reality is that marriage is the major investment

in their lives. Threats to that marriage, especially the
threat that the husband may withdraw his love and ultimately his financial support, are terrifying. Small wonder
that many women become hysterical when their husbands announce an impending affair or one already in progress.
While we think many women are possessive of their men for
self-destructive, although understandable, reasons, we also
recognize that jealousy is an emotion deeply ingrained in
most of us, one that will not disappear without a struggle.

Off My Chest

I learned about sex
from my husband's
girlfriend
She taught me
how to dress and
wear just-licked
lipstick   smile
move my body
without sweating
use my eyes like a weapon
the meaning of
cleavage
and fat is OK
in the right
places

So my chest goes
bare
even in winter
I catch colds a lot
but it's worth it
The men greet me
at parties
with glazed half-smiles
of lust   They pretend
to adjust a cufflink but
that's only an excuse
to linger hoping to
lay a finger
on me   before I walk
away and leave them
hanging.

Now my husband's
girlfriend is furiously

jealous   She thinks I've
become so attractive he'll
get interested

Maralyn Lois Polak
December 25, 1973

Those are some of the problems for women who are involved
in relationships that are not monogamous. There are obviously some benefits, or fewer people would be experimenting. Sometimes it is the woman who has her cake and
eats it too, by having a husband and a lover. Sometimes
in *ménages à trois* and group marriages women report that
once freed from the confines of a two-person marriage
they learn more about their sexuality and develop more of
a sense of self than ever before. Since married women are
supposed to be relatively sexless to all men but their
husbands, many women who are open to sexual experimentation
report feeling more sensually alive than at any time since
their marriage. Often these feelings benefit sex in the
marriage as well.

To be honest, very few couples we know or have read about
have worked out extramarital sexual relationships over a
really long period of time. Such relationships usually
result in one of two things: either the affair is broken
off with bitterness all around, or the original marriage
ends so that the new lovers can be together. Occasionally
a couple returns to the original relationship renewed and
refreshed by the extramarital activities that took place.
Some couples report that rather than destroying their
marriages, the affair--or swinging, or group sex, or
whatever--awakened the partners to new dimensions in themselves and heightened their appreciation for each other.
The partners say that in longer-term intimate relationships
outside their marriages they had the opportunity to be
somebody different, to escape the confining behavior patterns that married couples often get locked into. Women
report this to be especially true. For them to be able
to step outside the role of somebody's wife, even for a
short time, awakened them to the possibilities of their
own identity.

ANN

*I get much more of the pleasures of closeness from
my relationship with Vivian. Just tremendous*

intimacy, sharing, this whole business of feeling like the other person. Just the quality of the sharing and we understand each other's words so much better, because we're basically living through the same experience, which is just really different from Lou. Now with him, he looks independent in his life and he has tremendous interests that are outside of home. He's very committed to them and loves to spend time working. His rhythm of connecting and not connecting has been a huge help to me over the years. I used to be a real clinger, and he feels so comfortable with independence that he encouraged it and accepted it in me and still does. He assumes in the way he relates to me that I have my own life, own interests, and that these things merit time and he's just comfortable with me having a separate existence. Also, he operates in sort of a different realm so when we come together there's much more variety in the sharing, different people, different characters in the play, different skills, everything.

If you are faced with extramarital activity on your partner's part or are considering it for yourself, try to figure out how you really feel about what is going on. While husbands' affairs are usually upsetting to their wives, that may not be true in your case. Perhaps having some of his attentions turned elsewhere for a while can give you some free space without having to be available to him all the time emotionally and sexually. Don't feel the situation needs to be tit-for-tat and scurry around to find a lover yourself. If you have developed a relationship with someone else, how is this really making you feel? Alive and interesting, or stretched thin because you are sharing your energy with two other people and have little left over for yourself? If you and your partner are swapping mates, is it enjoyable for you or are you just going along with the crowd? Surely we women have the right to discover for ourselves what makes us feel good. The important thing is not to fall into the old trap of defining ourselves through our sexual relationships and failing to develop other parts of ourselves. You should also consider carefully how to handle feelings of jealousy that may arise. Couples who report that extramarital activities have enriched their relationships say that they had to spend much time discussing their feelings with each other and with their lover(s), providing reassurance that they still cared and respecting whatever limits their partners felt were necessary.

The "failure rate" of those experiments in opening up
marriage is high because there are years of conditioning
about sex roles and sexuality to be overcome as well as
the objective difficulties of women's economic and emotional dependence. That the failure rate is high, however,
does not mean that if you are stepping outside the traditional marriage roles you are foolish or irresponsible.
On the contrary, we feel you deserve support and encouragement as well as honest and critical feedback, because you
are attempting something very difficult. Just as we
believe the high divorce rates are not a national tragedy
and that the divorce experience can be one of growth, we
believe that attempts to open up marriages, as painful
as they may be to one or both of the partners, can result
in more autonomy for women. This is especially true when
the women don't focus solely on the sexual aspects of
opening up the marriage but try to develop many facets of
themselves. Provided that the woman's self-respect and
integrity are encouraged in those alternatives to traditional marriage, they can be an important step in changing
marriage into an institution that does not penalize and
restrict women.

CHARLOTTE

When Kay and George and I first made love together,
one of my first thoughts was, "I'm one of those
freaks my mother used to warn me about." Except that
I didn't feel freaky. I felt very close to both of
them as friends, and they to me, and we wanted to
experience sexual closeness as well. Kay and I had
both slept with George separately, and while we had
felt sexual feelings for each other, we were hesitant
to just hop into the sack together.

To get our courage up (none of us had ever done anything like it before) we drank a lot of wine and
then smoked some grass. We put some music on and
took turns undressing each other, which helped get
us into it. For the next two or three hours we took
turns touching and kissing and caressing each other.
Sometimes two of us focused our attention on the
third, and sometimes two of us made love while the
third one watched. There was some intercourse, but
George could only get it up so many times, so mostly
we all touched a lot.

*One of the nicest memories is of one of them, I can't
remember which, fondling my breasts while the other
one was licking my clitoris. One of my sexual fantasies had always been to have a cast of thousands
holding me down (not brutally, but in a caring way)
and doing delicious things to me, all over my body.
And it was happening to me!*

ANN

*I have a relationship with a woman which is outside
of my marriage. The worst problem has to do with
Vivian's acceptance of the fact that I'm married,
because she says that she accepts it, but I think
what she really means is that she believes I'm married. She knows on an intellectual level that, yes,
I am married, but there's no emotional ability to let
that be and just function with the limits that that
imposes. If I mention Lou, she tightens, makes sar-
castic cracks. If I do something with him that she
wishes we would have done together, then she resents
me. So I'm getting a lot of resentment that really
belongs on the whole marriage situation. For a long
time my main response was to feel guilty and evil for
imposing this pain on her, for staying married and for
wanting to stay married. The issue is of her really
coming to terms with the fact that I can love him
and be married and love her, and that doesn't make her
a second-class citizen. She feels she's not as important, which is unbelievable bullshit, but she feels
it, because he has my name on paper and she doesn't.*

Common-Law Marriage and Living-Together Arrangements

On the West Coast there is a common expression for describ-
ing two people living together without having a licensed
marriage. This expression is LTA, or Living-Together Arrangement. Common-law marriage, an expression that describes the same situation, has been in use for some time
but has usually implied low-income or minority couples.
Now that more white, middle-class people of all ages are
living together in this way, other expressions are developing. While we aren't completely enthusiastic about the

term LTA, we use it here because it is a convenient term
to describe a growing trend.

There is more than just a semantic difference, however,
between living together and common-law marriage. Many
people think that common-law marriage is just a polite
name for no marriage at all. Others believe that "if you
live together for seven years, you're common-law married."
Neither of these popular myths is true. But common-law
marriage does exist in seventeen states. Chapter 3 explains the legal aspects of common-law marriage and living-
together arrangements. Here we explore some of the emotional issues involved.

There is considerable adverse public opinion about couples
who live together without being married, particularly
in white middle-class communities. Many people--political
figures, mental health professionals, religious leaders,
parents, relatives, neighbors, teachers--can go on at
length about how such arrangements are eroding the fabric
of American society. Yet more and more couples are
choosing to live this way, either before becoming formally
married or as a long-term arrangement. LTAs are obviously meeting the needs of a number of people.

Those who object to LTAs do so on several grounds. They
have moral and religious objections: couples who live
together without benefit of clergy are considered to be
living in sin. Other critics feel that the woman in an
LTA is at a disadvantage, that she is denying herself the
legal and social protections available to a married women
and that in the end she will be taken advantage of, especially if she becomes pregnant. Finally, there are
those who object to LTAs on the grounds that the lovers
are irresponsible; if they were truly mature they would
not be afraid to make a commitment of marriage to one
another.

RUTH

*Are there advantages for me to not being legally
married? I was brought up with traditional values.
You must get married, that type of thing, and have
that piece of paper, but I feel the commitment is
mental, and emotional. It's stuck in my head, not
on a piece of paper. I don't really look at it as
an advantage or a disadvantage. I find it a*

complication when I meet a certain type of person who doesn't see things that way or can't understand it. I don't care what they want for themselves, but they can at least understand it for me.

Like with my parents. I think my mother would rather see us married with a piece of paper, knowing that I might walk out tomorrow and pay six hundred dollars for a divorce, knowing that it would be legal. To me that's crazy. I don't know how much I consider it a temporary thing or a permanent thing. I don't think there is any structure. It's a day-to-day thing. As long as it lasts, it's there. But I can't see what difference a piece of paper makes, except to make you get a six-hundred-dollar divorce. If it's over, it's over. Why should you have to pay for it?

If he had said to me, "Let's get married," I don't know how I would feel. I haven't thought of it. I think I'd rather stay the way it is now. I think it gives me more of a sense of my own identity. Sometimes people say I don't want to because it leaves me free to split or whatever I want to do. But I don't think of it that way. If I want to leave, I'm going to want to leave, whether I've got that paper and a thousand other papers and a hundred wedding gifts and the whole bit.

The stereotype of the living-together couple is that they are young, white, middle-class, reckless, and flaunting these objections in the faces of their elders and more conservative friends. Our experience is that this is the exception rather than the rule. LTAs come in all ages (there has been a dramatic upsurge of elderly LTAs in recent years for economic and companionship reasons), are from a variety of backgrounds, and are generally quite sensitive to the criticism of those around them. They endure the criticism because they feel that their life-style is right for them at this time. Obviously most couples who live together do so because they are attracted to each other and want to share their lives in significant ways. Usually it is cheaper and more convenient to live with someone you are intimately involved with than to maintain separate residences. The reasons for not legalizing the union vary. Some are opposed to marriage on any grounds and do not want to be forced into the roles of "wife" and "husband." Others feel they could not possibly commit themselves to marriage

without having lived with the other person first. They
think that learning about each other's annoying habits
and developing problem-solving mechanisms together
should prevent any rude shocks after marriage. Some have
been through a painful previous marriage and are reluctant
to commit themselves in that way again. Many low-income
people are not free from a previous marriage because of
the high cost of divorce and so they simply live together
with the new partner.

Our feelings about living-together arrangements are
generally positive. While there are a few legal protections for women within marriage, in general married
women are *not* protected by law, so the argument about
women being taken advantage of legally is not very persuasive. Chapters 3 and 4 outline the ways in which we
feel women are legally and financially disadvantaged by
marriage. There are, however, definite disadvantages to
nonlicensed marriages--in the areas of taxes, insurance,
and housing. Those are also spelled out in Chapter 3.
Pregnancy can present other problems; we explore the
question of "illegitimacy" in Chapter 3.

We have mixed reactions to the objection about maturity
and commitment. On the one hand, we have observed a
tendency for living-together couples to flee from each
other when the going gets rough. Most of us have been
encouraged to want instant gratification--instant mashed
potatoes, easy courses in high school, love at first
sight. When a relationship starts to falter, some LTAs
immediately look around for something better. However,
this is happening with greater frequency in marriage
also, and while a marriage certificate may provide some
impetus for staying in a relationship and working things
out, it also provides no guarantees. On the other hand,
we know a great many living-together couples who have real
commitment to each other and have struggled through some
very stormy periods in their relationships. They have
invested a great deal of time, energy, and love in one
another and won't easily abandon their relationships. We
know of a number of couples who lived together for many
years, decided to become legally married, and were divorced
within a year or two. They report that the expectations
which others put on them about living up to the wifely and
husbandly roles were too much to handle. They had much
more flexibility and comfort when they were just living
together.

BARBARA

I thought about getting married, but right now I feel like I'm married, in that sense of marriage. I thought about it, and at first it was a positive, but now to me it's a negative, because I feel like once there's that piece of paper with my name on it, everything is going to really change. He's going to run around here saying, "You're my wife, and you're supposed to do this and that," and really be dominating me.

LTAs do break up, and the pain of the breakup is usually as traumatic as with formal marriage. But, as with marriage, that does not necessarily mean that the partners are failures or that the relationship was a waste of time. The couples may have learned from each other, enjoyed good times, supported each other in bad times, and in general enriched each other's lives. They may have more to bring to future relationships because of this.

Coping with the disapproval of family, neighbors, friends, and employers can be something else again. Since the woman is thought to be at a greater disadvantage in this kind of relationship than the man, the criticism can come down more heavily on her. For many LTAs the pressure to marry was so great that they decided to legalize their arrangement. They say it took more of a toll on them to resist marrying than to contend with the problems of being husband and wife. Couples from working-class families often have great difficulty with this kind of pressure, although in some lower-income communities common-law marriage is frequent and there is less stigma attached to it.

If you are thinking about a living-together arrangement or are already involved in one, our suggestions are in many ways the same as for women who want to achieve some degree of independence within their marriages. We know many LTAs whose relationships are just as restrictive as legal marriages. The men are the major breadwinners and make most of the decisions; the women are dependent and have few interests outside the home. This is especially true in hippie communities, where an "old lady" provides her "old man" (and sometimes several "old men") with food, children, tender loving care, and "liberated" sex. Probably, if you are in a living-together arrangement, you are doing so because in some way you question the legitimacy of the marriage institution to control your life.

It makes sense, then, to push those questions even further
and look at the way you and your partner relate, unless,
of course, you are living with someone whom you *would*
marry if you could. We hope your goal, the goal of many
legally married women today, is to achieve your own
personhood. Begin discussing with your partner, if you
haven't already, issues such as money, household chores,
privacy, and sex. If most people close to you are opposed
to your arrangement, look around for support from others
who are in similar situations or are at least sympathetic.
At this point in your relationship there are a number of
options open to you, and with the right kinds of encouragement you can exercise them wisely.

Group Living

During the last decade many young, white middle-class
people have begun to explore the concept of communal
living as a way of increasing their potential for personhood as individuals or within a close relationship. There
are many stereotypes about communes, as there are about
living-together arrangements. There are, of course, communes where nudity, dope, and group sex abound. There are
many more, however, that are a lot less flashy and therefore don't make the news. Communes vary considerably.
They are urban, suburban, and rural; they are made up of
just women, just men, or both; they are with and without
children; they contain people of varying ages (although
usually in their twenties and thirties); they are sometimes
organized along common religious, political, or therapeutic
beliefs; they can be highly structured or somewhat an-
archistic; income may or may not be shared; responsibility
for children may or may not be shared; and sex may be
strictly between couples or more open.

Group living is not new to the 1960s and 1970s. Extended
families have existed for centuries as mutual support
systems for people and continue to do so now within many
ethnic and racial groups.   The extended family is still
prevalent in low-income communities. Since low-income
people have fewer material resources to draw on, they must
depend on each other for emotional and economic support.
Some of us, however, grew up in nuclear families consisting
of a father, mother, and children. There were occasional
variations of that arrangement--a single-parent home or

an aging grandmother who lived with us. But by and large,
we were used to seeing families living as self-contained
units, alone in their "own" homes.

In our experience it has been the women in couple relationships who have pushed for group living more often
than the men. They perceive, and rightly so, that living
with others offers them greater potential for flexibility.
This is especially true for women who are not economically
self-sufficient and women with small children. Sharing
expenses for housing, appliances, food, utilities, and
even automobiles is usually cheaper than living as an
isolated family. Besides saving you and your partner money,
if you are economically dependent it will probably cause
less friction between you and him to be dependent on the
group (especially if incomes are shared) than on him alone.
The difficulties some couples experience about household
chores can also be reduced. In a group living situation
usually everyone, women and men, assumes responsibility
for one *part* (instead of all) of the housekeeping chores.
Sharing the cooking, laundry, and child care can create
more freedom for a woman who is used to doing most of
these things by herself. Groups can also be helpful
to couples who are experiencing difficulty in their
relationships by giving feedback and a different perspective
on what they observe. Many married women report that living
with a group rather than within the confines of a tight
couple relationship helps them to see themselves differently
and gives them the opportunity to develop more autonomy.
Single women who live in groups report relief from their
feelings of isolation and loneliness, and nonparents say
they enjoy contact with children.

Shared childrearing is a more complex matter, but many
parents are finding it worth trying. Living in a group
means that there are more adults around to share the responsibilities of children. Children have an opportunity
to know adults other than their biological parents and
children other than their brothers and sisters. Many of us
have, out of necessity, shared childrearing with our parents
or other close relatives, but living with responsible peers
who are willing to make a commitment to our children is
different. Sometimes those arrangements can be helpful in
breaking down destructive patterns we have developed in
our family relationships. At the very least, such an
arrangement can provide parents with more time away from
their children.

MEG

*When I brought my baby home from the hospital my
major problem was that I was exhausted all the time.
The folks in my commune were just terrific in helping
out me and the baby's father. We were living with
four other adults and one child at the time. They
took over all of my house chores, which was a good
thing, because I could barely do what I had to do to
take care of myself--eat, bathe twice a day (to heal
my stitches), and nurse the baby. Since I was nursing, I had to wake up at least every three hours,
but the rest of the time all I wanted to do was
sleep. So the people in my house changed her and
played with her and took her to a room far away when
she cried so I could get some rest. If it hadn't
been for their help, I think I would have been very
depressed about all I had to cope with. I remember
thinking, "I know that millions of women have babies
and don't live in communes, but I don't know how
they do it."*

There are definite disadvantages to group living. People
who have lived only as couples find themselves in a very
different world. Living in a group can mean more diverse
emotional responsibilities, and the group may not be able
to furnish the same intimacy or privacy as in a close
nuclear family. Living with other people requires the
ability to compromise and develop shared standards of
responsibility, cleanliness, and so on, and some people
find it more difficult than they had anticipated. Inevitably, old group members leave and new ones arrive, which
can be disruptive for everyone, especially the children.
In some groups the women are still the ones with major
responsibility for household tasks and raising children.
When responsibilities are not worked out equally, some
women find themselves taking care of two or three families
instead of just their own.

Living in mixed groups can create complexities. If your
relationship is shaky, you or your partner may find yourselves attracted to others in the house. That does not
necessarily spell disaster. We have mentioned ways in
which couples have reinforced themselves and their relationships through emotional and sexual involvement with
others. Such involvements can be very disruptive to the
group, however, and those groups where sexual involvements
have occurred report that they had to spend much time and

energy dealing with what was happening so that the group
was not split apart by the tensions and confusion that
arose.

Most communes dissolve or re-form within a year or two.
That is not surprising because there are many people's
needs to be taken into account. There are some outside
pressures (in some localities, communes face hostility
and harassment) and few models to follow. As with marriage,
longevity is not the sole definition of success in group
living. Many ex-communards report that the experience was
valuable to them in learning about themselves and how they
interact with others. And as with marriage, groups that
have succeeded over time have done so because they have
kept their lines of communication open. They have found
it is destructive and unproductive to allow resentments
and grievances to pass by unacknowledged. This doesn't
mean that if you are part of a group you should be tearing
yourselves apart, but rather that honesty and willingness
to deal with conflicts help to prevent them from escalating.
Many groups have weekly house meetings to discuss what
the members are feeling and to keep communication flowing.
Most people who live in groups say that group living isn't
the answer to all of their problems, but that it has
allowed them to develop more fully as individuals.

CLARA GUTSCHE

A. C. WARDEN

A. C. WARDEN

EMIKO TONOOKA

7

CHRIS

I don't view my lesbianism as a choice--it was not a choice.
It just always was. It's the only life I know. It's the
only life I can exist in. There are many disadvantages to
it. One thing alone aggravates me a great deal: the
social aspects of it. I cannot have the same social activities that straight relationships have. Going out to
dinner, for example. One of the biggest social functions
in this whole country is having two couples go out to dinner. Well, two gay couples can go out to dinner, but two
straight couples can go out to dinner and <u>dance</u>.

I grew up in West Philadelphia. My father worked like
hell and so did my mother. Neither one had a college
degree. I liked girls as soon as I started feeling something for someone else, since I was twelve or thirteen.
The feelings didn't scare me, but I knew even then it was
something you didn't talk about with anybody. I never
discussed it with an adult. I wish I had. I think it
would have been helpful. I felt alone and isolated.

I didn't date boys to any great extent, but I did go to
formal dances and things like that. And I would go to
dances with other girls, because I enjoyed the social
aspect of it. I just enjoyed being out with people.

I had a girl friend and we always double-dated. And then
we would stay over at each other's house. That took care
of the parents and that took care of us. I didn't feel
guilty about that relationship, because it was the first
time I was in love, and it was very beautiful. I didn't
feel it was wrong. I had heard very little about homosexuality at that point. She and I didn't talk much about
it then, we didn't analyze things. I don't even know
where this girl is now, but I would love to talk to her
again in an analytical way about our relationship.

Her mother gave her a very hard time, because her mother
suspected, although she was never told. I was fifteen,
she was seventeen. This started in the third year of
high school, it went on as we graduated, and as we both
went out to work. It got to be too much for her to handle,
with her mother giving her a hard time, wondering how come
she wasn't dating or anything like that. And she went
through a bad emotional time, and had a mini-nervous breakdown. She ended up leaving home, joining the service, and
that really severed our relationship. I was eighteen then.
It was painful. I'm talking lightly about it now because
it's twenty-two years later, but then it was very, very bad.

Number two was a girl at work. She was a great help and a
great transition. I found out about gay bars and parties
at people's houses and the whole gay community. All of
a sudden I knew a hundred gay people instead of one. I was
eighteen and drinking and smoking, and I just had a great
time for three or four years. I went with two different
people before going with the person that I've now been with
for twenty years. I loved being a lesbian, because to
the rest of the world it was "bad," and when you're between
eighteen and twenty-two there's something exciting about
doing something "wrong." At that time the role-playing
was very heavy, and I used to love to dress up, not with
shirt and tie, but even then having short hair and wearing
slacks was kind of risqué. We would go to the shore for
weekends, and there were some really terrific gay bars
there that were nice-looking places. I had good times,
dancing all night long. . . .

I didn't think in terms of homosexuality being sick. That's
the way we were, and there were so many of us then, and
they were the only people that I dealt with in my social
life, so it wasn't questioned. I dealt with as many gay
fellows as I did gay girls, and they were a hell of a lot
of fun, too. Queens and faggots and going in drag--it

282

was just great fun. I have movies of it. There were a couple of gay fellows in particular that I really liked a lot.

I assume my parents assume I'm gay, but it has never been discussed. I never wanted to tell my mother, because she would die. I have enough people I can talk to about that so I don't need to. I think some people in my family would then feel sorry for me or wonder if I could change or some crap like that. So why should I burden them with that? I've got a pretty good relationship with almost everyone I want to have in my family. This way they can always think, "Maybe she really isn't."

When I was nineteen or twenty I met the girl I'm living with now. She had a daughter who was eight at the time. She's about five years older than I am. We took a beautiful apartment, and it was like a two- or three-year honeymoon. We had lots of friends and a couple of close friends. Her brother is also gay, kind of a key figure in the men's gay community, and we had a very happy life. We never told her daughter either, in all these years, even to this day. It was not a conscious decision not to tell her, we just assumed we wouldn't. It's not the kind of thing you tell kids. If society doesn't accept it, why are you going to go forcing it down somebody's throat and discussing it?

During this period we had some very bad times that strengthened our relationship. Her mother died at the end of this three-year period, which was very hard for her to handle.

Over time, the relationship changed. As I think any marriage does. Instead of being young and party-going, it got to be more that we were looking forward to vacations, we were fixing up the house together, and it just got to be broader-based. I think our love grew. It still grows. It's an amazing thing. It's not the same type of love, but the relationship just gets stronger. The mere fact of putting the years on it does something to it, too, that you can't explain unless you've lived through it. That's something that you don't throw away. How can I explain ten years? There were many times when we had fights, and they were bad fights. I would go out and maybe sit in a local bar drinking. But I would always come back, and we would get patched up.

As her daughter grew up and became more aware, I think we knew we couldn't be having these people who looked obviously gay at our house. This was in the sixties, and people looked more gay than they do today. So we went through this period of not having social activities at our house. That was another period that maybe strengthened our lives together. When her daughter left home to go to college, it was in the late sixties when kids were giving their parents a hard time. Again we went through a bad period because she was hurt so badly by her kid. Her daughter left home and was obviously shacking up with some fellow and then left school. We didn't know if she was messing into drugs. It was hard to live through, and there was no joy in our lives for a two-year period. But we lived through that too. Now the relationship with her daughter is good again. She's married and has a baby. We've had a whole life together with all the things that happen--a parent dies, a baby grows up, a kid breaks your heart.

My lover thinks her daughter knows about us. I can be very naïve at times, probably on purpose. If it's never been discussed, how can she really know? We share a bedroom and always have because that was how the furniture was arranged. We never touched or hugged or kissed in front of her. I didn't feel under a strain because it was part of our life. You learn to live a certain way. But, since she has left home, whenever she comes back into the house, or if anyone does, any straight person (I had an aunt stay with us while she was recuperating), yes, it's strained, because now I'm in the habit of having affection whenever I feel like it. Lots of touching, lots of physical contact. When there's someone else in the house and it's cut off, yes, that's very strained.

We certainly have lived our life playing out roles, but that's all we had to go on. In the beginning we both worked, but when I started earning enough money she stopped working. I think she has had a great deal to do with the fact that I have had a relatively successful career. She's not economically dependent on me because I've planned that she not be. I've been careful to put things in both names. I cannot sell the house out from under her. Each of us owns half. But she is more in the housewife role.

I've seen some good heterosexual marriages where I think that there's plenty of concern between the partners, but I do have a feeling there are more heterosexual marriages where there is no dialogue, where the woman is oppressed, and I like to think that our relationship isn't like that. I like to think that we do discuss things, that one of us doesn't do things on her own without consulting the other. One time when we had a very bad disagreement, that was one of the things we decided: that we would not make commitments for each other without discussing it. But I like to think that straight marriages are doing this more too. I have one sister that I think has a good marriage. If I were straight that would be the kind of marriage I would like to have. I think her husband is sensitive and she's sensitive, and they don't do things without discussing it with each other.

But my lover and I do play the roles. She does the housework and I go out to work. Especially in the wake of feminism and our awakening consciousness, she is hearing more of this and she comes back with statements like, "God, is there something wrong with me, because I really enjoyed being home?" I think feminism has affected our relationship in a good way. If nothing else, it has put another spark under us after being together for twenty years. You think that people can't change, yet it has changed my friend. In the period when her daughter was growing up, she was content with less social activity, but I wanted more. Now she almost wants more social activity than I do. I don't know if she's still doing that just to please me or not, but she listens to the radio stations, she wants this literature that I'm bringing home, she keeps wanting to go to that coffeehouse, and I keep dragging us back to the gay bar, which is my favorite place because I like to dance. Feminism has helped us, and I think I have only come to realize that lately. We have more meaningful conversations now. She is restructuring our relationship.

7 / Women Loving Women

What Is Lesbianism?

JANE

*Let me tell you how I feel about lesbianism. Lesbian-
ism is not simply sleeping with other women. Lesbianism is the time, energy, and love of women flowing
into each other, a reaffirmation of ourselves and
each other as women, an awakening to the harmony and
peace possible from within. Learning to love another
woman is learning to love yourself.*

Love. We search for it, long for it, are often controlled
by our need for it. Many women say that they have found
love through sharing their lives with other women.

KATHY

*The first thing I realized about being with Linda was
that she really loved me. It was so different than
when I was married and I was constantly trying to
reassure myself that my husband loved me. With
Linda there was no doubt. I saw that I was an im-*

portant person to her, that she cared about my
thoughts and feelings as much as she cared about her
own. She didn't try to keep me down like John did.
In fact, I found that I was gaining self-confidence
and self-respect. It was different from when I
was married and my husband could never feel good
about himself unless he felt that I wasn't as good
as he was; unless he was constantly sure that he had
me underneath him.

How to Make Love to a Woman If You're a Woman

Think of yourself
and what you like
*   then do that*
Ask her
what she wants
*   then please her*
Imagine the most delicate
caress you have ever known
*   and give it to her*
*   everywhere, slowly*
Speak her name
into the openings
of her body
*   and listen*
*   to her answer.*
Remember
the fierceness and power
of all our great grandmothers
*   who rode horses*
*   and plowed fields*
*   and bore children*
*   in anguish*
and share that with her.
Love her in daylight
Treasure what you learn.

Jennie Orvino

Lesbians are generally committed, either consciously or
unconsciously, to building relationships based on equality.
Often they are convinced that such relationships are not
possible between men and women, usually having tried
unsuccessfully with men or having observed patterns of
dominance and submission in heterosexual relationships.
How many men, they ask, can really accept women as their

equals? How many men are really ready to consider the
needs and feelings of women as important as their own? Not
many, and most lesbians are not or never have been willing
to undertake the struggle of trying to find one of those
few. In fact, why should they, when they know that loving
women brings them happiness?

Lesbians, along with all women, were taught that they would
be loved and cared for by men; that other women were no
more than competition in the race for male approval; but
what they have found is that they are being loved and
cared for by women, not men, and in ways that are fulfilling.

TONI

*The first time that I made love with a woman, I was
scared to death but I knew that I was in love, so I
was sure that it was right. How amazed I was when
I found all the things that had been missing with
men. Tenderness, gentleness, and an intimate knowledge of my body, although it was the first time.
I thought, This woman knows my body because she
knows hers. But it wasn't just a body thing. That
was what made it so different. She touched my cheek
and kissed me and I knew that that was just as important to her as whatever genital contact we had.
It blew my mind because my fantasies were finally
coming true. I had long ago resigned myself to a sex
life that would never quite reach the levels that
I had sensed were possible. It was overwhelming when
I realized that not only was it possible to reach
those levels but we were, in fact, going there. When
I made love to her, I realized that I was making
love to myself. Soon there were no distinctions
between the two.*

Many lesbians would be upset if we devoted a major part of
this chapter to comparing lesbianism with heterosexuality.
They feel that it is important to understand lesbianism
not as a negative reaction to men, but rather as a natural,
rewarding, and fulfilling means of realizing their potential
as women and as lovers. There *is* no comparison, they say,
because women loving women has nothing to do with the dynamics that go on within male-female relationships. The
ingredients are different, the needs are different, the
expectations are different. Lesbianism is a celebration

of womanhood, an expression of freedom, a stand against
the age-old subservience of women to men. While it may
be true that lesbianism is "the rage of all women condensed
to the point of explosion,"* it is also true that lesbianism is the creative expression of the love, intensity,
and respect possible between women.

Who Are Lesbian Women? What Are Their Lives Like?

Those women who make up the lesbian community are as
varied as the total population. They come from the suburbs
and the ghetto; they live alone and in pairs, sometimes
with husbands, sometimes with friends. It is estimated
that there are 20 million gay people in this country. We
assume that lesbians make up about half that number. Where
did they come from? How did they become gay?

There are different routes to becoming a lesbian. Some
women turned to lesbianism after their exposure to feminism
first taught them to love and respect other women. They
were determined to overcome the notion that women should
see each other mainly as competition for men. Many of
them began by thinking that they would use their feminism
to build equal relationships with men. As they grew
closer to other women, however, their respect for male
behavior declined and they found very few, if any, men
willing to accept them as equals. They found themselves
drawn more and more to other women emotionally and realized
that the love and support they needed was coming from
women, not men.

Other women became lesbians not so much out of a conscious
choice, but because their lives had always been complete
without men, or because they found the lesbian life-style
more to their liking, or simply because they just found
that they were gay rather than straight. They found,
perhaps early in life, that they could obtain all the love
and companionship they needed with other women. Sometimes
lesbians, from blue-collar and low-income families in

*New York Radicalesbians, "Woman-Identified-Woman," Boston:
New England Free Press, 1970.

particular, looked around and saw the difficulties of
their friends who were frustrated in early marriages and
decided that such a life was not for them.

JEAN

*I've been gay all my life. When I was young, I never
liked the way that the boys acted. It seemed like
they were always doing things like playing dirty
tricks on the girls and making fun of us. During
most of my childhood I was a tomboy, but later my
parents forced me to wear dresses and to go out with
boys. I did not enjoy dating boys. I felt that they
were nasty and always had one thing on their mind.
I could not understand the other girls and why they
always tried to act so cute and dumb around the
boys. They didn't act like that when it was just
the girls around. I did not want to be part of what
they were getting into--I thought it was phony and
foolish. I felt that I could always be myself with
girls, but if I was myself with the boys, they didn't
like it because they said I wasn't acting like a
girl is supposed to. When I got into my late teens,
I saw many girls getting married. I had no desire
at all to get married. I couldn't stand the way that
men treated women. I tried to talk to the other
girls and tell them they should make sure that they
knew what they were getting into, but they didn't
always listen. I thought that they were making
mistakes. I think that being gay was the best
thing that could have happened to me. I never felt
that it was wrong or abnormal. Sometimes I thought
the straight girls were abnormal--they acted so
strange when the boys came around. I feel that the
gay life is better because I can be myself and because I think women are great.*

Most lesbians are women who at one time or another began
to realize that they were not feeling the things toward
men that they were "supposed to" and instead were wanting
to spend their time and energy with other women. Acting
this out is one of the most difficult things that lesbians
have to do, because it is not easy to be gay in this society.
People assume that gays are sick, perverted, and dangerous
to heterosexuals. Lesbians are often faced with strong economic and legal penalties if their lesbianism becomes known.
Many have lost their jobs or have not been hired because

of their life-style. That kind of discrimination is still
a real threat for most gay people. In addition, lesbian
mothers risk losing custody of their children if their
lesbianism is brought out in court.

There is a lot of social and psychological pressure on the
lesbian. Growing up in a society in which heterosexuality
is considered normal and healthy has caused many lesbians
to consider themselves sick and develop enormous res-
ervoirs of self-hate. Sometimes it is very difficult for
them to believe in themselves and what they are doing.
Many gay women feel forced to hide what they are rather
than face the scorn of heterosexual friends and family.
Traditional psychotherapists have added to this burden by
labeling lesbianism a sickness and working to "cure" their
patients. While this has been changing in recent years,
there is still a great deal of prejudice and misinformation
that need to be overcome by mental health professionals.

Enter Feminism

Feminism is beginning to influence the lives of many lesbians, particularly the white and middle-class. Low-income
and minority lesbians are less likely to have been significantly exposed to feminism, largely because the lesbian
feminist movement has failed to reach out to gay women
in the low-income community. Although low-income women,
lesbians in particular, have always been strong and independent, feminism as a political ideology has been
developed by middle-class women. The low-income woman
has had to focus primarily on survival and has not had
the option of developing a political understanding about
anything other than her most basic economic needs.

One of the results of recent lesbian feminist activity has
been the opportunity for lesbians to socialize in a non-
exploitative atmosphere. Many gay bars, to which most
lesbians turn for social interaction, are depressing and
exploitative. Instead, gay women in many areas can now
find coffeehouses, softball teams, and dances organized
by lesbian feminist groups. Lesbian centers and counseling
groups have also sprung up to serve as clearinghouses for
lesbian projects and to provide needed services in a
warm, supportive atmosphere. The Resources section for
this chapter lists some of these programs. In addition to

providing places and activities for lesbians to get together comfortably, lesbian feminists have been thinking about how people perceive lesbianism in this society. They refuse to accept the notion that heterosexuality is healthy and normal and homosexuality is sick. They are saying that it is not the lesbian who is sick, that perhaps it is the society that rejects her that is a little less than healthy. Gay people are condemned because they reject the sex roles that are dictated to us all from birth. Gay men are despised because they are seen as feminine. Since female qualities such as softness and gentleness are not really valued, those who adopt them are not really valued. Lesbians are despised because they refuse to behave out of a need for male approval; they refuse to "know their place" and submit to men.

Lesbians are called unnatural for not wanting or needing men, but many lesbians feel it is unnatural for women to be the weak, passive, submissive beings many men seem to require. They question the value system that says women were created to serve men and to be dominated by them, that it is their "nature" to enjoy it, and that something is wrong with them if they have any quarrel with this arrangement. Lesbians ask, "Is it sick to desire an equal relationship, a relationship that promotes a woman's strength and self-confidence, a relationship that reinforces her independence and self-reliance?" Those are often the dynamics of the lesbian relationship which, far from being sick, frequently provides a healthy climate for growth and development. That is not to say that all lesbian relationships are automatically healthy and productive. There are unhappy and unhealthy lesbian relationships. The reasons behind unhappiness for lesbians are often tied up in how society perceives them and in how they perceive themselves.

FRAN

I got so tired of trying to keep my husband happy. I wanted to have a life of my own and he was against it. I went out to work anyhow and he never stopped punishing me for that. God forbid that he should ever so much as wash a dish or change the baby. I really don't know how I did it all those years, but I was determined that I wasn't going to let him stop me. After about six years of fussing and fighting I realized that my husband was more concerned about having everything neat, clean, and in its place, including me, than he was about a loving relationship. Now, I am living with Sharon. Although I would never say that it's been easy, I feel that together we form a partnership. We share the load equally, and neither person is considered more important than the other. We are both working at things that give meaning and direction to our lives. She is going to school and I am writing. I feel as if I am building something good.

Lesbians are questioning the so-called health of a heterosexual society. They feel that heterosexuality does not seem to be all that healthy, with its rape, violence, pornography, and abuse of women. Lesbians also say no to the notion that homosexuals present a danger to the heterosexual community. Statistics show that it is heterosexual men who rape--certainly not women, gay or straight, and generally not gay men. Gay people also point out to their heterosexual brothers and sisters that gays are already very much a part of everyone's lives. Gay people have been teaching children, providing health care, driving buses and planes, directing traffic, and trying to keep the streets safe.

Many lesbians say that once society begins to eliminate sex-role channeling and allows both men and women to behave in whatever ways seem most natural, the prejudice against gays will decrease significantly. Perhaps when a little boy exhibits enough tenderness, gentleness, and *parental* instinct to want to play with a doll, he will actually be encouraged instead of punished. It is not unmanly to be sensitive and caring; rather it is unmanly and inhuman to be cold, constantly controlled, unable to express feelings, and unable to cry. Perhaps when a little girl exhibits enough bravery and ingenuity to want to climb trees and build bridges, she will be encouraged instead of redirected into acceptable feminine activity. It is not unwomanly to be self-confident, strong, and independent; it *is* unwomanly and unnatural to be weak, dependent, and insecure.

It is clear that without sexism, inequality of the sexes, and sex-role stereotyping, gay people would be left alone by the rest of society. Gay people are hassled not simply because they are "deviant" but because they violate the very fabric of a society that insists on categorizing people along lines of sex, race, and class. We hope that

as the roles for women and men begin to be less rigidly
defined, gay people will be less terrifying to heterosexuals. When women in general have achieved a true measure
of freedom it is logical to assume that then lesbians will
achieve it also. When women are no longer conditioned to
believe that they must submit to men, lesbians should no
longer be labeled unnatural in their refusal to submit.
And when men can feel free to reject the macho, he-man
image that so many believe is a true indication of manhood,
then gay men should no longer be labeled unnatural because
they reject that image for themselves.

Lesbian Relationships

The social climate of the straight world has led many lesbians into behaving in ways that have not always been in
their best interests. Role-playing (when one partner
adopts a "female" role and the other adopts a "male" role)
stands out as the aspect of gay life most offensive to
straight people and most damaging to gays. Role-playing
is a survival mechanism for many lesbians. Lesbians need
to be strong in order to survive. To many it means trying
to be aggressive, tough, assertive--what is usually labeled
"acting like men." Lesbians, like everyone else, have
been taught that it is the "nature" of the female to be
weak, passive, and inferior. Since men appear to be
the only strong people around, many lesbians adopt behavior
that is traditionally considered "male" as a way of becoming strong and independent and as an unconscious rebellion against falling into their "proper" place as women.
Some gay women have not withstood the pressures to see
lesbianism as sick and have decided, perhaps unconsciously,
that since it is wrong to love a woman if you are a woman,
you had better become a man.

Straight people always get upset when they see lesbians
playing out butch-femme (male-female) roles. What they
forget is that lesbians have no other behavior models to
go by. It is considered normal, for example, for men to
control women, to dominate women, but when two lesbians
show anything less than complete respect for each other,
everyone is horrified. Most people fail to realize that
role-playing among lesbians is only a manifestation of a
deeper need to find a place within the existing society.
Since the society is based on roles, it is only natural

that lesbians have tried to fit into the only available
model. It is true that some lesbians wish they were men.
They probably feel that way about themselves because they
see that women generally do not have the freedom of movement and action that men do, that men are socially and
economically superior and women despised and discriminated
against. They may even have bought the lie that men are
the better people, the smarter people, the stronger people.
But to deny what you are is to deny yourself totally and
can only result in unhappiness and frustration. The
answer for those women is to see that you don't have to
be male to be strong, independent, and assertive. In a
way it is difficult to find fault with women who would
prefer to be men. After all, men are the people with the
advantages that give them better-paying jobs, greater
respect, greater importance, greater educational and
athletic opportunity. Small wonder that many more women
don't want to become men!

SHIRLEY

*I guess that I'm into roles because I believe that
someone has to be the head, someone has to take the
responsibility, make the final decisions. I'm in
the male role because I tend to be strong, independent, and demanding. I want to take care of the
person that I love. I like to think that I take care
of the business matters and my lover takes care
of the home front. I guess I do do a lot around the
house, though, but that's because I like to do things
for my lover. I have thought about not being in a
role but it seems to me that everything would be too
confusing. Lately people in the women's movement
have been saying that women are just as capable of
being strong and independent, and I think that's
probably true.*

LUCY

*I became gay because I don't believe in roles. I
didn't like the role-playing that I saw within
heterosexual relationships. Although it has been
confusing without roles, I feel that the benefits
outweigh the disadvantages. I feel that I can be a
whole person. I am not restricted to what is considered the traditional role for women; there is a*

*broader definition of women in a non-role-playing
relationship. When I was involved in a heterosexual
relationship, I wanted to be respected as being
strong, but I had to be constantly demanding that
recognition. I couldn't show any weakness for fear
of being too vulnerable. Within a lesbian relationship without roles, I can get in touch with both
parts of myself, both parts of me are accepted.
There is significantly less rigidity when there are
no roles. Role-playing goes against the nature of
lesbianism.*

Since role-playing has for so long been the accepted life-
style within the lesbian community, many gay women think
that they are much more role-identified than is the actual
case. When one really looks at how lesbians live their
lives, it becomes apparent that even those who most vocif-
erously defend role-playing actually live in an egalitarian
manner. Shirley, who believes that her lover should "take
care of the home front," but who does most of the housework
and cooking, is a good example.

Role-playing has not brought most lesbians the happiness
they seek, and many gay women are now trying to find other
solutions. Straight feminists as well as lesbians are
struggling to free themselves of limiting sex roles as both
come to understand the destructiveness of such behavior
patterns.

How does a lesbian seek fulfillment? Generally lesbians
look for partners with whom they can share their lives.
There is a minimal amount of cruising and one-night stands
in most lesbian communities. Lesbians are not generally
promiscuous and tend to want sex within the context of a
love relationship.

Some lesbians, like everyone else, are not always successful at finding long-term mates. There are several
factors involved in the breakdown of lesbian relationships.
It is clear that many of these factors stem from our
conditioning as women. It could be said that women are
like puzzles. Our conditioning has left us with many
missing parts, parts needed for complete personhood. The
missing parts vary according to background, environment, and
other factors. Some women have no self-confidence; some
have no inner strength; some are unable to control their
emotions. When women look to other women to fill in these
missing pieces, they are doomed to failure because each

woman must herself begin the long process of overcoming her
conditioning and completing herself. It is only when a
woman becomes a whole person herself that she will have
anything to offer anyone else. Lesbians are women, and
women have been taught to see themselves as unworthy. As
a result, many are often unable to love themselves and
unable to accept love from another. As women begin to
achieve more good feelings about themselves, they will be
more capable of developing fulfilling relationships with
each other and with people in general.

If You Are Bisexual

Many women feel that lesbianism is not for them, although
they have found themselves attracted to other women. Perhaps they have recently been thinking about women as a
result of the feminist movement and have realized that they
are growing to care for and respect women more as they
gain a greater understanding of themselves and all women.
If you feel this way, or even if you have had only vague
and unformed thoughts and feelings in this direction, you
are not alone. There are women at a hundred different
points long the line from straight to gay. We know that
you may be feeling confused and scared. You may not know
how to deal with the men or man in your life; you may not
even know what you want to do about these feelings, if
anything. It is important for you to find support from
other women as you go through the process of defining and
redefining your sexuality and life-style. There are gay
counseling centers and programs that are running emotional
support groups for bisexual as well as gay people. The
Bibliography can give you more information on this. If it
is not possible for you to be in a structured group, you
should try to make contact with other women who may be
going through a similar process. There are many women
within the women's movement who have been struggling with
these questions who do not consider themselves gay. Communication with some of these women would undoubtedly be
helpful. The most important thing is to see these feelings
in a positive light and to recognize them as natural and
normal. Many lesbians believe that most women have some
part of them that wants to get closer to other women
sexually, emotionally, or in other ways. These feelings
are positive and creative. There's no reason to deny them.

If You Are a Gay Woman

If you are a lesbian, you probably know gay women who have gotten married to each other. Perhaps you are considering gay marriage for yourself or have been involved in one. Legally, of course, there is no such thing as gay marriage; Chapter 3 describes recent attempts to allow gay people the right to marry.

What are some of the advantages and disadvantages of lesbian marriage? On the positive side, many lesbians feel that they should have the same right to make a life-time commitment to the person they love that straight people have. Often lesbians want to get married for pretty much the same reasons that straight people do: security, companionship, economic benefits, social recognition, peer group and family pressure. These are all common human needs, and because this society is very couple-oriented, being part of a couple seems to be a natural way to get those needs met.

We have to say honestly, however, that we have strong reservations about marriage for gay women. Is imitating heterosexuality really in the interest of lesbian women? Is it not possible that getting married draws you closer to the negative aspects of heterosexuality which you were trying to avoid by becoming gay in the first place? Lesbianism can allow women the opportunity to build equal relationships, something that many women found difficult within the confines of heterosexuality. When two women get married, they are often not aware of the ways that marriage has stifled women throughout the centuries, or if they are, they feel that they can make it different.

As we have outlined in previous chapters, marriage is an institution developed by men to benefit men, not women as we have been led to believe. We strongly urge you to read Chapters 2, 3, and 4 if you are considering entering into a lesbian marriage. Even if you think that you will not fall into the patterns prevalent within a heterosexual marriage, we have found that it is very difficult, if not impossible, to avoid adopting the mentality and value system of an institution such as marriage once you have entered into it.

As we see it, one of the most negative aspects of lesbian marriage is that it encourages role-playing. Who is going

to be the husband? The wife? If straight women are trying
to move away from those roles, it seems absurd for lesbians to perpetuate them. When role-playing is involved
in a lesbian relationship, it leads to the same kinds of
problems found in heterosexual relationships. Being
dominated and controlled really does not promote anyone's
mental health. Role-playing automatically excludes the
possibility of an equal relationship since one person has
more power and control than the other.

Another negative aspect of gay marriage is that any marriage, gay or straight, tends to trap people in couple
definitions, possessiveness, and stifling behavior patterns.
The implication that one partner "owns" the other, or that
both partners "belong" to each other, is often unhealthy.

The choice of whether or not to enter into a gay marriage
is, of course, yours. But as we have stressed throughout
this book, there are other options. It is important for
all women to become economically independent and emotionally
self-reliant so that they can develop relationships based
on mutual caring and respect, not crippling dependency.
A marriage ceremony or piece of paper will not guarantee
that your relationship will last or that it will be a
fulfilling one if it does. Only your self-awareness,
willingness to risk, and hard work will make that happen.

What are some of the major difficulties you face in an
important one-to-one relationship with another woman?
Chances are you and your lover are struggling with such
issues as whether or not to be monogamous; learning to
share time and space; dealing with questions of property
ownership; dealing with children; dealing with the outside
world; and coping with the tensions and intrigues of your
particular lesbian community. These issues, of course,
can be compounded by feelings common to many of us, such
as jealousy and insecurity. We will discuss some of
these concerns. We don't have a lot of answers, but we
have included the experiences, knowledge, and feelings
of many lesbians.

There are many reasons why it is difficult for lesbians
to build healthy, productive lives either singly or in
pairs. When a man and woman get married the dynamics of
the institution are such that things are very clearly
spelled out. The man is supposed to be the breadwinner;
the woman, the nurturer, the mother, the wife. Although
we have tried to point out most emphatically throughout

this book the destructiveness of the stereotyped sex roles, it is still true that there is supposed to be very little variation within the traditional marriage setup. The relationship is even governed by laws, so that one spouse may not be unfaithful to the other, so that neither spouse can stray too far from what society says is acceptable behavior. When two women decide to live together, things are very different. There are no rules, no established modes of operation. Often, we find lesbian couples living very isolated lives, each couple trying to figure out for themselves how to deal with the monumental questions facing them. One thing that we wholeheartedly recommend is the formation of groups of lesbians who come together to work out some of these questions within a supportive atmosphere. These groups can be leaderless or not. Either way, we think that they can be very helpful for many gay women who want to work on their relationships and who are exploring such questions. These groups could be formed very loosely among couples who already know each other. Often gay community or counseling centers run such groups. See the Bibliography for further information.

MONOGAMY

VIRGINIA

I don't believe in monogamy. I see it primarily as an outgrowth of the patriarchal male-dominated family. I feel that it has been used to limit and control people, and through the laws and legal system, it perpetuates the power of the state in the intimate lives of individuals. I don't think that one person can be all things to another. My lover and I have been living together for five years and we both see our relationship as the most important one in our lives, but we also have relationships in addition. I'm not only talking about sexual relationships, I'm also talking about deep friendships with other women. I feel that each of us is a separate person within the relationship with separate needs. Of course, I think that this can work only when both people are agreeable, and even then it is not an easy thing to work out. In the beginning, there were feelings of jealousy and resentment. But going through some

*experiences and talking them out has helped tre-
mendously. I also think that each of us feels very
secure in the relationship so we don't feel threatened when one or the other gets close to someone else.*

To be or not to be monogamous is a question widely discussed by many lesbians. Many women, like Virginia, feel
that monogamy, another one of those male institutions we've
been talking so much about, is not in the interests of
women. It is unrealistic, many feel, to think that one
person will meet all your needs forever. Furthermore, it
promotes the practice of women seeing each other as property (you belong to me) rather than promoting each partner's sense of herself as an individual.

It is extremely important within a lesbian relationship
that each woman feel she is growing within that relation-
ship--not being stifled by it. To the extent that monogamy confines, it probably has a negative effect. On the
other hand, many gay women feel that just managing one
relationship successfully is such a challenge that they
can't possibly imagine themselves involved in more than
one. In addition, many say, it is idealistic to think that
most women are capable of adopting the maturity and openness
that such an open relationship requires. Some lesbians say
that the whole idea smacks too much of those heterosexual
"understandings" where the man goes out and does what he
wants while the woman goes along so as not to lose him.

While it is true that almost every woman experiences
jealousy and insecurity to some extent, it may also be
true that there are some women mature enough to undertake
such a relationship. It is our feeling that women are
more prone to these negative emotions because they have
always been taught that they are incomplete within them-
selves--that it is only when they are attached to the
appropriate man that they will ever feel that they are
complete persons. The extent to which a woman is capable
of overcoming these feelings is often the extent to which
she is capable of giving and receiving love from another.
And love, we feel, is the key in determining what the best
course is in these situations. If two women feel that they
can have outside relationships without *using* the other
women or each other, then such an arrangement may be
appropriate. It is important that *whatever* happens, respect
is maintained.

SEX

Many women are drawn to the gay life because they feel that their partner will not be using them sexually, and for many this knowledge goes a long way to making them feel loved and cared for. In addition, the technical aspects of lovemaking are rarely a problem since, as many gay women say, "only another woman can understand your body the way you do."

SUE

It wasn't until I made love with a woman that I really understood what an orgasm was. Always before, I had orgasms, but they were mostly physical sensations in a specific part of my body. The first time I made love with Carol, though, I realized that she was asking for much more than my body. She wanted me to share our love, our common struggle, our sisterhood. She asked me for everything and when I gave it to her, I could feel all of me pouring into her, my mind, my body, my feelings. For the first time I felt the connection between my mind and body, and I realized how men had managed to separate the two, and how unnatural and unfulfilling it had been.

THE OUTSIDE WORLD

How much do lesbians deal with the outside world in their day-to-day lives? A lot of that can depend on how each couple sees themselves and each other; how positive they feel about their lesbianism; how healthy they think it is. Most lesbians have had to learn not to care too much about what straight people think about them. Often it is difficult for lesbians to block out completely what society thinks of them, and a particularly nasty experience can sometimes come between lovers.

KAY

The other day I was out shopping and two women were staring at me. I'm not sure whether or not they knew that I saw and heard them. One of them said, "Oh my God, what is it? Is it a boy or a girl?" Well, I don't like to wear particularly feminine clothes. It's not that I'm trying to be a man or look like a man. I'm just not comfortable in feminine clothing. At the time, I didn't think it bothered me that much but later that evening I found myself snapping at my lover and I realized that it had really gotten me down.

In our opinion, the key to dealing with the way the rest of the world perceives you lies in how you perceive yourself. If you are a lesbian who is not only not ashamed of being gay, but who feels proud in her lesbianism, then you have the battle half won. As a lesbian you must work at building your own positive self-image. You must not let others make you feel insecure or inadequate as a person. In the event that you are considering therapy, make sure that you do not enter into any therapeutic situation that does not promote a complete acceptance of your life-style. Nothing could be more damaging than to enter into therapy with a therapist who either overtly or subtly puts you down because you're gay. The ideal, of course, would be to see a gay therapist. If that is impossible, a straight therapist with a feminist consciousness is your next best bet. Under *no* circumstances should you go to a therapist to be "cured." There is nothing wrong with you! Our *Therapy Information Packet for Women,* listed in the Bibliography, gives you information on how to select a therapist and how to evaluate a therapy experience.

THE LESBIAN COMMUNITY

Your peers can play an important part in your life. Whether or not your particular lesbian community can be helpful and supportive depends on a number of factors. These days the white middle-class lesbian community has strong feminist consciousness that has proved very helpful for those within that community. There are the alternative social activities mentioned before; it is likely that there are support groups operating for you to join and become involved with. There are many ways for you to become active in helping other lesbians, such as working to set up a lesbian center. All of this support and political awareness, however, does not negate the fact there is a lot of intrigue that goes on. Lovers leaving one another, new matches constantly being formed, flirting, fighting can lead to tension, tension within the group at large, and tension at home once the party or dance is over. First, it is important to understand why the lesbian community is

not the citadel of sisterhood that we would like it to be.
Once again, lesbians are women, and they have not been
completely capable as yet of overcoming society's expectations of them. They are working at it, but all oppressive
behavior will not disappear overnight just because there
is a new political understanding of how and why women act
as they do. The lesbian community faces a long struggle as
each woman within it moves to define herself on her own
terms rather than society's. That struggle has begun, and
we are hopeful that it will continue and succeed. In the
meantime, one has to cope with the behavior patterns that
now exist. It can be gratifying to your ego to know that
you are attractive to women other than your lover, but more
harm than good can come out of one of those "harmless"
flirtations. It can be exciting to "break up just to
make up" but it can also leave scars. Lesbians must take
each other seriously enough to resist falling into these
destructive patterns.

WHEN THERE ARE CHILDREN

Many lesbians have children. Contrary to popular belief,
almost half of all lesbians have had some heterosexual
experience at some time in their lives. For many of those
women, a desire to act out society's expectations of them
as women is what prompted the heterosexual experience.
For others, heterosexuality was a cover for their lesbian
activities. Whatever the reasons, there are literally
hundred of thousands of lesbian mothers, many of whom
are living with their lovers. What to tell or not tell
the children can become a major issue for them.

Since most people think lesbians are sick, crazy, perverted,
or dangerous, this is what lesbians' children are hearing
in school, in the media, and on the street. Some women
believe it is important to tell their children that they
are lesbians so they can begin to counteract all that
prejudice. They feel that not telling their children
would be to live a lie and set an example of dishonesty
which might stifle communication with their children.

Many lesbians feel the heterosexual norm is dangerous and
must be attacked head-on by offering a positive alternative
to the kind of sex-role stereotyping and nuclear family
models the children are exposed to in school and elsewhere.
That belief almost always provokes the classic heterosexual
question "Aren't you afraid they'll turn out to be

homosexual?" The classic response, of course, is that all
homosexuals came out of heterosexual unions and a culture
that promotes a strongly heterosexual norm. Why shouldn't
children know that there is more than one way to live
and then choose for themselves?

Some lesbian mothers feel that their children's knowing
they are lesbians is too great a burden. It forces the
children to face the social rejection that their mother
may have chosen but they did not. Conformity is very
important to most children, they will point out. It's
terrible for children to feel different, and they can be
cruelly rejected by peers whose parents may not tolerate
any variation from the norm. They may also be forced to
live a double life, acknowledging their mother's lesbianism
at home but hiding it from friends and relatives.

When two women in a love relationship decide to live
together, the children will eventually figure things out
anyway. It does seem to us that more harm can come from
trying to keep the knowledge of your lesbianism from your
children. The children can become confused and resentful,
knowing that they are not being told the truth about their
mother's life. If they are picking up negative messages
from others about homosexuality, their resentment and
confusion will only be increased. It may be in your
children's best interests to tell them, and to present
your life-style in a positive manner. This can contribute
to creating a basically honest atmosphere in the household
and will better prepare them to deal with reactions from
the outside world.

Children are adaptable. Telling your children about your
lesbianism may end up being a lot easier than telling
anyone else. If they are young enough, they may not have
developed the antigay attitudes that permeate our society.
On the other hand, maturity can be a positive factor and
can help you evaluate just how much your child is capable
of taking in and understanding. If your children are
asking questions, we feel that it is best to answer them
as honestly as possible. If they are not asking questions,
they probably have them in mind anyway. We suggest that
you open up discussion in this area. It may seem more
convenient to avoid sexuality discussions with your
children, but it probably won't be as beneficial for them
in the long run. If your child already has antigay
attitudes, we think it best slowly and systematically to
create a more progressive understanding and tolerance

of *all* life-styles. The most important ingredient in any child's life is love. If the child is living in a home where the adults, gay or straight, love each other and the child, positive things are likely to result.

There are several other problems often faced by lesbian mothers. A major issue for many is what to say to the father of their children and how to cope with a custody battle if one arises. The most important thing to realize is that admitted lesbians almost never win when child custody cases go to court, so it is crucial to proceed carefully and with adequate legal representation. Whether or not and what to tell your children's father depends on his attitude toward you and toward lesbianism and whether he is likely to use the information against you. If he is angry with you or likely to see your love for other women as a total rejection of his masculinity, then it is better not to tell him. If he already knows, try not to antagonize him by flaunting your lesbianism. Our previous book, *Women in Transition: A Feminist Handbook on Separation and Divorce*, has extensive sections for lesbian mothers. We suggest you take a look at the book if you are faced with custody difficulties.

One problem that many lesbian mothers face is how to relate to a lover who has never had children, has never been interested in motherhood. Many lesbians have rejected the notion that a woman must have children to be fulfilled and have decided not to have children themselves. Sometimes they can feel resentful when they find themselves saddled with a lover's children after they had decided that motherhood was not for them.

JOAN

I do not want to be a mother. Because I have not experienced motherhood myself, I feel somewhat removed from the process of parenting. When you're living in a situation where you're expected to be a full-time mother and adopt the same attitudes and feelings toward the children as their natural mother, a great deal of hostility can result if you are incapable of doing so. It's not that I don't love and care for my lover's children, and in fact, I consider them my own in many ways. It's just that I can't stand the nuclear family. It seems that my lover has a greater tolerance for the misbehavior and squabbling that goes on. I guess at times I have also felt that her children oppress her and take up too much of her time and energy, time and energy which is badly needed to deal with the struggles and differences between us. Over a period of years I feel that these problems could take on monumental proportions within the relationship.

There can also be adjustment difficulties when two lesbians, each with children, move in together. There are no easy answers for these problems. In many ways they are similar to the problems faced by any stepparent, and we refer you to the Stepfamilies section in Chapter 5. One possible solution is to become part of a lesbian mothers' group. In the last few years more and more lesbian mothers have been seeking out other lesbian mothers to share ideas, problems, and support. Lesbian mothers' groups have been formed in many major cities and are accessible through lesbian hotlines, women's centers, and gay switchboards and counseling centers. The Bibliography can give you an idea of additional resources.

Whatever the problems you face as a lesbian, we feel that they are problems that can be solved, in spite of the fact that you must exist in an unsympathetic society. Somewhere along the line of learning to love other women you must have decided that it was worth it. We hope that this chapter has been helpful. We wrote it because we believe that women can come to love one another in spite of the ways that we have been taught to compete, to envy, to hate. We salute you for your courage, your determination, your love for yourself and all women.

JOANNE KANDER

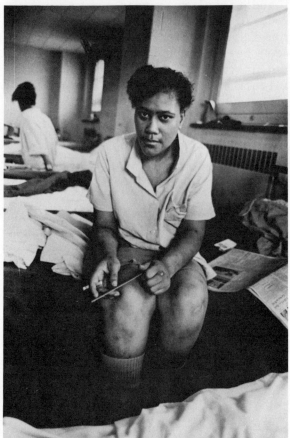

EMIKO TONOOKA

EVA SHADEROWFSKY

EVA SHADEROWFSKY

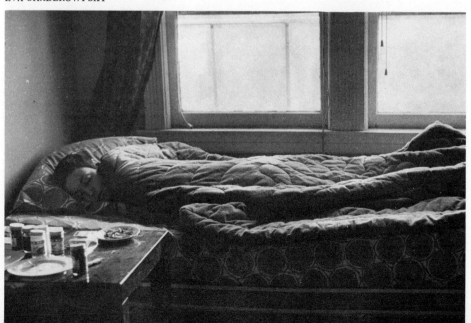

EVA SHADEROWFSKY

JOANNE KANDER

8

GERRI

I was introduced to my husband through my brother. At the
time he seemed like a very nice young man. We went out
occasionally, and I thought truly that I was madly in love
with him. My parents were very hostile to the other
fellows I was going out with due to the fact that they
drank and my husband didn't drink. He was an ideal husband for me. They kept nagging me that he was the right
man for me. It got to the point that I had to escape. I
was fifteen at the time. All I wanted to do was get out
of the house. I figured that if I got married I would be
a grown woman and my parents would no longer be able to
tell me what to do. I would be on my own.

But then problems started. I was never allowed to go out
of the house, not allowed to have any friends because most
of my friends were single, and he had these feelings that
if I went out with my friends I would meet some other guy.
And I lived in total fear when my friends came around,
because I knew what I was in for when they left. I completely isolated myself from my friends and neighbors. The
only people I had any contact with were my family.

I was really afraid of him because he was a man and he
could beat me. The first time he hit me I was standing with

my parents. This discussion we were having turned into an argument. I said quite a few bad things to him because I was frustrated. My father--and I never will forgive this for the rest of my life--told him, "You go beat that woman. Beat her. She's my daughter, but she deserves it." So my husband jumped on me until my mother heard it. She was the one who pulled him off of me. She said she wasn't going to have this in her house, and he wasn't going to beat on her daughter like this.

When an argument would start, naturally I was upset and would argue back with him. So the more I would say, the worse it would get. And he would get totally deranged. Before you knew it, he would grab me and hit me. The only thing I could do was hold my arms up to block, and scream. Now the majority of times that I would scream, this is where I would get choked because he didn't want anybody to hear me screaming. I would try to hit him back, but he would kick at me. I would also try to block it and sometimes fall to the floor. If he knew he was really hurting me, he would stop. It seemed like he would be scared and he would take off.

Sometimes he would stay away when the cops would come. But if he was there, he would say, "I didn't do nothing to this woman." Sometimes the cops would listen to me, and sometimes they would say, "Well, look, you have to take this up at domestic problems court." I would say then, "You mean you can't do nothing? Here he is beating me up!" The majority of times they would tell him to go walk around the block. After they would go, my husband would say, "You called the cops on me. That's a big threat to a man. Don't ever call the cops on me." Then he would say he was sorry and we would start all over again, peaceful. Every time he did something to me, he would try to buy something to make up for what he had done.

One time we got in an argument. I was carrying triplets at the time. When you're pregnant, the last thing in your mind is that your husband is going to hit you. He never hit me in the stomach, but he would hit me so I would fall and people would say that I done it. Some women will fly up into a man's face when they're pregnant, thinking that he won't hit them. But a lot of times they do, and the women are clumsy and fall. And that's what happened to me. I was about seven months pregnant.

310

It was a very scary feeling when I knew I was going to
get hit. Each woman knows when her husband is about to
strike her. It's like a panic button. For a moment the
expression on their face changes, the whole disposition
changes. And then he comes after you and you think,
"O God, this is it. He's going to kill me." Mine used to
hit me in the temples, he used to hit me with his fists.
I always got up in a corner. It was some kind of security
feeling for me. But the only bad thing about it was that
my head would slam against the wall. So it was a double
blow, and at that moment I just lost myself--something
would crack inside my head. I would come out and fight
with all the strength I had in my body. And I would win
a lot of times. It's strange now to think that I did
win a lot of those fights, because when I struck out it
shocked him. Before then I was not hitting him back. He
was only hitting me to his satisfaction, and when he decided to stop, he stopped. But when I started hitting back,
I found the parts on his body to hit him and get him to
back off. My husband had nosebleeds, so I would concentrate around the face, on the bridge of his nose. When
he would back off me, I would take anything in the house
and throw it at him. And he ran. Striking back probably
saved me from getting killed. But some women fight their
husbands back as violently as their husbands fight them, and
that's when you find a lot of killing. Because neither
one is going to give in and stop.

You get emotionally very wrecked up. It hurts deep,
because this man is supposed to love you very much. For
him to beat on you like that, you think, "This man can't
love me if he could beat me like this." And in front of
the children. The children are hollering and screaming and
he wouldn't even stop in front of his own kids.

Finally I had no choice and took my husband to court. He
was very afraid to go to court. What was the big change
in this woman? She went and put me in court, and she never
did this before. His boss notified the judge to put in
a good word that he was a good worker and all, which had
nothing to do with him beating me. The judge turns to him
and asks why did he do it. He first said he didn't do it.
But I said I wouldn't be standing here, going through all
this, scared to death, if he hadn't done it. The judge
asked how long we had been married, which was eight years,
and how many kids we had, which was four, and she said
couldn't we sit down and talk about this and reconsider,
because we had a lot at stake with the children. She said,

"If I should see you in this court again on these charges, I'll put you up for two years."

It was a big relief when that was over. When we got home he was very nice. Everything was just beautiful. For a while. But I'll be doggone if he didn't start all over again. At that point I just didn't know what to do. I didn't really want to put the man in jail, but I just wanted him to leave me alone. Besides, if he went to jail, I wouldn't have no more money. If he goes to jail, how am I going to make it with these children here?

The arguments were getting worse. I was hospitalized four times. One time we were arguing and I went in the bathroom and slammed the door. He came in, and as I got up off the toilet he fought me, and I fell in the tub. I have phlebitis and this activated my blood clots. My legs swelled and I couldn't hardly walk and I had to go in the hospital for three weeks. Another time he went to kick me in the stomach and I caught it with my hand and I thought it was broken. That was on record at the hospital, because I always told them the truth about what happened, which I'm glad I did. The third time I was hospitalized I don't know whether he hit me with his fist or an object. He had put me out, but I didn't have no money because my wallet was in the house. I went back to the house, and when I went in he had turned all the lights out. He hid behind the door and hit me on the back of the head. I went limp and just went right out. I didn't know anything until I saw my mother there in a nightgown. The neighbors called her. At the hospital they said I had a mild head concussion. When I was back from the hospital, he came back to get his clothes and my mother and sister were waiting for him. My sister had a gun, and she backed him up the stairs. I was groggy from the medication and I said, "What's the commotion here?" He begged me to tell my family to leave him alone. He was really pitiful, and I felt sorry for him regardless of what he done to me. Now that I think about it, I wish I had reminded him that that's how I felt.

So I stayed with him for the sake of the children, always hoping that he would change. I tried to do everything to please him. I never went back to court to tell them that he didn't stop, because I was afraid. I knew he would go to jail. One time he got me so upset I was screaming, and he thought I was going to jump out the window. He called the cops and they took me to the psychiatric ward. I tried to tell the psychiatrist that I wasn't crazy, I

312

was just upset about my husband. They were going to admit me that night, but they didn't have a bed. Thank God they didn't have a bed. After that we had a marriage counselor, but my husband didn't want no part of her, and she wouldn't see me alone.

One day I really got out of myself and started wrecking the house, throwing grease around, turning over the fish tank. I stopped because the kids were scared to death of me. So I sat down and said, "Gerri, you got to get out of here. Either you're going to kill that man or he is going to kill you or you'll be in a mental institution. And then what are your kids going to do?" So I hid the money he gave me for paying bills under the rug, and I kept putting off the collectors until I had enough money. I was lucky. My girl friend found an apartment for me. I had one day to move, because if he would have caught me, that would be it for me. I had to run around and get everything in my new place. I made sure I left him one of everything. I didn't think about how I was going to support myself and the kids, I was just thinking about survival. But then I went and applied for welfare, which was a sickening thought because I never wanted to get on welfare. The way those people treat you is like dirt. But I'm now on welfare, and I'm making it by the grace of God.

8 / Violence within Marriage

Wilma O. is thirty years old. She has been married for three years. When she called Women in Transition she said that her husband had recently beaten her because she had misplaced his pack of cigarettes. At the time of the beating she was six months pregnant. Her husband had beaten her into unconsciousness while threatening her with a butcher knife.

Sally L. is fifty years old and has been crippled for life from repeated beatings by her husband. She has been hospitalized at least a half-dozen times in the last ten years. Asked why she has put up with it for so long, she says, "Doesn't he have the right to beat me? After all, he is my husband and the law says I have to obey, doesn't it?"

Margaret C. is the wife of an attorney for a prominent big-city firm. On nights that he works late he often has a few drinks with some of the other lawyers. When he gets home he has a few more drinks, and by the time they are ready for bed he is quite drunk. When Margaret refuses to make love with him under those circumstances, he yells at her and strikes her. The commotion awakens and terrifies their five-year-old daughter.

Barbara M. told her story to a counselor in a family-planning clinic: "This is the first time I have been out

314

of his earshot in six months. He doesn't work, he just
follows me around the house all day beating and threatening
me. I am afraid for the baby, too. Last week he hit me
with a baseball bat and I had to crawl down the street to
a neighbor's house for help. When I called the police
they told me there was nothing they could do."

Minnie G. was locked in a closet for two weeks by her
boy friend. By the time the police had found her, she
was barely alive and had been mutilated with a knife.

We wish we could say that these stories are made up, but
we can't. They are just a few of the many that we have
heard in the Women in Transition office during the last
few years. They are representative of the millions of
women who are being abused by their husbands, a pattern
so common that we have come to feel it is a national
pastime.

"Women, like walnut trees, should be beaten every day."
This quaint injunction was dropped from the Napoleonic Code
only within the last few decades, according to Betsy
Warrior, author of a recently published pamphlet entitled
Wifebeating (see Bibliography). Ms. Warrior also points
out that in some Arab countries women accused of adultery
are still stoned to death; Sato, the former prime minister
of Japan, was awarded the Nobel Prize for Peace only a few
years after his wife had publicly accused him of wife-
beating; and, to bring it a little closer to home, at the
turn of the century in this country, women who found more
sexual pleasure through the clitoris rather than the vagina
often had their clitorises surgically removed under recom-
mendation of their physicians.

Violence against women is a natural extension of the male-
female relationship in societies and cultures that are
male-dominated. Wife-beating, rape, and sometimes death
have been and in many cases still are very real possibilities for most women. During the Middle Ages literally
millions of women were executed for "being witches." Under
the guise of purifying and purging society of unnatural
and evil influences, countless numbers of women were tor-
tured and executed, often for "crimes" such as nagging or
refusing to perform "wifely" duties. Judeo-Christian
religion has always taught that women were doomed to lives
of pain and suffering because of Eve's transgression. In
more modern times the psychiatric establishment has in
effect sanctioned violence against women by concluding that

women are innately masochistic and desirous of being hurt.
In *Three Essays on the Theory of Sexuality* Sigmund Freud
said, "Women are like the masses in wanting to be mastered
and ruled." The legal system in this country reinforces
this antiwoman folk wisdom and culture. Until recently
husbands had the right to "chastise" their wives. Our
legal system, based on English common law, held that
women were the property of their husbands. As such,
they had no legal existence independent of their husbands
(hence the custom of the wife's taking the husband's surname). The husband had absolute control over the person
of his wife. It was not until the mid-nineteenth century,
for example, that married women acquired the right to own
property in their own names. Even today, there is no
legal remedy for rape within marriage, and many men and
some women make the assumption that if rape is legal, then
wife-beating must be legal also. In fact, some states
still have laws on the books that regulate the husband's
behavior--such as limiting the hours when he may beat his
wife! It is not surprising, then, that with these kinds
of legal and cultural attitudes a great deal of violence
occurs today within the American family.

What happens to the woman who finds herself in an abuse
situation? Usually she goes through several stages of
frustration and powerlessness as it escalates into a life-
and-death battle. Let us examine some of the forces she
runs up against as she tries to deal with her situation.
They include the attitudes of the police and the courts,
women's economic dependence within marriage, and women's
psychological powerlessness.

The Police and the Courts

Many women have told us that calling the police just doesn't
help. Sometimes the police won't come at all if they know
that it's a domestic disturbance. If they do come, chances
are they won't do anything. One reason is that they are
hampered by the law which, in most cases, states the police
must witness the assault to make an arrest. In addition,
more than 40 percent of all police injuries occur in response to domestic calls--so the police are understandably
reluctant to put themselves in high-risk situations. Further, the police often tend to empathize with the husband
and to blame the wife for "aggravating" him. They sometimes

decline to advise the woman what legal procedures she can
take. These procedures usually include filing a complaint
against the husband--which generally proves to be a waste
of time. First, the woman may find it difficult to file a
complaint unless she has bruises or cuts to display in the
D.A.'s office. Second, a woman may be afraid to press
charges against her husband for fear of retaliation. If
the case does come to court, it probably takes months,
during which time the woman is living with her assailant.
It is ludicrous for a woman to have to live with the person
she is prosecuting. One woman said to us, "If he put me
in the hospital for serving him lukewarm coffee, what will
he do to me if I prosecute?"

In addition to all this, the court encourages her to drop
the charges against her husband if he promises to leave
her alone. Intimidated by the authority of the court, she
usually agrees. If she says no, however, and pushes the
case through to conviction, the usual sentence is a short
nonreporting probation--not very effective when it comes
to protection. If it's his second or third conviction, he
may be incarcerated but, once again, there's no telling
what he'll do when he gets out, and if a woman has been
economically dependent on her husband, his incarceration
may only increase her problems by removing her sole source
of income.

The courts tend to view the problem as a social rather than
a legal one, taking the attitude that what goes on behind
closed doors is between husband and wife. While we would
not like to see an invasion of privacy, there certainly
should be a point of intervention. A woman should be as
safe--if not safer--in her own home as she is on the street.
(Of course, she's not very safe there either, as rape and
mugging statistics show.) In a recent study conducted in
Kansas City, police statistics showed that homicides due to
marital violence had been preceded by at least one phone
call to the police in 85 percent of the cases, and five
or more calls to the police in 50 percent. It is clear then
that these violent situations are not all hidden away
behind closed doors. Often, someone knows what is going
on. Often, it is apparent that tensions are building up
to a tragedy--yet nothing is done. Although one in four
homicides occurs between spouses, and although the FBI
says that reported cases of wife-beating outnumber rape by
three to one (1973 figures), we find that there is little
or no help for the victims of such crimes.

So Why Doesn't She Leave Him? Women's Economic Dependence within Marriage

Many people assume that women must actually enjoy physical abuse or they would simply get up and leave. What we have found, however, is that it's not that simple. For the woman who is economically dependent on her husband, the reality is that there is no place for her to go. With no money to find a place of her own, especially if she has children, the situation looks bleak. Many realtors are reluctant to rent to a single woman with children. If she considers going home to her family or to friends, she may fear inflicting her husband's violence on them as well. For the low-income woman, going home may be impossible anyway, since quite likely there is no room or money. If a woman decides to leave alone without her children, she may feel guilty about exposing them to her husband's violence. If she tries to get a job, her husband will often prevent it or follow her to work and harass her, jeopardizing her job. If she tries to get welfare, she is usually told that she must be living apart from her husband in order to qualify. In addition to all that, in most localities there is no legal way to force a man from his property, and invariably the abusive husband refuses to leave. Even for the woman who does manage to escape, the problems are not necessarily over. Often, the husband will follow her to her new address, break in, and beat her. Many women find that the only way that they will ever again feel secure is to disappear completely--a difficult thing to accomplish.

In addition to the harsh economic realities facing her, the abused woman finds little, if any, support from friends and family. Often, people are reluctant to believe what is happening. Quite frequently the abusive husband exhibits a totally different image to the surrounding community. Many are well liked and are even pillars of their particular community. At Women in Transition we've taken to calling it the Dr. Jekyll/Mr. Hyde syndrome. As with rape, this is a situation in which the victim tends to be made into the criminal. The assumption is that she must have asked for it, must have provoked it in some way. Many women are too ashamed to admit what is going on. They feel that they must be failing in their roles as wives and mothers, or that people will see them that way. As a result, most abused women will not talk about what is happening to them. They assume that they are the only ones going through it.

They may not be aware that the woman down the block or
across the street is experiencing the same problem. If
they admit the problem to anyone, they feel that they will
then look like fools to stay in the marriage. They tend to
blame themselves, not their husbands. The woman who does
share her problem may hear things like "Well, you made
your bed, now you have to lie in it," "You should try to
save the marriage at any cost," or "Are you sure that
you don't really like it?"

How Does She Get in the Situation in the First Place? The Psychology of Powerlessness

Usually the abused woman has no knowledge before the marriage that her husband is going to be violent. It is not
until after the wedding and she becomes "his" that the
violence begins. Her first reaction is usually one of
disbelief that she is being betrayed to such an extent.
She loves him, she's sure that he won't do it again. It
takes her a while to face it. Then she thinks that she
can change him, that they can work it out in some way.
When this doesn't succeed, she sometimes tries to get help.
Traditional marriage counselors, however, prove to be not
very helpful, since they usually do not deal with the
power dynamics within the family and since most abusive
husbands refuse to seek help or go to a counselor with
their wives anyway, seeing it as a sign of weakness.

Once a woman has gone through these processes, some time has
gone by; perhaps several beatings have occurred. Although
she may not realize it, the abuse has begun to take an
emotional as well as a physical toll. There is a psychological process. Many people are familiar with the effects
that terrorism has on a community of people. Individuals
become jumpy, fearful, insecure, never knowing when the
next bomb may go off, when the next attack may occur.
Wife abuse is terrorism on a personal basis. The wife finds
herself living in fear. She never knows when the next
violent act may occur. Feelings of powerlessness and hopelessness develop as she tries to escape and finds that she
can't. Living in that manner begins to affect her general
outlook, and paranoia may develop. An atmosphere of fear
and violence does not support emotional health. The woman
begins to lose whatever self-confidence she may have had

before the abuse and she often transfers that attitude to
other areas of her life. She starts to think less and less
of herself as a person because she isn't fighting back,
she isn't getting out. Her family and friends are iso-
lating her more and more, and she withdraws. She tends to
make herself into the criminal, thinking, "Oh, I must have
asked for it. If only I hadn't said this or done that,
maybe he wouldn't have exploded."

Guilt is a major factor. Many women internalize the concept
that they are responsible for the emotional well-being of
family members and blame themselves when their husbands
become violent or uncontrollable. These factors combine
with the feelings of powerlessness that are reinforced with
every beating. She is constantly being told how powerless
she is: "Look at what I can do to you with a flick of my
wrist, just try to stop me and see what happens." She
becomes paralyzed, emotionally as well as physically
crippled. Most of the women who call Women in Transition
are literally trapped within their situations but even
those women who can get out often don't. The reason that
they don't is that they *think* that they can't even when
they can. So what we have here is an insidious undermining
of the abused woman's mental as well as physical health.
That leaves her in the position of reinforcing the myth of
her own masochism by her inability to leave her violent
husband.

In her *Wifebeating* pamphlet Betsy Warrior gives a startling
view of the ways the psychiatric establishment has been
responsible for perpetuating the physical abuse of women.
In *Time* magazine an article on "Wife Beaters and Their
Wives"* gave an account of the "findings" of three Massachusetts psychiatrists who dealt with thirty-seven cases of
wife-beating referred to them by the courts. Some of the
traits found in the wives were "aggressive, efficient, masculine and sexually frigid." The article goes on to say,
"The wife, whose father had also been a wife beater, would
resist. The ensuing fight had, however, helpful overtones."
The period of violent behavior by the husband, the doctors
observed, "served to release him momentarily from his anxiety
about his effectiveness as a man, while giving his wife
apparent masochistic gratification and helping probably to
deal with the guilt arising from intense hostility expressed
in her controlling, castrating behavior."*

Time magazine, September 25, 1964.

That report clearly illustrates the sexist attitudes that
pervade traditional psychiatric thinking: the assumptions
that aggressiveness and efficiency are characteristics
that should belong only to men, and that women who are not
passive and weak are neurotic; the attitude that wife-
beating might not be all that bad since it gives a man
the chance to feel better about his masculinity; the
automatic assumption that women are inherently masochistic.
It is no wonder that many abused women feel no alternative
but to stay and "take it."

In fact, within some ethnic communities women are taught
that it is part of the wifely role to take a certain
amount of abuse, that it is part of the "worse" of the "for
better or for worse" in the marriage ceremony. We have
found that some women have so internalized the idea that
women are inferior that they actually feel if their husbands
don't hit them their husbands don't love them.

In these situations the woman actually needs to be abused
to have her negative self-image reinforced. When her
husband abuses her, she can feel satisfied that she has
performed her female function of feeding and building his
ego. She lets him "feel like a man." She has become the
proper object and servant that society has taught her is
her "natural" function. In many ways we can compare male-
female relationships to parent-child relationships. The
parent (husband) knows what is best for the child (wife),
makes all the important decisions, takes care of the money
because children (women) just "don't know how to handle
these things," and, of course, is responsible for "discipline." We are considered inadequate parents if we don't
properly discipline our children; perhaps many husbands
would feel inadequate if they didn't properly "discipline"
their wives. Husbands and parents can control through fear;
by being bigger and more powerful they can intimidate their
"lessers" into desired behavior. And although adult women
may be more able than children to escape physical abuse,
they are often too controlled by fear to take the necessary
steps. As the beatings continue over a period of time,
they tend to escalate in severity. The abused woman finds
that just when things are getting totally out of hand, she
is least capable of fighting back and getting out, since
the emotional crippling has become so severe.

Sometimes the woman will be the first to become violent.
That usually happens when she has been goaded beyond her
power to control her feelings. Men, having been conditioned

to maintain control over their emotions, can often stay calmer longer. Once a man has succeeded in making his wife violent, he then has an excuse to respond with further violence. Occasionally when a homicide results from patterns of abuse, we find that it is the husband rather than the wife who gets killed. Generally that comes about in the wife's self-defense. Recently, in Philadelphia, a Common Pleas judge set free a woman who had killed her husband by grabbing his shirt collar and strangling him as he leaned her back over a burning stove and threatened her with a knife. The incident was witnessed by the couple's children, who testified that he had been abusing her for years. The judge's comment upon acquittal: "What took you so long?"

What Kind of Man Abuses His Wife?

Generally the abusive husband is a man who is insecure about his masculinity. Perhaps he has not done well living up to the "he-man" image that society has created for him. If he feels inadequate about his manhood, the more an abusive husband can put his wife down, the more he can build himself up. Many men cannot feel "manly" without dominating and controlling women; they measure their own self-worth by how willingly women submit to them. Alcohol often plays a part in the abusive situation. Quite frequently the husband is drunk when beating his wife. Some of those men are alcoholics, some are not. We don't think that the use of alcohol creates the abuse. Generally it is used as a crutch by the abuser. It allows him to go ahead and become violent. Later, he can forget what happened, say he is sorry, and promise never to do it again--a common pattern. Many men who abuse their wives, however, do not use alcohol in this way.

Wife Abuse and Child Abuse

We have observed some correlation between these two forms of abuse. The man who beats his wife is likely to beat his child as well. Often this happens when the husband/ father feels that his authority is being challenged by his children or his wife. In that situation, he resorts to

violence to keep them "in their place." The same frustrations that lead a man to beat his wife may lead him to beat
his child (extreme insecurity, failure in the business
world).

Sometimes women who are themselves beaten will turn around
and beat their children, the only people in the family
with less power than them. This is a tragic extension of
the powerlessness of women within the nuclear family. We
discuss this further in Chapter 5.

Class and Race Differences

We have found that wife-beating crosses lines of class and
race. Many people think that it happens only in low-income
neighborhoods, but that is untrue. There are several
reasons why wife-beating is considered a low-income phenomenon. First, police statistics seem to indicate that
domestic violence occurs more frequently in low-income
neighborhoods, but that is because they are more involved
in the lives of low-income people in the first place.
Second, it is easier to hide abuse in the suburbs where
people do not live on top of one another. In the city,
where people are crowded together, everyone knows what's
going on in the next apartment. Third, middle-class
violence, like white-collar crime, tends to be more subtle
and sophisticated and ignored by law enforcement agencies.
The middle-class man has learned to express hostility in
roundabout ways that do not jeopardize the image that he
has attained. The white-collar man quite possibly has
others, besides just his wife, underneath him in the
pecking order, such as secretaries or other employees that
he supervises. He has the opportunity to take some of
his frustrations and resentments out on these people
rather than bringing it all home to his wife. The low-
income man, however, has only his wife "underneath" him,
so she is more likely to become his sole target.

We have found that the middle-class woman is less likely
to fight back on a physical level than the low-income
woman. The low-income woman is usually more accustomed to
physical violence because often she has had to know how
to fight to survive in the streets. The middle-class
woman, trained to be dependent and passive, tends to sit
and "take it" longer. Although she has more resources

to fall back on (money, family), she tends to use them
less. She may be more controlled by feelings of fear and
terror. She probably feels more ashamed, partly because
"those things" aren't supposed to happen in her community.
If she has any history of emotional breakdown or psychiatric treatment, she will have a harder time convincing
friends and family that what is happening is real. They
may not believe her. The low-income woman is more likely
to fight back physically and emotionally because she has
virtually no resources but herself to fall back on. The
institutions that she is forced to rely on not only do not
help, but very often actually contribute to her desperation
by failing to respond in positive, constructive ways.
The welfare system, for example, often forces people to
lie about their situations in order to get any help
whatsoever.

The psychological effects of abuse can be particularly
damaging for the low-income or minority woman, who is
constantly getting mixed messages. On the one hand, she
is encouraged to be strong and independent and to get
out there and fight. On the other hand, she is encouraged
to adopt submissive, subservient attitudes on the home
front to satisfy her man. Those contradictions have forced
many low-income women into damaging internal conflict
as they move to gain control over their lives.

What Are the Solutions?

On a large scale, temporary shelters for battered women
and their children need to be created so that they will
have someplace to go to escape the abusive husband. Supportive services such as day care, job counseling, legal
help, and self-defense instruction need to be developed.
Emotional support groups need to be created so that
battered wives can come together to share their feelings
and survival techniques. Significant community education
and outreach are needed to make people aware of and knowledgeable about the problem. There must be changes within
police practices and the criminal justice system so that
battered women will receive every protection of the law.
Mental health personnel need to intervene so that both
the husband and wife can receive help before the situation
gets out of hand. Sensitivity training for those who come
into contact with the abused wife and special domestic

relations squads within the police department should be
established. The antirape groups in this country have
changed the national consciousness regarding rape. Whereas
sympathy and concern for the criminal rather than the
victim once was the prevailing norm, the situation is
changing and women are now receiving better and fairer
treatment by both the police and the courts. These kinds of
attitudinal and procedural changes need to occur with wife
abuse as well. Funds should be appropriated to deal with
the problem, as with child abuse. There are many women's
groups throughout the country that are beginning to deal
with the wife abuse problem; they are listed in the back of
the book. We realize, of course, that most of those needed
measures will be a long time in coming, but some steps are
being taken, and as more are carried out, we hope to begin
seeing some solutions to a problem that for too long has
been swept under the rug.

How Does Wife Abuse Affect You?

If you are thinking about marriage, we strongly urge you
to give this issue some consideration. Even though you
may scoff at the notion that the important person in your
life would ever resort to violence, we must remind you that
the millions of women who have found themselves in this
position at first scoffed as well. As we have said, there
is no way to know beforehand that your husband-to-be will
become violent. You should not assume that such a thing
could not happen. Rather, you should be aware that it
could happen and be prepared to deal with it if necessary.
Economic dependence on your husband will ensure your being
trapped by his violence should it occur. It is very important that you know that you can get a job if you don't
have one or that you will have the resources to get out
if necessary. It is usually those women who are most
trapped who end up losing their lives. We don't mean to be
dramatic, but these are the realities that we have discovered. Try to pay attention to any warning signs that
may appear in your fiancé's behavior before the marriage:
reluctance to talk about his past, extreme insecurity,
frequent references to rape, violence, guns. Although it
may seem foolish to make a big deal out of some offhand re-
mark, you may be doing yourself a favor in the long run.
We realize that the last thing a prospective bride wants to
do is to be suspicious of her mate, but it is as important

to be practical as it is to be romantic. We know that it
would be very hard for you to start thinking that this
particular person is not for you, but you can always
change your mind later if you begin to feel more secure
about him. Premarriage counseling may be helpful. If he
is reluctant to try this, you should question his reasons.

If you are already married and have discovered that your
husband is violent, we make the following suggestions.
First, make sure you read the legal chapter of this book
for suggestions about prosecution. Usually it doesn't
do much good but you may want to try it anyway. We have
found that most men fall somewhere on the line between
those who just slap their wives around a little on the
weekend and those who have undertaken a systematic program
of torture and abuse. It is our feeling that if your
husband falls anywhere along this line beyond very mild
slapping around, you should seriously think about getting
out. We should remind you that wife abuse escalates.
Violence begets violence. Chances are that your husband's
beatings will increase in number and severity as time goes
by. And the more time goes by, the more difficult it
becomes to get out. It is crucial that you don't sit and
falsely hope that he will change. Most likely he won't,
not unless he gets extensive counseling. If he did get help
after you left, you could always go back with him once you
felt that he had made substantial changes. It is extremely
important not to let fear and feelings of frustration and
hopelessness control you. You should remember that you
are being affected emotionally by the abuse, and probably
just getting out will make a huge difference.

If there are children, you must put their welfare and yours
before any considerations of wifely duty or obligation.
It is important to recognize that it is time to give up and
move to protect yourself and your children. Once again,
don't let time pass. One or two severe beatings should
be enough to convince you to leave, even if the beatings
are far apart. They *will* become more frequent. Facing the
reality that your husband is a wife-beater is difficult,
but holding on to the vain hope that it won't happen again
can end in destruction.

Once you have made the decision to leave, evaluate your
resources. If you have family or friends who will help, do
not hesitate to take advantage of their support. Using
a friend's address, try to get on welfare without your
husband's knowledge; save a couple of checks and use them

for a security deposit and a month's rent. If you have
any money of your own, don't let your husband know about
it. If you do leave, don't let him know where you are, if
you can help it. Talk to someone! Tell someone you trust
about your situation. Don't hesitate to ask for help and
support. Don't be too ashamed to talk about your situation.
It is *not your fault*. Contact any women's group, women's
center, or wife abuse program in your area (see the Resource section for this chapter). If you can afford it,
get good legal help. If you qualify for a community legal
service program, seek help there (forcefully). Take concrete steps. No matter how boxed in you may feel, there
is a way out. Succumbing to feelings of powerlessness will
only ensure that you feel even more powerless later on.
Develop your emotional strength and independence. We know
that you are probably afraid, but keep thinking about how
good you are going to feel once you are free. True, you
may have to go through some rough times to reach your goal,
but nothing could be rougher than what you are going
through now. You are entitled to a life free from terror
and abuse. You have tried to be a good wife. You have
paid the price of silence and submission. You have more
than earned the *right* to survive as a human being. Now
you face the fact that you have tremendous obstacles to
overcome as you try to exercise that right. We guarantee
that the situation is not as hopeless as it seems. Recognizing that fact can be the first step as you move to
build the life that you deserve.

BARRY KOHN

BARRY KOHN

9

JACK

Deborah and I got married in 1965 and we separated in 1974. Since we did separate, some people think that our marriage was a failure, but I do not see it that way. Even though I was the one who wanted it to end, I think there were many really good parts to our relationship and that we grew a lot as a couple over the ten years we were together.

One of the big things that happened to us was that Deborah got involved in the women's movement after our being together for about ten years. She got into a consciousness-raising group and it really meant a lot to her. As a result, she thinks of herself as a strong feminist and feminism influences a lot of the choices she makes for herself.

Over the years I have become very enthusiastic about feminism. I believe in it politically as a broad movement and concretely in my own life. I think it had a deep and positive influence on Deborah and me. I didn't always think this way, though. At the beginning I was very threatened by the changes Deborah was going through as she got into it. She challenged a lot of things in me and in our marriage and I fought back. But I did change a lot and I gained a lot.

Feminism affected us in four ways: housework, friendships, sexuality, and parenting. They became issues in our lives in about that order.

Housework: When Deborah and I started living together, we just fell into a way of sharing housework without any self-conscious planning. I don't remember any talk between us about who would do what. We just seemed to agree automatically, even though she wound up with a bigger share of the load and with the psychological burden of being responsible for everything. Though we were both working she got the job of planning the meals and cooking. She also did all the clothes washing and ironing. We split shopping and we split cleaning, though there wasn't much of that except when our parents visited. I did the "man's work," of course, like taking care of the car and putting up shelves. I think it was pretty typical for people who were not yet questioning sex roles, but who had some general ideas that people should not exploit one another too much or too obviously.

After about two years she began to raise some questions about me helping with cooking. It seemed reasonable that I should help out when she asked me specifically and I don't remember thinking that cooking was "women's work" or beneath me. But I didn't like her suggestion that I should take on an equal share of cooking as my basic duty. I wanted her to thank me whenever I did a job that I saw as being above and beyond my limited responsibility. For a long while Deborah did thank me. That made it easier for me to do work because I was still doing things as a favor to her.

For the next couple of years Deborah pushed slowly and I continued slowly to take on more. I still wanted her to thank me though. Obviously there was more at stake than a few minutes a day of housework, though neither of us could have said then what it was. She was starting to challenge my view that it was basically her job to take care of me and to please me. This tension was a forerunner to the struggles that were to come. Still, it was not until she was already in her consciousness-raising group that she called a stop to the thank-yous. By then I was doing about half of the housework. (Holding out on clothes washing was my last line of defense.) But dealing with the thank-yous and what they represented was harder than dealing with the actual work load. I felt a lot of resentment. I gave up my demand for thank-yous because I had no choice

330

and because I got to feeling pretty silly for pushing it. It was so petty, and there was no way I could win once Deborah had made up her mind. Still, it took a while for my emotions to catch up with the fact that we were going to be fully equal partners in housework, in spirit as well as in practice.

In fact, when our son was born shortly after, I regressed. I felt that Deborah should take a larger share of the work since she stopped working outside the house at that point. She felt that the dirt was still partly mine and that cleaning it was not how she wanted to spend her time. I was not at all pleased and we wrestled with the problem again until she returned to a paying job. During our last several years together we had finally worked out the issue to a point of equal sharing of work and sense of responsibility.

All in all, it was not the hardest change we went through, though it got nasty and was serious for us at the time. Finally, I came to feel more comfortable as an equal partner than I had felt when I was in the position of being served and I felt good about having moved what seemed like a long way. (I didn't know then the other struggles that were to come which made this seem easy.)

Besides appeasing Deborah and feeling more consistent ideologically, there was another reason why I changed. Even as I was just starting to take on more responsibility, and even though I was resenting and resisting, I also took pleasure in my growing accomplishments as a homemaker. Now I really enjoy my ability to organize my house and I like to serve people I care about. When someone chooses to serve me, I can accept that with more ease. I feel that I have gained a lot.

Friendships: My relationships with friends, especially with men, were much influenced by Deborah's feminism. Her closeness with other women was a model for me as I began to form friendships with men in the years she and I were together. This has finally led me to a strong commitment to men and to male liberation, though my struggles with the issues that keep me from being more involved with men are far from over.

Most of Deborah's and my friendships at the beginning of our marriage were shared friendships. We presented a "couple front" to the world and our friends tended to be people in couples. When the various foursomes got together, Deborah and the woman of the other couple usually had the most lively and personal discussions. The next most lively parts were between the other woman and myself and the other man and Deborah. The least exciting things happened between the other man and me. I had enough awareness to more or less realize that this was going on, but I didn't understand why and I didn't know what to do about it. I just assumed that I could not be a good friend. I also felt Deborah was very good at relating to people, which was intimidating to me. I felt that our couple friends were basically attracted to Deborah and were nice to me because she and I came together as a package. Also I would be angry with the other man for not being able to reach out to me. Time after time, at the end of an evening, I would complain to Deborah about the shortcomings of the men we knew.

Friendships did matter to me, but I had no doubt that the relationship with Deborah was where I had to go for closeness and sharing. Friendships were mostly entertainment--good entertainment for Deborah and fair entertainment for me. Neither of us saw them as basic to our sense of well-being.

Deborah was the first to change. Gradually, her women's group helped her to experience a new way of relating to women that was different from the way she related to them when men were around. Her relationships with several women were very loving. They stopped being entertainment and started being part of the support which Deborah counted on every day.

I had mixed reactions. Partly I was envious of her relationships. Often I would ask Deborah what she and her friends had talked about and what was going on in their lives. I wanted to be part of a relationship like the ones I saw her in, even vicariously. My way of experiencing the contact I needed with other people was often through Deborah. My own involvement with my male friends, or more realistically with my male acquaintances, did not have the vitality I experienced Deborah's friendships as having. Deborah was onto something important that I was missing.

I also felt left out and even abandoned by her. For example, on the nights Deborah would go to her consciousness-raising group, I would get more and more angry as the evening wore on. By the time she got home, I was often

332

furious, for reasons I couldn't even fully explain to myself. Looking back, I think I half knew that things were going on with her and other women that would lessen her need for me. I also did not like the fact that she might be discussing me with the women in her group, who were women I knew. It was only after we talked when she came home from her group, and I felt that I was still important to her, that I got less angry. But then, as her group got more personal, and as her friendships became closer, there was more that she wouldn't share with me. I had to face the fact that there were some important things going on with her that I was just not going to know about. At that point I was really worried. I was jealous of Deborah's other relationships, envious of them, and frightened of being more alone.

At that time I was going through a three-year psychoanalysis which was a big help in freeing me to get closer to men. In the analysis I talked about my sexual feelings toward men and about my fears of those feelings. Since college I had been aware of homosexual feelings and they had been very upsetting to me. One of the ways I tried to control them was by being more formal and distant with men. As I started to be less afraid of the homosexual feelings, I was able to let men into my life more fully-- though with false starts and retreats.

About a year later I became part of a group of men. Several of us who had known one another from political work found ourselves at a meeting joining together as a leftist minority. It felt so good to have support for a position we all felt deeply about but were accustomed to defending alone that we suggested to each other that we get together again. We all had been through experiences that made us ready for each other and shortly after we formed a group that continued for over two years. Our little collective was part men's group, part therapy group, part play group, and part study group. At times we were very close to one another and very helpful to each other through a wide range of life crises. When the group ended, we all felt that it had been quite important to us, though we were also aware that there had been some issues we could not get into, and that there were some important barriers remaining.

During this time I also had a number of false starts in individual friendships with men. As I look back I can recount a fairly long list of men I made overtures toward as friends that didn't work out for one reason or another.

333

Within a few years, however, I found myself involved in friendships with two separate men that were closer than any relationships with men I had had. In both cases they grew out of couple friendships Deborah and I had been in, so the men and I had had a while to get to know one another in a "safer" situation before we struck out on our own. It was very exciting for me to have those friends. The simplest things, like talking on the phone at night and chatting over the day's events with one or both of them, made me high. I felt as though I were becoming a whole new person. I loved the friendships, I loved the men, and I was very pleased with myself.

Those friendships have since had their ups and downs. My relationship with one of the men had setbacks because of split loyalties when Deborah and I separated, and my other friend moved out of the city. Even so, both relationships continue and I value them both. But I am dissatisfied with the extent and depth of my male friendships at this point.

Sexuality: There is a period of about five years of Deborah's and my sexual relationship that I don't remember. I can remember the very beginning, and I remember what happened around the fifth year of the marriage when the clitoris was discovered (rediscovered, really) in our family. In between is largely a blank.

For the first couple of months our sex was mostly a little foreplay and then intercourse with me coming pretty quickly. After I came, Deborah sometimes had the courage to ask me to caress her clitoris. But usually I lost interest in touching her after my own orgasm. In fact, touching her clitoris at all became more and more dis- tasteful to me and I didn't do it often. I was also very uncomfortable with her touching herself, which she wanted to do, and before too long I had discouraged her doing it. Despite this, I thought of myself as a good lover. I thought Deborah had problems, though, because she didn't come more quickly and because she made so many demands on me.

After the first couple of months, we settled into having sex perhaps twice a week. We experimented quite a lot with positions though not with anything else, and we never talked over what we were feeling about sex or what was happening with us. I did not have any great joy in sex and I certainly didn't think of myself as much of a sexual or sensual person. In fact, I think that I was pretty removed from the sex that was going on. It doesn't surprise me that I can barely remember that time.

Anne Koedt's "The Myth of the Vaginal Orgasm"* changed a lot of things for me and Deborah, as it did for many people. Deborah had gotten hold of it first. She showed it to me and we talked about it, but at first we didn't change the way we were with each other sexually. In not too long a time, though, Deborah put out two strong expectations. The first was that she fully expected to, and planned to, have an orgasm every time we made love. The second was that she wanted direct clitoral stimulation from my hand or mouth since she did not and would not have an orgasm from my penis being in her. I got unhinged.

I would hardly talk to her and we stopped making love for several weeks. Having to help doing laundry had made me unhappy, but it was manageable. This was not. I felt that Deborah was telling me that she did not need my penis, and I reacted just as though she were telling me that she didn't need me. A lot of my sense of myself as a lover and lot of my own sexual pleasure involved my penis. If that was not going to be the prime source of Deborah's sexual pleasure, then she might as well make love just to my finger or tongue or perhaps to a woman.

The idea that Deborah expected to have an orgasm each time we had sex was also a big problem for me and seemed like an enormous imposition. It meant that I would have to be involved with her clitoris again. It also meant that I would have to make a serious effort to please her, when the whole pattern of our relationship had been for her to please me. She was demanding that our sex shift from me masturbating with her help to a shared experience between us. One of the scary parts of that was the pressure for me to recognize her as a sexual person. Over the years I had come to see her as not being too sexual as a way to cope with some of the fears I had about sexuality. The more we were really in contact with each other sexually, the harder it was to keep those fears down.

After this initial shock and more talking, my resistance did weaken and we started to make love again, though at first not too often. I had to summon up an energy for lovemaking that had not been called on before. One thing

*Information on obtaining this article is found in the Bibliography.

335

that meant is that we made love only when we both were more interested in doing so. It also meant we had to talk more than we had before about what was happening during sex. It was not an easy process and I brought a lot of anger into our lovemaking for several months. However, after a period under this new set of rules, some important changes began to take place in me.

I was forced to think about what felt good to Deborah. She insisted on it, and since I was not prepared to do without sex, I had to respond. In the process I began to learn not only what felt good to her, but also woke to the fact that there was pleasure for me in bringing her pleasure--at first just a little, but then more and more. Also I could be more open myself about what was happening between us which meant more freedom to ask for the things I enjoyed sexually. I could also discuss more fully the fears I had of my own inadequacy as a sexual partner. As a consequence of some of this discussion, for example, I got out from under the burden of constantly struggling with "coming too soon." I had been in the position of always being a failure in that respect, since whenever I came it was before Deborah's orgasm. Even though biology was destiny in this case, I had felt inadequate. Having an orgasm that was overcast with worries about premature ejaculation was quite a different experience from having an orgasm that seemed well deserved and that was happily received. We were both freed from the tyranny of the vaginal orgasm. We understood the clitoris more fully and did not see it as a last resort when all else failed. Our sex life improved a lot.

These changes led me to a broader understanding of my own sexuality. As I learned that my penis was less important to Deborah than I had thought it was, or at least had hoped it was, I discovered that it was less important to me also. The demands she made eventually opened up our range of sexual activity. We got more into touching, licking, and casualness. That sense of the variety and playfulness and fullness of sexuality has continued to grow for me. Coming is still important. But when sex is good, it is just one of the pleasures to be found in being with another person in a physical way. It is startling to me, and embarrassing, to think about where I was in those early days, especially about not wanting to touch Deborah after I came. Now when I am fully turned on to another person, my sensuality is still alive after I come, and touching and caressing in a variety of ways can be as fresh and delightful after coming as before.

There have been a lot of forces leading me to where I am sexually. But a crucial one was Deborah's demand on me, her insistence on having a satisfying sex life and her willingness to push me until she got it. I'm glad now that she did push.

Parenting: For many years I said no to Deborah's desire to have a child. It wasn't that I had thought a lot about what being a parent would mean, or about the loss of freedom to do other things. I did know that I was living with painful feelings about my marriage. At the time having a child seemed to guarantee that Deborah and I could never separate.

Deborah felt strongly about it, however. As her thirtieth birthday got closer, she put more pressure on me. Since I could not get clear that I would or could leave the marriage, and did not seem to be getting less ambivalent as time went on, I agreed. To be more accurate, I gave in. Once I agreed to have a child I buried my doubts about the marriage (they stayed buried for several more years) and got into the pregnancy with enthusiasm. The delivery itself was long and hard, but having gone through natural childbirth classes and being together in the labor room made it easier. The actual birth was, and remains, the single most exciting event of my life. I was awed and I was ecstatic.

We basically assumed a "liberal" stance toward shared parenting at the beginning. I did not make any special plans to free myself from my other work but I did feel that I should be involved in childrearing in the time that was left over. That wasn't much and I was not really motivated to make it more. For the first half year there were few pleasures for me in parenting. Aaron was born in January and I remember fantasies as I would try to rock him back to sleep in the middle of the night of wanting to throw him out the second-floor window into the snowy backyard. But I also remember a fantasy of regretting that I could not nurse him which was often such a nice experience for him and for Deborah.

Over time two things happened. Aaron became more respon- sive and more interesting as he got older. I felt I could be useful and even important to him and I saw that he was beginning to develop an attachment for me. The other thing that happened was that Deborah went back to work, a day a week when Aaron was six months old, half-time when he was a year old, and full-time two years later. Her

337

women's group gave her support for this. Without it that decision would have been much harder and maybe impossible. The women's movement also shaped the way I was thinking about how involved I would be in raising Aaron. I was getting it from Deborah as well as from other people I was meeting and from the things I was reading. When Deborah went back to work a day a week, I spent half that day with Aaron and when she worked full-time I was often the one to pick Aaron up at his babysitter's house, feed him supper, and put him to bed.

Over the four years we all lived together we got to the point of sharing parenting just about equally. In fact, I got involved with Aaron at a level that surprised both of us and felt love for him that was as rich and clear as any love I had ever felt. I looked forward to weekends and vacations a great deal for the chance to be with him more and I missed him if a night or two went by with meetings that kept me from being with him.

When Deborah and I separated, we both felt that we wanted to work out a joint parenting arrangement. We each needed our involvement with Aaron for our own sakes, and we knew that he was actively involved with both of us. After a few months we established the pattern we still have. He is with me from Thursday after school until Sunday morning and with Deborah from Sunday morning until Thursday morning. We generally split vacation times equally and each of us has been comfortable in taking over with Aaron on the fairly frequent occasions when the other wanted a weekend or week away on business or pleasure. We share responsibilities such as keeping up with school meetings, running birthday parties, arranging doctor visits, and the like. These child care arrangements work out well for all of us partly because Deborah and I live near one another and partly because we still see eye to eye on most issues. Aaron is not something we disagree about. He and we have adapted well to the arrangements. Despite our fears, and a lot of what we had heard, we learned that a so-called broken home does not have to be a disaster for kids and in fact can have much that is positive.

The women's movement did a lot for Deborah, for me, and for us. It helped Deborah feel more sense of self-worth and competence, and this showed up in many places in her life. In turn, she pushed me to become more than I had been. What we were moving toward was frightening at first

338

because it was different and it was unknown. But we became fuller people as a result and our relationship became richer. We got closer to one another and at the same time we learned to allow each other to be more separate.

At the end, however, I came to feel strongly that the separation was necessary. Deborah did not want to separate, though she believes that she too has grown from the experience. Despite the pain the separation caused, especially for Deborah, our relationship since then has been mostly friendly. We got a divorce in 1976 without bitterness or disagreement.

I said earlier that I believe that feminism not only strengthened our marriage but that it also contributed to the separation. Deborah and I disagree somewhat on what that contribution is. She feels that I got too threatened by her growth and independence. There may be some truth in this, though honestly, I am more aware of the part of me that was excited and challenged by each new breakthrough we made.

In the first years our experiences together were not very rich; we did not really expect them to be. We made few demands on each other for deep satisfaction and we got little. This allowed us to continue safely, though painfully, in our old patterns. It wasn't a good way to live, but it was a way to live. As we both changed, we started to want more and we had the courage to press for more. There was considerable give in our relationship. But the limitations that had been built in from the start could not be overcome, at least for me.

At some point I would like to be involved once more in a close love relationship. That relationship will surely have its own issues and struggles, but some of what has already been achieved will not need to be repeated. For this I owe much to the women's movement, and, more recently, to the men's movement. I don't feel that I have "arrived" as some kind of fully liberated person. I do feel that I am better equipped than I was to keep working to liberate myself and perhaps to make a small contribution to other people's efforts to do the same.

9 / Not for Men Only

Taking the Risk

If you are a man reading this chapter, chances are it's
because you have noticed changes in your wife or partner
which are unsettling to you. Perhaps she is insisting that
you help with the housework, or she wants to get a job
outside the home, or she tells you that you don't satisfy
her in bed. Your first response probably is to get angry
and defensive. Housework? Only a henpecked husband would
agree to help with that. It's women's work. A paying job?
Isn't my salary enough? Disappointed in bed? Who do you
want, Robert Redford? You discover, however, that your
resistance only increases her determination to change the
way things are. If the two of you are going to stay to-
gether--and at this point you may wonder if that is pos-
sible--you realize that some change is inevitable, but the
prospect is frightening. You may be worried that upsetting
the roles that you feel comfortable and familiar with will
leave you both uncertain about what is expected of you.
You may fear that in the long run those changes will wreck
your marriage.

This is a difficult chapter for us to write. We are not
men; our ideas and feelings have been shaped by our

340

experiences as women. Sometimes we are angry about the
ways we have been kept down, both by individual men and
by "the system," which often benefits men at our expense.
When our anger subsides, we find ourselves feeling
compassion for men, especially for those of you who are
not satisfied with the established roles. We recognize
the dilemmas you face and the difficulty of the risks you
are taking. It may not be clear to you how you have been
victimized as well as rewarded for living out the male
role. You probably have no clear guidelines to follow if
you are earnestly trying to be supportive of women's struggles for equality, whether on the job, among friends, or
at home. Other people, men and sometimes women, may not
support you during this process of change. Further, there
are many myths about what women's liberation is, most of
which stem from the sensationalist way feminism is
usually portrayed in the media. You may have preconceived
negative ideas about egalitarian relationships that prevent
you from responding honestly and undefensively to what your
partner is asking.

For most men, responding to women's demands for change
requires that you go against the grain of everything you
were taught about being a man in this society. But in many
ways the socialization of little boys into he-men is as
damaging as the socialization of little girls into little
ladies. This is especially true within the marriage
relationship. Redefining the role of "husband" can be as
beneficial for you as redefining the role of "wife" can be
for your spouse. Such redefining is painful for everyone,
but especially for men. It may often appear to you that
your efforts are unappreciated; you may feel frustrated and
quite isolated. However, you may also experience the satisfaction of overcoming behavior patterns that have been destructive to you and to the woman or women in your life.
We know such victories are possible. We know a number of
men who are struggling to make concrete changes in their
behavior toward women and toward other men and are suc-
ceeding, slowly, in doing so. We will try to share with
you, without letting our own biases intrude too much, the
struggles and joys of these men. We admire them and you
for daring to change.

What Does It Mean to Be a Man?

Many of the problems that men have in their intimate relationships are a direct result of having successfully adapted
themselves to the image of American manhood that was held
before them from childhood on. What thoughts come into
your head when you think of the term *manly*? Someone who
is strong, assertive, tough, sexy, brave, athletic? Boys
and men are bombarded with messages about how they are
supposed to look and behave, and most of these messages
stress that strength is synonymous with masculinity,
weakness with femininity. Demonstrating that strength
on a day-to-day basis can take different forms, depending
on your background, but there are many characteristics
that all men are supposed to exhibit. Actual physical
strength, or at least the appearance of it, is particularly
important. Men who are short or slight may spend a good
part of their lives trying to make up for this supposed
inadequacy in other ways, such as being overly aggressive
at work or in personal relationships.

Athletic ability is another definition of maleness. Sports
culture in this country is saturated with "maleness" and
the emphasis is usually on the stars rather than on each
person developing her or his athletic capabilities to the
fullest. Many boys in grade school and high school struggle
to be stars and are crushed if they don't make the first
string. Some boys, especially those who are middle-class
and academically motivated, may be able to compensate for
their lack of athletic success by getting good grades or
being student leaders. But they may still feel they are
not quite acceptable and doubt their own masculinity.
Those who are successful in sports may get an inflated
sense of their own importance, only to discover that being
captain of the football team in high school does not
guarantee success for the rest of their lives.

PETER

*I'm somewhat of a mixture in temperament in that I'm
extremely competitive but not that aggressive. This
has caused some ego problems in my original family,
since both my mother and my brother are extremely
successful professionally and in their public life.
I've always compared myself to them in judging my*

*own success. As ideals, my image of them is so high
that it's almost impossible to meet. This has been
a real benefit of having a family which requires as
much time as Judy and the kids have. You might almost
say that I sought that out as a way to prevent myself
from being totally caught up in the inevitable
frustration of trying to be the complete professional
and public citizen that I saw my mother being.*

*Being successful is still very important to me. I
think I've been fortunate to be able to find jobs
where I've not been part of a hierarchical structure,
either reporting up or down through a large number of
people or having to time my work time precisely, for
example by a teaching schedule. I feel very lucky.
This has given me the freedom to visit the kids'
schools in the earlier years, to wait at home for
the appliance repairman before going to work, and to
make these kinds of telephone calls during the day.
This is because my job involves a lot of writing and
reading and fewer highly structured meetings than
many professional people. This has reduced a lot of
the pressure and strain that attempting to play a
broad-ranging family role would induce in many men.
To put it simply, I think I've been lucky.*

Throughout their lives men are expected to *produce*: to get
a good job and hold it, work hard, succeed, and preferably
make a lot of money, or in less well-paid occupations, such
as academics, to build prestige and honor for themselves.
On the job and among friends most men are acutely aware
of who has greater or lesser status, who makes more money
and who makes less, and they rate themselves accordingly.
Husbands are expected to be good providers for their families and not to take risks that would jeopardize their job
security. Men are expected to be competitive and to have
answers to all kinds of problems; to be able to take
charge in almost any situation. A man who admits that he
doesn't know something, or that he is confused or insecure,
can be seen as weak.

The behavior men are supposed to exhibit on the job is
usually carried over into personal relationships. Men's
relationships with each other are often based on competition and ego-building. Many men feel uncomfortable sharing
intimate feelings or insecurities with their male friends
and often spend time talking in a superficial way about
work, sports, and women. In many men there is a deep-

seated fear of homosexuality which keeps them from touching
each other except in prescribed ways (a slap on the rump
after a touchdown) and from growing close emotionally.
In their relationships with women most men expect that they
need to be strong and aggressive, that they need to take
the lead in asking a woman for a date, deciding what to
do, and initiating sexual activity. As a man gets closer
to a particular woman, their roles may become even more
rigidly defined.   Since it is considered a sign of
weakness for men to cry and show emotions such as tenderness
or sadness (as opposed to anger and joy, which are more
acceptable), he may look to his woman partner to express
those things for the two of them. He may feel uncomfortable if she expects support from him when she experiences
painful or confusing feelings.

Many of these definitions of manhood are reactionary ones,
that is, reactions to being not-female. Because female
characteristics are not as valued in this culture as male
characteristics and because over the centuries women have
been seen as unclean and mysterious, many men in fact perceive women as frightening, incomprehensible creatures.
Historically, women have been seen as wicked, destroying
the many virtues of hard work and rational thought, or as
immaculate, to be put on a pedestal and worshiped there.
Some men cope with those mixed, contradictory images by
avoiding closeness with women and by striving to prove
themselves as unlike women as possible.

The difficulty with all of these role expectations is that
they are very difficult to live up to and quite stifling
when you do live up to them. Perhaps you have already
found yourself acting in ways that you are not comfortable
with but that you don't understand and feel powerless to
change. You may not like having to be strong all the
time, to have answers, to take the initiative. It can be
exhausting. Yet because there is little support in this
society for men who do exhibit so-called feminine traits,
you may feel that there is something wrong with you and try
all the harder to live up to what you think is expected
of you.

JIM

*Some men feel that they must have an answer for
everything--when they're asked a question, they've
got to have an answer. My kids are always asking me*

*a million questions, and when I don't know, I just
tell them I don't know.*

In a country that values profit more than the physical and
mental well-being of its workers, most jobs, even at managerial and professional levels, are boring and frustrating.
But because many men are caught up in the common belief
that the amount of money they earn determines their worth,
they have no perspective for understanding why their lives
seem so meaningless. The deteriorating physical and
mental health of competitive career men has been well
documented. Blue-collar workers and poor men often find
their jobs even more frustrating because they have less
control over their working conditions. Men who cannot
find work or who are chronically underemployed often feel
extremely worthless. Hard-driving, competitive men who
are willing to work long hours may make excellent workers
in the eyes of a corporation president, but they usually
have difficulty making the transition to warm, sensitive
husbands and fathers. Most men try to get relief from
their lack of satisfaction at work by turning to their
wives for support, comfort, and the reassurance that they
are really O.K. people.

Many wives try to do that for their husbands, but it is
a huge task. It is really not possible to give someone
self-respect if he can't develop it by himself. In addition, most women are faced with their own frustrations,
from which they are hoping to find relief through their
husbands. If your partner does not work outside the home,
she may look to you for contact with the world outside
and feedback that *she* is really an O.K. person; if she
works at a paid job and takes care of the home and family
as well, she probably hopes for an encouraging word and
some concrete help with the housework. The two of you may
get into vicious patterns of not being able to give each
other what is needed and then penalizing each other for
not being able to do so. While women traditionally have
given each other support (what else did you think was going
on at those "hen sessions"?), the usual competition and sense
of reserve between men has kept them from developing meaningful relationships with each other, which contributes
further to a sense of isolation.

By trying to live up to the "manly" image a man can contribute heavily to the destructive patterns that exist between
husbands and wives. You may be vaguely aware that you are
uncomfortable in the role of sexual aggressor, under-

standing that this sets you up for rejection and stifles
the development of your own sensuality as well as your
sexuality. By sensuality, we mean the ability to touch
and caress without having to be striving for a sexual goal,
usually orgasm. Men have been trained to see women as
sexual objects (the *Playboy* ideal) and have consequently
suffered from the resulting lack of harmony among mind,
body, and feelings. A great deal of sexual frustration
for both men and women can result when men continue to
separate sex from love while women continue to try to
connect the two. Yet you may have no other models for
male sexual behavior and may be afraid of women who are
sexually aggressive. You may also be handicapped by the
distorted relationships that can develop when a man
allows the woman he is close to, to be responsible for
the emotional aspects of their relationship. Many men
are out of touch with what they really want and with what
will contribute to their psychological well-being. By
letting your "better half" be responsible for the feelings
and the crying and the nurturing, you may fail to develop
these characteristics in yourself. You may be missing
half of the qualities that are necessary to be a full
human being, just as women often lack strength and assertiveness. That inability to nurture themselves shows
up dramatically for some men. Divorced and widowed men,
for example, are often not only unable to take care of
their housekeeping needs but find themselves at a loss
to meet their emotional needs as well.

She bore three sons, and thus must live
Part of her life in a house of men,
A house of wiry hair in the shower,
Sticky semen on the sheets,
Moldy socks on the floors,
And air steamed up with sweat.

In vain did she dress her babies in fancy suits.
   They just spit up all over them and once, she told
     me, she cried.
In vain did she laughingly put ribbons in Keith's curls.
   Abe would have none of that.
In vain did she plan a twenty-fifth anniversary party.
   Abe only pounded his chest with masculine pride in
     front of everybody.
In vain does she buy new dresses.
   Abe <u>always</u> says "Very pretty, dear"--as he does
     when <u>I</u> get a new dress.

*"Could you please sort-of spray the tub after you
        take a shower?" she asks them.
And it reminds me of the man on TV who, about to be
        tortured, said,
"Couldn't you sort-of do it slowly."*

                              Marion D. Cohen

The inability to nurture oneself or others is evident less
dramatically but more frequently in many men's inability
to relate well to their children. Most men have been used
to having their needs met by women in various ways--mother,
girl friend, wife, secretary. Since they have not been
raised to see themselves as caretakers in any way but instead expect to get *their* needs met, it is difficult for them
to extend themselves emotionally to their children. You
may find yourself annoyed by, or frightened of, your children's demands. You may feel most comfortable disciplining
or instructing them and may be more relaxed with older
children who need less physical care and can relate to you
on a more adult level. Close contact with your children
may be limited to occasional family playtime or outings,
while the rest of the nurturing is left to their mother.

Why Men Get Married

Men--perhaps as much as women--live out what is expected of
them by family, friends, teachers, co-workers, and society
at large. Many men get married to bring into their lives
those qualities which they have been unable to develop
for themselves--nurture, tenderness, caring. They expect
to be the breadwinners and expect their wives to make a
comfortable nest for them. Most men have expectations
about marriage that are just as unrealistic as women's,
although because men also have job responsibilities to
worry about, they may not be as singlemindedly focused on
marriage as many women are. Many men think that in order
to be normal they must get married. Being married will
provide someone to keep house, a steady sexual partner, a
good image at work and in the community, and a mother for
their children. Men as well as women are influenced by
the widespread couple orientation in this country and want
the security and comfort that a close friendship can bring.
And many men feel that an attractive wife is a reflection
of their own success and power. Sometimes they may not be

so much interested in her as a person as in whether she
meets external standards of acceptability.

Men's expectations for marriage usually are not met, just
as women's are not. There may be a great deal of disillusionment after marriage. You may feel trapped by the
breadwinner role, frustrated in your job, and resentful
of the "free ride" you think your wife is getting. For
a time some men can convince themselves that they have
options in their lives by buying things or changing jobs
or moving to a new neighborhood or taking a lover, but
in the end they still feel locked in. Men who are unable
to find work or who are stuck in low-paying, boring jobs,
or whose wives earn more than they do, may feel worthless
and emasculated. You may have found yourself getting out
of touch with what pleases you sexually, focusing on sex
to the exclusion of other sensual experiences and developing powerful sexual fantasies about women other than your
wife. This happens to many men. Sometimes they act out
these fantasies and other times not; generally, though,
there is a lot of guilt and anxiety connected with whatever they choose to do. Perhaps you have simply lowered
your expectations about what will make you happy and what
life is all about. If you have done what was expected of
you and still aren't happy, you may blame your wife, or
the job you're in, or even yourself. But since you were
probably not encouraged before marriage to get in touch
with your own needs and feelings and were not made aware
of alternatives to traditional marriage, you may have few
resources and little motivation to explore what deep or
varied relationships can be about. You may have assumed
that after marriage everything would fall into place and
did not understand that a good relationship needs to be
worked at--that it is a process rather than a fixed thing.

PETER

*I had grown up living with my mother, who was
widowed, from the time I was four, and she worked
full-time from then on. So I had an image of a
professional woman who did not spend all her time
with her children. When Judy and I married she was
very much into the blossoming women's liberation
movement. I had the typical liberal attitudes to
race and class and so moved fairly easily into the
question of sex roles. I found gratification in
taking care of a lot of household chores, laundry,*

her kids' school contacts, etcetera. This gave me
a clear family role and satisfied my penchant for
making order of clutter.

Making Changes in Your Life

Occasionally it is the husband who pushes for the marriage
to become more egalitarian. That is usually the case if
a man is exposed to new ideas and life-styles when he
continues his education after his wife stops hers, or when
he gets a challenging job. He may feel he has outgrown
her and that she is an embarrassment to him around his
new friends or business associates. Sometimes the husband's dissatisfaction leads him to suggest that he have an
affair or that the two of them get involved in mate-swapping
(there is more on this in Chapter 6). Or the husband may
encourage his wife to get further education or training
or to get a job outside the home. He may also be willing
to assume more responsibility for home and family to
enable her to do this. A wife's responses to this pressure
from her husband can vary from enthusiastic acceptance to
threatened defensiveness, depending on how secure she
feels about herself and how dependent she is on the marriage.

For the Househusband

vacuum cleaner whines like a cat
while doing the dishes i work at
straightening out these lines
i'm the housewife of the poems
always ready for minding them
peeling through the surfaces of consciousness
like the purple turnips in the refrigerator
peeling and warming them up
feeling for the right sizes

you have chosen your lot
chosen to seal the cracks in the door
you have decided to bake the crackers today
you unhang your apron from a hook on the wall
you sweep behind closed window blinds
the carpeting gets fluffy
the vacuum cleaner bagging your hopes

you have chosen your lot
though without learning to weep as women can

Mary McGinnis

More often, however, it is the wife who is pushing for
more equality, for all the reasons we have explored in
previous chapters. We share with you here some of the
typical demands women put on their husbands, how the
men respond, and some ways of looking at the pluses and
minuses of the situation.

(For information on some of the legal and financial implications for men of ERA-related legislation, see the end of
Chapter 3.)

WHAT THE WOMEN DO

It sometimes happens that when a woman starts honestly to
look at her marriage, she may discover in herself considerable bitterness and anger that have been building up
over the years that she dedicated to serving others. Many
women go through a period of intense reaction against their
own submissiveness, and you, the husband, may be the
closest and most vulnerable target. Different women
demand different changes. Some demand that the men share
equally in the housework--immediately. Others want to
develop outside interests and friends or get a paying job.
Some women insist on a more satisfying sex life--no more
faking orgasms, no more masturbating in the bathroom
because you fell asleep after intercourse. For other
women, developing real communication is the key question--
they no longer want you to grunt at them from behind the
newspaper but want a real interchange to go on. Still
other women feel that nothing is more important than having
their husbands take an active, caring role with the children. Different women demand these changes in different
ways. Some women can be very clear about which of their
own behaviors they want to abolish and which of yours they
want done away with. They know that change takes
time, however, and are willing to negotiate and compromise.
Other women push their husbands to the wall, refusing to
cook or have sex until they get some results. Still other
women have difficulty in giving up old patterns of manipulation and control because those are the skills they
always felt were necessary for survival.

Change Is in the Air

Wrapped tightly
In a thick cocoon
Of layer upon layer
Of programmed behaviors,
The men are stirring.

Wiping cobwebs from their eyes,
Pulling cotton from their ears,
Stumbling on butterfly feet,
They are trying to overcome
The fear of flying.

The dying summer air
Smells of change.
The Red Sea parted for the women.
Now men are rowing across
In lifeboats.

Women and children
Always go first
To safety and warm, new worlds.
Men stand shivering
And naked in their need.

                    Judith Bondy Brigham

HOW THE MEN RESPOND

If you have been faced with any of these situations, you
are undoubtedly bewildered and probably somewhat frightened.
You may find yourself acting in ways you don't like but
can't stop. Some men immediately become defensive and
hostile, insisting that their wives have a "soft life" and
that it is unfair to be asked to help with housework or
child care or whatever. Some men respond by accusing their
wives of going nuts; others withdraw into silence. Other
men talk as if they are in favor of equalizing marriage
but in fact are more threatened and vulnerable than they
realize or are willing to admit. You may feel very hurt
and betrayed, especially if your wife is developing close
friends outside the marriage. You may feel the trust and
confidentiality of the marriage has been violated. If
your wife is starting to work outside the home again, you
may fear that friends and family will think less of you as
a husband and a provider. You may fear that your wife will
leave if she is no longer dependent on your money. You may

need to reassure yourself by knowing every detail of what
goes on when she is away from you. You may feel bitter
that you wife seems to want you to do all the changing
without being willing to change much herself. Still other
men are put off by the rhetoric of feminism but find themselves responding favorably to their wives' requests
for change.

WHAT'S IN IT FOR YOU?

Those reactions are all very natural, especially if your
relationship up to now has been a fairly traditional one.
Change is threatening for everyone and can be especially
frightening if you are not the one initiating it. You may
be asking, "What's in it for me?" To many men it may appear
that relating to a woman who is in the process of becoming
more self-confident and independent is just too painful.
A woman who wants to be a traditional helpmate may seem
much more appealing. We have talked with a number of men
whose relationships are going through these changes or have
already gone through them, and they generally report that
despite the pain and the struggle, it can be worth it.
These men now feel that keeping a woman down is ultimately
self-destructive. They report that what began as their
partner's move toward independence resulted in their own
liberation as well, even though their original marriages
may not have withstood all the upheaval. The things those
men learned about themselves and the new behavior they
developed have enabled them to relate to women and men in
new and fulfilling ways.

   JIM

   I'm a printer, coming from a working-class family.
   My father insisted that I get some sort of vocational
   training, so I went to a vocational-technical high
   school. I like my job simply because I'm good at it
   and it requires no great concentration on my part.
   The pay is good, and I live within my income. I love
   the hours, which are eleven thirty P.M. to seven A.M.,
   because it gives me a great deal of flexibility and
   freedom. When I come home my routine is that I get
   the kids up, get them ready for school, make breakfast, and then my wife gets up and makes lunches for
   them for the day. I take them to the bus stop. Then
   I can either play tennis or sleep. When the kids come

home, there's time for messing around with them,
taking them to the park or whatever. I also put them
to bed. The girl is going to be eleven next month,
and David will be seven.

Pat is here with me all the time, and she also
spends a lot of time with the kids. She knows that
I have to go out and earn a living, and whatever I
decide is fine with her. She never pushes--it's very
important. This job offers me a lot of time to do
things like fencing, which opens up a new circle
of acquaintances for me. Pat is loose about my
outside friends. And when she wants to go somewhere,
it's no problem. We help each other to make escapes.
We recognize that we each need our own time to
ourselves.

Work

Many men say that when they were finally able to see their
wives' jobs in a positive way and not as a threat to their
own competence, they began to view their own work in a
new light. Because more money is coming in, there is
usually an easing of the financial tensions that can strain
so many marriages. If your wife goes back to work, you
may find that you feel less trapped in your own job because
you are no longer the sole breadwinner. Taking risks
that might get you fired, or changing to a lower-paying
job that is more interesting or provides opportunities to
develop new skills, may now be possible for you. A few
men, although unfortunately still a small number, report
that they see work from a new perspective and are no
longer as driven to succeed. No longer so wrapped up in
their work, they find that they are getting new pleasure
from family, friends, and activities.

On the Home Front

Many men report a great deal of excitement and enthusiasm
about the emotional changes they experience as a result of
their wives' growing independence. When a woman has
interests outside the home and family and is no longer
dependent on husband and children to meet her needs for
companionship and approval, the husband and children are
freer to develop their own interests. The husband and
children are also freer to get to know each other, often
simply because the father is expected to do more child
care. You may not be as pressured to succeed at work or

your children to succeed at school. Your wife is feeling
better about herself through her own activities and interests
and no longer needs her husband's or her children's success to define her existence. You may also find that you
are free to develop close friends of your own and to
begin to break down the competition and isolation which
is so characteristic of male relationships. Both of you
may be relieved when you don't have to be the sole providers of each other's happiness and well-being. If you
share household chores, men will learn firsthand how
repetitive and unrewarding much of housework can be. Together you can then develop joint standards of cleanliness
and your wife may be less anxious about meeting unneces-
sarily high standards. You may also find that there are
household tasks you enjoy and find relaxing; some men
develop great pride in their ability to produce clean
clothes or to cook and serve a meal to family and friends.

IAN

*My three-year-old daughter lives with me; her mother
is in another state finishing up a job and will move
out here to live with us in a few months. The
housework is getting out of hand. I find that no
matter how much I do, I can't keep ahead of Jessie,
and the result is that the apartment is never clean
and orderly as I want it to be even though I am
spending more time cleaning and trying to make it
orderly than I ever have before. Is this the script
of a soap opera, a plot from a feminist consciousness-raising group, or my life?*

Sex

When couples learn to share lovemaking rather than fall
into aggressive and passive roles, their sex life usually
benefits. Freed from the pressure to perform, to take
the initiative, you may feel much less anxious about sex.
As your wife gets in touch with what gives her pleasure
and communicates it to you, and you do the same, you will
probably get more turned on to each other sexually. You
will also be able to explore ways of being physical and
sensual but not necessarily sexual. Many couples report
that they have been able to free themselves from monot-
onous or destructive sexual patterns because they can be
open with each other about what they really want.

Children

Many men whose marriages are becoming less conventional report that they are developing new relationships with their children that bring them great joy. Spending more time and a better quality of time with their children helps many men get in touch again with their own playfulness and tenderness. You may find that observing closely the growth and development of your children not only will bring back memories of your own childhood but also will help you feel connected to other families and children and give you a perspective on your own life. Ideally you will understand more about parenting and be able to make joint decisions with your wife where you both have significant input. You will probably also have many frustrating and tension-filled experiences with your children, but on the whole you should find it very satisfying to receive the unconditional love of a child and to return that love by providing care and support and nurture.

IAN

Carolyn and I have each made the conscious choice to not get married. Doing this has enabled me to escape one more expectation that society has placed on me, that is, the role of the happily married man providing for his wife and children. As I look back over my life, I see how strongly I was raised to be productive, to dominate, to excel, to be ambitious, to achieve a successful career, to work hard, to compete, to exploit others, to provide for a family, etcetera. I now rebel against many of these roles.

Living my life this way has provided many rewards. Carolyn has always worked and earned her own money. All our common expenses are divided proportionately according to how much each of us makes, so that over the years I have been able to save some money, because my expenses are much less than they would be if I were the sole wage-earner. Carolyn has also encouraged me to develop my own friends outside the relationship, so that I have maintained rich male friendships which offer me comfort and love in areas where she is not available. I have most profited from our decision not to have a traditional marriage in relation to our daughter, Jessie. Having been intimately involved in her upbringing ever since her *birth, I truly feel sorry for men whose lives are so devoted to work and are so heavily structured that they don't get to spend much time with their children. My relationship with Jessie is the most satisfying relationship I have ever had with another human being. If I hadn't been so committed to sharing her upbringing I might have missed all these good feelings I get from being with her.*

On the other hand, the going has not always been easy. Carolyn and I have had our share of troubles over the years. I don't want to try to convince anyone that the type of relationship we have strived to create is any easier than any other type of relationship. A year ago we separated and went into therapy. On Thursday evenings we met jointly with our therapists in a desperate attempt to hold the relationship together. (Contrary to the common assumption, just because we're not married does not mean that we will split when the going gets rough. We are committed to making it go.) The therapy seems to have done some good, for by now we have moved to a new city and are looking forward to a new phase in the relationship.

WHAT YOU HAVE TO GIVE UP

Chances are that up until now you have had the power in your relationship, even if you weren't aware of it. If you have a secure job and your wife has not worked for a number of years, if she wanted to get married (and wants to say married) more than you, if she is dependent on your conversation at dinnertime because she has been at home with the kids all day--then you have had the upper hand in the relationship. Even if your marriage is the shrew-henpecked husband variety, you may still have had more power. Your wife has probably felt, as most women do, that men are basically better people than women and she is lucky to be married to one. By trying to live through you, she has most likely been expressing her frustrations at not being a self-fulfilled person. Now that your wife, whatever her feelings about herself and you have been up until now, is reexamining the notion that she is a second-class citizen, she may want to equalize the power in the relationship or even have more power for herself. This means that you will have to give some things up. As we see it, some of this giving up can be quite painful but

most of it can be a relief. The painful part is giving up
the privileges: being taken care of physically and
emotionally, being freer to come and go, getting your
sexual needs met without having to be too concerned about
hers--in general feeling that there is a woman behind the
man and that man is you. If you want to respond con-
structively to the changes your wife is initiating, you will
need to reach out to her--perhaps for the first time in
your life. You will need to listen, to talk about your
real feelings, and to give another person your support and
caring. The relief comes when you can experience sharing
your life with another adult human being, rather than
having to take care of her or letting her take care of you.
If you have felt that you always needed to be strong,
knowledgeable, and in control, then as your wife develops
her strengths you can relax about feeling you have to
hold up the world singlehandedly. You can make a mistake,
let yourself be vulnerable, allow someone else to be in
charge for a change. You can allow yourself to develop
qualities that you may never have thought possible.

WHERE TO FROM HERE?

Only you--we hope with the help of your partner--can look
at your life and decide if and how you want to change it.
Expect that it will be difficult for you to overcome your
resistance and hostility right away. For most of your
life you *have* been told that women exist to serve you, and
it will be very hard to rid yourself of those ideas,
especially when what is immediately expected of you is
boring or unpleasant (such as housework) and the long-range
payoffs are not so obvious. Whatever your situation, you
need to look at your role and your level of resistance.
It may be that your wife's demands are unreasonable at times,
but it may also be that you are refusing to recognize the
validity of her requests. Changing an ingrown relationship
is a back-and-forth process which requires honesty and
caring on both sides. Sometimes there are not enough
reserves of love in each partner to carry the relationship
through the rough periods, and the partners feel they could
do better alone or with someone else. Other times, one or
both partners will revert to behavior that is totally
offensive to the other, but such backsliding is only normal
when human beings try to change and grow.

Changes do not happen overnight in this kind of struggle,
and the special difficulty for you, unlike your wife, is

that there is still relatively little encouragement for
men who want to redefine themselves and their behavior in
relation to women. Women can usually count on the support
of a consciousness-raising group or sympathetic friends,
but men who are struggling to change must usually do so
in isolation. If you have decided you want to work on
equalizing your marriage, it is important for you to get
support for yourself during this process. Talking honestly
with men friends who may be going through similar struggles,
participating in a men's consciousness-raising group, or
attending a men's therapy group through a mental health
center are all possibilities.

It may not seem to you now that your story will have a
happy ending. But we know from talking with numerous
couples who have struggled through these changes that in
the end it is all worth it. You may feel that your life
was a lot more pleasant in the good old days when everyone,
men and women, knew their places. We agree that sometimes life gets overwhelmingly complicated and we wish we
could play by the traditional rules again. But having
experienced the pleasure and satisfaction of working for
a mutually fulfilling relationship, we can't settle for
anything less. And we suspect that you won't be able to
either, at least not if you want to stay married to the
woman who is pushing you to be your own best self. Try
not to get too discouraged, and remember to congratulate
yourself from time to time for doing something that is
very difficult.

JUDITH

When my marriage of nine and a half years ended in 1966, I
was absolutely sure I would never marry again. I knew
my childbearing was ended, and I doubted I could ever find
a man who suited me and could also suit my four sons. For
a long while I dated men away from the house, because I
didn't want the boys to wonder if each Saturday night date
was a prospective stepfather. I'd often avoid the whole
question of sex with a date by asking him to drive my
babysitter home and then shutting off the lights and going
off to bed, alone. I had divided men into two groups,
those who were possible sexual partners and those who were
"friends." I looked to male friends to provide the male
role model I still believed was important back in the
mid-sixties.

Eventually, after three years of being on my own, one of
my "friends" became more and more special to me, and important also to my kids. It was something of a relief
to have someone share in my kids' lives and also be supportive to my own struggling growth. Yet I feared getting
into a relationship just because of my need for help with
raising four kids, working full-time, and going to school
at night. So we took it very slowly, spending bigger and
bigger chunks of time together. At first we were both
against marriage for different fearful reasons. After a
year or so, partly because of pressure from our parents,
partly to give Peter a more legitimate role with people
in the boys' lives, and mostly because we were less afraid,
we decided to marry. We decided to work on the kind of
marital relationship that would give us each the security
and acceptance that marriage can bring, while still maintaining our individual lives and needs.

We knew that traditional marriage and its confinements was
not for us. One area of great concern to me was economic
dependency, not wanting to be financially dependent on
Peter, who earned three times the amount I did, and who had
some money in the bank. When an accidental fire brought
me eleven hundred dollars in insurance compensation, I was
able to feel like I was approaching the marriage on a more
equal footing.

It was very hard to establish our own marital contract
without the presence of four kids pervading every issue.
Many times I tormented myself with the question of whether
I'd be marrying Peter if I didn't have the kids. (The boys'

father had remarried by then, and his involvement with them was minimal.)

I think this is an issue with which every woman with kids has to struggle. And the kids and I had developed our own way of life, our own system, our own holiday rituals-- how would Peter fit into all this? What kind of controls would I have to give up in terms of discipline? How would I know when giving up control was appropriate, for he'd never been a parent and had been raised virtually as an only child. How could I allow Peter to learn from his mistakes with my children? I was also strongly into the women's movement and feared at times that my emerging politics might make marriage untenable.

Fortunately, Peter's fears never struck him at the same time as mine, so we were able to help each other work out, as best we could, our many anxieties about marriage.

Peter and I felt that one problem with marriage as it existed in the sixties was stagnation--people taking each other and the relationship for granted. We decided on a year-to-year contract, and that each year we'd go away by ourselves to review and renegotiate our contract. Of course we spent lots of each day processing what was happening, so there haven't been any surprises in our contract talks to date.

I did give up my name then, although I don't think I'd do that today. I insisted upon both joint and separate money (what I called my get-out-of-town money). We agreed that neither of us would give up any friends, and that as individuals we had rights to times with those people we cared about. Both of us continued to spend time with friends of the opposite and the same sex, although we did share new friends with each other sometimes. We didn't always like each other's friends, which was O.K. We focused a lot on the politics of housework and how to share equally what had to be done. While our feelings for each other kept us fairly monogamous, we felt that sex with other friends would not automatically mean destruction of our marriage, for neither of us felt we "owned" the other. We did see many of our friends' relationships scuttled in the name of "sexual freedom," so we were cautious about jumping on any sexually trendy bandwagons.

During the first few years of our marriage, the oldest kid entered some turbulent adolescent years. We agonized

360

daily over what we were or weren't doing wrong. In a way the focus on the kids' problems kept us from dealing with some of our own differences. I resented the fact that Peter could be as involved or as uninvolved with the kids as he chose, that ultimately if things were wrong, he might say (he never did), "Well, after all, they aren't really my kids." I got in touch with the fact that kids are ultimately the responsibility of mothers and that fatherhood is often an option for men.

Eventually, due to lots of hard work, things fell into place, and we finally became the family we'd all been hoping for. I think the fact that the boys' biological father dropped out of the picture completely helped a lot. While he was there, there were lots of blurred authority lines (who really is the father?) and divided loyalties on the part of the kids.

After seven years of being a "legal family" we've learned a lot. We've all learned that kids are capable of being responsible if they're treated respectfully and given clear support and clear limits. Peter and I have learned that time to ourselves is precious and renewing, so we get away by ourselves whenever we can. Sometimes we ask the kids to make plans so we can have the house to ourselves. A quiet evening by the fire just isn't the same with four teen-agers (plus friends) sharing in it.

Sometimes I feel overwhelmed by role strain and lack of privacy, and I flee to a friend in the country for a few days. Sometimes in the summer I'll house-sit for vacationing friends, stocking the refrigerator with my favorite foods. I usually invite each kid to have dinner out and spend special time with me. We review our ways of being with each other, make a list of changes we'd each like to see, and make a commitment to try to make changes.

Watching the boys grow into men has been exciting, and at times wondrous. They are now nineteen, eighteen, fifteen, and fourteen. Family life definitely gets easier as they get older and more responsible. Cooking, shopping, maintenance, and laundry are all shared equally. I often end up the house nag, though, because my female socialization has made me more aware of "hidden dirt," etcetera.

And as things get easier, Peter and I feel freer to spend more time alone with each other, rediscovering ourselves a lot. Having been through so much struggle, we have a

real sense of each other's capacities. Our main commit-
ment this year is awareness, to ourselves and to each
other. We still keep the possibility of freedom from the
relationship open, but neither of us has wanted to be
free from the other because we've built in freedom as part
of what our marriage is all about. We feel we have a
responsibility to treat each other the way we'd like to be
treated. And the kids, too. So far, it's working.

Bibliography and Resources

Note: Whenever a book is available in paperback, we have made a note of it and have listed that edition only.

General

BOOKS AND ARTICLES

Cisler, Lucinda. *Women: A Bibliography*. Box 241, New York, N.Y. 10024. 50¢ per copy. A useful list of books and articles for and by women.

Grimstad, Kirsten, and Rennie, Susan. *The New Woman's Survival Sourcebook*. New York: Alfred A. Knopf, 1975. Paperback. Successor to *The New Woman's Survival Catalog,* this is a very useful compilation of resources for women throughout the country.

Women in Transition, Inc. *Women in Transition: A Feminist Handbook on Separation and Divorce*. New York: Charles Scribner's Sons, 1975. $7.95 paperback, $12.95 hardcover. This book is terrific! What else can we say? It has useful information on many aspects of separation and divorce: emotional, children, legal, financial,

housing, and physical and mental health. It is useful
not only for separating and divorcing women but for
any women alone.

2

BOOKS AND ARTICLES

Allen, Pamela. *Free Space: A Perspective on the Small
     Group in Women's Liberation*. Times Change Press.
     Washington, N.J. 07882. 1975. $1.75. The story of
     a women's consciousness-raising group and how it grew.

Barbach, Lonnie Garfield. *For Yourself: The Fulfillment
     of Female Sexuality*. Garden City, N.Y.: Anchor Books,
     1976. Paperback. This is one of the most useful books
     on female sexuality to appear in a long time. Read it
     yourself and share it with your partner.

Bernard, Jessie. *The Future of Marriage*. New York:
     Bantam Books, 1972. Paperback. The language is
     somewhat academic, but it is an important and interesting
     book.

Boston Women's Health Book Collective. *Our Bodies, Our-
     selves*, 2nd ed. rev. New York: Simon & Schuster, 1976.
     Paperback. If you haven't read this book, do so. It
     is an excellent source of easily readable information
     about how our bodies work. Useful sections on
     sexuality and birth control.

Burton, Gabrielle. *I'm Running Away from Home but I'm
     Not Allowed to Cross the Street: A Primer on Women's
     Liberation*. New York: Avon Books, 1975. Paperback.
     One woman's account of how she began to grow and how
     her family responded.

Chesler, Phyllis. "Marriage and Psychotherapy." KNOW,
     Inc., P.O. Box 86031, Pittsburgh, Pa. 15221. 40¢.
     1971. (Also in *The Radical Therapist*. New York:
     Ballantine Books, 1971. Paperback.) A classic and
     a "must" for any married woman in therapy or thinking
     about it.

Chesler, Phyllis. *Women and Madness*. New York: Avon Books, 1973. Paperback.

Curry, Barbara. *O.K. I'll Do It Myself*. New York: Random House, 1971. Paperback. A handywoman's primer.

Gettleman, Susan, and Markowitz, Janet. *The Courage to Divorce*. New York: Simon & Schuster, 1974. An excellent book which we recommend highly. The authors challenge many of the assumptions about divorce that are common among mental health professionals and in the media. The sections on remarriage and stepfamilies are especially helpful.

Koedt, Anne. "The Myth of the Vaginal Orgasm." Somerville, Mass.: New England Free Press, 1969. The now-famous article that opened the eyes of many women and their partners about the nature of female orgasm. (Appears in *Radical Feminism*, Koedt, et al., eds. New York: Quadrangle Books, 1973.)

McBride, Angela Barron. *A Married Feminist*. New York: Harper & Row, 1976.

Mainardi, Pat. "The Politics of Housework." New England Free Press, 60 Union Square, Somerville, Mass. 02143. 1968. 10¢ plus 13¢ postage. A classic.

O'Neill, Nena, and O'Neill, George. *Open Marriage*. New York: Avon Books, 1972. Paperback. As we mention in Chapter 2, the theme of this book, which encourages both partners to become separate people, is similar to ours. We would like to have seen the special difficulties of women (economic and emotional dependency) taken into account more, but basically this book is helpful. Oriented toward middle-class people.

Peele, Stanton, and Brodsky, Archie. *Love and Addiction*. New York: Taplinger Publishing Co., 1975. A realistic and useful look at "romantic love" in this country.

Reingold, Carmel Berman. *How to Be Happy If You Marry Again*. New York: Harper & Row, 1976.

Rogers, Carl R. *Becoming Partners: Marriage and Its Alternatives*. New York: Dell Publishing Company, 1972. Paperback. This book has meant a lot to a lot of people.

Sex books (not pornography, but the how-to-do-it-better books). In general, we are wary of them. These books are usually written by men whose motives for writing about female sexuality should be questioned in the first place and who, it turns out, are often simply wrong about what pleases women. In addition these books usually emphasize that sex is the key to happiness in our lives. While sex is usually an important part of a good relationship, it cannot make up for a lack of meaning in other areas of our lives and cannot, in the long run, save a relationship that is basically unfulfilling. *For Yourself* by Lonnie Garfield Barbach (listed above) is a good introductory book about women's sexuality. *Analysis of Human Sexual Response*, edited by Ruth and Edward Brecher (New York: New American Library, 1966, paperback) and *The Pleasure Bond: A New Look at Sexuality and Commitment* by William H. Masters and Virginia E. Johnson (New York: Bantam Books, 1976, paperback) are well known. There are literally thousands of others, as "frigidity," impotence, and "swinging" have become best-selling subjects. Use your judgment.

Sheehy, Gail. *Passages: Predictable Crises of Adult Life*. New York: E. P. Dutton & Co., 1976. If you and your husband seem to have conflicting needs and goals at this point in your lives, this book can help you understand why.

Slater, Charlotte. *Things Your Mother Never Taught You*. Mission, Kans.: Sheed & Ward, 1974. Collection of articles from Charlotte Slater's syndicated how-to-do-it column.

Women in Transition, Inc. *Therapy Information Packet for Women*. KNOW, Inc., P.O. Box 83061, Pittsburgh, Pa. 15221. 1975. A collection of articles on how to decide if you need and want therapy, how to choose a therapist, and how to evaluate a therapy experience. Up to the usually high Women in Transition, Inc., standards. KNOW, Inc., specializes in articles about psychology and women; write to them for a price list.

3

BOOKS AND ARTICLES

Alexander, Shana. *Women's Legal Rights*. Los Angeles: Wollstonecraft, 1975. Paperback. State-by-state guide covering marriage, divorce, children, work, abortion, rape, death, and taxes.

Babcock, Barbara A.; Friedman, Anne; Norton, Eleanor Holmes; and Ross, Susan. *Sex Discrimination and the Law: Causes and Remedies*. Boston: Little, Brown & Co., 1975. Another good casebook.

Boggan, E., et al. *The Rights of Gays*. New York: Avon Books, 1975. Paperback.

The Center for a Woman's Own Name. *Booklet for Women Who Wish to Determine Their Own Names after Marriage*. Write to them at 261 Kimberly, Barrington, Ill. 60010. Facts on the use of one's own name, state by state. Further topics covered are common-law procedure for name change, court procedures, and other related topics.

Citizens' Advisory Council on the Status of Women. *The Equal Rights Amendment and Alimony and Child Support Laws*. Write to the Council at the Department of Labor Building, Washington, D.C. 20210. It sounds dry but is a real eye-opener about the child support scandal in this country.

Davidson, Kenneth; Ginsburg, Ruth Bader; and Kay, Herma Hill. *Sex Based Discrimination: Texts, Cases and Materials*. New York: West Publishing Co., 1974. An important casebook on women and the law.

DeCrow, Karen. *Sexist Justice*. New York: Random House, 1974. Of general interest and readable.

Equal Opportunities Task Force of Eastern Massachusetts NOW. *Sex Discrimination in Employment: What to Know about It, What to Do about It*. Eastern Massachusetts NOW, 45 Newbury Street, Boston, Mass. 02116. 1973.

Ford Associates, Inc. *Women's Legal Handbook Series on Job and Sex Discrimination.* 701 South Federal Avenue, Butler, Ind. 46721. 1974.

Freedman, Anne; Babcock, Barbara; Norton, Eleanor H.; and Ross, Susan C. *Women and the Law: A Collection of Reading Lists.* KNOW, Inc., P.O. Box 86031, Pittsburgh, Pa. 15221.

Gager, Nancy, ed. *Women's Rights Almanac.* New York: Harper & Row, 1975. Paperback.

Homemakers Committee, National Commission on the Observance of International Women's Year. *The Legal Status of Homemakers.* Different booklets for each state. To be published soon by the Department of State.

Kanowitz, Leo. *Sex Roles in Law and Society: Cases and Materials.* Albuquerque: University of New Mexico Press, 1973. Hardcover and paperback. A textbook on women and the law.

Kanowitz, Leo. *Women and the Law: The Unfinished Revolution.* Albuquerque: University of New Mexico Press, 1969. Paperback. Major work on women's legal oppression. Covers divorce, rape, employment, and marriage.

Ross, Susan C. *The Rights of Women.* An American Civil Liberties Union Handbook. New York: Avon Books, 1974. Paperback.

Samuels, Catharine. *Legal Remedies: Tools to Eliminate Sex Discrimination in State and Local Governments.* Women's Action Alliance, 370 Lexington Avenue, New York, N.Y. 10017. 1975. A superb handbook delineating legal strategies for fighting discrimination against women in public employment.

Scott, Ann, and Komisar, Lucy. *And Justice for All.* National Organization for Women, 5 S. Wabash, Suite 1615, Chicago, Ill. 60603. 1971. A thoroughly researched indictment of the federal agencies whose job it is to enforce laws prohibiting job discrimination based on sex.

Switzer, Ellen. *The Law for a Woman: Real Cases and What Happened.* New York: Charles Scribner's Sons, 1975. Hardcover and paperback.

U.S. Commission on Civil Rights. *A Guide to Federal Laws Prohibiting Sex Discrimination.* Superintendent of Documents, U.S. Government Printing Office, Washington, D.C. A comprehensive and easily understood description of all federal laws prohibiting discrimination on the grounds of sex.

Women's Law Caucus, Temple University School of Law. *Women and the Law: Symposium on Sex Discrimination.* March 1976.

PERIODICALS

Pro Se: National Law Women's Newsletter. Northeastern University Law School, 400 Huntington Avenue, Boston, Mass. 02115. A bimonthly newsletter giving news on women and the law.

Women's Rights Law Reporter. 180 University Avenue, Newark, N.J. 07102. An important feminist law journal which began publication in 1971.

RESOURCES

American Civil Liberties Union, Women's Rights Project, 22 E. 40th Street, New York, N.Y. 10016. (212) 725-1222.

Center for Law and Social Policy, Women's Rights Project, 1751 N Street N.W., Washington, D.C. 20036. (202) 872-0670.

National Organization to Improve Support Enforcement, 12 W. 72nd Street, New York, N.Y. 10023. Group working on improving divorce and support process for both men and women.

NOW Legal Defense and Education Fund, 9 W. 57th Street, New York, N.Y. 10019. (212) 688-1751.

4

BOOKS AND ARTICLES

Albrecht, Margaret. *A Complete Guide for the Working Mother*. New York: Award Books, 1970. If you can still find this book, it may be one of the best buys of the day. It answers a lot of questions about working that women who haven't worked before, or who are returning to work, might have.

Bird, Caroline. *Everything a Woman Needs to Know to Get Paid What She's Worth*. New York: Bantam Books, 1974. Paperback. This book is geared to women who already have job options and who are mostly interested in up-grading themselves.

Bolles, Richard Nelson. *What Color Is Your Parachute? A Practical Manual for Job-Hunters and Career-Changers*. Berkeley, Calif.: Ten Speed Press, 1972. Paperback. Available in bookstores or from the publisher for $4.95 plus 25¢ postage, handling, and sales tax. Write Ten Speed Press, Box 4310 Berkeley, Calif. 94704. This book has been getting rave reviews, from both the people who are job-hunting and career-changing and the career counselors who are helping them do it.

Borrowing Basics for Women. First National City Bank, Public Affairs Department, P.O. Box 939, Church Street Station, New York, N.Y. 10008. 1975. Free. An excellent book on establishing and maintaining credit; has up-to-date information taking into account the Equal Credit Opportunity Act.

Burton, Gabrielle. *I'm Running Away from Home but I'm Not Allowed to Cross the Street*. See Bibliography listing for Chapter 2. If moving from home into the world of work seems overwhelming right now, this book should help.

Catalyst. *Self-Guidance Series* for women who want to return to the job market. Write to them at 6 East 82nd Street, New York, N.Y. 10028.

Chesler, Phyllis, and Goodman, Emily Jane. *Women, Money and Power*. New York: William Morrow & Co., 1976. There have been mixed reactions among feminists to this book. Some say it is an important, pioneering analysis of women and economics; others say it misses badly. The fact that there is such controversy means that the book is probably useful reading.

Epstein, Cynthia Fuchs. *Woman's Place: Options and Limits in Professional Careers*. Berkeley: University of California Press, 1971. Paperback.

Fiske, Heidi, and Zehring, Karen. "How to Start Your Own Business." *Ms*. Magazine, April 1976.

Friedman, Sande, and Schwartz, Lois C. *No Experience Necessary: A Guide to Employment for the Female Liberal Arts Graduate*. New York: Dell Publishing Company, 1971. Paperback.

Gornick, Vivian. "Why Women Fear Success." *Ms*. Magazine, Spring 1972. After you have been working for a while out there in the big world, this article can give you some insights into your working self.

Gray, Eileen. *Everywoman's Guide to College*. Available for $3.95 from Les Femmes Publishers, 231 Adrian Road, Millbrae, Calif. 94030. 1974. Very good.

Loring, Rosalind, and Wells, Theodora. *Breakthrough: Women into Management*. New York: Van Nostrand, Reinhold, 1972. Paperback.

Porter, Sylvia. *Sylvia Porter's Money Book: How to Earn It, Spend It, Save It, Invest It, Borrow It--And Use It to Better Your Life*. New York: Avon Books, 1976. Paperback. Make no mistake: Sylvia Porter is not a feminist, is heavily invested in this country's economic system (except for complaining about some small-scale consumer fraud practices), and doesn't understand what life is like for people with very little money. Nevertheless, the book is a gold mine of information.

Rapoport, Rhona, and Rapoport, Robert. *Dual Career Families*. New York: Penguin Books, 1972. Paperback.

Schwartz, Felice; Schifter, Margaret; and Gillotti, Susan. *How to Go to Work When Your Husband Is against It, Your*

*Children Aren't Old Enough, and There's Nothing You Can
Do Anyhow.* New York: Simon & Schuster, 1972.

Scobey, Joan, and McGrath, Lee P. *Creative Careers for
Women: A Handbook of Sources and Ideas for Part-Time
Jobs.* New York: Simon & Schuster, Essandess Special
Editions, 1968.

Tillmon, Johnnie. "Welfare Is a Women's Issue." *Ms.*
Magazine, Spring 1972.

"Volunteerism: Your Money or Your Life?" Several articles in the February 1975 issue of *Ms.* Magazine.

Women's Bureau, U.S. Department of Labor. *A Working
Woman's Guide to Her Job Rights.* Leaflet 55, Revised
1975. Available from Women's Bureau, U.S. Department
of Labor, Washington, D.C. 20210. A concise summary
of women's job rights.

Women's Bureau, U.S. Department of Labor. *Jobfinding
Techniques for Mature Women.* 1970. Available from
Women's Bureau, U.S. Department of Labor, Washington,
D.C. 20210.

RESOURCES

"The Sky's the Limit." An excellent film available for
groups through the Bureau of Apprenticeship and Training regional offices. About women in apprenticeships
in "nontraditional" occupations.

Women's Work. A magazine listing jobs and employment resources and carrying articles of interest to working
women. Recent issues have had articles about innova-
tions such as jobs with flexible hours. $5.00/year.
Wider Opportunities for Women, 1649 K Street N.W.,
Washington, D.C. 20006.

Throughout the country there are numerous nonprofit
agencies that can counsel you for free on how to budget
your money, consolidate your bills, eliminate unnecessary expenditures, and so on. Contact the national
office to see if one of these agencies is near you:
The National Foundation for Consumer Credit, Federal
Bar Building West, 1819 H Street N.W., Washington, D.C.
20006. Also, local Y's, community colleges, adult

evening schools, and similar agencies often provide
counseling and courses on money management. Investigate these resources in your community.

CETA Regional Manpower Services Council Contacts
   REGION I: Connecticut, Massachusetts, New Hampshire,
   Vermont, Rhode Island, Maine. Regional Administrator
   for ETA, U.S. Department of Labor, Room 1703, JFK
   Building, Boston, Mass. 02203.

   REGION II: New York, New Jersey, Puerto Rico, Virgin
   Islands. Regional Administrator for ETA, U.S. Department of Labor, Room 3713, 1515 Broadway, New York, N.Y.
   10036.

   REGION III: Pennsylvania, Virginia, Delaware, District
   of Columbia, Maryland, West Virginia. Regional Administrator for ETA, U.S. Department of Labor, P.O. Box
   8796, Philadelphia, Pa. 19101.

   REGION IV: Alabama, Florida, Georgia, Kentucky, Missis-
   sippi, South Carolina, North Carolina, Tennessee.
   Regional Administrator for ETA, U.S. Department of Labor,
   Room 405, 1371 Peachtree Street N.E., Atlanta, Ga. 30309.

   REGION V: Michigan, Ohio, Illinois, Minnesota, Wisconsin,
   Indiana. Regional Administrator for ETA, U.S. Depart-
   ment of Labor, 6th Floor, 230 South Dearborn, Chicago,
   Ill. 60604.

   REGION VI: Arkansas, Louisiana, New Mexico, Oklahoma,
   Texas. Regional Administrator for ETA, U.S. Department
   of Labor, Room 316, 555 Griffin Square Building, Dallas,
   Tex. 75202.

   REGION VII: Iowa, Nebraska, Missouri, Kansas. Regional
   Administrator for ETA, U.S. Department of Labor, Federal
   Building, Room 1000, 911 Walnut Street, Kansas City,
   Mo. 64106.

   REGION VIII: Colorado, Montana, Utah, North Dakota,
   South Dakota, Wyoming. Regional Administrator for ETA,
   U.S. Department of Labor, 16122 Federal Office Building,
   1961 Stout Street, Denver, Colo. 80202.

   REGION IX: California, American Samoa, Arizona, Guam,
   Hawaii, Nevada. Regional Administrator for ETA, U.S.
   Department of Labor, Box 36084, San Francisco, Calif.
   94102.

REGION X: Alaska, Idaho, Oregon, Washington. Regional
Administrator for ETA, U.S. Department of Labor, Room
1145, Federal Office Building, 909 First Avenue, Seattle,
Wash. 98174.

For further information see *A Guide to Seeking Funds from
CETA* (1976), available from the U.S. Department of
Labor, Employment Standards Administration, Women's
Bureau and Employment and Training Administration,
Washington, D.C. 20210.

5

BOOKS AND ARTICLES

Albrecht, Margaret. *A Complete Guide for the Working
Mother*. See Bibliography listing for Chapter 4.

Barber, Virginia, and Skaggs, Merrill McGuire. *The
Mother Person*. Indianapolis: Bobbs-Merrill, 1975.

Boston Women's Health Book Collective. *Our Bodies, Ourselves*. See Bibliography listing for Chapter 2. In-
formative and readable information on pregnancy, childbirth, and postpartum.

Breibart, Vicki. *The Day Care Book*. New York: Alfred
A. Knopf, 1974. Paperback.

Faber, Adele, and Mazlish, Elaine. *Liberated Parents,
Liberated Children*. New York: Avon Books, 1974.
Paperback.

Fraiberg, Selma. *The Magic Years: Understanding and
Handling the Problems of Early Childhood*. New York:
Charles Scribner's Sons, 1959. Paperback.

Gettleman, Susan, and Markowitz, Janet. *The Courage to
Divorce*. See Bibliography listing for Chapter 2. Their
sections on stepfamilies are especially useful.

Ginott, Dr. Haim G. *Between Parent and Child*. New York: Avon Books, 1965. Paperback. Had Dr. Ginott lived to be influenced by the women's movement, some of his sexist assumptions might have been changed in later editions of this book. Nonetheless, much of his advice has been useful to parents for a number of years.

Klein, Carole. *The Single Parent Experience*. New York: Avon Books, 1973. Paperback.

Lazarre, Jane. *The Mother Knot*. New York: McGraw-Hill, 1975.

McBride, Angela Barron. *The Growth and Development of Mothers*. New York: Barnes and Noble, 1974. Paperback.

Maddox, Brenda. *The Half-Parent: Living with Other People's Children*. New York: Signet Books, 1976. Paperback.

Radl, Shirley. *Mother's Day Is Over*. New York: Warner Books, 1974. Paperback.

Rosser, Phyllis. "Making Time: A Housewife's Log." *Ms.* Magazine, March 1976. If anyone still thinks that housewives eat chocolates and read novels all day, read this. More important, the article explains how, by keeping the log, the author found out that not only did she not have time for herself, but she spent most of her time responding to her children's demands rather than providing a "stimulating, creative environment for intellectual growth" which she had hoped to do by staying home with them while they were young.

Rozdilsky, Mary Lou, and Banet, Barbara. *What Now? A Handbook for New Parents*. New York: Charles Scribner's Sons, 1976. Paperback. Carolyn read this in its original pamphlet form just after her daughter was born in 1973 and thought it was the best of all the books of its kind that she read. The revised edition is even better.

Seaman, Barbara. "How Late Can You Wait to Have a Baby?" *Ms.* Magazine, January 1976.

Sidel, Ruth. *Women and Child Care in China*. Baltimore: Penguin Books, 1973. Paperback.

Whelan, Dr. Elizabeth M. *A Baby Maybe*. Indianapolis:
   Bobbs-Merrill, 1975. Paperback.

RESOURCES

Momma. An organization for single mothers, with chapters
   around the country. Headquarters: P.O. Box 5759,
   Santa Monica, Calif. 90405. They also publish
   (from time to time) a newsletter available from P.O.
   Box 567, Venice, Calif. 90291.

National Center for Prevention and Treatment of Child
   Abuse and Neglect, University of Colorado Medical
   Center, Denver, Colo. (303) 321-3963.

Nonsexist books for children. A growing number of
   presses today specialize in "nonsexist" books for
   children. You may want to look for the books in your
   local bookstore or write for catalogs at these
   addresses:
   Feminist Press, Box 334, S.U.N.Y., Old Westbury, N.Y.
   11568.
   Lollipop Power, P.O. Box 1171, Chapel Hill, N.C. 27514.
   Sojourner Truth Press, 432 Moreland Avenue N.E.,
   Atlanta, Ga. 30307.

Stepparents' Forum. Bimonthly newsletter. $5.00/year
   (sample $1). Westmount, P.O. Box 4002, Montreal
   H3Z 2X3, Canada.

6

BOOKS AND ARTICLES

Adams, Margaret. *Single Blessedness: Observations on
   the Single Status*. New York: Basic Books, 1976.

Bernard, Jessie. *The Future of Marriage*. See Bibliography
   listing for Chapter 2. This book helps put into perspective alternative arrangements that people are
   developing today.

Constantine, Larry L., and Constantine, Joan M. *Group Marriage*. New York: Collier Books, 1973. Paperback. This is a pioneering work, although its approach (half sociological, half personal) is a bit confusing. Not as juicy as the title might suggest.

Edwards, Marie, and Hoover, Eleanor. *The Challenge of Being Single*. New York: New American Library, 1975. Paperback. A very supportive book for singles which is open and readable, basically covering the options and pitfalls of being single. Oriented toward middle-class people and doesn't take into account enough the special problems single women face.

Houriet, Robert. *Getting Back Together*. New York: Avon Books, 1972. Paperback. The experiences of a man who has lived in and visited a number of communes.

Kanter, Rosabeth Moss. *Communes: Creating and Managing the Collective Life*. New York: Harper & Row, 1973. Paperback.

Rimmer, Robert. *The Harrad Experiment* (New York: Bantam Books, 1973), *Proposition 31* (New York: New American Library, 1971), *The Rebellion of Yale Marratt* (New York: Avon Books, 1971). Fictionalized accounts of people who try alternative living arrangements such as group marriages, triads, and others.

Van Deusen, Edmund L. *Contract Cohabitation: An Alternative to Marriage*. New York: Avon Books, 1975. Paperback.

Yates, Martha. *Coping: A Survival Manual for Women Alone*. Englewood Cliffs, N.J.: Prentice-Hall, 1976.

RESOURCES

COST (Committee of Single Taxpayers), 1628 21st Street N.W., Washington, D.C. 20009. A lobbying group concerned with equalizing taxes for single and married people.

Momma. An organization and newsletter for single mothers. See the Resources listing for Chapter 5.

Parents without Partners. Headquarters: 7910 Woodmont Avenue N.W., Washington, D.C. 20014.

The Singles Register. A national newspaper for divorced, widowed, and never-married people. P.O. Box 40, Lakewood, Calif. 90714.

7

BOOKS AND ARTICLES

Abbott, Sidney, and Love, Barbara. *Sappho Was a Right-On Woman.* Briarcliff Manor, N.Y.: Stein & Day, 1972. Paperback. An account from personal experience by two women who were lesbian/feminist activists in New York.

Birkley, Phyllis, et al., eds. *Amazon Expedition: A Lesbian Feminist Anthology.* New York: Times Change Press, 1973. Paperback.

Boggan, E., et al. *The Rights of Gays.* See Bibliography listing for Chapter 3.

Brown, Rita Mae. *Rubyfruit Jungle.* Plainfield, Vt.: Daughters, Inc., 1973. Novel about growing up lesbian in America.

Damon, Gene, and Watson, Jan. *The Lesbian in Literature,* 2nd ed. Ladder, 1975. Paperback. An alphabetical listing by author of all books in the English language, in the general field of literature, concerned with lesbianism or having lesbian characters.

Grahn, Judy, et al. *Lesbians Speak Out.* Oakland, Calif.: Women's Press Collective, 1974. A collection of lesbian writings including poetry, photographs, and drawings.

Jay, Karla, and Young, Allen. *After You're Out.* New York: Quick Fox, 1975. Paperback. Personal experiences of gay men and lesbian women.

Johnston, Jill. *Lesbian Nation: The Feminist Solution.* New York: Simon & Schuster, 1974. Paperback. Exposition of the sexual underpinnings of patriarchy.

Klaich, Dolores. *Woman Plus Woman: Attitudes Towards Lesbianism*. New York: William Morrow & Co., Inc., 1975.

Martin, Del, and Lyon, Phyllis. *Lesbian-Woman*. New York: Bantam Books, 1972. Paperback. A thorough account of their experiences with a wide variety of lesbian women by the two founders of the Daughters of Bilitis.

Miller, Isabel. *Patience and Sarah*. New York: McGraw-Hill, 1972.

Myron, Nancy, and Bunch, Charlotte. *Lesbianism and the Woman's Movement*. Baltimore: Diana Press, 1975. Outlines the essence of lesbian/feminist politics and documents how the women's movement has responded to it.

Nachman, Elana. *Riverfinger Women*. Plainfield, Vt.: Daughters, Inc., 1974. Novel about the youth and lesbian cultures of the last ten years.

Radicalesbians. *Woman-Identified-Woman*. Somerville, Mass.: New England Free Press, 1970. A presentation of lesbian politics and the concept of the woman-identified-woman.

Rule, Jane. *Lesbian Images*. New York: Pocket Books, 1976. Paperback. The lesbian experience of twelve women writers.

Women in Transition, Inc. *Therapy Information Packet for Women*. See Bibliography listing for Chapter 2.

Women Loving Women. Chicago: Womanpress, 1975. A select and annotated bibliography of women loving women in literature.

PERIODICALS

Ain't I a Woman. Box 1169, Iowa City, Iowa 52240.

ALFA Newsletter. Atlanta Lesbian Feminist Alliance, P.O. Box 7684, Atlanta, Ga. 30309.

Amazon. 2211 East Kenwood, Milwaukee, Wis. 53211.

Amazon Quarterly. Box 434, West Somerville, Mass. 02144.

Cowrie. 359 East 68th Street, New York, N.Y. 10021.

Desperate Living. Box 7124, Baltimore, Md. 21218.

Dykes Unite. S.U.C. Genesee, Fraser Box 354, Genesee, N.Y. 11454.

Focus: A Journal for Gay Women. c/o Boston D.O.B., Room 323, 419 Boylston Street, Boston, Mass. 12116.

HERA. A Philadelphia feminist publication. 2041 Walnut Street, Philadelphia, Pa. 19103.

It's Time. Newsletter of the National Gay Task Force, Inc. Room 506, 80 Fifth Avenue, New York, N.Y. 10011.

Lavender Woman. Box 60206, Chicago, Ill. 60660.

Lesbian Connection. Ambitious Amazons, P.O. Box 811, East Lansing, Mich. 48823.

Lesbian Feminist, The. Box 243 Village Station, New York, N.Y. 10014.

Lesbian Tide, The. 1005 Ocean Avenue, #B, Santa Monica, Calif. 90403.

Lesbian Visions. c/o The Lesbian Collective, Box 8265, Stanford, Calif. 94305.

Long Time Coming. Box 161 Station E, Montreal, Quebec H2T 3A7, Canada.

Purple Cow, The. Box 10, 1739 High Street, Columbus, Ohio 43210.

Sappho. BCM/Petrel, London WC 1V, England.

Sisters. 1005 Market, Suite 401, San Francisco, Calif. 94103.

Tres Femmes. Gay Center for Social Services, 2250 B Street, San Diego, Calif. 92102.

Wicce. Box 15833, Philadelphia, Pa. 19103.

RESOURCES

ACLU

Listed below are chapters of the American Civil Liberties
   Union which is pioneering in advocating civil rights
   for gay people.

Alabama CLU
P.O. Box 1972
University, Ala.   35486
(205) 758-2301

Alaska CLU
SRA 89-P
Fairbanks, Alaska   99507
(907) 349-1270

Arizona CLU
1429 North 1st Street
Phoenix, Ariz.   85004
(602) 254-3339

ACLU of Arkansas
P.O. Box 2832
Little Rock, Ark.   72203
(501) 374-2660

ACLU of Northern California
814 Mission Street
San Francisco, Calif.   94103
(415) 777-4545

ACLU of Southern California
633 South Shatto Place
Los Angeles, Calif.   90005
(213) 487-1720

ACLU of Colorado
1711 Pennsylvania Street
Denver, Colo.   80203
(303) 825-5176

Connecticut CLU
57 Pratt Street, Room 713
Hartford, Conn.   06103
(203) 247-9823

Delaware. See Pennsylvania listing

District of Columbia. See National Capital Area

ACLU of Florida
7210 S. Red Road, Room 213
South Miami, Fla. 33143
(305) 666-2950

ACLU of Georgia
88 Walton Street
Atlanta, Ga. 30303
(404) 523-5398

Guam. See National Chapters listing

ACLU of Hawaii
217 South King Street, Suite 210
Honolulu, Hawaii 96813
(808) 538-7336

Idaho. See National Chapters listing

Illinois Division, ACLU
5 South Wabash Avenue, Suite 1516
Chicago, Ill. 60603
(312) 236-5564

Indiana CLU
445 North Pennsylvania Street, Suite 604
Indianapolis, Ind. 46204
(317) 635-4056

Iowa CLU
102 East Grand Avenue, Suite G-100
Des Moines, Iowa 50309
(515) 243-3576

Kansas CLU
629 Quincy, Suite 203
Topeka, Kans. 66603
(913) 235-2405

Kentucky CLU
134 Breckinridge Lane
Louisville, Ky. 40207
(502) 895-0279

ACLU of Louisiana
535 Gravier, Room 507
New Orleans, La.   70130
(504) 522-0617

Maine CLU
193 Middle Street
Portland, Maine 04111
(207) 774-5444

ACLU of Maryland
1231 North Calvert Street
Baltimore, Md.   21202
(301) 685-6460

CLU of Massachusetts
68 Devonshire Street
Boston, Mass.   02109
(617) 742-8020

ACLU of Michigan
808 Washington Boulevard Building
234 State Street
Detroit, Mich.   48226
(313) 961-4662

Minnesota CLU
628 Central Avenue
Minneapolis, Minn.   55414
(612) 332-2883

ACLU of Mississippi
520 North President Street
Jackson, Miss.   39201
(601) 355-7495

ACLU of Eastern Missouri
8011 Clayton Road, Suite 315
St. Louis, Mo.   63117
(314) 721-1215

ACLU of Western Missouri
823 Walnut, Room 608
Kansas City, Mo.   64106
(816) 421-1875

384   For Better, For Worse

ACLU of Montana
534 Northwestern Bank Building
Great Falls, Mont. 59401
(406) 453-6851

ACLU of the National Capital Area
1345 E Street N.W., Suite 301
Washington, D.C. 20004
(202) 638-6263

Nebraska CLU
1030 Q Street
Lincoln, Nebr. 68508
(402) 432-8091

ACLU of Nevada
401 East Fremont, Room 12A
Las Vegas, Nev. 89101
(702) 386-4837

New Hampshire CLU
1 South Street
Concord, N.H. 03301
(603) 225-3080

ACLU of New Jersey
45 Academy Street, Room 203
Newark, N.J. 07102
(201) 642-2084

ACLU of New Mexico
510 Second Street N.W., Room 220
Albuquerque, N.Mex. 87102
(505) 842-1448

New York CLU
84 Fifth Avenue, Suite 300
New York, N.Y. 10011
(212) 924-7800

North Carolina CLU
P.O. Box 3094
Greensboro, N.C. 27402
(919) 273-1641

North Dakota. See National Chapters listing

ACLU of Ohio
203 E. Broad Street, Suite 200
Columbus, Ohio 43215
(614) 228-8951

ACLU of Oklahoma
P.O. Box 799
Oklahoma City, Okla.   73101
(405) 235-9209

ACLU of Oregon
601 Wilamette Building
534 S.W. 3rd Avenue
Portland, Oreg.   97204
(503) 227-3186

ACLU of Pennsylvania
260 South 15th Street
Philadelphia, Pa.   19102
(215) 735-7103

Rhode Island CLU
55 Eddy Street, Suite 508
Providence, R.I.   02903
(401) 831-7171

ACLU of South Carolina
533-B Harden Street
Columbia, S.C.   29205
(803) 799-5151

South Dakota.   See National Chapters listing

ACLU of Tennessee
81 Madison Building, Suite 1501
Memphis, Tenn.   38103
(901) 521-9875

Texas CLU
600 W. Seventh Street
Austin, Tex.   78701
(512) 477-5849

ACLU of Utah
211 E. 3rd South
Salt Lake City, Utah 84111
(801) 521-9289

Vermont CLU
43 State Street
Montpelier, Vt.   05602
(802) 223-6304

ACLU of Virginia
1001 East Main Street, Suite 515
Richmond, Va.   23219
(804) 644-8022

ACLU of Washington
2101 Smith Tower
Seattle, Wash.   98104
(206) 624-2180

West Virginia CLU
Box 2893
Huntington, W.Va.   25738
(304) 696-6789

Wisconsin CLU
1840 North Farwell Avenue
Room 1, Lower Level
Milwaukee, Wis.   53202
(414) 272-4032

Wyoming.   See National Chapters listing

National Chapters

Guam National Chapter, ACLU
P.O. Box 1891
Agana, Guam 96910
477-9751

Boise Valley (Idaho) National Chapter, ACLU
2312 Jean Street
Boise, Idaho 83705
(208) 336-0862

Southeast Idaho National Chapter
2810 Holly Place
Idaho Falls, Idaho 83401
(203) 523-4664

Ward County (North Dakota) National Chapter, ACLU
Political Science Division
Minot State College
Minot, N.Dak. 58701
(701) 838-6101

Missouri Valley (North Dakota) Chapter
609 N. 4th Street
Bismarck, N.Dak. 58501

South Dakota Chapter, ACLU
P.O. Box 362
Vermillion, S.Dak. 57069
(605) 624-8191

Laramie (Wyoming) Chapter, ACLU
Box 3282, University Station
Laramie, Wyo. 82071
(307) 766-4371

Gay Organizations

This listing was compiled from information in the March
1976 issue of *Ms.* Magazine. It includes both lesbian groups
and groups that are not all lesbian but include lesbian
feminists active in their ranks. They can provide information and referrals.

Arizona

Gay Women's Liberation
1414 South McAllister
Tempe, Ariz. 85281

Lesbian Feminists
646 South 6th
Tucson, Ariz. 85701

California

Lesbian Activists
P.O. Box 2023
Culver City, Calif. 90230

Colorado

Lesbian Task Force of NOW
1400 Lafayette Street
Denver, Colo. 80218

Connecticut

Gay Women's Group
Box 3438
Yale Station
New Haven, Conn. 06520

District of Columbia

NOW Task Force on Sexuality
1424 16th Street N.W. #104
Washington, D.C. 20009

Washington Area Women's Center
2453 18th Street N.W.
Washington, D.C. 20009

Illinois

Midwest Women's Legal Group
c/o Renee Hanover
54 W. Randolph Street
Chicago, Ill. 60601

Lesbian Feminist Center
3523 North Halstead
Chicago, Ill. 60657

Maine

Maine Freewoman's Herald
P.O. Box 488
Brunswick, Maine 04011

Massachusetts

Gay Media Action
c/o Gay Community News
22 Bromfield
Boston, Mass. 02108

Minnesota

Lesbian Resource Center
2104 Stevens Avenue South
Minneapolis, Minn. 55404

New Hampshire

Women's Group
P.O. Box 137
Northwood, N.H.   03216

New York

Sisters of Sappho
1350 Maine
Buffalo, N.Y.   14209

Task Force on Respect for the Individual
National Women's Agenda
c/o Women's Action Alliance
370 Lexington Avenue
New York, N.Y.   10017

Ohio

Gay Women Sapphonified
c/o Women's Liberation
1739 N. High Street
Columbus, Ohio 43210

Texas

Houston NOW Lesbian Task Force
c/o Women's Center
3602 Milam
Houston, Tex.   77002

Washington

Lesbian Mothers' National Defense Fund
2446 Lorentz Place North
Seattle, Wash.   98109

Wisconsin

Lesbian Switchboard
306 N. Brooks
Madison, Wis.   53715

Daughters of Bilitis

There are seven DOB chapters around the country:

Tampa DOB
c/o Warner
Route 1, Box 110
Lithia, Fla.   33547

Women's Group
P.O. Box 137
Northwood, N.H.   03261

DOB in New Jersey
P.O. Box 62
Fanwood, N.J.   07023

Boston DOB
419 Boylston Street #323
Boston, Mass.   02116
(617) 262-1592

Dallas DOB
P.O. Box 1242
Dallas, Tex.   75221

Fort Worth DOB
P.O. Box 1564
Fort Worth, Tex.   76101

San Francisco DOB
1005 Market Street #404
San Francisco, Calif.   94103
(415) 861-8689

8

BOOKS AND ARTICLES

Ann Arbor-Washtenaw County Chapters of NOW. *Wife-Beating: How to Develop a Wife Assault Task Force and Project.* NOW, 1917 Washtenaw Avenue, Ann Arbor, Mich. 48104.

Bannon, James. *Law Enforcement Problems with Intra-familial Violence.* 1975. Available from the author at Detroit Police Department, Second Precinct, 2801 W. Vernor, Detroit, Mich. 48216. A speech given to a conference of the American Bar Association.

Edmiston, Susan. "The Wife Beaters." *Woman's Day*, March 1976.

Eisenberg, Susan, and Micklow, Patricia. "The Assaulted Wife: 'Catch 22' Revisited." *Women's Rights Law Reporter*, June 1976. A study of wife-beating in Michigan.

Gelles, Richard J. *The Violent Home: A Study of Physical Aggression between Husbands and Wives*. Beverly Hills, Calif: Sage Publications, 1974. Paperback. Gelles has also written several articles on wife abuse, available from the author at the Department of Sociology, University of Rhode Island, Kingston, R.I. 02881.

Gingold, Judith. "One of These Days, Pow, Right in the Kisser." *Ms.* Magazine, August 1976.

"In Her Own Words." *People* Magazine, May 1976. Article on battered wives.

Martin, Del. *The Battered Wives of America*. San Francisco: Glide Publications, Inc., 1976. An excellent feminist study of wife-beating in America.

Pizzey, Erin. *Scream Quietly: Or the Neighbors Will Hear*. Women's Liberation Workshop. 38 Earlham Street, London, England. The first book ever published on wife-beating; it led to the establishment of several shelters for abused wives throughout England.

Steinmetz, Suzanne K., and Strauss, Murray A., eds. *Violence in the Family*. New York: Dodd, Mead & Co., 1974. Paperback. A study of wife-beating as a sociological phenomenon in the United States.

Strauss, Murray. *Sexual Inequality, Cultural Norms and Wife Beating*. Available from Betsy Warrior, 46 Pleasant Street, Cambridge, Mass. 02139. 1976. A sociological study of violence in the family.

Strauss, Murray A., ed. *The Social Causes of Husband-Wife Violence*. Publication now being arranged.

Warrior, Betsy. *Wifebeating*. Available from Betsy
    Warrior, 46 Pleasant Street, Cambridge, Mass. 02139.
    May 1975. An excellent booklet describing and analyzing
    the phenomen of wife abuse.

Warrior, Betsy. *Working on Wife Abuse*. Available from
    the author, 46 Pleasant Street, Cambridge, Mass. 02139.
    1976. Listing groups and individuals who are involved
    in all areas of helping battered wives.

RESOURCES

The following list from the August 1976 issue of *Ms*.
Magazine is a sampling of people and places dedicated to
meeting the specific needs of battered women.

National

Center for Women Policy Studies
2000 P Street N.W.
Suite 508
Washington, D.C. 20007
(202) 872-1770
Has applied for a grant to establish clearinghouse for
victims of rape, child abuse, and wife abuse. Particular
concern is legal problems of battered women.

National Organization for Women National Task Force on
    Battered Women
c/o Del Martin
651 Duncan Street
San Francisco, Calif. 94131
(415) 928-2480
or
c/o Nancy Kirk-Gormley
7 Aloha Drive
Pittsburgh, Pa. 15239
(412) 327-5077
Recently established as a result of 1975 NOW national
resolution on battered women. Welcomes information from
around the country. Planning national conference.

Regional

California

Haven House, Inc.
644 S. Marengo Avenue

Pasadena, Calif. 91106
(213) 681-2626
Limited to families of alcoholics. Can stay three weeks.

La Casa de las Madres
1800 Market Street
Box 137
San Francisco, Calif. 94102
(415) 626-7859
Refuge which can accommodate up to thirty battered women
and children. Hot line, counseling, advocacy program, and
emergency rescue service.

Women's Transitional Living Center
c/o Susan Maples, Director
Community Development Council
1140 S. Bristol Street
Santa Ana, Calif. 92704
(714) 992-1931
Provides shelter up to forty-five days for women and
children as well as counseling and referrals.

Florida

Joanne Richter
Fort Lauderdale Police Department
Victim Advocate Office
1300 W. Broward Boulevard
Fort Lauderdale, Fla. 33312
(305) 761-2143
Provides crisis intervention counseling with follow-up
sessions; referrals; child care centers and job training
available.

Citizens Dispute Settlement Center
Metro Justice Building
1351 N.W. 12th Street
Miami, Fla. 33125
(305) 547-7062
Provides counseling, referrals.

Florence Morgenroth
Task Force on Battered Women
YWCA
100 S.E. 4th Street
Miami, Fla. 33168
(305) 377-8161, ext. 416
Has set up task force to provide shelter, to work with

wide range of county agencies, and to develop local and
state legislation.

Women in Distress
Jackson Memorial Hospital
122 N.E. 24th Street
Miami, Fla. 33137
(305) 573-5528
Will provide food and shelter for battered women without
children.

Maryland

Battered Wives Task Force
Chairperson Evelyn Bata
5403 Queens Chapel Road
West Hyattsville, Md. 20782
(202) WA7-5877
Fully funded shelter working with county representatives,
police department, government agencies.

Massachusetts

Women's Transition House
c/o Jimenez, Womendez, and Foulis
46 Pleasant Street
Cambridge, Mass. 02139
(617) 547-5942
Twenty-four-hour hot line. Limited accommodations for
women and children.

Elizabeth Stone House
128 Minden Street
Jamaica Plain, Mass. 02130
(617) 522-3417
Temporary residency and therapeutic community which can
house four women and two children for up to two weeks;
twenty-four-hour paraprofessional care.

Respond, Inc.
Box 555
Somerville, Mass. 02143
(617) 776-5931
Currently runs support group for battered women. Plans to
establish a refuge.

Michigan

Ann Arbor County NOW Domestic Violence/Spouse Assault
   Task Force
1917 Washtenaw Avenue
Ann Arbor, Mich.   48104
(313) 995-5444

Booklets entitled "How to Develop a Wife Assault Task
Force," "Counselor Training Manual," "Handbook for Victims of Domestic Violence," are available for $1.50, $2,
and 50¢, respectively.

Minnesota

Women's Advocates
584 Grand Avenue
St. Paul, Minn.   55102
(612) 227-8284
Refuge for women and children offering collective atmosphere.
Provides support, advocacy, and a twenty-four-hour information and referral service.   Their newsletter is available
for a $4 donation.

New York

Marjory D. Fields
South Brooklyn Legal Services
152 Court Street
Brooklyn, N.Y.   11201
(212) 855-8003
A divorce lawyer who considers herself a clearinghouse for
material on battered women, Fields is seeking a grant for
support systems.

Abused Women's Aid in Crisis (AWAIC)
c/o Maria Roy
P.O. Box 431
Cathedral Station
New York, N.Y.   10025
(212) 473-8181 or hot line: (212) 473-8182
Currently provides hot line, daytime counseling, and
monthly evening outreach meetings.   Plans to establish
refuge.

Oregon

Bradley Angle House
c/o Women's Place

1915 N.E. Everett
Portland, Oreg. 97232
(508) 243-7044
Refuge where women and children can stay up to eight weeks.

Pennsylvania

Women's Center South
2929 Brownsville Road
Brentwood, Pa. 14227
(412) 885-2888
Refuge for battered women and their children. Provides
referrals, rap groups. Maximum stay six days.

Women Against Abuse
Germantown Women's Center
5519 Wister Street
Philadelphia, Pa. 19144
(215) 848-7327
Published "Off the Beaten Track--A Resource List for
Abused Women in Philadelphia," $1.

Washington

Women's Emergency Housing Project
1012 W. 12th Street
Vancouver, Wash. 98660
(206) 695-0501 or (206) 694-8366
Provides temporary housing, food, counseling, and
referral for women and children who would otherwise be
without shelter.

Wisconsin

Women's Coalition, Inc.
Task Force on Battered Women
2211 E. Kenwood Boulevard
Milwaukee, Wis. 53211
(414) 964-6117 or (414) 964-7535 after 5 P.M.
Plans to establish a refuge. Currently offers daytime
counseling, evening counseling by appointment.

Canada

Interval House
596 Huron Street
Toronto, Canada M5R 2R7
(416) 924-1491
Will accommodate women with children for two to six weeks.

9

BOOKS AND ARTICLES

Barbach, Lonnie Garfield. *For Yourself: The Fulfillment of Female Sexuality*. See Bibliography listing for Chapter 2. Get this book for yourself and your partner if she doesn't get it for you first.

Faber, Adele, and Mazlish, Elaine. *Liberated Parents, Liberated Children*. See Bibliography listing for Chapter 5.

Farrell, Warren. *The Liberated Man: Beyond Masculinity. Freeing Men and Their Relationships with Women*. New York: Bantam Books, 1974. Paperback.

Koedt, Anne. "The Myth of the Vaginal Orgasm." See Bibliography listing for Chapter 2. If you still think that women have orgasms in their vaginas, read this.

McGrady, Mike. *The Kitchen Sink Papers: My Life As a Househusband*. New York: Doubleday, 1975. Hardcover.

Nichols, Jack. *Men's Liberation: A New Definition of Masculinity*. New York: Penguin Books, 1975. Paperback.

Unbecoming Men: A Men's Consciousness-Raising Group Writes on Oppression and Themselves. New York: Times Change Press, 1971. Paperback.

Appendix/
Common-Law Marriage

Many people wonder why it is so easy to get married and so
hard to get divorced. It has been suggested that states
should make it harder to get married. Ironically, "common-
law" is the easiest of all marriages to get into. However,
it is just as hard as any other kind of marriage to get
out of. Many people think that "common-law marriage" is
just a polite name for no marriage at all. Others believe
that "if you live together for seven years, you're common-
law married." Neither of these very popular myths is true.
But common-law marriage does exist in seventeen states.

The following states currently recognize common-law marriages as having the same legal effect as licensed marriages:

Alabama	Georgia	Oklahoma
Alaska	Idaho	Pennsylvania
Colorado	Iowa	Rhode Island
District of	Kansas	South Carolina
Columbia	Montana	South Dakota
Florida	Ohio	Texas

The following states have recently repealed their laws
recognizing common-law marriage and will not recognize any
new common-law marriages. They do recognize common-law
marriages entered into before the dates specified below:

398

Indiana, January 1, 1958
Michigan, January 1, 1957
Minnesota, April 26, 1941
Missouri, April 4, 1953
Nebraska, March 3, 1921
Nevada, 1923
New Jersey, March 29, 1943
New York, December 1, 1939
Mississippi, April 29, 1933

Common-law marriage is forbidden in all other states. Some states that do not recognize common-law marriages entered into within the state do recognize those that were entered into in another state that does recognize them.

People involved in a valid common-law marriage are just as legally and permanently married as those who have a license. The same duties and rights arise from common-law and official marriages, and the children of common-law marriages are as officially "legitimate" as those of formal marriages. Common-law wives are entitled to support from their husbands and may sue for support if they are separated.

The problem with common-law marriage is not that it is a less official or less valid form of marriage, but that you have a hard time proving that you are married without a certificate or other concrete proof of marriage. Before a court will enforce any of your marital rights, you must prove that you were in fact living as husband and wife with a mutual understanding that you were married and not just "living together."

In order to prove this marriage, you will have to show evidence of the following things:

1. Intention and promise or agreement that the relationship is a permanent husband-wife relationship.

2. Actual cohabitation--that the two of you did live together at the same address for some length of time. The longer the time, the more convincing, but in most states the number of years will not prove anything without other evidence.

3. Your reputation in the community as married people. A lease in both your names, your using his last name, bills, accounts in both your names, joint tax returns, testimony of neighbors and other disinterested people in the com-

munity, and children born of the common-law marriage
are all considered pieces of evidence tending to show
you had a valid marriage.

Warning: Many courts and legislators are hostile to common-
law marriages. In Pennsylvania, where they are still recognized, they have been called "a fruitful source of perjury
and fraud . . . to be tolerated, not encouraged" (*Baker* v.
Mitchell, 143 Pa. Super. 50).

The parties claiming to have a common-law marriage have to
bring a significant amount of convincing evidence into
court with them. And the judge will be skeptical.

A final warning about common-law marriage: It is just as
hard to get out of as an official marriage. You can't end
a common-law marriage by walking out the door either. If
you want to be free to get legally married again, you must
get a divorce. In order to get a divorce, you must prove
that you are married, which is not easy for people in a
common-law marriage. If this reminds you of a dog chasing
its own tail, you've got the picture.

Instances in which you might want to prove a common-law
marriage include the following:

1. If you are going to have a baby and don't want the
    hospital records or birth certificate to indicate that
    the child is "illegitimate," insist that you are mar-
    ried. You don't have to call yourself Mrs. John Jones
    if your name is Sarah Smith, but it would probably
    make things a lot easier.

2. If he has left you without any support and has a decent
    income, you might get him to sign a separation agree-
    ment, or you can sue him for support. But note:
    fathers of "illegitimate" children are also legally
    obligated to support their offspring, so you can get
    support for the children regardless of any kind of
    marriage.

3. If he should die and there are widow's and/or other
    survivor's benefits for you and/or your children, you
    will want to prove that you are his wife. Sometimes
    these benefits go only to "legitimate" children (which
    is probably unconstitutional), so it's important even
    if you only want to collect for them. These benefits
    might include social security, worker's compensation,

life insurance, employee benefits, death benefits, and inheritable property.

4. If he should later try to get "officially" married to someone else and you are concerned that he will end up supporting the second family at the expense of yours, or if you are afraid he will try to use his official marriage to get custody of your children, you might warn him that he will continue to be legally obligated to support your children, and you can get a support court to order him to do so; and that unless there is a divorce between the two of you, his second marriage is bigamous and the children born of it will be "illegitimate."

Index

Abolitionist movement, 74
Abortion, 77, 108, 145, 203
Advocates for Women, 173
Age of consent, 76
Agoraphobia, 39–40
Alcoholics, abusive type of, 322
Alimony, 115, 116, 125, 184
Alternative life-styles, 247–80; being
    single, 253–60; common-
    law marriage, 104–6, 272–77,
    398–401; equality and, 263–64;
    group living, 277–80; open marriage,
    260–63; sexuality and jealousy and,
    265–72; togetherness and, 264
American Civil Liberties Union (ACLU),
    108
American Trade Schools Directory, 170
Apprenticeship, job training, 171
Apprenticeship Information Centers, 172
Apprenticeship Outreach Programs, 172
Athletic ability, male, 342

Baker v. *Nelson,* 107
Bernard, Jessie, 38, 39, 263
Better Jobs for Women program, 169, 173
"Big Giveaway, The: What Volunteer Work
    Is Worth" (Sanborn and Bird), 77
Bird, Caroline, 77, 138
Birth control, 202–3
Birth name, 110–11

Bisexuality, 297
Blackstone's Commentaries, 73
Borrowing Basics for Women
    (First National City Bank), 186
Bove v. *Pinicotti,* 79
Bureau of Apprenticeship and Training
    (Department of Labor), 172

Center for a Woman's Own Name, 111
Chesler, Phyllis, 61
Child abuse, 238–39, 322–23
Childbirth, 198; decision and
    planning for, 203–7
Child care, drudgery of, 214–15
Child care centers, 225–27
Children, 199–202; chores for, 217;
    decision to have (or not to have),
    195–96; divorce and, 211–12; in
    group living situation, 278; legal
    system and, 98–104; lesbian
    relationships and, 304–7; men's role,
    woman's demand for change and,
    355–56; -mother relationship, 207–8,
    217; playing with dolls, 198; shared
    custody of, 230; sibling rivalry, 211,
    255; surnames of, 111–14; time spent
    "playing" with, 218; tomboyishness,
    198. *See also* "Illegitimate" children
Child support, 115. *See also* Alimony
Close friends, separate friendships with, 51
"Clutching mother," 214

College, going (back) to, 173–82; campus
  survival and, 178–79; financing,
  180–81; questions to consider,
  175–76; two-year certificate programs,
  174; women's studies programs,
  179–80; "work-study" programs,
  181–82
College Level Examination Program
  (CLEP), 177
Common-law marriage, 104–6, 272–77,
  398–401; objections to, 273; reasons
  for not legalizing the union, 274–75
Communal living, 277–80
Community property, 91, 93
Comprehensive Employment and Training
  Act (CETA), 166–67
Consciousness-raising groups, 41, 59–60
Constantine, Joan M. and Larry L., 248
Coping, 34; learning, and sharing, 46–47
"Coupleness," 26
Courage to Divorce, The (Gettleman and
  Markowitz), 235
Coverture, doctrine of, 73, 77
Credit rating, 182–86

Dependency, healthy types of, 41–42
Desertion, 79–80; and nonsupport, 80
Discrimination: employment, 156–61;
  against lesbians, 290–91; marriage
  law, 71–81
Disillusionment, 28–29
Divorce, 12–13, 38, 41, 71, 72, 75, 90,
  248; children and, 211–12; for
  desertion, 76; no-fault, 80; right to
  retake own name after, 110
Divorce counseling therapy, 63

Economic dependency, 77–78, 90;
  avoiding, 125–26; violence within
  marriage and, 318–19
Economic factors, motherhood experience
  and, 236–38
Economic independence, 44–46, 57, 78, 79
Ehrenreich, Barbara, 138
Emotional independence, 47–51; issues
  connected with, 48–51
Employment, 147–82; away from home,
  153–56; considered "masculine," 165;
  discrimination, 156–61; education
  and, 163–65; going (back) to college
  for, 173–82; at home, 151–52;
  insurance and income protection,
  161–63; job training resources,
  165–73; labor force statistics, 148–49;
  volunteer work, 150–51
English, Deirdre, 138
Equal Credit Opportunity Act, 95, 182,
  183–84, 186

Equal Employment Opportunity
  Commission (EEOC), 157
Equality: alternative life-style and, 263–64;
  in lesbian relationships, 287–88
Equal Rights Amendment (ERA), 81,
  115, 142

Federal income taxes, 96–98
Feminism, lesbian, 291–94
Finances, 124–86; attitudes and behavior
  toward, 128–33; class background
  and, 129–30; credit accounts and
  creditors, 128–86; education and
  reeducation, 163–65; employment
  discrimination, 156–61; federally
  funded jobs, 166–69; food stamps,
  145; going back to college, 173–82;
  insurance and income protection
  plans, 161–63; job training resources,
  165–73; labor force statistics, 148–49;
  miscellaneous job programs, 170–71;
  paid outside employment, 152–56;
  parents and, 129; personality factor
  in, 128; private training schools,
  169–70; Social Security, 147; state
  subsidy programs, 143–47; supplemental security income, 146–47;
  support from a spouse, 137–41;
  supporting yourself, 133–37;
  unemployment compensation,
  145–46; value system, 130–32;
  volunteer work, 150–51; wages for
  housework, 141–43; welfare, 144–45;
  women's work, 147–56; working at
  home, 151–52
Food stamps, 145
Fourteenth Amendment, 162
Freud, Sigmund, 316
Future of Marriage, The (Bernard), 38,
  39, 263

Gay marriage, 106–8
Geduldig v. Aiello, 162
Gettleman, Susan, 235
Gilman, Charlotte Perkins, 141
Giving, emotional, 29–33; expectation of,
  29–30; unequal problem in, 32–33
Group living, 277–80; disadvantages to,
  279–80; shared childrearing, 278;
  variations of, 277–78
Group Marriage (Constantine), 248

Haft, Marilyn, 108
Health care rights, 108–9
Healthy dependency, 41–42
"His" and "hers" marriages, 38
Homicides (due to marital violence), 317
Homosexuality. See Lesbianism

"Housewife syndrome," 39
Housework, 82; wages for, 141–43
Housing protection, legal system and,
    94–95
Husband's name, 49
Hyphenated surnames, 113–14

Identity problems, motherhood and,
    212–14
"Illegitimate" children, 80; custody of,
    102–3; inheritance law and, 100–101;
    legal system and, 98–104; mother's
    surname, 111–12
Income protection plans, 161–63

Jealousy, alternative life-styles and,
    265–72
Job Opportunities in the Business Sector
    (JOBS), 170–71
Job training resources, 165–73;
    apprenticeship, 171; federally
    funded, 166–69; miscellaneous,
    170–71; private training schools,
    169–70; suggestions for, 171–73
Joint income tax returns, 97, 132–33

Koob v. Koob, 73

Lady Carpenters' Institute, 173
Laks (Eliot) v. Laks, 113
Legal system (marriage and parenthood),
    71–118; background of, 72–75;
    benefits, 71–83; children's names,
    111–14; common-law marriage,
    104–6; conclusions about, 118; future
    and, 81–83; health care rights,
    108–9; housing protection, 94–95;
    hyphenated surnames, 113–14;
    lesbian marriage, 106–8; making it
    work for you, 83–118; marriage
    contract, 83–89; in the 1970s, 75–81;
    name (after marriage), 110–11;
    property law, 91–94; rape (within
    marriage), 115; reproductive freedom,
    108–9; Social Security, 95–96; state
    laws and, 89–90; tax system, 96–98;
    trends (of interest to men), 115–18;
    wife abuse and, 114. See also names
    of law cases
Lesbianism, 286–307; bisexuality and,
    297; butch-femme (male-female)
    roles, 294; children and, 304–7;
    community relationships, 303–4;
    discrimination against, 290–91;
    equality and, 287–88; feminism and,
    291–94; monogamy and, 300–301;
    number of lesbians (U.S.), 289;
    reason for, 289–91; relationships,

294–97; role-playing, 294, 296,
    298–99; self-image and dealing with
    others, 302–3; sex, 302; social and
    psychological pressures, 291
Lesbian marriage, 106–8
Living-together arrangements (LTA),
    272–77; objections to, 273
Love and Addiction (Peele), 47
Love and marriage, 23–70, 72;
    dependency in, 33–34; developing
    separateness (within an intimate
    relationship), 41–70; disillusionment
    about, 28–29; giving and, 29–33;
    "his" or "hers," 38 39; power and,
    34–37; reasons for marrying, 23–28;
    sexual needs and, 37–38; unequal
    problems in giving and, 32–33
Lucy Stone League, 110

McGuire, Mrs. Ruth, 75
McGuire v. McGuire, 75
Maiden name, 49
Mandamus action, 107
"Manufacture of Housework, The"
    (Ehrenreich and English), 138
Markowitz, Janet, 235
Marriage: alternative life-styles to, 247–80;
    finances and, 124–86; legal system
    and, 71–118; lesbian, 298–300; love
    and, 23–70; men's role in, women's
    demand for change and, 340–58;
    motherhood role in, 192–242; "to
    have and to hold" and "to love,
    honor, and obey," 74; unrealistic
    expectations in, 8–22; violence within,
    314–27
"Marriage and Psychotherapy"
    (Chesler), 61
Marriage contract: how to make, 83–89;
    as a practical matter, 83–84; purpose
    and value of, 84–85; sample
    agreement, 87–89; standard items
    in, 85–87
Marriage counseling therapy, 63
Marriage counselors, 12, 319
Maynard v. Hill, 79
Medicaid, 145
Ménage à trois, 266
Men's role in marriage, women's demand
    for change and, 340–58; children,
    355–56; home and family change,
    353–54; how men respond, 351–52;
    husband's desire for equality, 349–50;
    male role expectations, 342–47;
    mutually fulfilling relationship,
    357–58; reasons men marry, 347–49;
    relationship changes, 352–53; sex,
    354; taking risks, 340–42; what

women do, 350–51; what you have to give up, 356–57; wives' jobs, 353
Money. *See* Finances
Monogamy, lesbian, 300–301
Motherhood, 192–242; abuse of children, 238–39; attitudes, beliefs, and traditions about, 194–202; changing goals of, 214–22; -child relationship, 207–8, 217; as choice or chance, 202–3; conclusions about, 240–42; decision and planning for, 203–7; economic factors and, 236–38; employment and, 214, 223–30; identity problems, 212–14; labor force statistics, 227–28; lesbian, 304–7; pressures of, 208–12; redefining, 193–94; single-parent role, 230–33; stepfamily situation, 233–35; support from other mothers, 239–40
Mother's Day, 207
Ms. (magazine), 77, 138, 144

"Nagging mother," 213
Name changes, 110, 111
Names (birth names), 110–11
National Organization of Women (NOW), 60
National Urban League, 166
Neuberg v. *Bobwicz*, 73
New York Radicalesbians, 289
1975 Handbook on Women Workers (Department of Labor), 149, 228
No-fault divorce legislation, 80

O'Neill, Nena and George, 260
Open marriage, 260–63; couples experimenting with, 261–62; meaning of, 260; reasons for not legalizing the union, 274–75
Open Marriage (O'Neill), 260
Opportunities Industrialization Centers (OIC), 168
Our Bodies, Ourselves (Boston Women's Health Book Collective), 203

Peele, Stanton, 47
Pendente lite, doctrine of, 116
Personality clash, 35
Postpartum depression, 199
Power, struggle for, 34–37
Powerlessness, violence within marriage and, 319–22
Preconceived notions about marriage, 8–11
Pregnancy, 198–99; decision and planning for, 203–7
Premartial counseling therapy, 63
Pressures, mother role, 208–12

Privacy, constitutional right to, 108
Property law, 91–94; issues to keep in mind, 93–94; joint tenancy, 93; tenancy in common, 92–93
Property ownership, 74–75, 81–82; "illegitimate" children and, 100–101
Psychotherapy, 61–70

Rape (within marriage), 77, 115
Remarriage, 12–13, 38
Reproductive freedom, 108–9
Rights of Gay People, The (Haft), 108
Robinson v. *Hansel*, 113

Sachs v. *Sachs*, 76
Sanborn, Margaret A., 77, 138
Separate friendships, 51
Separate interests, pursuing, 49–51
Separateness, developing (within an intimate relationship), 41–70; coping (learning and sharing), 46–47; economic independence, 44–46; emotional independence, 47–51; healthy dependency and, 41–42; making it work, 51–58; professional support for, 61–70; self-love, 43; women as friends and support, 58–61
Sex: alternative life-styles and, 265–72; lesbian, 302; men's role, women's demand for change and, 354; outside marriage, 250
Sex-role stereotyping, 212, 214, 219
Sexual needs, 37–38
Sibling rivalry, 211, 235
Single. *See* Unmarried, being
Single parenthood, 230–33
Social Security, 95–96, 125, 143, 147
Social Security Administration, 147
Spinsterhood, 39, 40, 256
Spouse, support from, 137–41
Standen v. *Pennsylvania R. Co.*, 76
State Apprenticeship and Training Councils, 172
State Employment Security Agency (SESA), 168
State subsidy programs, 143–47
Stepfamilies, 233–35, 307
Stone, Lucy, 110
Supplemental Security Income (SSI), 146–47
Support arrangements, 133–37; paid employment (inside or outside the home), 147–56; from spouse, 137–41; state subsidy programs, 143–47; wages for housework, 141–43

Tax system, marriage and, 96–98, 132–33
Therapy, 61–70; criticism of, 62; positive

effects of, 62–63; types of, 63
Therapy Information Packet for Women,
    61–63, 303
Thirteenth Amendment, 141
Three Essays on the Theory of Sexuality
    (Freud), 316
Tillmon, Johnnie, 144
Togetherness, alternative life-styles and,
    264
Tomboyishness, 198

Unemployment compensation, 143,
    145–46
Union for Experimenting Colleges and
    Universities, 177
U.S. Constitution, 141, 162
U.S. Department of Health, Education
    and Welfare, 167
U.S. Department of Housing and Urban
    Development (HUD), 95
U.S. Department of Labor, 149, 160,
    167, 228
U.S. Supreme Court, 77, 79, 107, 108,
    162, 236
Unmarried, being, as an alternative life-
    style, 253–60; with children, 258;
    living with others and, 258–59;
    social situations and, 255–56
Unrealistic expectations about marriage,
    8–22; divorce and remarriage, 12–13;
    preconceived notions and, 8–11
Upper Division Scholarship Competition,
    180, 182

Violence within marriage, 314–27; class
    and race differences, 323–24;
    considerations (before marriage),

325–26; decision to leave, 326–27;
    economic dependency and, 318–19;
    historical background of, 315–16;
    masculine insecurity and, 322; police
    system and court attitudes, 316–17;
    psychology of powerlessness, 319–22;
    solutions to, 324–25
Volunteer work, 150–51

Warrior, Betsy, 315, 320
Welfare, 143, 144–45
"Welfare Is a Women's Issue" (Tillmon),
    144
What Now? (Rozdilsky and Banet), 203
Wider Opportunities for Women, 173
Widowhood, 90
Wife abuse, legal aspects of, 114
Wifebeating (Warrior), 315, 320
Wife-swapping, 262
Women and Economics (Gilman), 141
Women in Skilled Trades, 173
Women in Transition, Inc., 1–2, 44, 57,
    61, 71, 78, 125, 129, 314
*Women in Transition: A Feminist
    Handbook on Separation and
    Divorce,* 2–3, 144, 212
Women's Bureau (Department of Labor),
    149, 160, 172, 228
Women's Liberation Center
    (Philadelphia), 1
Women's Survival Manual, 2
Women Working in Construction, 173
Work Incentive Program (WIN), 167
*Working Woman's Guide to Her Job
    Rights, A* (Department of Labor),
    160

Yohey v. *Yohey,* 76